LAWS OF VERMONT

EDITED BY JOHN A. WILLIAMS

State Papers of Vermont

VOLUME SIXTEEN

HARRY H. COOLEY

Secretary of State, Montpelier, Vermont

1968

PRINTED IN THE UNITED STATES OF AMERICA

BY THE MODERN PRINTING COMPANY, INC., BARRE, VERMONT

LAWS OF

VERMONT

1796-1799

State Papers of Vermont

I. INDEX TO THE PAPERS OF THE SURVEYORS-GENERAL. Prepared by Franklin H. Dewart. 170 pp. 1918. *OUT OF PRINT*

II. CHARTERS GRANTED BY THE STATE OF VERMONT: being Transcripts of Early Charters of Townships and Smaller Tracts of Land Granted by the State of Vermont; with an appendix containing . . . Historical and Bibliographical Notes Relative to Vermont Towns, Continued and Brought up to Date. [In front: Map of Vermont by James Whitelaw, 1796.] Edited by Franklin H. Dewart. 424 pp. Indexed. 1922. *OUT OF PRINT.*

III. JOURNALS AND PROCEEDINGS OF THE GENERAL ASSEMBLY OF THE STATE OF VERMONT . . . with explanatory notes. Edited by Walter H. Crockett. In four separate parts or volumes, all indexed:

> PART I. March, 1778 through June, 1781. With an Introduction by James B. Wilbur, 288 pp. 1924. *OUT OF PRINT.*
>
> PART II: October, 1781 through October, 1783. 232 pp. 1925. *OUT OF PRINT.*
>
> PART III: February, 1784 through March, 1787. 359 pp. 1928.
>
> PART IV: October, 1787 through January, 1791. 307 pp. 1929.

IV. REPORTS OF COMMITTEES TO THE GENERAL ASSEMBLY OF THE STATE OF VERMONT March 9, 1778 to October 16, 1801; with Explanatory Notes. Edited by Walter H. Crockett. 257 pp. Indexed. 1932.

V. PETITIONS FOR GRANTS OF LAND 1778-1811. Edited by Mary Green Nye. 547 pp. Indexed. 1939.

VI. SEQUESTRATION, CONFISCATION AND SALE OF ESTATES [*Loyalist material, 1777-1822*]. Edited by Mary Greene Nye. 476 pp. Indexed. 1941.

VII. NEW YORK LAND PATENTS 1688-1786. Covering Land Now Included in the State of Vermont (Not including Military Patents). Edited by Mary Greene Nye. 537 pp. Indexed. 1947.

VIII. GENERAL PETITIONS 1778-1787. Edited by Edward A. Hoyt. 458 pp. Indexed. 1952.

IX. GENERAL PETITIONS 1788-1792. Edited by Edward A. Hoyt. 506 pp. Indexed. 1955.

X. GENERAL PETITIONS 1793-1796. Edited by Allen Soule. 470 pp. Indexed. 1958.

XI. GENERAL PETITIONS 1797-1799. Edited by Allen Soule, 494 pp. Indexed. 1962.

XII. LAWS OF VERMONT. Constitution of 1777, Laws of 1778-80. Edited by Allen Soule. 249 pages. Indexed. 1964.

XIII. LAWS OF VERMONT, 1781-1784. Edited by John A. Williams, 327 pages. Indexed. 1965.

XIV. LAWS OF VERMONT, 1785-1791. Edited by John A. Williams, 629 pages. Indexed. 1966.

XV. LAWS OF VERMONT, 1791-1795. Constitution of 1793. Edited by John A. Williams, 504 pages. Indexed. 1967.

XVI. LAWS OF VERMONT, 1796-1799. Edited by John A. Williams, 528 pages. Indexed. 1968.

FOREWORD

THIS is the sixteenth volume of the *State Papers of Vermont,* the fifth and last in the law series, which includes all of the session laws from 1779 through 1799. Volume XII includes the Constitution of 1777 and the laws of 1779 through 1780; volume XIII includes the laws of 1781 through 1784; volume XIV includes the Constitution of 1786 and the laws of 1785 through the January session of 1791; volume XV includes the Constitution of 1793 and the laws from the October session, 1791 through 1795; while this volume completes the session laws through 1799.

When the *"Index to the Papers of the Surveyors General of Vermont"* was published fifty years ago (1918), it was decided after due consideration to style it *State Papers of Vermont, Volume I,* and thus to make a beginning, however modest, upon the belated task of printing the extremely interesting and valuable official papers of Vermont.[1]

The present volume continues that purpose by setting forth the laws of the new State during the last four years of the eighteenth century. As in previous volumes, these laws have been transcribed directly from the *Manuscript Laws of Vermont* in chronological order of enactment. Imprints of the session laws of this period are rare, and in some instances non-existent. This publication, therefore, will serve the purpose of making available a basic source of early Vermont law and history, not heretofore available in full.

This volume is published at the direction of the Secretary of State, under the authority vested in him by Number 259 of the Acts of 1912-13, entitled, "An Act to Provide for the Publication of State Papers." This act authorizes him to prepare for publication certain specific public documents, and "such other of the manuscript records of his office as in his judgment are of general public interest." These manuscript records consist of official papers and documents in use during the early years of the State's history, which have become known as the *Manuscript Vermont State Papers,* including the early manuscript laws.

---

1. Dewart, Franklin H.: *State Papers of Vermont,* Volume II, Vermont Charters, Introduction, iii.

This volume is intended for reference purposes for the student, scholar, or general reader in the fields of law, political science and history. There are a number of peculiarities in spelling, capitalization and grammar. Where corrections were in order, to preserve clarity, they appear in square brackets.

The editor is indebted to the Honorable Harry H. Cooley, Secretary of State, who authorized publication of this volume, and to Mrs. Betty L. Barclay, who painstakingly transcribed from the manuscript, typed, proofread, and indexed the volume.

Through this publication, the basis of the legislative history of the State prior to 1800 is made accessible to the public. Accordingly, the editor is indebted to the Legislature for authorizing funds for the completion of this worthy project.

TABLE OF CONTENTS

INTRODUCTION

THE period covered by this volume, 1796 to 1800, represents the fifth through the eighth years of Statehood following Vermont's acceptance into the Union on March 4, 1791. The unicameral General Assembly met at Rutland, Windsor, Vergennes, and again at Windsor during these years (See Table of Contents). The laws enacted reflect the major issues and events of the period, especially those concerned with the establishment in 1796 of the revised Constitution of 1793 as the supreme law of the State; the adoption of the Common Law of England;[1] taxation, particularly to build roads and bridges; lotteries, also to provide funds for building roads and bridges; legislative authorization for James Whitelaw, Surveyor General, to print and sell maps of the State (See Whitelaw's map of 1796, inside front cover); establishment of Caledonia and Franklin Counties; legislative approval for a grammar school at Middlebury, known as the Addison County Grammar School; and many others. These were the subjects of concern to the population of Vermont during the last four years of the eighteenth century.

During the years 1796 through 1799, petitions continued to be the source of a great part of the legislation considered by the General Assembly, as they had been since 1778. The laws passed during the period had their origins, in many instances, in those petitions coming from the grass roots of the people. Volume X, *General Petitions, 1793-1796*; and Volume XI, *General Petitions, 1797-1799, State Papers of Vermont*, include the most significant petitions for those years, and are therefore closely related and corollary to the laws of the period, as evidenced by footnotes throughout the volume.

Contemporary events during the period include: Washington's Farewell Address, 1796; arrival in England in 1796 of General Ira Allen to purchase various goods for shipment to New England. He then proceeded to France where he purchased arms for Vermont, for shipment on the *"Olive Branch,"* seized enroute by the British, thus initiating the events which lead to Ira Allen's failure, but which brought forth his book: *"The Capture of the Olive Branch."* Other events of the period include: publication of *Descriptive Sketches of Vermont*, by John A. Graham, a Vermont lawyer who was sent to England in 1797 as an agent of the Episcopal Church, which gives much informa-

---

1. See this volume, 36, 87.

tion about Vermont after admission to the Union; Governor Thomas Chittenden's death while in office, in 1797, after serving continuously since 1778, except for one term; erection of a blast furnace at Sheldon in 1798; publication of *"A History of Vermont,"* by Ira Allen, containing as an appendix a letter addressed by the author to the Duke of Portland, in which there is an argument in favor of a ship canal from Lake Champlain to the St. Lawrence River. The author also mentioned the products of the farms of the State, including winter wheat and rye, spring rye, barley, oats, Indian corn; peas, hemp, flax, red and white clover, timothy, beef, pork, butter and cheese. In 1798, the mail was carried once a week each way between Windsor and Burlington, passing through Woodstock, Randolph, and Montpelier. The whole number of letters received at the Post Office in Woodstock during the year was one hundred and eighty; the number sent out was one hundred and twenty. Other events include: construction of a forge at Swanton in 1799; dispatch of oak and pine timber to Quebec from Ira Allen's mill at Winooski; news of the death of George Washington, received at Bennington on Christmas Day, 1799. Announcement was made in the County Court which apparently met during the Christmas holidays. A service was attended by members of the court, the bar, and citizens both old and young. Governor Tichenor served as chairman of the arrangements committee. A procession was formed, including military officers in uniform, a mounted troop recruited from Bennington and Pownal, a company of light infantry from Shaftsbury, and groups of men of all ages, Free Masons, civil officials, the Governor and clergy, described as "the most solemn and well ordered procession that ever was seen in Bennington," as it marched to the meeting house to the music of muffled drums, playing a solemn dirge.[1]

During the first nine years of Vermont's statehood, the population increased from 85,539 in 1791, to 154,396, in 1800.[2] These were the *Good Years* for Vermont. "The quarter-century between the close of the American Revolution and the passage of the Embargo Act [1807] was the happy time in Vermont's history. The pressures of controversy were lessened; the hardships of pioneering decreased; population flowed in; land values increased; and every one had big plans for the future. It was not a time of unmixed paradise, of course; and certainly there

---

1. Crockett, Walter Hill: *Vermont, The Green Mountain State,* Volume II, Chapter XXIX, 499-628.
2. *The First Census of the U. S., 1790,* page 8; and *The Second Census of the U.S., 1800,* page 10.

was no feeling of contentment or of realization anywhere among the people. But in general these were the years when striving was buoyant, and small successes seemed to justify great visions of the future."[1]

JOHN A. WILLIAMS,
Editor

Montpelier, Vermont
December 29, 1967

---

1. Stillwell, Lewis D.: *Migration from Vermont,* Chapter III, The Good Years, 1783-1808, 95-124.

LAWS OF VERMONT

1796 - 1799

ACTS AND LAWS PASSED BY THE LEGISLATURE OF THE STATE OF VERMONT AT THEIR SESSION HOLDEN AT RUTLAND ON THE SECOND THURSDAY OF OCTOBER A. D. 1796

AN ACT DIRECTING THE TREASURER TO PAY SAMUEL WALKER THE SUM THEREIN MENTIONED

OCTOBER 20TH, 1796

It is hereby Enacted by the General Assembly of the State of Vermont, That the treasurer of this State be, and he is hereby directed to pay to Samuel Walker, captain of the artillery in Rutland, the sum of twenty six pounds, eighteen shillings and nine pence, in compensation for powder consumed on the last election day.[1]

AN ACT PROTECTING DANIEL KING FROM ARRESTS DURING THE PRESENT SESSION OF THE LEGISLATURE

OCTOBER 20TH, 1796

It is hereby Enacted by the General Assembly of the State of Vermont, That all actions, suits, processes or executions, against Daniel King of Rockingham, in the county of Windham, and State of Vermont, arising upon any civil matter or contract, be, and they hereby are suspended for and during the present session of the Legislature.[2]

AN ACT ESTABLISHING A BOUNDARY LINE BETWEEN THE TOWNS OF SALISBURY AND LEICESTER

OCTOBER 20TH, 1796

Whereas, disputes and controversies have subsisted for a long time between the said towns, respecting a line of division, and that the towns have mutually agreed, and by their Committees petitioned this assembly to establish a permanent boundary line of jurisdiction between the aforesaid towns. Therefore,

---

1. State Papers of Vermont, Vol. X, *General Petitions,* 1793-1796, "For Compensation for Powder Expended on Election Day," 384.
2. State Papers of Vermont, Vol. X, *General Petitions,* 1793-1796, "For a Temporary Suspension of Prosecution in Civil Rights," 359.

It is hereby Enacted by the General Assembly of the State of Vermont, That the line of division between the towns of Salisbury and Leicester be as follows: beginning at the southwest corner of Lot No. twenty in the first division of the town of Salisbury, thence westerly until a direct line shall run thirty rods south of John Fyfe's dwelling house; and then to continue the same point until it strikes Otter Creek, and also to run east from the aforesaid corner of lot number twenty, until it strikes Captain White's west line; thence north 'til an east line will run thirty rods north from said White's dwelling house, thence east until it comes parallel with the southeast corner of said lot number twenty, thence south to the aforesaid corner, thence east to the east line of Salisbury; which line as aforesaid shall be a perpetual line of division and jurisdiction between the towns aforesaid.[1]

AN ACT EMPOWERING JOEL LINSLY AND JEREMIAH BINGHAM TO SELL
ALL THE REAL ESTATE OF JACOB LINSLY LATE OF CORNWALL,
IN THE COUNTY OF ADDISON, DECEASED, AND LAY OUT
THE MONEY FOR THE BENEFIT OF THE HEIRS

OCTOBER 21ST, 1796

It is hereby Enacted by the General Assembly of the State of Vermont, That Joel Linsly and Jeremiah Bingham, are hereby empowered to sell and dispose of all the real estate of the said Jacob, lying in the township of Cornwall and county of Addison, aforesaid, subject to the widow's dower, if any widow hath right of dower therein, and a deed of conveyance from the said Joel and Jeremiah shall be good and valid in law to convey to the purchaser all the title to the said property which was vested in the said Jacob Linsly at the time of his decease, subject to the right of dower aforesaid.

Provided, the said Joel Linsly and Jeremiah Bingham shall give bonds with sufficient surety, to the acceptance of the Judge of Probate for the county of Addison, for the faithful disposal of the property aforesaid, and for the appropriation of the avails thereof, in such manner as the Judge of Probate for the county of Addison, aforesaid, shall direct.[2]

---

1. State Papers of Vermont, Vol. X, *General Petitions,* 1793-1796, "For Confirmation of Boundary Line," 97.
2. State Papers of Vermont, Vol. X, *General Petitions,* 1793-1796, "For Right to Sell Real Estate," 351.

AN ACT EMPOWERING JEREMIAH BINGHAM AND EBENEZER HURLBUT TO
SELL ALL THE REAL ESTATE OF HILAND HALL ESQR., LATE
OF CORNWALL IN THE COUNTY OF ADDISON, DECEASED,
AND APPROPRIATE THE MONEY FOR THE USE AND
BENEFIT OF THE HEIR

OCTOBER 24TH, 1796

It is hereby Enacted by the General Assembly of the State of Vermont, That Jeremiah Bingham and Ebenezer Hurlbut, are hereby empowered to sell fifty four acres of the real estate of the said Hiland Hall, Esquire, lying in the township of Cornwall aforesaid, and a deed of conveyance from the said Jeremiah and Ebenezer shall be good and valid in law to convey to the purchaser all the title of said land which was vested in the said Hiland at the time of his decease.

Provided, the said Jeremiah and Ebenezer shall give bonds with sufficient sureties to the acceptance of the Judge of Probate for Addison County; that the monies arising from the sales of the aforesaid lands shall be laid out to good advantage under the direction of the aforesaid judge of Probate, for the benefit of the heirs, until they shall arrive at proper age to take care of said interest themselves.

Provided also that this act shall in no wise operate to deprive the widow of the deceased of her right of dower.[1]

AN ACT DIRECTING THE STATE'S ATTORNEY FOR THE COUNTY OF
BENNINGTON TO PAY CONSTANT BROWN FIFTEEN POUNDS
LAWFUL MONEY FOR THE PURPOSES THEREIN
MENTIONED

OCTOBER 24TH, 1796

Whereas, it hath been made to appear to this Legislature that one Barnabas Allen, formerly of Bennington, was complained of, and bound to the supreme court to be holden at Bennington in February 1796, in the sum of fifty pounds, for the crime of stealing a certain quantity of leather from the said Constant Brown, of the value of fifteen pounds, and that the said Barnabas Allen did not appear, but suffered his bonds to be called out against him, and absconded to parts

---

1. State Papers of Vermont, Vol. X, *General Petitions,* 1793-1796, "For Right to Sell Real Estate," 293.

unknown, by which the said Contant Brown is wholly without remedy, for the loss he has sustained, and the contents of the said bond became forfeit to this State. And the said Brown having petitioned for a sum to be allowed him out of the avails of said bond. Therefore,

It is hereby Enacted by the General Assembly of the State of Vermont, That the state's attorney for the county of Bennington be, and he is hereby directed to pay to the said Constant Brown, the sum of fifteen pounds, out of the monies to be collected on the said bond, whenever the same shall come into the hands of said attorney, taking said Brown's receipt for the same.[1]

AN ACT ASSESSING A TAX OF ONE PENNY HALF PENNY PER ACRE ON THE TOWNSHIP OF KINGSTON FOR THE PURPOSE OF MAKING AND REPAIRING ROADS AND BUILDING BRIDGES IN SAID TOWN.

OCTOBER 24TH, 1796

It is hereby Enacted by the General Assembly of the State of Vermont, That there be, and hereby is assessed a tax of one penny half penny on each acre of land in the township of Kingston, in the county of Addison (public rights excepted), for the purpose of making and repairing roads and building bridges in said town, to be expended by the order and under the direction of Joseph Patrick, Newman Scarlet and Peter Thatcher, all of Kingston, aforesaid, who are hereby appointed a committee to superintend the expenditure of said tax. And any justice of the peace within the county of Addison is hereby empowered to issue a warrant to Ezra Ball to collect said tax, and said collector is hereby made accountable to said committee for the amount of said tax, and said collector and committee are hereby directed to govern themselves in collecting, disposing, and accounting, for the monies raised by said tax agreeably to an act entitled "an act regulating the disposition of monies raised by tax on the several towns for the purpose of making and repairing roads and building bridges," passed March 8th, 1787, and the act in addition to said act passed the 24th October 1788.

And it is hereby further Enacted, That the collector of said

---

1. State Papers of Vermont, Vol. X, *General Petitions,* 1793-1796, "For Compensation for Stolen Goods," 274.

tax be, and he hereby is empowered to sell so much land of any delinquent owner, as will pay said tax and legal costs after advertising the same as the law directs. And,

It is hereby further Enacted, That if the owner of any lands sold as herein directed, shall pay or tender to said collector the full sum for which such land was sold, with legal cost and twelve per cent interest thereon, within one year from the day of such sale, the collector shall not execute a deed for such lands so redeemed, and the title shall not be conveyed by such vendue sale, and the collector shall pay the purchaser such money so by him received.[1]

AN ACT GRANTING A SUSPENSION OF SUITS, ACTIONS &.C. AGAINST ABIA COLBURN, FOR THE TIME THEREIN LIMITED

OCTOBER 24TH, 1796

It is hereby Enacted by the General Assembly of the State of Vermont, That all suits, actions, processes or executions of a civil nature against Abia Colburn of Hartford, in the county of Windsor, be, and they hereby are suspended for the term of one year.

Provided, this act shall not take effect until the said Abia execute a bond to his creditors, with surety, to the satisfaction of one of the judges of Windsor county court, in the sum of two thousand dollars (and the same lodge with the clerk of Windsor county court), conditioned that the said Abia shall not waste, destroy, secrete or embezzle any part of his estate, attested copies of which bond shall by said clerk, be delivered to any of the creditors on application. And on breach of the conditions of said bond, each creditor respectively, shall have a right to maintain an action on the copy of said bond, in his own name, the same as he might on the original bond, and the same as if said bond had been severally executed to him by name.[2]

---

1. State Papers of Vermont, Vol. X, *General Petitions,* 1793-1796, "For a Tax on Land to Build and Repair Roads and Bridges," 324.

2. State Papers of Vermont, Vol. X, *General Petitions,* 1793-1796, "For Suspension of Civil Prosecution," 386.

AN ACT IN ADDITION TO, AND EXPLANATION OF, AN ACT ENTITLED
"AN ACT ASSESSING A TAX OF ONE PENNY PER ACRE ON THE TOWN-
SHIP OF MORETOWN AND TWO PENCE PER ACRE ON THE TOWN-
SHIP OF MIDDLESEX FOR THE PURPOSE OF BUILDING A
BRIDGE OVER ONION RIVER," PASSED
OCTOBER 22ND, 1795

OCTOBER 24TH, 1796

Whereas, by the said act, the taxes aforesaid were solely appropriated to building a bridge over Onion River, and the Committee
appointed for that purpose by said act, having built said bridge, find
a considerable part of said tax not yet laid out, and whereas the said
bridge will not be of any benefit to the public, unless the roads to and
from the same be repaired and made good. Therefore,

It is hereby Enacted by the General Assembly of the State of
Vermont, That a sufficient part of said taxes be expended on the public
river road through Middlesex, and that part of the public river road
through Moretown, which lies between said bridge, and the old ford-
way, to make the same comfortable and convenient to travellers. The
remaining part of said taxes (if any be) to be laid out as follows, the
tax on Moretown, to be laid out on the road leading from Onion
River to Waitsfield, and the tax on Middlesex on such road in said
town as will best accomodate the public by the order and direction of
the Committee appointed by the before mentioned act to superintend
the expenditure of said taxes. And,

It is hereby further Enacted, That, that part of said act appointing Joseph Wilson the collector of said taxes, be, and the same
is hereby repealed. And that Seth Putnam, be, and he hereby is appointed collector of said taxes, and any justice of the peace in the
county of Chittenden, may issue his warrant to said Seth Putnam,
to collect said taxes, and the said collector is made accountable, and
vested with the same powers in the same manner, as the said Joseph
Wilson was, by the before mentioned act.[1]

---

1. State Papers of Vermont, Vol. X, *General Petitions,* 1793-1796, "For Appointment of a Committee to Lay Out a Land Tax," 310.

AN ACT IN ADDITION TO AND FOR REPEALING PART OF AN ACT PASSED
OCTOBER THIRTIETH ONE THOUSAND SEVEN HUNDRED AND NINETY
FOUR, ENTITLED "AN ACT IN ADDITION TO AN ACT ENTITLED
AN ACT GRANTING A TAX OF TWO PENCE ON EACH ACRE
OF LAND IN THE TOWNSHIP OF ISLE LA MOTT, IN
CHITTENDEN COUNTY," PASSED NOVEMBER
THIRD ONE THOUSAND SEVEN HUNDRED
AND NINETY TWO

OCTOBER 24TH, 1796

Whereas, it is represented that Enoch Hall, who was dismissed by said act as one of the committee for the expenditure of said tax on account of his removal out of said town, has moved back, and that it will be of public utility to the land owners, that the said Enoch should be reappointed as one of the said committee. Therefore,

It is hereby Enacted by the General Assembly of the State of Vermont, That so much of the said act passed October thirtieth, one thousand seven hundred and ninety four, as discharged the said Enoch Hall from said committee be, and hereby is repealed.

And whereas, it is also represented that William Blanchard, who was appointed by the said act, which passed November third, one thousand seven hundred and ninety two, collector of said tax on said Isle la Mott, has not attended, and will not attend to his duty, and has not collected any part of said tax. Therefore,

It is hereby Enacted, That the said William Blanchard be, and he is hereby discharged as a collector of said tax, and Jesse Holcomb of said Isle la Mott be, and is hereby appointed a collector in the room of the said William, with all the powers granted by said act to the said William, and the said Jesse shall be accountable in the same way and manner for the amount of said tax.

AN ACT ANNEXING THE TOWN OF CRAFTSBURY TO THE
COUNTY OF CALEDONIA

OCTOBER 24TH, 1796

It is hereby Enacted by the General Assembly of the State of Vermont, That the town of Craftsbury, in that part of the county of Orleans now by law annexed to the county of Franklin, be, and the said town is hereby annexed to the county of Caledonia, to remain a member and part of the last mentioned county, until the county of Orleans shall become organized by law, and no longer.

AN ACT LEVYING A COUNTY TAX ON THE COUNTY OF ADDISON

OCTOBER 24TH, 1796

I *It is hereby Enacted* by the General Assembly of the State of Vermont, That a tax of two pence on the pound be, and hereby is granted on the list of the polls and rateable estates of the county of Addison, for the year of our Lord one thousand seven hundred and ninety seven, one half of said tax to be collected in hard money, the other half in due bills or notes issued by the treasurer of said county, or in hard money, and paid into the county treasury by the first day of December, A.D. one thousand seven hundred and ninety seven; and the said treasurer is hereby directed on the receipt of such part of said tax as is collectable in hard money only, to pay the same to Gamaliel Painter, Daniel Chipman, and Samuel Mattocks, Jun., Esquires, who are hereby appointed a committee to receive such monies from said treasurer, and to lay out the same in finishing the courthouse in Middlebury, for which purpose said money is hereby appropriated.

II *And it is hereby further Enacted,* That if any part of that half of said tax which is collectable in due bills, or notes issued by the county treasurer, or in hard money, said treasurer is hereby directed to pay the same to the holders of orders on said treasury, or notes or due bills issued by said treasurer, if such orders, notes or due bills shall be presented to him for payment by the first day of March, A.D. one thousand seven hundred and ninety eight. And if any part of said monies shall remain in said treasury on the said first day of March A.D. one thousand seven hundred and ninety eight, the said treasurer is hereby directed to pay the same to the aforesaid Committee, to be by them laid out in manner aforesaid. And said Committee are hereby made accountable to the county court of said county for the expenditure of such monies agreeably to the intention of this act.

III *And it is hereby further Enacted,* That the treasurer of said county shall have the same power in issuing his warrants and extents for the collection of said tax as is by law given to the state's treasurer. And that the selectmen of the several towns in said county, shall proceed in the assessment of the same in the same manner as in the assessment of town taxes; and that the first Constables of the respective towns in said county shall proceed in the collection of said tax in the same manner as in the collection of state taxes.

IV *And it is hereby further Enacted,* That the town clerks of the several towns in said county are hereby directed to certify the amount of the grand list of their respective towns for the year one thousand seven hundred and ninety seven (as taken for the payment of town taxes), to said county treasurer before the fifteenth day of October next.

AN ACT ANNEXING PART OF THE TOWN OF CORNWALL TO MIDDLEBURY

OCTOBER 25TH, 1796

It is hereby Enacted by the General Assembly of the State of Vermont, That the north eastwardly part of the Town of Cornwall, in the county of Addison, herein after described, be, and the same hereby is annexed to the town of Middlebury in said county; bounded as follows, viz., beginning at the south west corner of said Middlebury, thence running west, so far that a north line will strike the west end of the long cause-way, so called; thence on a straight line to the South-east corner of Ethan Andrus's farm on which he now lives; thence on a straight line to a large white pine stump, from which was cut the "shingle tree," so called; thence north to the north line of said Cornwall; thence East on the north line of said Cornwall to the west-wardly side line of Middlebury; thence southwardly on the said west-wardly line of Middlebury, to the first bound; and the inhabitants, who do or may hereafter inhabit the above described tract of land, shall, in common with the other inhabitants of said Middlebury, be entitled to all the privileges and immunities of inhabitants of said Middlebury.

AN ACT DISCHARGING CALVIN KNOULTON FROM THE PAYMENT OF A CERTAIN NOTE THEREIN MENTIONED

OCTOBER 26TH, 1796

Whereas, in the month of August in the year of our Lord seventeen hundred and ninety five, Calvin Knoulton Esqr. of Newfane in the county of Windham, executed to the treasurer of this State his note of hand for about the sum of twenty one pounds, thirteen shillings and eight pence, as security for the payment of the fines and costs assessed by the supreme court, holden in Windham county in August, 1795, against Nathaniel Bennett, Sybil Bennett, Jonathan Bennett and Nathaniel Bennett, Junr. And whereas it appears to this Assembly, that the said fines and cost ought not be paid. Therefore,

It is hereby Enacted by the General Assembly of the State of Vermont, That the said Calvin Knoulton be, and hereby is discharged from the payment of the aforesaid note. And the treasurer of this State, the state's attorney for said county of Windham, or any oher person in whose hands and possession the said note now is or hereafter may be, are hereby directed to deliver to the said Calvin Knoulton, the aforesaid note, and for their so doing this act shall be sufficient evidence, to discharge them, and each of them, from being accountable to the State for the money thereupon due.[1]

AN ACT DIVIDING THE STATE INTO DISTRICTS FOR ELECTING
REPRESENTATIVES TO THE CONGRESS OF THE UNITED
STATES, AND DIRECTING THE MODE
OF THEIR ELECTION.

OCTOBER 27TH, 1796

I *It is hereby Enacted* by the General Assembly of the State of Vermont, That the counties of Bennington, Rutland and Addison, and that tract of country heretofore included in the counties of Chittenden and Franklin, be, and they hereby are formed into one district for the purpose of electing one Representative, to represent this state in the Congress of the United States: and that the counties of Windham, Windsor and the tract of country heretofore included in the counties of Orange and Caledonia be, and they are hereby in like manner formed into one other district for the purpose aforesaid.

II *And it is hereby further Enacted,* That the first constables, and in their absence the town clerks of their respective towns in this State, and in the absence of both the selectmen of such towns, without further order, shall set up a notification, at such place or places

---

1. State Papers of Vermont, Vol. X, *General Petitions,* 1793-1796, "For Remission of Fines and Costs," 374.

as shall have been appointed by the inhabitants of their several towns, for notifying town meetings, at least twelve days before the first Tuesday of September, that is to say, twelve days before the first Tuesday of September, which will be in the year of our Lord, one thousand seven hundred and ninety eight, and twelve days before the first Tuesday of September, which will be in the year of our Lord one thousand eight hundred, and thus once in two years, forever thereafter, warning the freemen to meet on the said first Tuesday of September at eleven o'clock before noon, at the usual places of holding freemen's meetings in said town, for the purpose of electing a person to represent this state in the Congress of the United States, at the opening of which meeting this act shall be publickly read.

III *And it is hereby further Enacted*, That the first constable, and in his absence the town clerk, one of the Selectmen, or a justice of the peace, shall then call on the freemen of such town, from time to time, for the space of two hours, to give in their ballots for a person to represent this State in the Congress of the United States; which ballots shall be given in the following manner, that is to say; each person voting shall deliver his ballot folded together, to the presiding officer, in the presence of the meeting; which ballot shall be a paper ticket, containing the name of the person he would elect; And the presiding officer, on receiving the ballot, shall direct the town clerk, whose duty it is hereby declared to be, to write the name of the elector, in a roll to be by him provided for that purpose, and preserved on file in his office; and the said presiding officer shall, without inspecting the name of the person voted for, examine the ballot, so far as to determine whether the same contains more than one ticket, and if it does not, he shall place it in the balloting box; but if said ballot contains more than one ticket, he shall make it manifest to the meeting, and reject the same, and no vote shall be afterwards received from such elector in said meeting; and after the ballots have been received in manner aforesaid, and at hte expiration of the time aforesaid, the ballots may be sorted and counted by the presiding officer, with the assistance of the town clerk, magistrates and selectmen. And a certificate of the number of votes for each candidate (of which a record shall be made in the town clerk's office) signed by the presiding officer, shall be by the said presiding officer, sealed and superscribed with the name of the town, and these words, "Vote for a Representative to Congress." And the said certificate, so sealed and superscribed, the said presiding officer shall deliver to the representative chosen to attend the General

Assembly for that town, or a representative from some adjacent town, at their next session. And the said representative shall deliver the same to a committee to be elected by the general assembly for each respective district; Which committee on the Monday next after the second Thursday in October, shall sort and count the said votes and declare the person having a majority thereof, in their respective districts, to be elected to represent the people of this State in the Congress of the United States, and give notice thereof to the chief magistrate.

IV *And it is hereby further Enacted,* That if no person shall have a majority of votes in a district, given in by the freemen on the first Tuesday of September as aforesaid, the Committee for such district, with a statement of the number of votes for each candidate. And it shall be the duty of the treasurer of this State to furnish the chief magistrate with a list of all the towns in each district, where no choice shall have taken place as aforesaid, in which there shall be town-clerk, constable and selectmen in sufficient season for the issuing of warrants as herein after provided. And it shall be the duty of the chief magistrate to issue his warrant to the first constables of the several towns, in the district or districts in which such failure of choice shall happen, notifying them of the number of votes for each candidate in the former meeting, and directing them, or in their absence the town-clerks, and in the absence of both, the selectmen, to warn the freemen in their several towns, in the manner aforesaid, to meet at the usual places in the several towns for holding freemen's meetings, on the first Tuesday of December then next, at one of the clock afternoon to elect a person to represent this state in the Congress of the United States. And the said meeting shall be governed and conducted as in this act as before directed, which said warrants the chief magistrate shall cause to be delivered to the respective sheriffs of such district or districts, whose duty it is hereby declared to be, to deliver the said warrants to the said first constables, or in their absence, to the town clerk, or one of the selectmen of the respective towns.

V *And it is hereby further Enacted,* That a certificate of the number of votes for each candidate, signed as in this act before directed (a record of which shall be made in the town clerk's office), shall be sealed, as before in this act directed, and shall by the presiding officer of said meeting, be delivered to the county clerks of the respective counties, within ten days after the holding of said meetings; whose duty it shall be, to meet at Middlebury and Windsor in their respective districts, on the second Tuesday of January then next following, with the said votes, and then, publickly proceed to sort and count the same, and to declare the person, having a majority of all the votes, to be elected to represent this State in the Congress of the United States; of which election they shall notify the chief magistrate within ten days from such meeting.

VI   *And it is hereby further Enacted,* That in case the county clerks at such meeting shall find that no person has a majority of votes as aforesaid, that then the said clerks shall return to the chief magistrate, in ten days after such meeting, the names of all the candidates, with a statement of the votes for each of them. And it shall be the duty of the chief magistrate to issue his warrants as before directed in this act, requiring the freemen to meet, as before in this act directed, within six weeks after the report of such clerks. And the presiding officers of such meetings shall return the votes so taken, certified and recorded as herein before directed, to the respective clerks, within ten days from such meeting. And such clerks shall meet at the places herein before appointed, on the twentieth day next after such meetings, unless the same shall be on Sunday, in which case they shall meet on the Monday next following, and proceed, publickly, to sort and count the votes and to declare the person having a majority of votes elected to represent the people of this State in the Congress of the United States, and notify the chief magistrate thereof, as last aforesaid; and in case there shall be no such choice, it shall then be the duty of such clerks, to report to the chief magistrate as before in this act directed. And it shall be the duty of the chief magistrate to issue his warrants, and of the constables, clerks and other persons herein before mentioned, to continue in the discharge of their several duties from time to time as is last before in this act directed, until some one person shall have a majority of all the votes, as aforesaid.

VII   *And it is hereby further Enacted,* That in case of absence, or disability of either of the county clerks, or where there shall have been no clerk appointed in either of the counties in this state, it shall be the duty of the presiding officers of the respective freemen's meetings in such county, to deliver the votes sealed as aforesaid, to the sheriff of such county, who is hereby fully authorized and required to do the duty by this act enjoined on the clerk of said county.

VIII   *And it is hereby further Enacted,* That the presiding officers of such freemen's meetings, clerks of counties, or sheriffs, shall be allowed five cents per mile travel each way; and the clerks or sheriffs, two dollars per day for each day's attendance while sorting and counting said votes. And the judges of the supreme court are hereby authorised and directed to settle such accounts and draw orders on the treasurer of this state for the payment, and the treasurer is hereby required to pay the same.

IX   *And it is hereby further Enacted,* That any person neglecting to do the duties enjoined on him by this act, shall forfeit and pay into the treasury of the State, the sum of twenty dollars for every such offense. And it shall be the duty of all informing officers to make due presentment of every breach of this act.

X   *And it is hereby further Enacted,* That it shall be the duty of the chief magistrate of this State, to cause to be executed under his hand, and the seal of this state, proper credentials to the persons declared to be elected agreeable to this act.

XI   *And it is hereby further Enacted,* That no vote shall be received for a person to represent this state in the Congress of the United States, in any meeting for that purpose, after the setting of the sun.

XII   *And it is hereby further Enacted,* That if any person shall be guilty of using any indirect, sinister or corrupt means, in the execution of any of the trusts by this act reposed in him, or with intent to corruptly influence any elector, or electors, in giving in their ballots at any such election; or to corruptly influence any officer or officers in the discharge of any of the duties in this act pointed out; or who shall give in, or attempt to give in more than one vote, or shall, unasked, offer votes to any other elector, or give his own vote in any other town than that wherein he resides at any such election, each person so offending, and being thereof convicted, shall forfeit and pay the sum of fifty dollars; to be recovered by action of debt, before any court proper to try the same, one half with costs, to the prosecutor, and the other half to the treasury of this State. And if any person shall, by bribery, menace, or other corrupt mean, or device, either directly or indirectly, attempt to influence or to procure any person to attempt to influence as aforesaid, any person to give his vote for him; or to deter him from giving his vote for any other person, at any election for the choice of a person to represent this State in the Congress of the United States, and be thereof convicted, he shall forfeit and pay the sum of two hundred dollars, to be recovered and applied as aforesaid; and be disabled from holding any office in the gift of this State.

XIII *And it is hereby further Enacted,* That to supply the present vacancy of election in the Western District, the same mode of proceeding shall be had as in this act is before provided, where the freemen shall make no choice at their meeting on the first Tuesday of September. And, until the present vacancy is supplied, the freemen of Craftsbury shall vote with the county of Franklin, and thereafter with the county of Caledonia.

XIV *And it is hereby further Enacted,* That the act entitled "An act dividing the State into Districts, for electing Representatives to the Congress of the United States, and directing the mode of their election," passed October the twenty eighth, A.D. one thousand seven hundred and ninety four, be, and the same hereby is repealed.

AN ACT DIRECTING THE CLERK OF WINDSOR COUNTY COURT TO ENTER AN ACTION ON THE DOCKET OF SAID COURT

OCTOBER 28TH, 1796

It is hereby Enacted by the General Assembly of the State of Vermont, That the clerk of Windsor county court be, and he hereby is directed to enter on the docket of said court, at their next adjourned term, an appeal from the order of removal, which was made on the seventeenth day of May, seventeen hundred and ninety six, by Benjamin Emmons, Esqr., for the removal of Polly Rouse from the town of Woodstock, to the town of Pomfret, which said appeal was entered on the docket of said court at their last session, and by them ordered to be dismissed from the docket. And the judges of said court are hereby empowered and directed, to hear, try, and determine said appeal upon the merits thereof, in the same manner as they would have done had it not have been dismissed from the docket of said court, and in the same manner as if the justice had regularly allowed an appeal. And if said orders shall be reversed, the appellees shall recover all cost and damage they have sustained by reason of said order.[1]

---

1. State Papers of Vermont, Vol. X, *General Petitions,* 1793-1796, "For Entry of an Appeal against a Judgment onto the Court Docket," 325.

AN ACT TO DIRECT THE COUNTY COURT, IN THE COUNTY OF RUTLAND
TO ENTER ACTION JOHN PARTRIDGE VS ROBERT KNOULTON,
ANEW, AND TO PROCEED THEREIN AS THOUGH THE SAME
HAD NOT BEEN DEFAULTED

OCTOBER 28TH, 1796

Whereas, it appears to this Assembly that John Partridge of Benson, in the county of Rutland, now residing in some part of the State of New York, by the consideration of the county court holden at Rutland, within and for the county of Rutland, on the Monday next preceding the third Tuesday in March, in the year of our Lord seventeen hundred and ninety four, recovered judgment by default against Robert Knoulton of Woodstock, in the county of Windsor, in an action brought for the non-performance of certain promises; which said judgment as appears to this Assembly, was recovered by fraud, collusion, and imposition on the part of the said John Partridge, and without the said Knoulton's having any day in court, in the said action. Therefore, to prevent injustice in the premises:

It is hereby Enacted by the General Assembly of the State of Vermont, That the said judgment be, and it is hereby declared null and void, and that no execution shall issue thereon, and any execution already issued thereon, is also hereby declared null and void; and that all sheriffs, under sheriffs, constables, or other officers to whom the same may be directed, are hereby required to govern themselves accordingly. And the said county court, and the clerk thereof, are hereby directed to proceed no further in carrying the said judgment into effect. And,

It is hereby further Enacted, That the clerk of the said county court, at the next session thereof to be holden at Rutland, within and for the county of Rutland, on the Monday next preceding the third Tuesday in November next be, and he hereby is directed at the request of the said Knoulton, to enter the said action anew on the docket of the said court, and to bring forward the original files in the said action. And the said court is hereby empowered and directed to proceed in the trial of the said cause, in like manner, as though the same had not been defaulted, and as though the same had been continued from term to term in the said court, 'til this time, any law, usage or custom to the contrary notwithstanding.[1]

---

1. State Papers of Vermont, Vol. X, *General Petitions,* 1793-1796, "For Re-entry of a Civil Suit to the Court Docket," 252.

AN ACT LAYING A TAX OF ONE PENNY ON THE POUND ON THE POLLS
AND RATEABLE ESTATES IN THE COUNTY OF WINDHAM

OCTOBER 28TH, 1796

Whereas for the purpose of discharging the debts due from said county it appears necessary to lay a tax on said county. Therefore,

I *It is hereby Enacted*, by the General Assembly of the State of Vermont, That a tax of one penny on the pound be, and hereby is granted on the list of the polls and rateable estates of the inhabitants in the county of Windham for the year one thousand seven hundred and ninety six, to be paid in orders drawn by the county court in said county, on the treasurer of said county, or in notes or certificates issued by the treasurer of said county, or in dollars, current money of the United States, to be collected and paid into the treasury of said county by the first day of June next.

II *And it is hereby further Enacted,* That the treasurer of said county, shall have the same power in issuing his warrants and extents, for the collection of the aforesaid tax, as is by law given to the treasurer of this State, in the collection of state taxes. And the first constables in each of the respective towns in said county of Windham be, and they are hereby empowered to proceed in the collection of the aforesaid tax in the same manner as they are directed by law to proceed in the collection of state taxes.

III *And it is hereby further Enacted*, That the town clerk of each of the towns in said county, shall, within two months from the passing of this act, make returns to the treasurer of said county of the list of the polls and rateable estates of the inhabitants of the town where such clerk may belong, proper to calculate the aforesaid tax by. And in case the said clerk shall neglect or refuse to make such return within two months from the passing of this act, he shall forfeit and pay into the treasury of said county the sum of three dollars and fifty cents for every month he shall so neglect or refuse to make such return. And the state's attorney for said county is hereby directed to prosecute such delinquent or delinquents in the name of the treasurer of said county, before any court of competent jurisdiction; and such court is hereby directed to render judgment with costs, and issue execution accordingly.

AN ACT IN ADDITION TO AN ACT ENTITLED "AN ACT TO ENABLE THE
LAND OWNERS OF THE TOWN OF FAIRLEE, IN ORANGE COUNTY,
TO MEET AND TRANSACT THE BUSINESS THEREIN MENTIONED

OCTOBER 28TH, 1796

Whereas, in and by said act the land owners in said Fairlee were empowered to meet and confirm the doings of the proprietors of said Fairlee respecting the division of said town, and laying of taxes as they should think proper. And whereas, no provision was made by said act, whereby the land owners were enabled to agree unto, and settle the amounts and demands against said proprietors.

It is hereby Enacted by the General Assembly of the State of Vermont, That it shall be lawful for, and the land owners of said Fairlee are hereby enabled to procure a meeting or meetings, of themselves, to be warned in the same manner as is provided by said act, and when they shall meet pursuant to said warning, to agree unto, and settle the accounts and demands against said proprietors. Which agreement and settlement, when so made, shall be as good and valid as if the proprietors in a legal meeting had agreed unto, and settled the same.

AN ACT GRANTING A SUSPENSION OF PROSECUTIONS AGAINST
DANIEL KING FOR THE TIME HEREIN LIMITED

OCTOBER 28TH, 1796

Whereas, Daniel King, Esqr., of Rockingham, in the county of Windham, hath represented to this Assembly that he hath met with sundry losses by unavoidable providences, which has so embarrassed his circumstances, that some of his creditors must be greatly injured, unless he can obtain by act of government, a suspension of prosecutions for a short time, 'til he can turn some of his property for their benefit. Therefore,

It is hereby Enacted, by the General Assembly of the State of Vermont, That the the said Daniel King have, and he hereby hath granted to him a suspension of prosecutions for the term of one year, from the passing of this act, upon all suits, actions, and causes of action, arising upon any civil contract either expressed or implied. And all actions, suits, and processes already pending, on any such cause, are hereby ordered to be no further pursued during the term aforesaid, except by continuance of the actions now pending from term to term, during said term, without costs, other than to the clerk for continuance fees.

Provided, this act shall not be construed to lessen the claim, or injure, or in any manner abridge the security already obtained by any creditor, by attachment of property or otherwise.

Provided also, This act shall not take effect until the said Daniel execute a bond to his creditors, with surety, to the satisfaction of one of the Judges of Windham county court, in the sum of five thousand dollars (and the same lodge with the clerk of Windham county court), conditioned that the said Daniel shall not waste, destroy, secrete or embezzle any part of his estate; attested copies of which bond shall, by said clerk, be delivered to any of the creditors on application. And on breach of the conditions of said bond, each creditor respectively, shall have a right to maintain an action on the copy of said bond, in his own name, the same as he might do on the original bond, and the same as if said bond had been severally executed to him by name.[1]

AN ACT TO ERECT A PART OF FAIRLEE, IN THE COUNTY OF ORANGE
INTO A SEPARATE PARISH

OCTOBER 28TH, 1796

It is hereby enacted by the General Assembly of the State of Vermont, That all that part of Fairlee in the county of Orange lying west of the line hereafter mentioned, be, and the same hereby is erected into a parish by the name of the West Parish in Fairlee; to have and enjoy all the privileges and immunities to which any other parish in this State is entitled by law, which line shall begin at the north line of said Fairlee, and on the line which divides the seventh from the eighth ranges of hundred-acre lots, thence to run southerly on the line last mentioned, to the north line of lot number three, thence easterly on the line last mentioned to Fairlee Lake, thence southerly in the deepest channel of said lake to the south line of said Fairlee.

---

1. State Papers of Vermont, Vol. X, *General Petitions,* 1793-1796, "For Suspension of Prosecution for Civil Suits," 259.

AN ACT TO SUSPEND PROSECUTIONS AGAINST EDWARD FULLERTON
OF NEWFANE IN THE COUNTY OF WINDHAM

OCTOBER 29TH, 1796

Whereas, Edward Fullerton of Newfane in the county of Windham, hath petitioned this Assembly, setting forth that by reason of misfortune, he has become unable at this time to pay all his creditors. And hath prayed that an act may be passed to suspend prosecutions on civil contracts against him. And whereas it appears to this Assembly, that the facts set forth in said petition are true. Therefore,

It is hereby Enacted by the General Assembly of the State of Vermont, That all suits, prosecutions, and processes against the said Edward Fullerton, arising upon any civil contract either express or implied, be, and they hereby are suspended for the term of one year from the passing hereof. And that all suits now pending against the said Edward Fullerton be continued for the said term, without cost to the said Edward, excepting clerks fees. *Provided*, that at the end of said term the creditors of the said Edward, shall be entitled to the same advantages by virtue of judgments already recovered, or property attached or otherwise secured at the end of said term as they now enjoy. *Provided also*, that this act shall not take effect until the said Edward execute a bond with sufficient surety to the accepance of one of the Judges of the county court, for the county of Windham, in the sum of five thousand dollars, to his the said Edward's creditors, generally, conditioned, that he shall not waste, secrete or destroy any of his property; and lodge the same with the clerk of the same court, attested copies of which bond shall be furnished by said clerks to each creditor on application. Which copies shall be considered by the several courts, as equal evidence with the original. *And* each creditor on a breach of the condition of bond, shall have a right to maintain a separate action, in his own name, on the same bond, as fully as if the same bond had been executed to each of said creditors by name.[1]

---

1. State Papers of Vermont, Vol. X, *General Petitions,* 1793-1796, "For Suspension of Civil Prosecutions," 403.

AN ACT DIRECTING THE TREASURER TO PAY THE SELECTMEN OF
DUMMERSTON THE SUM OF THIRTEEN POUNDS TWO
SHILLINGS & SIX PENCE

OCTOBER 31ST, 1796

Whereas, the selectmen of Dummerston have been at expense in supporting one Hannah Knowle, a foreigner. Therefore,

It is hereby Enacted by the General Assembly of the State of Vermont, That the treasurer be, and hereby is directed to pay the selectmen of Dummerston the sum of thirteen pounds two shillings and six pence, in hard money orders.[1]

AN ACT DIRECTING THE TREASURER TO CREDIT THE TOWN OF HINSDALE
A CERTAIN SUM THEREIN MENTIONED

OCTOBER 31ST, 1796

Whereas, it appears to this assembly by the report of the committee appointed to settle with the treasurer of this state, in October one thousand seven hundred and ninety four, that the town of Hinsdale is in arrear the sum of eight pounds, sixteen shillings and two pence, on the two penny tax granted in the year 1782. And whereas it appears that the said arrear has been paid by the town of Hinsdale. Therefore,

It is hereby Enacted by the General Assembly of the State of Vermont, That the treasurer be, and he hereby is directed to credit the town of Hinsdale, the sum of eight pounds, sixteen shillings and two pence, being the arrear of the two penny tax on the said town of Hinsdale, granted by the legislature in the year 1782.

AN ACT REPEALING AN ACT ENTITLED "AN ACT TO ANNEX PART OF THE
TOWNSHIP OF NEWHAVEN [NEW HAVEN], TO THE CITY OF
VERGENNES," PASSED NOVEMBER FIRST ONE THOUSAND
SEVEN HUNDRED AND NINETY ONE, AND TO
INCORPORATE THAT PART OF SAID NEWHAVEN
DESCRIBED IN SAID ACT, INTO A TOWNSHIP
BY THE NAME OF *Waltham*

OCTOBER 31ST, 1796

I   *It is hereby enacted* by the General Assembly of the State of

---

1. State Papers of Vermont, Vol. X, *General Petitions,* 1793-1796, "For Compensation for the Support of an Indigent Foreigner," 340.

Vermont, That the act entitled "An act to annex part of the township of New Haven to the city of Vergennes," passed the first day of November A.D., one thousand seven hundred and ninety one, be, and the same is hereby repealed.

II *And it is hereby further enacted*, That such part of said township of Newhaven, as was annexed to said city of Vergennes, by said act, be, and the same is hereby formed into a distinct town by the name of *Waltham*; and the inhabitants which do, or shall hereafter reside in said town, shall be entitled to all the privileges and immunities which the inhabitants of other towns in this State have and do enjoy; excepting that the said town shall not be entitled to send a representative to the General Assembly and State convention; and they shall be entitled to their equal proportion of all the public lands, in the town from which they were originally taken.

III *And it is hereby further enacted*, That the freemen of said town of Waltham be, and they are hereby fully authorised and empowered to meet annually, and vote with the freemen of the city of Vergennes, at their annual meeting, to elect a representative to represent said city and town in General Assembly and State convention. And the freemen of said town shall, with the freemen of said city, at such meetings give in their votes for Governor, Lieutenant-Governor, Treasurer, Councillors, and Representatives to Congress; anything in this act to the contrary notwithstanding.

IV *And it is hereby further enacted*, That it shall be the duty of the first Constable of said town of Waltham to warn the freemen of said town annually, according to law, to meet at the place for holding freemen's meetings in said city, to elect a Representative to the General Assembly &c. And it shall also be the duty of the clerk of said town, annually, to furnish the clerk of said city, previous to the annual freemen's meeting in September, with a list of the freemen of said town, who shall have been admitted and sworn since their last meeting.

V *And it is hereby further enacted*, That this act shall not take effect until the first monday of March next.

AN ACT DIVIDING THE COUNTIES OF ORANGE, CALEDONIA,
AND ESSEX INTO PROBATE DISTRICTS

NOVEMBER 1ST, 1796

I   *It is hereby Enacted* by the General Assembly of the State of
Vermont, That all the towns and gores of land, within the following
bounds be, and hereafter shall be one entire probate district, called and
known by the name of the District of Bradford, to wit, beginning at
the north east corner of the county of Windsor, thence running west-
wardly on the north line of said county of Windsor to the southwest
corner of Strafford, thence running northwardly on the west lines of
Strafford, Vershire, Corinth and Topsham to the south line of Caledonia county; thence on the south line of Caledonia county, to the east
line of this state; thence on the said east line of this State to the place
of beginning.

II   *And it is hereby further Enacted*, That all the remainder of
the lands included in the county of Orange, according to the lines
established by the law dividing the county of Orange from the county
of Caledonia, shall be and remain one entire probate district by the
name of the District of Randolph.

III   *And it is hereby further Enacted*, That the county of Caledonia be, and remain one entire probate district, known by the name
of the District of Caledonia, any act or law to the contrary notwithstanding.

IV   *And it is hereby further Enacted*, That the judges of the
probate districts of Newbury and Thetford, shall respectively cause to
be delivered to the judge of probate for the District of Bradford, all
the records and files belonging to their respective probate offices on or
before the first day of January next.

V   *And it is hereby further Enacted*, That the county of Essex
be, and shall remain, one entire probate District to be called and known
by the name of the Probate District of Essex.

AN ACT TO RECOVER DAMAGES IN CASES WHERE SHEEP ARE KILLED
OR WOUNDED BY DOGS

NOVEMBER 2ND, 1796

It is hereby Enacted by the General Assembly of the State of
Vermont, That when any sheep shall be killed or wounded by any

dog or dogs, in any town in this State, the owner or owners, keeper or keepers of such dog or dogs, shall be liable to pay to the owner or owners of such sheep so killed, or wounded, all such damages occasioned by the bite of such dogs, to be recovered by an action on the case, to be brought before any court in this State proper to try the same; any law usage or custom to the contrary notwithstanding.

AN ACT REGULATING THE DISPOSITION OF MONIES RAISED BY TAX ON
LANDS IN THE SEVERAL TOWNS FOR THE PURPOSE OF
MAKING AND REPAIRING ROADS AND BUILDING
BRIDGES

NOVEMBER 2ND, 1796

I *It is hereby Enacted* by the General Assembly of the State of Vermont, That all lands within this State, which are or shall be liable to the payment of taxes, for making and repairing roads and building bridges, shall not be exposed to sale for the payment of such tax until a fair and correct account of the labour, which shall have been done on such road, under the direction of the committee authorised by the act levying such tax to superintend the expenditure of the same, shall have been made out by the said committee and presented to the judges of the county court of the county in which the lands are situate, and approved by them at one of their stated sessions; and the clerk of such county court, shall record such accounts, and an attested copy of the same shall be good evidence in any court of law in this State.

II *And it is hereby further Enacted,* That no article of account shall be allowed by the said Judges unless they shall be satisfied by the oath of one or more of the committee aforesaid, that the labour was faithfully done and performed on such road or roads agreeably to the account which they exhibit; and that no account be allowed for any labour done on such road, except the same be done between the first day of May and the fifteenth day of November.

III *And it is hereby further Enacted,* That such Committee appointed to superintend such tax, and to lay out and determine the road or roads on which the same shall be expended, shall not consist of more than three persons. And such committee shall lay out the roads on which said tax is to be expended in the Month of May next after such tax shall be granted, and the land owner of such towns shall have liberty by applying to said Committee to work out their respective taxes in the months of June and July following. And it shall be the duty of such Committee to notify the land owners of such town by advertising the same three weeks successively in the Windsor, Bennington and Rutland Newspapers, either in the month of March or April preceding the time such work is to be done.

IV *And it is hereby further Enacted,* That the price of labour shall be seventy five cents per day, the person boarding himself, excepting in the months of November and December, in which it shall be fifty eight cents per day.

V *And it is hereby further Enacted,* That if any proprietor or landowner, shall refuse or neglect to perform the labour required by such act, within the term of time advertised by the Committee of superintendance as aforesaid, and also to pay his or her proportion of such tax in money, it shall be the duty of the collector, appointed by the act levying the tax, to advertise such delinquencies, in the paper printed at Windsor, Rutland and Bennington, three weeks successively, the last time of which shall be at least thirty days before the day appointed for the sale of delinquents' lands. And in case any part of such tax shall remain unpaid at the time appointed for such sale, such collector shall proceed to sell, at public vendue, so much of such delinquents' lands, as will pay such tax with costs, including, as well the costs of advertising, as those of the vendue. And such collector shall, at the expiration of one year after the day of such sale, unless such lands should be redeemed, as is hereinafter provided, make and execute a deed, or deeds, to the purchaser, or purchasers, containing a covenant of warranty, which deed or deeds shall be good and valid in law.

Provided always, That if the proprietor or proprietors of lands thus sold, or any other person shall appear and tender to such collector, or in case of his absence, shall leave at his last and usual place of abode, within one year from the day of such sale, that is to say, at any time previous to twelve of the clock at night of the day of the month next preceding the day of the month of the sale in the year next succeeding to the year of the sale, the full sum of money for which such land was sold, with the costs arising thereon, and twelve per cent interest, such collector shall receive the money, and not execute a deed to the purchaser, but return to him his money and interest as aforesaid; but no suit shall be maintained against such collector for such money until an actual demand has been made for the same. *And* the advertisement herein before directed to be published by such collector shall, as nearly as circumstances will permit, be in the words following:

"WHEREAS the Legislature of the State of Vermont, at their session at .... in the year .... assessed a tax of .... per acre, on all the lands, public lands excepted, in the town of .... in the county of .... in said State, for the purpose of making and repairing roads and building bridges, these are to warn the proprietors and land owners of said town of .... who have not paid their proportion of said tax, in labour or otherwise, to the Committee appointed to super-intend the expenditure of the same, or to the subscriber, that so much of their lands will be sold at public vendue, at the dwelling house of .... in the town of .... in the county of .... at .... oclock .... noon, as will be requisite to discharge their respective taxes with costs. Dated at .... this .... Day of .... A.D.

　　　　　　　　　　　　　　　　　　　Collector."

Which sale shall be advertised to be, and be holden in the town in which the lands are situate, if the same be incorporated and or-ganized as a town, but if not, it may be holden in any other town within the county. And the blanks in the form of the advertisement herein before directed shall be filled with the place of the session of the Legislature where the tax was assessed, the year in which it was assessed, the quantity of the tax per acre, the name of the town taxed and county; and the day, place and hour of the sale; which collectors shall be entitled to receive the same fees as are by law allowed to proprietors' collectors.

VI *And it is hereby further Enacted,* That no one person shall be appointed a member of such Committee of superintendance with relation to more than one tax at the same session of the Legislature.

VII *And it is hereby further Enacted,* That the Committee of superintendance as aforesaid, or any two of them, are fully authorised and empowered, and it is hereby made their duty, to lay out all the roads, and affix on the place or places, for building a bridge or bridges, as the case may be, in all unorganized towns, subject to the payment of such tax. And such Committee, or either of of them appointed as aforesaid, are to superintend the work or labour necessary for the expenditure of said tax. And the said Committee shall, each of them, while actually and necessarily employed in said business, be allowed for such service one dollar per day.

VIII *And it is hereby further Enacted,* That the several Committees and Collectors, who have been appointed the present session of the Legislature, or shall hereafter be appointed, for the purpose of collecting and expending such taxes, shall govern themselves in the disposition of monies raised by such taxes, and in the sale of lands for the collection of the same, according to the directions of this act.

IX *And it is hereby further Enacted,* That the act entitled, "An act regulating the disposition of monies raised by tax on lands in several towns, for the purpose of making and repairing roads and building bridges," passed March eighth one thousand seven hundred and eighty seven, and the act in addition to said act, passed October the twenty fourth, one thousand seven hundred and eighty eight, be, and the same are hereby repealed.

Provided, That the repealing clause in this act, shall not be construed to affect any proceedings already had, or that may be had on any tax granted previous to the present session of the Legislature.

AN ACT EMPOWERING THE ADMINISTRATORS OF THE ESTATE OF PAUL DAVISON, LATE OF HARTLAND, DECEASED, TO DEED CERTAIN LANDS THEREIN MENTIONED

NOVEMBER 2ND, 1796

Whereas, it is represented, That Dan Davison of Hartland, in the county of Windsor, deeded part of his farm to his son, Paul Davison, since deceased, on certain conditions, which conditions have not been fully complied with. And whereas it is represented that it will be for the interest of the heirs of the said Paul, that the said land should be re-deeded back to the said Dan Davison, and that the heirs of the said Paul should have their equitable proportion of such estate in other lands. Therefore,

It is hereby Enacted by the General Assembly of the State of Vermont, That Asa Taylor and Belinda Davison, Administrators of the estate of the said Paul Davison, deceased, be, and they are hereby empowered to execute a deed of the farm (deeded by the said Dan

Davison to the said Paul) unto the said Dan Davison, upon such equitable conditions and considerations as the court of probate for the district of Hartford, in said county of Windsor, shall order and direct.[1]

AN ACT DIRECTING THE MODE OF APPOINTING AN ATTORNEY-GENERAL IN THIS STATE AND STATE'S ATTORNIES IN THE SEVERAL COUNTIES, AND REGULATING THEIR OFFICE AND DUTY

NOVEMBER 2ND, 1796

I *It is hereby Enacted* by the General Assembly of the State of Vermont, That there shall be appointed annually, at the October session, by the joint ballot of both Houses, an attorney general, who shall be duly sworn for that purpose, and under a bond to the treasurer of this State, with sufficient sureties in the sum of ten thousand dollars, for the faithful discharge of his office; whose duty it shall be to prosecute all matters and causes in behalf of this State, that are properly cognizable before the supreme court; to advise with the judges of said court in settling the form of all mandatory and other select writs; to file information *ex-officio,* in said court, in all matters proper therefor; and who shall have full power to take all legal measures to collect all such fines, penalties, costs and sums of money, that may have been, or shall be adjudged, laid, or assessed by said court, and which by law, belongs to the State's treasury; and pay the same over to the treasurer when collected; and who shall annually account with the auditor appointed to settle with the State's treasury.

II *And it is hereby further Enacted,* That it shall be the duty of the said attorney general, as soon as may be, after the end of every session of the supreme court, to cause to be made a schedule of such fines, penalties, costs and sums of money as accrued to the State during their circuit as aforesaid; and also a fair statement of the expenditures and costs, in each prosecution, for actions so by him prosecuted as aforesaid, and return the same to the treasurer of the State, for the time being, on or before the eighth day of the session of the General Assembly in October annually.

III *And it is hereby further Enacted,* That the attorney general shall be authorised to appoint a deputy, by the advise and with

---

1. State Papers of Vermont, Vol. X, *General Petitions,* 1793-1796, "For the Right to Convey by Deed the Land of a Deceased Person," 327.

the consent of the judges of the Supreme court, when unable to attend the same in person, and on the neglect of the attorney general to concur in such choice, it shall be the duty of the judges of the supreme court to make such appointment and to take bonds of the persons so appointed, and accepting the same, to the treasurer of this state, in the sum of one thousand dollars for the faithful discharge of his duty in said office. Which said deputy so appointed by said attorney general, or by the judges of the supreme court, shall within one month after the session of the court to which he is appointed, make out and transmit to the attorney general, a full and accurate statement of all the fines, monies and expenditures of the criminal business in said court, unless the session of the Legislature shall intervene, in which case he shall make such return, either to the attorney general or the treasurer of this State, by the eighth day of the session thereof.

IV *And it is hereby further Enacted,* That the said attorney general or his deputy, shall be entitled to the same fees and perquisites as allowed by law to the several states attornies within this State.

V *And it is hereby further Enacted,* That in case of the death or resignation of the attorney general the judges of the Supreme court shall have power to appoint an attorney general, who shall have [the] same powers, and be under the same regulations as the attorney general by law is, until the said office can be filled agreeably to this act.

VI *And it is hereby further Enacted,* That there shall be appointed by the Legislature, at their October session annually, in the same manner as other county officers are appointed, one state's attorney, within and for the several counties in this State, who shall be duly sworn for that purpose, and under a bond with sureties by way of recognizance, taken before either of the judges of the several county courts to which they belong, in the sum of one thousand dollars for the faithful performance of the duties of the office; whose duty it shall be to prosecute all matters and causes within their respective counties, which are properly cognizable by the several county courts in behalf of this State, and who shall have full power to take all legal measures to collect all such fines, penalties, costs and sums of money that may have been or shall hereafter be adjudged, laid, or assessed by said court, and which by law belongs to the county treasury, and to advise with the judges of said courts in settling the form of all mandatory and other select writs; to file informations *ex officio* in said courts in all matters proper therefor.

VII *And it is hereby further Enacted,* That the said state's attornies shall account with such auditors as shall be appointed by the judges of the several county courts in their respective counties, for all demands and monies due or by them collected, and belonging to the treasury of such county; and shall also lodge with such treasurer a fair statement of all the monies due and payable into such treasury, with the names of the suits and expenditures of the same.

VIII *And it is hereby further Enacted,* That in case of death, removal or resignation of either of said state's attornies, the judges of county courts, in their respective counties, shall have power to appoint others to officiate in said office until the next session of the Legislature.

IX *And it is hereby further Enacted,* That the several acts heretofore passed, appointing an attorney general and state's attornies, and regulating their office and duty, be, and the same are hereby repealed.

AN ACT GRANTING A NEW TRIAL TO ABNER MILES

NOVEMBER 3RD, 1796

Whereas, at the supreme court holden at Newfane, within and for the county of Windham, in September A.D. one thousand seven hundred and ninety four, Isaac Beard of West-Springfield, in the county of Hampshire, and commonwealth of Massachusetts, recovered judgment in an action of ejection against Abner Miles of Putney, in said county of Windham, which said action of ejectment was commenced by said Isaac Beard against the said Abner Miles to recover the possession of an hundred acres of land in said Poultney, on which the said Miles now lives, and by said judgment recovered the possession of fifty acres, part of said farm. And the said Abner Miles having made it appear to this Assembly that he is greatly injured in the premises; therefore,

It is hereby Enacted by the General Assembly of the State of Vermont, That the clerk of said supreme court for said county of Windham, be, and he hereby is directed to enter the said action anew on the docket of said court; and that a new trial be had in the same manner as if no judgment had been had or rendered thereon in said supreme court. And the party recovering shall be entitled to his cost

in said suit, to be taxed in the same manner as though no final judgment had heretofore been rendered in said suit.[1]

AN ACT ESTABLISHING A TURNPIKE ROAD FROM BENNINGTON TO
WILMINGTON, IN THIS STATE, UNDER THE REGULATIONS AND
LIMITATIONS THEREIN EXPRESSED

NOVEMBER 3RD, 1796

Whereas the road from Bennington to Wilmington, in this State,
is exceedingly rocky and mountainous, and there is much travelling
over the same; and the expense of straightening, making and repairing
an highway across said mountains, so that the same may be safe and
convenient for travellers with horses and carriages, would be much
greater than ought to be required of the Town through which the same
would pass, under their present circumstances. Therefore,

I *It is hereby enacted* by the General Assembly of the State of
Vermont, That Samuel Safford, Luke Knoulton, David Robinson,
Jonas Whitney, Timothy Castle, Jabez Foster, Calvin Knoulton, Josiah
Arms, Samuel Thompson, and all such persons as shall be associated
with them, and their successors shall be a corporation by the name of
the *First Vermont Turnpike Corporation;* and shall by that name sue
and be sued, and shall have a common seal and enjoy all the privileges
and powers which are by law incident to corporations, for the purpose
of laying out and making a turnpike road from the east line of said
Bennington to the east bank of Deerfield-River in said Wilmington,
in such place or places as the said corporation shall choose for the same.
And when said turnpike road shall be sufficiently made, and shall be
allowed and approved by the Judges of the county court in Windham
county, said corporation shall be authorised to erect a turnpike gate or
gates on the same, not exceeding two, in such manner as shall be necessary and convenient, and shall be entitled to receive from each traveller
and passenger the following rate of toll, viz.,

For every coach, phaeton, chariot, or other four wheeled carriage drawn by two horses, seventy-five cents; and if drawn by four
horses, one dollar; and if more than four horses, an additional sum of
six cents for each additional horse. For every cart, waggon, sled or

---

1. State Papers of Vermont, Vol. X, *General Petitions,* 1793-1796, "For a New
   Trial in an Ejectment Suit," 313.

sleigh drawn by two oxen or horses, fifty cents; and if by more than two, an additional sum of six cents for every such ox or horse. For every chaise, chair or other carriage drawn by one horse, thirty seven cents. For every man and horse, twenty five cents. For every foot passenger, four cents. For all horses, oxen, and other neat cattle, besides those in teams and wheel carriages, six cents each. For sheep and swine, one cent each; one half of such toll to be paid at each gate.

II *And it is hereby further Enacted*, That the said corporation or a committee by them appointed, be, and they are hereby authorised to lay out and make and alter said road, through any lands where it shall be necessary and convenient, under the same regulations and restrictions, which the selectmen in the several towns within this State are under, in laying out and altering highways.

III *And it is hereby further Enacted*, That if said corporation, their toll-gatherers, or others in their employ, shall unreasonably delay or hinder any traveller or passenger at such turnpike gate, or shall demand or receive more toll toll than is by this act established, the corporation shall forfeit and pay a sum not exceeding ten dollars, to be recovered before any justice of the peace in the same county where the offense shall be committed, by any person injured or defrauded, in a special action on the case, in which case the writ shall be served on the said corporation, by leaving a copy of the same with the treasurer or with some individual member of the said corporation living within the county wherein the offense shall be committed, or by reading the contents thereof to said treasurer or individual member at least six days before the day of trial. And the treasurer of said corporation or individual member shall be allowed to defend such suit, in behalf of the corporation. And the corporation shall be liable to a fine or presentment of the grand jury for not keeping such turnpike way, and the bridges thereon, in good repair.

IV *And it is hereby further Enacted*, That if any person shall cut, break down, or destroy such turn-pike gate, or shall forcibly pass or attempt by force to pass, without having first paid the legal toll at such gate, such person shall forfeit and pay a sum not exceeding forty dollars, nor less than two dollars, to be recovered by the treasurer of said corporation, to their use, in an action of trepass, before any justice of the peace or court proper to try the same. And if any person shall, with his carriage, team, cattle, or horse, turn out of the said road to pass the said turnpike gate, on ground adjacent thereto, with intent to avoid the payment of the toll due by virtue of this act, such person shall forfeit and pay three times so much as the legal toll would have been, to be recovered by the treasurer of said corporation to the use thereof, in an action of debt on the case. *Provided,* That nothing in this act shall extend to entitle the said corporation to demand toll of any person who shall be passing with his horse, or carriage, to, or from public worship, or with his horse, team or cattle, or on foot, to, or from his common labour on his farm, or on the common and ordinary business of family concern within the same town.

V   *And it is hereby further Enacted,* That the shares in the said turnpike road shall be taken, and deemed and considered to be personal estate to all intents and purposes.

VI   *And it is hereby further Enacted,* That there shall be a meeting of the said corporation held at the house of Col^o. Samuel Thompson in said Wilmington, on the third Tuesday of January next, for the purpose of choosing a clerk and such other officers as may then and there be agreed upon by the said corporation, for regulating the concerns thereof. And the said corporation may, then and there, agree upon such method of calling meetings in future as they may judge proper; and may also at said meeting, or any other meeting warned for that purpose, make and adopt such bye-laws as they shall think fit and expedient for regulating the affairs of said corporation, as shall not be repugnant to the constitution or laws of this State.

VII   *And it is hereby further Enacted,* That the said corporation, at the place or places where the toll shall be collected, shall erect and keep constantly exposed to view, a sign or board with the rates of toll, of all the tollable articles, fairly and legibly written thereon in large or capital letters.

VIII   *And it is hereby further Enacted,* That the Legislature of this State may dissolve the said corporation, when it shall appear to their satisfaction that the income arising from the said toll, shall have fully compensated the said corporation, for all monies they may have expended, in purchasing, making, repairing and taking care of the said road, together with an interest thereon at the rate of twelve percent by the year, and there upon the said road shall become public property and be laid open for public use.

IX   *And it is hereby further Enacted,* That the books of the said corporation shall, at all times, be subject to be inspected by the judges of the Supreme court, or a committee by them appointed, and the said corporation shall, within one year after the said road is compleated, lodge in the offices of the county clerks in the counties of Bennington and Windham an amount of the expense thereof. And the said corporation shall annually exhibit to the said county clerks a true account of the income or dividend arising from the said toll, with their necessary annual disbursements on said road.

Provided, That if the said corporation shall not expend five hundred dollars on said road, within two years, or neglect to complete the said turnpike road for the space of five years, from the passing of this act, the same shall become void and of none effect.[1]

AN ACT ADOPTING THE CONSTITUTION OF VERMONT AS THE SUPREME LAW OF THE STATE AND DESCRIBING THOSE PERSONS ENTITLED TO THE PRIVILEGES OF LAW AND JUSTICE

NOVEMBER 3RD, 1796

I *It is hereby Enacted* by the General Assembly of the State of Vermont, That the Constitution of this State as revised and established by Convention, holden at Windsor in July one thousand seven hundred and ninety three, subject to such alterations and additions as shall be made agreeably to the forty third section in the plan or frame of government, shall be forever considered, held and maintained as the supreme law of this State.

II *It is hereby further Enacted,* That all the Citizens or Subjects of the United States of America shall, within this State or Commonwealth, be equally entitled to the privileges of law and justice, with the citizens of this State, in all causes proper for the cognizance of the civil authority and courts of judicature in the same, and that without partiality or delay; and that no person's body shall be restrained or imprisoned unless by authority of Law.

---

1. State Papers of Vermont, Vol. X, *General Petitions,* 1793-1796, "For Incorporation of a Turnpike Company," 301.

AN ACT LAYING A TAX OF AN HALF PENNY ON THE POUND ON THE POLLS
AND RATEABLE ESTATES IN THE COUNTY OF WINDSOR

November 3rd, 1796

Whereas, for the purpose of discharging the debts due from the county of Windsor it appears necessary to lay a tax on said county. Therefore,

It is hereby Enacted by the General Assembly of the State of Vermont, That a tax of a half penny on the pound be, and hereby is granted on the list of the polls and rateable estates of the inhabitants in the county of Windsor, for the year one thousand seven hundred and niney six; to be paid in orders drawn by the county court, in the county aforesaid, on the treasurer of said county, or in notes issued by said treasurer, or in dollars, to be collected and paid into the treasury of said county by the first day of June next.

II *And it is hereby further Enacted*, That the treasurer of said county shall have the same power in issuing warrants and extents for the collection of the aforesaid tax, as is by law given to the treasurer of this State, in collection of State taxes; and the first constables in each of the respective towns, in the said county of Windsor be, and they are hereby empowered to proceed in the collection of the aforesaid tax in the same manner as they are by law directed to proceed in the collection of state taxes.

III *And it is hereby further Enacted*, That the town clerk in each of the towns in the county aforesaid, shall within two months from the passing of this act, make return to the treasurer of said county of the list of the polls and rateable estate of the inhabitants of the town where such clerk may belong, proper to calculate the aforesaid tax by, and in case the said clerk shall neglect or refuse to make such return within two months from the passing of this act, he shall forfeit and pay into the treasury of said county the sum of five dollars for every month, which he shall so neglect, or refuse to make such return, and the state's attorney for the county of Windsor is hereby directed and empowered to prosecute such delinquent or delinquents in the name of the treasurer of said county, before any court proper to try the same, and such court is hereby directed to render judgment therefor and issue execution accordingly.

AN ACT GRANTING A TAX ON THE COUNTY OF ORANGE

NOVEMBER 4TH, 1796

It is hereby Enacted by the General Assembly of the State of
Vermont, That there be, and hereby is granted, a tax of one penny on
the pound on the list of the polls and rateable estate of the inhabitants
of the present county of Orange, for the year one thousand seven
hundred and ninety six, to be paid into the treasury of said county, on
or before the first day of June next, in hard money, notes issued by the
treasurer of said county, or orders drawn on said treasurer by order of
the county court.

II   *And it is hereby further Enacted*, that the treasurer of the
county of Orange shall have the same power in issuing warrants and
extents for the collection of said tax, as is by law given to the treasurer
of this State in the collection of state taxes, which warrants and extents
shall run into the county of Caledonia; and each first constable in their
respective towns, in the said present county of Orange be, and they are
hereby empowered to proceed in the collection of said tax, in the same
manner as they are directed by law to proceed in the collection of state
taxes.

III   *And it is hereby further Enacted*, That all debts, dues and
demands which now are or shall be due, from the present county of
Orange, on the first day of December, shall be presented for payment
to the treasurer of said county, within one year from said first day of
December, or the person having such debts or demands shall be forever debarred from collecting the same, and the treasurer is hereby
directed to pay said demands out of the monies arising from the aforesaid tax.

IV   *And it is hereby further Enacted*, That said treasurer shall
keep a fair entry of all such demands as he shall pay as aforesaid; and
he shall pay no debts with the money arising from said tax, which shall
not be due before the first day of December next, and when the said
debts, so due as aforesaid, shall be all paid and discharged, if any of the
money arising from said tax shall remain in said treasury, that then and
in that case, the said treasurer of the county of Orange shall pay over
to the treasurer of the county of Caledonia, on demand, so much of
said money as shall be so remaining, in proportion to the list of the two
counties, on which said tax is assessed.

Provided, That no part of the expense of laying out and surveying a post road through said county on Connecticut River shall be paid by the county of Caledonia.

V *And it is hereby further Enacted*, That the several town clerks, within the present county of Orange, shall within two months from the passing of this act, make return to the treasurer of said county, of the amount of the grand list of their respective towns, proper to assess said tax by, and in case any such clerk shall refuse or neglect to make return of such list, within two months as aforesaid, he shall pay into the treasury of said county, the sum of four dollars for every month's neglect; and the state's attorney for the county of Orange is hereby direced and empowered to prosecute such delinquents in the name of the treasurer of said county before any court proper to try the same, and such court is hereby directed to render judgment thereon and issue execution accordingly.

VI *And it is hereby further Enacted*, That it shall be the duty of the treasurer of the county of Orange, before the first day of April next, to publish the time at which the limitation for the allowance of demands against the aforesaid county will expire by inserting an advertisement for three weeks successively in the newspapers printed in Newbury, in said Orange county, and Windsor, in the county of Windsor.

AN ACT FOR THE RELIEF OF GENERAL ROGER ENOS

NOVEMBER 4TH, 1796

Whereas, Roger Enos is now confined in gaol in Woodstock, in the county of Windsor, on an execution in favor of the treasurer of this state, on a judgment obtained by default, in the absence of the said Roger, for about five hundred pounds lawful money. And whereas, it is represented by the said Roger, that he has paid a considerable part of said demand, which he could make appear, provided he was liberated and enabled to make a settlement with the treasurer. Wherefore,

It is hereby Enacted by the General Assembly of the State of Vermont, That the keeper of the gaol in Woodstock, in said county of Windsor, be, and hereby is directed, to liberate the said Roger, on his paying gaoler's fees, and entering into bonds with sufficient sureties, to the treasurer of this state, to the acceptance of the state's attorney for the county of Windsor, in the sum of two thousand dollars, conditioned that the said Roger shall pay the ballance which shall be due to the state, at the expiration of one year from the day of passing of this act, or on failure, that the said Roger shall immediately after the expiration of said term, confess judgment, in presence of said state's attorney, for the amount of the judgment, and costs, for which he is now committed, or for the ballance which shall be found due and certified by the treasurer of this state; and the said state's attorney shall take out execution on such judgment, and deliver the same to a proper officer of said county, of which he shall notify the said Roger. And if the said Roger shall, in the life of such execution deliver his body to the officer having such execution, to be committed thereon, or shall otherwise satisfy the same, according to law, the bonds so taken shall be void; or otherwise shall be, and remain in full force and virtue.[1]

AN ACT CONSTITUTING AND ESTABLISHING THE PERSONS THEREIN
NAMED, AS A COMPANY OF ARTILLERY, TO BE ANNEXED TO THE
SECOND REGIMENT IN THE FIRST BRIGADE IN THE
FOURTH DIVISION OF THE MILITIA IN THIS STATE

NOVEMBER 4TH, 1796

Whereas, Huggin Storrs, Daniel Bissell, Junr., Chauncey Hayden, Enoch Cleveland, Martin Pinney, Alexander Plumley, Samuel Case, Alexander W. Tucker, Nathan Tinkham, Heman Miller, Remember Carpenter, William Rice, Moses Bates, Elisha Wilcox, Stephen Parker, Nathaniel Dyer, Matthew Pratt, Calvin Bragg, John Snow, Isaac Chadwick, Caleb Blodget, John Smith, Andrew D. Williams, Dan Parker, Benjamin Blodget, Stephen Fisk, Ezra Edgerton, Israel Kibbee, Ellis Fish, Elias Bissell, Peter Edson, Nehemiah Curtis, Abner Morse and Dudley Chase, inhabitants of Randolph in the county of Orange, have petitioned the Legislature of this State to be formed into a company of artillery. And whereas it is expedient that a company of artillery be constituted in the town of Randolph aforesaid. Therefore,

It is hereby Enacted by the General Assembly of the State of Vermont, That the persons above named, be, and they hereby are constituted and established a company of Artillery, to be annexed to the second regiment, the first brigade in the fourth Division of the militia

1. State Papers of Vermont, Vol. X, *General Petitions,* 1793-1796, "For Release from Gaol," 349.

of this State, with powers of establishments, and all and singular the powers, privileges and rights, which by right and by law, belong to other companies of artillery within this State.[1]

AN ACT FORMING THE NORTH-HERO, ISLE-LA-MOTT AND THAT PART OF ALBURGH LYING WEST OF MISSISQUE BAY AND THE ADJACENT ISLANDS, INTO A PROBATE DISTRICT BY THE NAME OF THE DISTRICT OF ALBURGH

NOVEMBER 4TH, 1796

It is hereby Enacted by the General Assembly of the State of Vermont, That the town of North-Hero, the Isle-la-Mott and that part of Alburgh lying west of Missisque-Bay, with the adjacent Islands in the county of Franklin, be, and the same hereby is erected into a probate district by the name of the District of Alburgh.

AN ACT GRANTING A SUSPENSION OF PROSECUTIONS AGAINST THOMAS BUTTERFIELD FOR ONE YEAR

NOVEMBER 5TH, 1796

Whereas, Thomas Butterfield of Swanton, in the county of Chittenden, hath represented to this Assembly that owing to a series of misfortunes, he is greatly involved in debt, and is totally destitute of property to discharge the same, excepting a certain demand due him, which through unavoidable delay he cannot obtain, which has so embarrassed his circumstances that he is constantly harrassed, and that his body has been and still is liable to be arrested and detained in prison for his debts, aforesaid, without any kind of advantage to his creditors and to the great distress of himself and family, and prayed for a suspension of prosecution against him, and free his body from all arrests in civil process for the space of three years, or such time as this Assembly should judge reasonable. And whereas it appears by the report of our Committee, that the facts are so far supported, that in their opinion he ought to obtain a suspension from arrests in civil process for the term of one year, he giving bonds with surety, against the embezzlement of his property in the mean time. Therefore,

---

1. State Papers of Vermont, Vol. X, *General Petitions,* 1793-1796, "For Formation of a Company of Artillery," 347.

It is hereby Enacted by the General Assembly of the State of Vermont, That all suits, prosecutions and processes against the said Thomas Butterfield, arising upon any civil contract, express or implied be, and they are hereby suspended for one year after the passing this act, and that his body be free from all arrest in civil causes arising as aforesaid, for the aforesaid term, and that all suits now pending against him be continued without cost to the said Butterfield, excepting for clerk's fees.

Provided, That at the end of said term his creditors shall be entitled to the same advantages by virtue of judgements already recovered, or property attached, or otherwise secured, at the end of said term as they now have and enjoy.

Provided also, That this act shall not take effect until the said Thomas execute a bond with surety, to the acceptance of one of the Judges of the county court of Chittenden county in the sum of five thousand dollars to his creditors, generally, conditioned that he shall not waste, embezzle, secrete or destroy any of his property, and the same lodge with the clerk of Chittenden County, attested copies of which bond shall be furnished by said clerk, to any creditor on application, which copies shall be considered by the several courts as equal evidence with the original. And each creditor on a breach of the condition of said bond, shall have a right to maintain a several action in his own name, as fully as if said bond had been given to him by name.[1]

AN ACT GRANTING A SUSPENSION OF ALL CIVIL PROSECUTIONS AGAINST DANIEL CROSS OF WELLS, FOR THE TIME THEREIN LIMITED

NOVEMBER 5TH, 1796

It is hereby Enacted by the General Assembly of the State of Vermont, That all actions, suits, processes, or executions, of a civil nature, against Daniel Cross of Wells, in the county of Rutland, be, and they are hereby suspended, for the term of one year, to be computed from the passing of this act.

Provided, That this act shall not take effect until the said Daniel execute a bond to his creditors with surety, to the satisfaction of one of the judges of the county court of the county of Rutland in the sum of

---

1. State Papers of Vermont, Vol. X, *General Petitions,* 1793-1796, "For Suspension of Civil Prosecutions," 375.

two thousand dollars (and the same lodge with the clerk of the court of said county), conditioned, that the said Daniel shall not waste, destroy, secrete or embezzle any part of his estate. Attested copies of which bond shall, by said clerk, be delivered to any of the creditors on application. And on breach of the conditions of said bond, each creditor, respectively, shall have a right to maintain an action, on the copy of said bond, in his own name, the same as he might on the original bond, and the same as if said bond had been severally executed to him by name.[1]

AN ACT EMPOWERING THE PROPRIETORS OF THE TOWNSHIP OF
NEW HAVEN IN ADDISON COUNTY, TO PITCH THE UNDIVIDED
LANDS IN SAID TOWN, AND TO TAX THE LANDS IN SAID
TOWN, FOR THE PURPOSE THEREIN MENTIONED

NOVEMBER 5TH, 1796

Whereas, the proprietors of the town of New Haven, previous to the late war, laid out three divisions to each right in said town, and the votes and proceedings of said proprietors, having been lost and destroyed, so that to find the bounds of the said lots, the proprietors have been obliged to be at the expense of re-surveying said allotment. And whereas, the said proprietors have laid two other divisions, by pitches, which renders it very difficult to find the undivided lands in said town, unless the whole be resurveyed, and a plan thereof made. And whereas, the undivided lands which now remain in said town, consist of small pieces and gores, and that it would be of advantage to the proprietors to pitch the same. Therefore,

It is hereby Enacted by the General Assembly of the State of Vermont, That the proprietors and land owners of said town be, and they are hereby empowered, in a legal meeting warned for that purpose, to grant a tax not exceeding three farthings, on each acre, on all the lands in said town of New Haven, excepting public lands, for re-surveying and making a plan of the several divisions laid out in said town as originally granted. And they are also hereby empowered to choose a collector, treasurer, committee and other necessary officers. Provided, the said survey and plan be completed by the first day of October next.

1. State Papers of Vermont, Vol. X, *General Petitions,* 1793-1796, "For Suspension of Prosecution in Civil Suits," 352.

It is hereby further Enacted, That the said proprietors be, and they are hereby empowered in a legal meeting warned for that purpose, to lay out the remainder of the undivided lands in said town of New Haven, by pitching the same, in equal quantity, on such days as shall be drawn, to each respective proprietor, by a committee appointed in proprietors' meeting for that purpose. And the selectmen of said town, are empowered to pitch the public rights in said town agreeably to this act.[1]

AN ACT INCORPORATING CERTAIN PERSONS THEREIN MENTIONED A
SOCIETY BY THE NAME OF BRADFORD SOCIAL LIBRARY SOCIETY

NOVEMBER 5TH, 1796

Whereas certain persons in the county of Orange influenced by a conviction of the many advantages that have arisen from literary societies and public libraries, have associated themselves under the name and title of the "Bradford Social Library Society." And whereas said society are desirous to promote and encourage literature, and considering that well regulated Library Societies tend, in a very great degree, to promote knowledge more universally, have petitioned the Legislature that the members of said society may be created a body corporate forever, with the power of choosing their own officers and of making laws and regulations, necessary for the government of said society, in such manner as may best answer the laudable purposes which the members of said society may have in view; wherefore to assist and encourage the member[s] of said society in promoting useful knowledge and literature,

I   *It is hereby Enacted* by the General Assembly of the State of Vermont, That the following persons, to wit, Gardner Kellogg, Micah Barron and Ezekiel Little, and their associates, be, and they are hereby created a body corporate, to be called and known by the name of *Bradford Social Library Society*, and they by the same name, and their successor are hereby constituted and confirmed a body corporate in law.

II   *And it is hereby further Enacted,* That the said society shall be capable in law, to sue and be sued, plead and be impleaded, answer and be answered unto, defend [and] be defended against, in all, or any

---

1. State Papers of Vermont, Vol. X, *General Petitions,* 1793-1796, "For a Tax on Land to Pay for Surveys and The Right to Pitch Undivided Lands," 39.

court of justice and other places, in all manner of suits, actions, complaints, pleas, causes and matters of what nature or kind soever by the name of "Bradford Social Library Society." And that it may and shall be lawful for the said Society, hereafter to have and use a common seal; and the same, at the will and pleasure of said society, to break, change, alter and renew.

III   *And it is hereby further Enacted,* That the said society shall have full power to make their own bye-laws and regulations, such as the appointing the time and place of holding their meetings, regulating the mode of electing their officers, determining the authority and duty of each officer, establishing the mode of admission of members and regulating all other concerns and interests of said corporation, and to enact penalties on such persons as transgress such rules and regulations. *Provided* That such penalties shall not extend to any thing more than the forfeiture of the share or shares of the respective delinquents. *And provided also,* That such bye-laws and regulations of said corporation, hereafter made shall not be repugnant to the constitution and laws of this State.

IV   *Provided also and it is hereby Enacted,* That no bye-laws or regulations of said corporation hereafter made shall be binding upon the officers, or members thereof, unless the same shall have been proposed at one regular meeting of the said society and enacted and received at another, after the intervention of at least twenty days.

V   *And it is hereby further Enacted,* That Micah Barron be, and he is hereby authorized to warn the first meeting of said society, and duly notify the members of the time and place.

Provided nevertheless, it shall be in the power of the Legislature of this State to regulate or disolve said corporation at any time when they shall see fit, any thing in said act to the contrary notwithstanding.

AN ACT GRANTING TO REUBEN E. TAYLOR OF ALBURGH THE EXCLUSIVE
RIGHT OF KEEPING A FERRY FROM THE NORTHWEST PART OF
SAID TOWN ACROSS LAKE CHAMPLAIN TO THE WESTERN
SHORE IN THE STATE OF NEW YORK

NOVEMBER 5TH, 1796

It is hereby Enacted by the General Assembly of the State of

Vermont, That the aforesaid Reuben E. Taylor shall have the exclusive right of keeping a ferry across Lake Champlain from the northwest part of Alburgh to the western shore of said Lake, for the term of eight years, under such restrictions and regulations as the authority and selectmen of said Alburgh shall direct.

Provided nevertheless, the said Reuben shall not take any benefit from this act, unless he provides sufficient boat or boats for carrying passengers, on horseback, and also teams; and keep the same in repair for the purposes aforesaid, and take no other fee or reward than shall be allowed by the authority and selectmen aforesaid.[1]

AN ACT GRANTING TO ENOCH HALL OF THE ISLE-LA-MOTT THE EXCLUSIVE RIGHT OF KEEPING A FERRY FROM THE ISLE-LA-MOTT TO ALBURGH

NOVEMBER 5TH, 1796

It is hereby Enacted by the General Assembly of the State of Vermont, That the aforesaid Enoch Hall shall have the exclusive right of keeping a ferry across that part of Lake Champlain that runs between the Isle-la-Mott and Alburgh to the western shore, for the term of eight years, under such restrictions and regulations as the authority and selectmen of said Isle-la-Mott shall direct.

Provided nevertheless, the said Enoch shall not take any benefit from this act, unless he provide sufficient boat or boats for carrying passengers, on horseback, and also teams; and to keep the same in repair for the purpose aforesaid, and take no other fee or reward than shall be allowed by the authority and selectmen aforesaid.

AN ACT POINTING OUT THE MODE OF NOTIFYING CREDITORS BY PERSONS APPLYING TO THE LEGISLATURE FOR ACTS OF SUSPENSION &. C.

NOVEMBER 5TH, 1796

It is hereby Enacted by the General Assembly of the State of Vermont, That hereafter all persons prefering petitions to the General Assembly for acts suspending prosecutions, acts of insolvency or for

---

1. State Papers of Vermont, Vol. X, *General Petitions,* 1793-1796, "For Exclusive Right to Run a Ferry," 405.

liberation from imprisonment, when at the suit of individuals, shall notify their intention of making such application, by publishing the same, with the time, place and nature of such intended application, in the newspaper, printed in Windsor and Rutland, three weeks successively, the last time of which publication shall be not more than sixty nor less than twenty days before such session of assembly.

Provided proof of personal notice in writing at least twenty days before such session of Assembly to the person or persons against whose right such privilege is claimed, shall be considered as good notice, without advertiseing as aforesaid. And that any petition prefered for any of the causes aforesaid without notice as in this act before directed, shall be dismissed.

AN ACT LAYING A TAX OF TWO PENCE ON EACH ACRE OF LAND IN THE TOWNSHIP OF FERRISBURGH IN ADDISON COUNTY

NOVEMBER 7TH, 1796[1]

It is Hereby Enacted by the General Assembly of the State of Vermont, That there be, and hereby is granted a tax of two pence on each acre of land in the township of Ferrisburgh agreeably to the original charter, public lands excepted, to be laid out and expended under the order and directions of Thomas R. Robinson, Abel Thompson, and Isaac Gage, who are hereby appointed a committee for that purpose; and any justice of the peace in said county is hereby empowered to issue his warrant to William Graves of said town to collect said tax. And said committee and collector are hereby directed to govern themselves in the collecting, disposing, and accounting for the monies raised by said tax agreeably to a law passed this session entitled "an act regulating the disposition of monies raised by tax on lands in the several towns for the purpose of making & repairing roads & bridges."

Provided nevertheless, That one half of said tax be laid out on the main post road from Vergennes to Burlington; the other half to be laid out as follows viz., one fourth part to be laid out on the roads west of Otter Creek, one quarter part on the roads between said Creek and the

1. Located at end of Laws of 1798. Placed in chronological order in this series, 1967.

main post road, one quarter part east of said post road and south of Little Otter Creek, the other fourth part on the roads north of Little Otter Creek. Provided, also that the tax raised on the lands lying in the bounds of Vergennes be laid out and expended on such roads in Vergennes as the said committee shall direct.

Passed November 7th one thousand seven hundred and ninety six. [Omitted to be recorded through mistake]

AN ACT REGULATING THE PAY OF THE COUNCIL AND GENERAL
ASSEMBLY FOR THE YEAR ONE THOUSAND SEVEN
HUNDRED AND NINETY SIX

NOVEMBER 7TH, 1796

Whereas the present pay by law allowed to the General Assembly is inadequate to their service and present expenditures; Therefore,

It is hereby Enacted by the General Assembly of the State of Vermont, That there be allowed to the Lieutenant Governor for his services while attending the Council, three dollars and fifty cents per day. Each member of the Council one dollar and forty five cents per day. And each member of the House of Representatives, and the auditors of accounts against this State, and the sheriff attending the Council, shall receive one dollar and twenty five cents per day for their services the present session, any law to the contrary notwithstanding.

AN ACT AUTHORISING GIDEON D. COBB AND EBENEZER COBB
ADMINISTRATORS ON THE ESTATE OF ELKANAH COBB
DECEASED TO EXECUTE AND EXCHANGE DEEDS
OF PARTITION OF THE LANDS THEREIN
MENTIONED WITH JAMES DUNSCOMBE

NOVEMBER 7TH, 1796

Whereas, Elkanah Cobb, late of Wells, deceased, died possed [possessed] of an equal half with James Dunscombe of Pawlet, of sixteen and an half acres of land lying at the south end of Wells Pond.

And whereas a division of said lands was agreed upon, between the said Cobb, in his life time, and the said Dunscombe; and by means of the death of the said Cobb, deeds were not executed. Therefore,

It is hereby Enacted by the General Asembly of the State of

Vermont, That Gideon D. Cobb and Ebenezer Cobb, Administrators on the estate of the said Elkanah Cobb deceased, be, and they are hereby authorised to execute and exchange deeds of partitions of the aforesaid lands with the said Dunscombe, or his assigns, agreeably to the tenor of the said agreement, between the said Cobb and Dunscombe. And such deed from the aforesaid administrators, shall be, to all intents and purposes as valid in law, as if given by the said Elkanah Cobb in his life time.

AN ACT ASSESSING A TAX OF ONE PENNY PER ACRE ON THE LANDS IN
THE TOWN OF CRAFTSBURY, FOR THE PURPOSE OF MAKING
AND REPAIRING ROADS AND BUILDING BRIDGES
IN SAID TOWN

NOVEMBER 7TH, 1796

It is hereby Enacted by the General Assembly of the State of Vermont, That there be, and hereby is assessed a tax of one penny per acre on all the lands in the town of Craftsbury in the county of Orleans (public lands excepted) for the purpose of making and repairing roads and building bridges in said town. And,

It is hereby further Enacted, That Ebenezer Crafts, Nehemiah Lyon, and Robert Trumbull be, and hereby are appointed a Committee to superintend the expenditure of said tax. And that any justice of the peace in the county of Caledonia is hereby empowered to issue a warrant to Elijah Allen to collect said tax. And said collector is hereby made accountable to said committee for the amount of said tax. And said committee and collector are hereby directed in the collecting, expending and accounting for said tax, to adhere and comply in all things with the directions of an act, entitled "An act regulating the disposition of monies raised by tax on lands in the several towns, for the purpose of making and repairing roads and building bridges," passed October session 1796.[1]

---

1. State Papers of Vermont, Vol. X, *General Petitions,* 1793-1796, "For a Tax on Land to Build and repair Roads and Bridges," 339.

AN ACT GRANTING A TAX OF TWO PENCE ON EACH ACRE OF LAND IN
THE TOWNSHIP OF CAMBRIDGE IN FRANKLIN COUNTY

NOVEMBER 7TH, 1796

It is hereby Enacted by the General Assembly of the State of
Vermont, That there be, and hereby is granted a tax of two pence on
each acre of land in the township of Cambridge, public lands excepted,
for the purpose of repairing roads and building bridges in said town, to
be expended by the order and direction of Robert Cochran, David
Safford and Solomon Walbridge who are hereby appointed a Committee for that purpose. And any justice of the peace in Franklin county
is hereby empowered to issue his warrant to Elias Green to collect said
tax. And said collector is hereby made accountable to said committee
for the amount of said tax. And said Collector and Committee are
hereby directed to govern themselves in collecting, disposing and accounting for the monies raised by said tax, agreeably to an act entitled
"An act regulating the disposition of monies raised by tax on lands, in
the several towns for the purpose of making and repairing roads and
building bridges," passed October session, A.D. one thousand seven
hundred and ninety six.[1]

AN ACT GRANTING A TAX OF TWO PENCE ON EACH ACRE OF LAND IN
THE TOWNSHIP OF FERDINAND IN THE COUNTY OF ORANGE FOR
THE PURPOSE OF MAKING ROADS AND BUILDING BRIDGES

NOVEMBER 7TH, 1796

It is hereby Enacted by the General Assembly of the State of
Vermont, That a tax of two pence of each acre of land in the township
of Ferdinand, in the county of Orange, and State of Vermont (public
rights excepted) be, and hereby is granted for the purpose of making
and repairing roads and building bridges in said town, to be expended
by the order and under the direction of James Lucas, Mills De Forest,
and Haines French, who are hereby appointed a Committee for the
purpose of superintending the same. And any justice of the peace in
the county of Caledonia is hereby empowered to issue his warrant
to Joseph Wait, who is hereby appointed collector of said tax. And the
committee and [collector] are hereby directed to govern themselves in

1. State Papers of Vermont, Vol. X, *General Petitions, 1793-1796,* "For a Tax on
Land to Build Roads and Bridges," 227.

the collecting and disposing of said money, agreeable to an act passed this session of the legislature.

AN ACT ASSESSING A TAX OF TWO PENCE PER ACRE ON THE TOWNSHIP
OF ENOSBURGH FOR THE PURPOSE OF MAKING AND REPAIRING
ROADS AND BUILDING BRIDGES IN SAID TOWN

NOVEMBER 7TH, 1796

It is hereby Enacted by the General Asembly of the State of Vermont, That there be, and hereby is assessed a tax of two pence on each acre of land in the township of Enosburgh, in the county of Franklin, public rights excepted, for the purpose of making and repairing roads and building bridges in said town, to be expended by the order and under the direction of Joshua Clapp of Montgomery, Stephen Royce of Berkshire, and Samuel Little of Enosburgh, aforesaid, who are hereby appointed a committee to superintend the expenditure of said tax. And any justice of the peace, within the said county of Franklin, is hereby empowered to issue his warrant to Stephen House of Bennington to collect said tax, and the said collector is hereby made accountable to said committee; and said collector and committee are hereby directed to govern themselves in the collecting, disposing, and accounting for the monies raised by said tax agreeably to an act entitled, "An act regulating the disposition of monies raised by tax on the several towns for the purpose of making and repairing roads and building bridges," passed this session of the Legislature in October 1796.

AN ACT ASSESSING A TAX OF ONE PENNY PER ACRE ON THE TOWNSHIP
OF GEORGIA AND TWO PENCE PER ACRE ON THE TOWNSHIP OF
ST. ALBANS FOR THE PURPOSE OF MAKING ROADS
AND BUILDING BRIDGES

NOVEMBER 7TH, 1796

It is hereby Enacted by the General Assembly of the State of Vermont, That there be, and hereby is assessed, a tax of one penny on each acre of land in the township of Georgia, and two pence on each acre of land in the township of St. Albans, in the county of Franklin, public rights excepted, for the purpose of making and repairing roads and building bridges in said towns, to be expended by the order and under the direction of Janna Churchill, Sardias Blodget, and Stephen Fairchild Junr., all of Georgia aforesaid, and William Coit, Silas Hathaway and Nathaniel Burton, all of St. Albans aforesaid, except William Coit, who are hereby appointed to superintend the expenditure of said taxes. And any justice of the peace within the county of Franklin is hereby empowered to issue a warrant to Reuben Evarts of said Georgia, and Alfred Hathaway of St. Albans, to collect said tax in each of their said towns, respectively; and said collectors are hereby made accountable to said committee for the amount of said tax, and said collectors and committee are hereby directed to govern themselves in collecting, disposing, and accounting for monies raised by said tax agreeable to an act entitled, "An act regulating the disposition of monies raised by tax on the several towns for the purpose of making and repairing roads and building bridges," passed October session 1796.[1]

AN ACT ASSESSING A TAX OF ONE PENNY PER ACRE ON THE LANDS
OF THE TOWN OF HINESBURG FOR THE PURPOSE OF MAKING
ROADS AND BUILDING BRIDGES

NOVEMBER 7TH, 1796

It is hereby Enacted by the General Assembly of the State of Vermont, That a tax of one penny per acre be, and hereby is assessed on all the lands of the town of Hinesburgh in the county of Chittenden (public rights excepted). And,

It is hereby further Enacted, That George McEwen, Salmon Bostwick, and Nathan Leavenworth, Junr., be, and they are hereby appointed a committee to superintend the expenditure of said tax; and any justice of the peace in said county is hereby empowered to issue a warrant to Justus Boynton to collect said taxes; and said collector is hereby made accountable to said committee, and the said committee and collector are hereby directed in the discharge of their duties, on this appointment to adhere and comply in all things, with the directions of an act entitled, "An act regulating the disposition of monies raised by tax on lands in the several towns, for the purpose of making and repairing roads and building bridges," passed at the October session A.D. 1796.

---

1. State Papers of Vermont, Vol. X, *General Petitions,* 1793-1796, "For a Tax on Land to Repair Roads and Bridges," 373.

AN ACT LAYING A TAX OF AN HALF PENNY ON EACH ACRE OF LAND
IN THE TOWNSHIP OF ROXBURY IN ORANGE COUNTY

NOVEMBER 7TH, 1796

It is hereby Enacted by the General Assembly of the State of
Vermont, That there be, and hereby is assessed a tax of an half penny
on each acre of land in the township of Roxbury in Orange county
(public rights excepted), for the purpose of making and repairing a
road leading from Braintree, through said town to Northfield, and a
road from Braintree, through said town to Waitsfield; that one third
part of the tax be laid on the first mentioned road, and the remainder
on the last mentioned road, to be expended by the order and direction
of Benjamin Wait and Samuel Richardson who are hereby appointed
a committee for that purpose. And any justice of the peace in said
county of Orange is hereby empowered to issue a warrant to Abel
Lyman to collect said tax, and said collector and committee are hereby
directed to govern themselves in the collecting, disposing, and accounting for the monies raised by said tax, agreeably to an act passed by
the Legislature of this State this session entitled, "an act regulating the
disposition of monies raised by taxes on lands for the purpose of making
and repairing roads and bridges."[1]

AN ACT ASSESSING A TAX OF ONE PENNY PER ACRE ON ALL THE LANDS
IN THE TOWN OF SHEFFIELD

NOVEMBER 7TH, 1796

It is hereby Enacted by the General Assembly of the State of
Vermont, That there be, and hereby is assessed a tax of one penny per
acre on all the lands in the town of Sheffield, in the county of Orange,
public rights excepted, for the purpose of making and repairing roads
and building bridges in said town. And,

It is hereby Enacted, That Reuben Miles, Jonathan H. Sand-
bourn, and John Bean Junr., be, and are hereby appointed a committee
to superintend the expenditure of said tax, and that any justice of the
peace in the county of Orange, is hereby empowered to issue a warrant
to Moses Foss to collect said tax; and said collector is hereby made

---

1. State Papers of Vermont, Vol. X, *General Petitions,* 1793-1796, "For a Tax on
Land to Build and Repair Roads and Bridges," 317.

accountable to said committee, and said committee and collector are hereby directed in the collecting, expending, and accounting for said tax, to adhere and comply in all things, with the directions of an act entitled, "An act regulating the disposition of monies raised by tax on lands in the several towns in this State, for the purpose of making roads and building bridges," passed at the General Assembly, October session, A.D. 1796.[1]

AN ACT GRANTING A TAX OF TWO PENCE ON EACH ACRE OF LAND IN THE TOWNSHIP OF WOODFORD IN BENNINGTON COUNTY

NOVEMBER 7TH, 1796

It is hereby Enacted by the General Assembly of the State of Vermont, That there be, and hereby is granted a tax of two pence on each acre of land in the township of Woodford, in the county of Bennington (public rights excepted), for the purpose of making and repairing public roads and bridges in said town, to be expended by the order and direction of Rufus Barney, David Wicks and Paul Phelps, who are hereby appointed a committee for that purpose; and any justice of the peace for the county of Bennington is hereby empowered to issue a warrant to William Parks to collect said tax. And said committee and collector are hereby directed to govern themselves in collecting, disposing, and accounting for the monies raised by said tax, agreeably to an act entitled "An act regulating the disposition of monies raised by tax on lands for the purpose of making and repairing roads and bridges," passed this present session.[2]

AN ACT GRANTING A TAX OF ONE PENNY PER ACRE ON EACH ACRE OF LAND IN THE TOWN OF UNDERHILL FOR THE PURPOSES THEREIN MENTIONED

NOVEMBER 7TH, 1796

It is hereby Enacted by the General Assembly of the State of Vermont, That there be, and hereby is granted, a tax of one penny on

---

1. State Papers of Vermont, Vol. X, *General Petitions,* 1793-1796, "For a Tax on Land to Build Roads and Bridges," 278.

2. State Papers of Vermont, Vol. X, *General Petitions,* 1793-1796, "For a Tax on Land to Repair Roads and Build Bridges," 312.

each acre of land in the township of Underhill in the county of Chittenden (public lands excepted), for the purpose of making and repairing roads and building bridges in said town, to be expended by the order and under the direction of Martin Chittenden, Esqr., Luther Dixon, and Udney Hay,[1] who are hereby appointed a committee for that purpose. And any justice of the peace within the county of Chittenden is hereby empowered to issue his warrant to Caleb Sheldon to collect said tax, and said collector is hereby made accountable to said committee for the amount of said tax. And said collector and committee are hereby directed to govern themselves, in the collecting, disposing, and accounting for the monies raised by said tax agreeably to an act entitled, "An act regulating the disposition of monies raised by tax on the several towns for the purpose of making and repairing roads and building bridges," passed this present session.[2]

AN ACT GRANTING A LOTTERY FOR THE PURPOSE OF MAKING A PUBLIC ROAD FROM CASTLETON TO MIDDLEBURY

NOVEMBER 7TH, 1796

It is hereby Enacted by the General Assembly of the State of Vermont, That leave is hereby given to Chancey Langdon, Arunah Woodward, Elisha Walker, Nathan Rumsey and Stephen Long, or any three thereof, to raise by lottery five hundred dollars, for the purpose of making and repairing the road from Castleton main street to Daniel Felton's, in Sudbury, under the direction of the aforesaid persons, who are hereby appointed managers of said lottery, and are authorized to enter upon the business, upon taking an oath and giving sufficient bonds, to the county court of the county of Rutland, for the full and due performance and management of the business herein assigned to them.

Provided always, That this State is by no means accountable for the said lottery.

---

1. Udney Hay of Underhill was deputy commissary general of purchases, [northern department of the Continental Army]: See Governor and Council, Vol. II, pages 19-50.
2. State Papers of Vermont, Vol. X, *General Petitions,* 1793-1796, "For a Tax on Land to Build and Repair Roads and Bridges," 286.

AN ACT ENABLING ALL THE ORGANIZED TOWNS IN THIS STATE TO TAX
THEMSELVES FOR THE PURPOSE THEREIN MENTIONED

NOVEMBER 7TH, 1796

Whereas, the Legislature of the State of New York have established a company in said State, called and known by the name of the President, Directors and Company of the Northern Inland Lock Navigation, for the purpose of opening a Lock navigation from the now navigable part of Hudson's-River to Lake Champlain, and have enabled said company to receive and enjoy certain profit, which may arise therefrom. And whereas the president of said company has made application to this Legislature to subscribe for fifty shares of the stock thereof. And altho' it appears to the Legislature that the purchase of said shares for the purpose of encourageing said undertaking would be highly beneficial to the State at large, yet as it would be more particularly beneficial to the western and northwestern parts thereof, the Legislature do not think fit to purchase said shares with money taken from the public treasury; but for the purpose of encourageing an undertaking so laudable and beneficial to mankind the Legislature have thought fit to enable such towns as from a Spirit of Liberality and enterprize shall have a wish to become stockholders in said company, to tax themselves for the purpose. Therefore,

It is hereby Enacted by the General Assembly of the State of Vermont, That the several organized towns in this State be, and they hereby are enabled, authorized and empowered, at a meeting legally warned for the purpose, to levy a tax on the list of the polls and rateable estate of such town or towns, not exceeding six pence on the pound, or on all the lands in such town (public lands excepted) not exceeding three pence on each acre, to raise money for the purpose aforesaid, and any justice of the peace of the town where such tax shall be voted or levied as aforesaid is hereby authorized to issue his warrant for the collection of the same to the first constable of such town, who is hereby appointed a collector of such tax; and such collector is hereby made accountable to the treasurer of such town for the amount of such tax; and such constable to whom shall be committed the collection of such tax laid on the list of such town as aforesaid, shall have the same powers and proceed in the same manner as the collection of other town taxes, and in case of delinquency, shall be proceeded against in the same manner as delinquent collectors of town taxes are; and any constable to whom shall be committed the collection of any tax so laid on the lands of any town as aforesaid, shall advertise such tax in the same manner as the collectors of taxes laid for the purpose of making and repairing roads and building bridges, are by law directed to do, except that such tax shall be advertised to be paid in money only, and at the time, which by the Town granting the same shall be set for payment thereof, and in case such tax, or any part thereof, shall remain unpaid after the day limited for the payment thereof in such advertisement, such collector is hereby empowered to sell so much of the land of each delinquent owner or proprietor as will pay his proportion of such tax with legal costs, and shall advertise such sale and shall proceed to sell and convey the lands of each delinquent proprietor or land owner in the same manner as the collectors of taxes, laid for the purpose of making and repairing roads and building bridges, are by law, empowered and directed to do; and the owner of such land, which shall be so sold for the collection of such tax as aforesaid, shall have the same time in which to redeem such land, and shall in all things have the same right of redemption as by law is given to those proprietors and land owners whose land may be sold for the payment of such road taxes as aforesaid.

II   *And it is hereby further Enacted,* That the inhabitants of any such town or towns as have been divided by act of Legislature, may lay a tax on such town, in the following manner, to wit, the inhabitants within the ancient or charter bounds of any township or gore of land, may after being duly warned thereto by notification from a justice of the peace living within the limits of such grant, lay a tax on all the lands contained in such charter or grant in manner aforesaid, and may appoint a collector of such tax, who shall be sworn to the fiaithful discharge of his duty, and shall thereupon be vested with all the powers herein before given to constables in the collection of such taxes, and shall proceed in the same manner in the collection such taxes, and such inhabitants, and those who may hereafter inhabit such tract, gore or township are hereby made a body corporate for the purposes aforesaid, and shall in all things be capable of suing and being sued, of prosecuting and being prosecuted, relative to the raising and disposing of such monies as aforesaid, for the purpose aforesaid, by the name of the inhabitants of a tract of land granted by the name of .... as mentioned in the original charter of such tract or township.

Provided, That this act shall not authorise any towns or any such inhabitants as aforesaid, to lay any tax for the purposes aforesaid after the expiration of three years from and after the passing of this act.

III *And it is hereby further Enacted,* That if any such town or inhabitants, who shall so lay any such tax as aforesaid, for the purposes aforesaid, on the land contained in any such town or grant as aforesaid, shall neglect to lay out such money for the purpose aforesaid, in the purchase of a share or shares in the stock of the company aforesaid, within two years from the time that such tax shall become payable, such money so raised by such tax shall become forfeit to the Treasury of the county in which such town or grant shall lie, to be recovered of such town or inhabitants by action of debt in the name of the treasurer of such county, for the time being, to be prosecuted by the state's attorney of such county.

AN ACT ASSESSING A TAX OF TWO PENCE PER ACRE ON THE LANDS
IN THE TOWN OF DUNCANSBOROUGH

NOVEMBER 8TH, 1796

It is hereby Enacted by the General Assembly of the State of Vermont, That there be, and hereby is assessed a tax of two pence per acre on all the lands in the town of Duncansborough, in the county of Chittenden, public rights excepted, for the purpose of making and repairing roads and building bridges in said town. And,

It is hereby further Enacted, That Martin Adams, Nathaniel P. Sawyer and Joseph Bean be, and are hereby appointed a Committee to superintend the expenditures of said tax. And that any justice of the peace in the county of Chittenden is hereby empowered to issue his warrant to John Bean to collect said tax; and said collector is hereby made accountable to said committee; and said committee and collector are hereby directed in the collecting, expending, and accounting for said tax, to adhere and comply in all things with the directions of "An act, regulating the disposition of monies raised by tax on lands in the several towns in this state, for the purpose of making and repairing roads and building bridges," passed at the General Assembly at their October session A.D. 1796.[1]

---

1. State Papers of Vermont, Vol. X, *General Petitions,* 1793-1796, "For a Tax on Land to Build Roads," 201.

AN ACT ASSESSING A TAX OF ONE PENNY PER ACRE ON THE LANDS IN
BROWNINGTON

NOVEMBER 8TH, 1796

It is hereby Enacted by the General Assembly of the State of
Vermont, That there be, and hereby is assessed a tax of one penny per
acre on all the lands in the town of Brownington, in the county of
Orange, public rights excepted, for the purpose of making and repairing roads and building bridges in said town.

And it is hereby further Enacted, That Benjamin Sias and Samuel
Chamberlain be, and are hereby appointed a Committee to superintend
the expenditure of said tax, and that any justice of the peace in the
county of Orange is hereby empowered to issue a warrant to Jeremiah
Sias to collect said tax, and said collector is hereby made accountable
to said committee, and said committee and collector are hereby directed
in the collecting, expending and accounting for said tax, to adhere and
comply in all things with the directions of "An act regulating the
disposition of monies raised by tax on lands in the several towns in
this State, for the purpose of making and repairing roads and building
bridges," passed at the General Assembly at their October session A.D.
one thousand seven hundred and ninety six.[1]

AN ACT GRANTING A NEW TRIAL TO WILLIAM SMITH, GIDEON SMITH
AND AARON ROWLEY

NOVEMBER 8TH, 1796

Whereas, at a County Court holden at Burlington on the last
Monday save one in September, A.D. one thousand seven hundred and
ninety three, in and for the county of Chittenden, John Hoffnagal of
Willsborough in the county of Clinton, and State of New York, administrator of the estate of Melcher Hoffnagal, late of said Willsborough,
deceased, brought his certain action against the said William Smith,
Gideon Smith and and Aaron Rowley, on a promissory note given to
the said Melcher Hoffnagal in his life time; which action the said
John Hoffnagal, at a county court holden at Burlington, within and for
the county of Chittenden, on the last Monday save one in September,
A.D. one thousand seven hundred and ninety six, recovered judgment

---

1. State Papers of Vermont, Vol. X, *General Petitions,* 1793-1796, "For a Tax on
Land to Repair Roads and Bridges," 373.

against the said William, Gideon, and Aaron, for the sum of fifty one pounds, seven shillings, and eleven pence, lawful money, for his damages and costs; and whereas, it has been made to appear to this Legislature that the said William, Gideon, and Aaron have been greatly injured by said judgment. Therefore,

It is hereby Enacted by the General Assembly of the State of Vermont, That the clerk of said Court be, and he is hereby authorised and directed to enter the said action anew on the docket of the said court, at their session in February next, and that a new trial be had in the same manner as though no judgment had ever been had and rendered thereon. *Provided,* that the said William, Gideon and Aaron shall notify the said John thereof by causing a true and attested copy of this act, to be delivered to the said John, or to his attorney in said cause, at least twenty days before the sitting of said court.[1]

AN ACT GRANTING A SUSPENSION OF PROSECUTIONS AGAINST
HARDING WILLARD FOR ONE YEAR

NOVEMBER 8TH, 1796

Whereas, Harding Willard of Hartland, in the county of Windsor, hath made it to appear to this Assembly, that by reason of a suspension of prosecutions against him the last year, he has been enabled to make very considerable remittances to his creditors, and that a like indulgence for another year would probably put it in his power to discharge the most of his debts. And whereas, it appears reasonable to this Assembly, that it may prove beneficial to grant a suspension of one year as aforesaid, and until the rising of the Legislature in October next; Therefore,

It is hereby Enacted by the General Assembly of the State of Vermont, That all suits, prosecutions and processes against the said Harding Willard arising upon any civil contract, either expressed or implied, be, and they hereby are suspended for one year from the passing hereof, and until the end of the session of the Legislature in October next. And that all suits now pending against him as aforesaid, be continued, without cost to the said Harding, excepting for clerk's fees.

Provided, the creditors to said Harding Willard, shall be entitled

1. State Papers of Vermont, Vol. X, *General Petitions,* 1793-1796, "For a New Trial," 305.

to the same advantages by virtue of judgments already recovered, or property already attached, or otherwise secured at the end of the term aforesaid, as they now have and enjoy. *Provided* also, that this act shall not take effect until the said Harding Willard execute a bond with surety to the acceptance of one of the judges of the county court for the county of Windsor, in the sum of five thousand dollars, to his creditors generally, conditioned that he shall not waste, embezzle, secrete or destroy any of his property, with intention to injure or defraud any one of his creditors; and the same lodge with the clerk of Windsor county court; attested copies of which bond shall be furnished by said clerk, to any creditor on application, which copies shall be considered by the several courts in this State, as equal evidence with the original bond; and each creditor, on a breach of the conditions of said bond, shall have a right to maintain a several action in his own name, as fully as if said bond had been executed to him by name.[1]

AN ACT EMPOWERING GROVE MOORE, ADMINISTRATOR, AND FANNY BAKER ADMINISTRATRIX, TO SELL THE REAL ESTATE OF PEMBERTON BAKER, LATE OF RUPERT, DECEASED

November 8th, 1796

It is hereby Enacted by the General Assembly of the State of Vermont, That Grove Moore of Rupert in the county of Bennington, administrator, and Fanny Baker now of Norwich, in the State of Connecticut, administratrix, on the estate of Pemberton Baker, late of said Rupert, deceased, be, and they are hereby authorised and empowered to sell an house, and about twenty acres of land situate in Rupert aforesaid, the real estate of the said Pemberton Baker, deceased, under the direction of the Judge of Probate for the district of Manchester, and appropriate the money arising from such sale to the maintenance and benefit of the heirs of the deceased.

Provided, that the said Grove Moore and Fanny Baker, enter into bonds to the satisfaction of the aforesaid Judge of Probate, whose duty it shall be to receive such bond, that the whole of the avails of such sale, excepting the dower to the widow, shall be faithfully applied to the support and maintenance of the said heirs, or be otherwise laid out, to the best advantage in their power for the said heirs, when they shall

---

1. State Papers of Vermont, Vol. X, *General Petitions,* 1793-1796, "For Suspension of Prosecution in Civil Suits," 335.

become of lawful age. And a deed executed by the said Grove Moore and Fanny Baker, to the purchaser, shall be good and valid in law, to convey to the purchaser all the title to said premises, which was vested in the said Pemberton, at the time of his decease.[1]

AN ACT AUTHORISING THE JUDGE OF PROBATE OF THE DISTRICT OF CALEDONIA TO EMPOWER WILLIAM C. ARNOLD AND JAMES WHITELAW, TO EXECUTE DEEDS IN CERTAIN CASES

NOVEMBER 8TH, 1796

Whereas, by an act of the Legislature of this State passed the second day of November, one thousand seven hundred and ninety three, the Judge of Probate for Newbury District was authorised to empower Josias L. Arnold Esqr., to deed certain lands. And whereas the said Josias L. Arnold has since deceased without completing some part of said business. Therefore,

It is hereby Enacted by the General Assembly of the State of Vermont, That the Judge of Probate for the District of Caledonia be, and is hereby authorised to empower William C. Arnold and James Whitelaw, executors to the last will of the said Josias L. Arnold Esqr. to complete that part of said business, that said Josias did not finish in his life time. And whereas said Josias L. Arnold had sold several lots of land in St. Johnsbury of which the purchaser had not obtained deeds at the time of his death.

It is hereby further Enacted, That said Judge of Probate be further empowered to authorise the said William C. Arnold and James Whitelaw to execute good and lawful deeds to the purchasers of all lands sold by the said Josias L. Aronld, Esqr. in the situation aforesaid, they the said William C. Arnold and James Whitelaw proving to the satisfaction of the said Judge of Probate, that said lands were *bona fide* sold and deeds not executed by the said Josias L. Arnold, previous to his decease.

It is hereby further Enacted, that all deeds executed by the said William C. Arnold and James Whitelaw, Executors as aforesaid, under the direction of the said Judge of Probate, shall be valid, to all intents and purposes, as though given by the said Josias in his life time.

---

1. State Papers of Vermont, Vol. X, *General Petitions,* 1793-1796, "For Right to Sell Real Estate," 407.

AN ACT TO RECTIFY THE ERRORS COMMITTED IN THE RECORDS OF THE
PROPRIETORS OF THE TOWN OF UNDERHILL

NOVEMBER 8TH, 1796

It is hereby Enacted by the General Assembly of the State of Vermont, That, *Whereas,* errors of various sorts appear to have been made in the records of the proprietors of the town of Underhill, in the county of Chittenden, which cannot be rectified without Legislative interposition, one sixteenth part or upwards of the proprietors of said town, may call a meeting of the proprietors thereof, to be held in the said town of Underhill, on any day or days between the tenth of February and twentieth of March next ensuing, (Sundays excepted.) *Provided always,* That due notification of the said meeting, shall be published for the space of three weeks respectively in each of the four public newspapers printed in this State, in the towns of Bennington, Rutland, Windsor, and Burlington, the last of which publication shall be at least one month prior to the day in which the said meeting shall be warned to be held.

It is hereby further Enacted, That the notification aforesaid shall be signed by some person or persons who are proprietors of above one sixteenth of said township, and be in the words following:

"This is to notify the proprietors of the town of Underhill, in the county of Chittenden, that they are warned to meet on the ————— day of February next, at the house of ————— in said town, at ten of the clock in the forenoon, of said day, to rectify such mistakes, and make such necessary amendments in the proprietors' records of said town respecting the divided, as well as the undivided lands therein, as they shall think proper, agreeable to the true meaning and intention of an act of the Legislature of the State of Vermont passed at their October Session 1796."

It is hereby further Enacted, That the present records of the said proprietors, as well as the proceedings of the said meeting, as far as respects the amendment or alteration of the said records, shall be laid before the supreme court, which shall sit at Burlington, in the said county of Chittenden next after the said meeting, whose duty it shall be to hear the complaints of any proprietor or proprietors, who may think himself or themselves aggrieved by the vote of the majority of the said proprietors, as well as such committee, not exceeding three in number, as shall be appointed by order of the majority of the said proprietors at their meeting aforesaid, and that such supreme court after hearing the assertions and allegations of both parties, and receiving as satisfactory proof as the nature of the case will admit, are hereby invested with full and complete power, finally to determine on the alterations which should take place in the said records, and whose determination is hereby declared to be equally valid and binding to all intents and purposes, as if the same had been heretofore done and established by the proprietors at a meeting legally warned and having full powers for that purpose, any law, usage or custom to the contrary notwithstanding.

It is hereby further Enacted, That it shall be the duty of the proprietors at their said meeting to provide for the payment of all the expenses which have already, or may hereafter accrue in the settlement of the above business, and enforce the collection thereof, in such manner as has heretofore practised, pursuant to an act entitled "An act regulating proprietors' meetings," passed ninth March 1787[1]

AN ACT FOR THE RELIEF OF JAMES GREENLEAF & UDNEY HAY[2]

NOVEMBER 8TH, 1796

Whereas, it appears by the petition of James Greenleaf and Udney Hay, that they are the proprietors of almost the whole of a large tract of land originally granted to John Kelly in the year one thousand seven hundred and ninety one, and designated, at that time, on the maps of this State by the name of Kelly's burgh, but now known by the titles of Belvidere, Kellyvale, No. 2 and No. 4, containing sixty nine thousand one hundred acres. *And Whereas,* the title of the said land has been, from sundry unfortunate circumstances, held in almost constant dispute, from the time it was first granted as aforesaid. And whereas it appears that the aforesaid James Greenleaf and Udney Hay had absolutely agreed for the survey of a considerable part thereof into small lots, for the purpose of commencing an immediate and extensive settlement, and for encouraging a number of inhabitants to reside on the land aforesaid. And whereas it further appears, that a writ of error was served upon the said Udney Hay, signed by one of the Judges of the supreme court in the month of September last, with a view of setting

---

1. State Papers of Vermont, Vol. X, *General Petitions,* 1793-1796, "For Correction of Errors in Proprietors Records," 328.

2. Udney Hay of Underhill was deputy commissary general of purchases, northern department of the Continental Army: See *Governor and Council,* Volume II, page 49-50.

aside a judgement formerly given in favor of the said Udney Hay, by which a large portion of the said land became vested in him, which writ of error in its present state has induced the aforesaid James Greenleaf and Udney Hay to desist from pursuing the intended settlement as mentioned aforesaid, 'til the month of the said writ of error be determined. Therefore,

It is hereby Enacted, by the General Assembly of the State of Vermont, That, for the relief of the said James Greenleaf and Udney Hay, their or either of their heirs or assigns, the time for performing the settling duties on the said land shall be protracted 'til the first day of January, which will be in the year of our Lord one thousand eight hundred and one; any thing in the original charter of the said land, any law usage or custom to the contrary notwithstanding.[1]

AN ACT APPOINTING A COMMITTEE AND COLLECTOR OF A LAND TAX IN JOHNSON IN FRANKLIN COUNTY

NOVEMBER 8TH, 1796

Whereas, William Coit of Burlington, Joseph Baker of Bakersfield, and John Wier and Daniel Coit, both then of Johnson, were appointed by the General Assembly of this State, in the year one thousand seven hundred and ninety four, a committee on a land tax of one penny on each acre of land in the township of Johnson aforesaid, and William Coit was appointed collector of said tax in and by the bill granting and assessing such tax. And whereas the said committee and collector previous to any work being done on the said roads have neglected to perform the business of said committee. Therefore,

It is hereby Enacted by the General Assembly of the State of Vermont, that William Coit of Burlington, John Wier and Robert Balch, of Johnson, aforesaid, be, and are hereby appointed a committee for the purpose of superintending the work to be done by money raised by said tax in the room of aforesaid committee. And that Silas Waterman of Cambridge, in said county, be, and he is hereby appointed collector, to collect said tax in the room of said William Coit, and any justice of the peace in the county of Franklin, is hereby authorised to issue his warrant to the said Silas Waterman, to collect the

---

1. State Papers of Vermont, Vol. X, *General Petitions,* 1793-1796, "For Extension of Time to Fulfill the Provisions of a Charter," 408.

said tax, the same as the said Coit was, by the act granting said tax. And the said new committee are made accountable and liable, and invested with the same authority and power, and in the same manner and respect as directed by the former act; and are to govern themselves in the laying out and expending said tax, agreeable to the petition praying for said tax. And said collector is made accountable to said committee last mentioned, the same as the said William Coit was to the former committee, and is vested with the same power and authority as the said William Coit was by the former act.[1]

AN ACT EMPOWERING THE ADMINISTRATORS TO THE ESTATE OF
NATHAN DELANO, LATE OF PANTON, DECEASED, TO DEED
CERTAIN LANDS THEREIN MENTIONED

NOVEMBER 8TH, 1796

Whereas, Nathan Delano, late of Panton, deceased, died seized of three undivided third division lots of land in the township of Whiting, in the county of Addison, which lots the said Nathan Delano, was by agreement, to have deeded to Ebenezer Wheelock, Jonathan Conick, and Ezra Allen. Therefore,

It is hereby Enacted, by the General Assembly of the State of Vermont, That Edmund Grandy and Ely Snow, administrators to the estate of Nathan Delano, late of Panton, deceased, be, and they hereby are empowered to execute deeds in as full and ample a manner as the said Nathan could have done in his life time, of three third division lots of land in the township of Whiting, which the said Nathan died seized of, unto the said Ebenezer Wheelock, Jonathan Conick and Ezra Allen, in such a manner and under such directions as the Judge of Probate in the district where such land lieth shall direct, any law usage, or custom to the contrary notwithstanding.[2]

---

1. State Papers of Vermont, Vol. X, *General Petitions*, 1793-1796, "For Appointment of a New Land Tax Committee," 366.

2. State Papers of Vermont, Vol. X, *General Petitions*, 1793-1796, "For the Right to Deed Lands to Settle an Estate," 369.

AN ACT, IN ADDITION TO AN ACT ENTITLED, "AN ACT APPOINTING
A COMMITTEE TO COLLECT, REVISE AND COMPARE THE
STATUTE LAWS OF THIS STATE," PASSED

OCTOBER 24TH, 1795

It is hereby Enacted by the General Assembly of the State of Vermont, That the honorable Nathaniel Chipman and Samuel Hitchcock, Esquires, be, and they are hereby appointed in addition to the Committee mentioned in said act, which Committee are hereby authorised and empowered to take all the existing laws of this state of a public nature, under consideration, and collect, compare, arrange, systematize and revise the same, and make such additions and amendments, as they shall judge will be the best calculated to insure a permanent system of public laws, and report their doings in proper bills to the next adjourned session of the Legislature in February next. And the said Committee are hereby authorised and empowered to report the constitution of the United States, and such laws and parts of laws of the United States as are immediately applicable to the situation and circumstances of this State; which committee, before they enter upon the business of their appointment, shall be duly sworn to the faithful discharge of their trust.

AN ACT DIRECTING THE TREASURER OF THE COUNTY OF CHITTENDEN
TO RECEIVE OF AARON ROWLEY, COLLECTOR, CERTAIN ORDERS
DRAWN ON THE TREASURY

NOVEMBER 8TH, 1796

Whereas, Aaron Rowley of Shelburne, in the county of Chittenden, was constable and collector for the town of Shelburne, in said county, of the tax assessed on said county by the Legislature in October 1795, and as collector on aforesaid, before the first day of September last past, received certain orders drawn by the clerks of the county court of said county, on the treasury of said county. And whereas by the act assessing said tax, the said treasurer was directed to receive no such orders as aforesaid after the said first day of September, of which direction the said Aaron Rowley had no knowledge, the laws of the last session not having been distributed in said county until after the said first day of September. Therefore,

It is hereby Enacted by the General Assembly of the State of

Vermont, That the county treasurer of the county of Chittenden for the time being, be, and he is hereby directed to receive of the said Aaron Rowley, such orders drawn on said treasurer as aforesaid, to the amount of said tax, on said town of Shelburne.

Provided Such orders bear date, previous to the said first day of September last past, and that the same be presented to the said treasurer, by the first day of December next.

AN ACT PROVIDING RELIEF TO SEVERAL TOWN CLERKS IN THE COUNTY OF CHITTENDEN WHO HAVE BEEN LIABLE, AND ARE STILL LIABLE TO PAY FINES IN CONSEQUENCE OF NOT TRANSMITTING A COPY OF THE GRAND LIST TO THE TREASURER OF THE SAME COUNTY BY THE FIRST DAY OF MARCH AGREEABLE TO AN ACT PASSED IN OCTOBER A.D. 1795

NOVEMBER 8TH, 1796

Whereas, the laws of the State of Vermont for the last session, by the negligence of a person appointed by the sheriff to distribute the same, were not sent to the several town clerks in the county of Chittenden, until the time expired, by which it was made the duty of the town clerks to return to the county treasurer the grand list for their several towns; and the state's attorney for said county, taking advantage of the delinquent town clerks, prosecuted them on the statute and put them to great cost. Therefore,

It is hereby Enacted by the General Assembly of the State of Vermont, That all fines, which have been recovered and paid into the treasury of the county of Chittenden, by virtue of any forfeiture obtained by said prosecutions, shall be remitted to said town clerks, and the treasurer of the county of Chittenden is hereby directed to remit said fines, to the several town clerks from whom they were received, any law to the contrary notwithstanding. And that no suit already commenced shall be further prosecuted; or any other suit be commenced against any of the clerks aforesaid, on account of the delinquency aforesaid.

AN ACT GRANTING A SUM OF MONEY THEREIN MENTIONED TO
STEPHEN CLARK

NOVEMBER 8TH, 1796

Whereas, it appears to this Legislature, that Stephen Clark, late collector of taxes for the town of Wallingford, has paid into the treasury of this State, one hundred and five pounds on the eight, seven and six penny taxes of the year 1781, for the collecting of which he has not received the usual and customary fees. Therefore,

It is hereby Enacted by the General Assembly of the State of Vermont, That the treasurer be, and he is hereby directed to pay to the said Stephen Clark, the sum of four dollars, it being the ballance due to him of collecting fees, on the aforesaid sum of one hundred and five pounds.

AN ACT DIRECTING THE TREASURER OF THIS STATE TO PAY
THE SEVERAL SUMS OF MONEY THEREIN MENTIONED

NOVEMBER 8TH, 1796

It is hereby Enacted by the General Assembly of the State of Vermont, That the treasurer of this State be, and he hereby is directed to pay out of the treasury the several sums of money annexed to the names of the following persons respectively, it being the amount of their accounts, as clerks of the supreme court of judicature, in the several counties in this State, to wit: to Samuel Robinson, Esquire, the sum of fifteen pounds, eleven shillings, and four pence; to Richard Whitney, Esqr., the sum of eleven pounds, nineteen shillings; to Nathan Osgood, Esquire, the sum of fourteen pounds, three shillings; to Lewis R. Morris, Esquire, the sum of thirteen pounds, thirteen shillings, and two pence; to Samuel Painter Esqr., the sum of six pounds, seven shillings; to Isaac Bayley Esqr., the sum of seven pounds, fourteen shillings; to John Law Esqr., the sum of ten pounds, nineteen shillings and six pence; and to Roswell Hopkins, Esqr., for services in receiving and receipting votes for members of Congress in January and February 1795, the sum of one pound, eighteen shillings. The said sums respectively, to be paid in hard money orders, on application for the same.

AN ACT FOR THE PURPOSE OF RAISING THE SUM OF
FIVE HUNDRED DOLLARS BY LOTTERY

NOVEMBER 8TH, 1796

It is hereby Enacted by the General Assembly of the State of Vermont, That George Sexton, Timothy Mead, Junr., and Robert Anderson, have liberty to raise the sum of five hundred dollars by lottery for the purpose of making a road through the northwesterly part of Winhall, to Bromley, it being where the old road goes, distance of near four miles.

And it is hereby further Enacted, That the above named persons be, and hereby are appointed managers of said lottery, and are hereby directed to lay out said money on said road.

And it is hereby further Enacted, That the aforesaid George Sexton, Timothy Mead, Junr., and Robert Anderson, give bonds to the county court of the county of Bennington, in the sum of one thousand dollars, for the faithful performance of their trust, before they commence the sale of said tickets.

And it is hereby further Enacted, That no defendant shall be liable to pay any cost, in any action brought to recover pay for said tickets, unless he appeals from the judgment that may be rendered against him.

Provided Nevertheless, That this State shall in no wise be accountable.[1]

AN ACT GRANTING A LOTTERY TO RAISE FOUR HUNDRED DOLLARS,
FOR THE PURPOSE OF BUILDING A BRIDGE OVER WHITE RIVER
IN THE TOWN OF STOCKBRIDGE

NOVEMBER 8TH, 1796

It is hereby Enacted by the General Assembly of the State of Vermont, That there be, and hereby is granted a lottery, to raise the sum of four hundred dollars, to be applied under the direction of managers herein after appointed, to the building of a bridge over White-River, in the town of Stockbridge, in the county of Windsor.

It is hereby further Enacted, That John Durkee, John Whitcomb,

---

1. State Papers of Vermont, Vol. X, *General Petitions,* 1793-1796, "For a Lottery to Repair a Road," 400.

and Robert Lyon, all of said Stockbridge, be, and they are hereby appointed managers of said lottery. And the said managers, previous to their entering upon the business of this trust, shall enter into a bond to the treasurer of the county of Windsor, with surety, to the satisfaction of the said treasurer, in the sum of ten thousand dollars, conditioned for the faithful performance of the trust. And the said managers are authorised to adopt such scheme for the said lottery, for raising the sum aforesaid, as they shall judge will be most expedient and eligible; transmitting to the clerk of the county court of the county of Windsor aforesaid, the said scheme, which the said clerk is hereby directed to keep on file in his office. And the said managers are hereby appointed a committee to superintend (in conjunction with the committee appointed by an act passed at the present session of the Legislature entitled "An act assessing a tax of one penny per acre on the lands in the town of Stockbridge"), the expenditure of the avails of said lottery, in the erecting of a bridge over White River as aforesaid. And the said managers, after drawing the lottery, and expending its avails, as before directed, shall exhibit their accounts of the lottery, and of the expenditure of its avails, aforesaid, to the said county court, for a settlement, which exhibition and settlement shall be made within two years from passing of this act. And the said county court shall, in the settlement of these accounts, proceed in the same manner as is directed by law, in allowing and approving the accounts of committees appointed to superintend the land taxes in the several towns, and they shall allow to the said managers what they shall judge just and equitable, for their trouble and expense, in the management of the said lottery, and upon a settlement of such management and superintendence, to the satisfaction and approbation of the judges of said court, an order shall be given by the said court, for the cancelling of the bond aforesaid. And the said managers shall publish a list of the prizes of said lottery, in at least the newspaper printed at Windsor, in this State. And such prizes as shall not be demanded within six months after such publication, shall be deemed as given to the purpose of the lottery, and of such undemanded prizes the managers shall render an account to the judges aforesaid. *Provided nevertheless,* That no cost shall be recovered in any action, brought against any person, for the recovery of any debt that shall accrue from the sale of the tickets in said lottery, unless by judgment on the defendant's appeal.[1]

---

1. State Papers of Vermont, Vol. X, *General Petitions,* 1793-1796, "For a Tax on Land to Build a Bridge," 381.

AN ACT ASSESSING A TAX OF TWO PENCE PER ACRE ON THE
TOWNSHIP OF SWANTON FOR THE PURPOSE OF
MAKING ROADS AND BUILDING BRIDGES

NOVEMBER 8TH, 1796

It is hereby Enacted by the General Assembly of the State of
Vermont, That there be, and hereby is assessed a tax of two pence on
each acre of land in the township of Swanton, in the county of Franklin, public rights excepted, for the purpose of making and repairing
roads and building bridges in said town, to be expended by the order
and under the direction of John Pratt, Clark Hubbard, and William
Green, all of Swanton, aforesaid, who are hereby appointed a committee to superintend the expenditure of said tax. And any justice of the
peace within the county of Franklin, is hereby empowered to issue his
warrant to Amasa How [Howe], to collect said tax, and said collector
is hereby made accountable to said committee for the amount of said
tax; and said collector and committee are hereby directed to govern
themselves in collecting, disposing, and accounting for monies raised by
said tax, agreeably to an act entitled, "An act regulating the disposition
of monies raised by tax on the several towns for the purpose of making
& repairing roads and building bridges," passed October session 1796.[1]

AN ACT GRANTING A TAX OF ONE PENNY HALF PENNY
ON EACH ACRE OF LAND IN THE TOWNSHIP OF
SALTASH FOR THE PURPOSE
THEREIN MENTIONED

NOVEMBER 8TH, 1796

It is hereby Enacted by the General Assembly of the State of
Vermont, That there be, and hereby is granted a tax of one penny
half penny on each acre of land in the township of Saltash, in the
county of Windsor (public rights excepted), for the purpose of making
and repairing public roads and bridges in said town, to be expended by
the order and under the direction of the selectmen of said town, chosen
for the year 1796. And any justice of the peace in said county is hereby
empowered to issue a warrant to Hart Marcy to collect said tax, and
said collector is hereby made accountable to the said selectmen for the

1. State Papers of Vermont, Vol. X, *General Petitions,* 1793-1796, "For a Tax on
   Land to Build and Repair Roads and Bridges," 321.

amount of said tax. And said selectmen and collector are hereby directed to govern themselves in the collecting, disposing, and accounting for said tax, agreeably to an act entitled, "An act regulating the disposition of monies raised by tax on lands in the several towns for the purpose of making and repairing roads and bridges," passed this present session.[1]

AN ACT ASSESSING A TAX OF ONE PENNY PER ACRE ON THE LANDS IN THE TOWN OF SALEM

NOVEMBER 8TH, 1796

It is hereby Enacted by the General Assembly of the State of Vermont, That there be, and hereby is assessed a tax of one penny per acre on all the lands in the town of Salem, in the county of Caledonia, public rights excepted, for the purpose of making and repairing roads and building bridges. And,

It is hereby further Enacted, That Ebenezer Strong and Jonathan Allen be, and are hereby appointed a Committee to superintend the expenditure of said tax; and that any justice of the peace in the county of Caledonia is hereby empowered to issue a warrant to John Bean to collect said tax. And said collector is hereby made accountable to said committee; and said committee and collector are hereby directed in the collecting, expending, and accounting for said tax, to adhere and comply in all things with the directions of "An act regulating the disposition of monies raised by tax on lands in the several towns in this State for the purpose of making and repairing roads and building bridges," passed [by] the General Assembly at their October session A.D. 1796.

AN ACT DIRECTING THE TREASURER OF THE STATE OF VERMONT TO PAY JOEL HAMILTON THE SUM THEREIN MENTIONED

NOVEMBER 8TH, 1796

Whereas, it appears to this assembly, that the sum in the debenture allowed to Joel Hamilton, sheriff's deputy, for his attending on this assembly the present session, is not for so long a time as he has actually attended. Therefore,

---

1. State Papers of Vermont, Vol. X, *General Petitions,* 1793-1796, "For a Tax on Land to Build and Repair Roads and Bridges," 315.

It is hereby Enacted by the General Assembly of the State of Vermont, That the treasurer be, and hereby is directed to pay to Joel Hamilton, eleven dollars and twenty five cents, in addition to the sum allowed him in the debenture.

AN ACT DIRECTING THE TREASURER TO CREDIT THE TOWNS OF
MONKTON AND FAIRHAVEN THE SUMS THEREIN MENTIONED

NOVEMBER 8TH, 1796

Whereas, it appears that the Listers of Monkton, for the year 1794, by mistake, made up their list eight hundred and ninety one pounds too large. And the listers of Fairhaven for the year 1795, by mistake, made up their list one hundred and eight pounds too large. Therefore,

It is hereby Enacted by the General Assembly of the State of Vermont, That the treasurer be, and is hereby directed to credit the town of Monkton seven pounds eight shillings and six pence on the tax granted in 1794. And he is hereby directed to credit the town of Fairhaven, one pound ten shillings on the tax granted in the year 1795.[1]

AN ACT DIRECTING THE TREASURER OF THE STATE TO PAY THE
SELECTMEN OF LONDONDERRY IN THE COUNTY OF WINDHAM
THE SUM OF NINETEEN DOLLARS

NOVEMBER 8TH, 1796

Whereas, the selectmen of Londonderry have expended the sum of nineteen dollars, for the support of Jonathan Brunt, a foreigner. Therefore,

It is hereby Enacted by the General Assembly of the State of Vermont, That the treasurer of this State be, and he hereby is directed to pay the selectmen of Londonderry, the sum of nineteen dollars in hard money orders, to defray the expense of supporting the aforesaid Jonathan.[2]

1. State Papers of Vermont, Vol. X, *General Petitions*, 1793-1796, "For Tax Credit for an Error in the Grand List," 209.

2. State Papers of Vermont, Vol. X, *General Petitions*, 1793-1796, "For compensation for the Support of an Indigent Foreigner," 336.

AN ACT DIRECTING THE TREASURER OF THE STATE TO PAY TO THE
SELECTMEN OF THE NORTH HERO, THIRTY ONE POUNDS,
FOUR SHILLINGS & THREE PENCE

NOVEMBER 8TH, 1796

It is hereby Enacted by the General Assembly of the State of
Vermont, That the treasurer of this State, be, and he is hereby directed
to pay to the selectmen of the North-Hero, in hard money orders, the
sum of thirty one pounds, four shillings and three pence lawful money,
in payment for the support, nursing and doctoring, one Peter Willson,
a foreigner.[1]

AN ACT DIRECTING THE TREASURER TO PAY THE SELECTMEN OF
STOCKBRIDGE THE SUM OF TEN POUNDS,
TEN SHILLINGS LAWFUL MONEY

NOVEMBER 8TH, 1796

Whereas, the said town of Stockbridge hath been at expense in
supporting a foreigner in said town. Therefore,

It is hereby Enacted by the General Assembly of the State of
Vermont, That the treasurer be, and he hereby is directed to pay to
the selectmen of Stockbridge the sum of ten pounds, ten shillings lawful
money, in hard money orders, on application for the same.[2]

AN ACT DIRECTING THE STATE'S ATTORNEY FOR THE COUNTY OF
RUTLAND TO PAY TO TITUS WATSON AND REUBEN STEVENS,
THE SEVERAL SUMS AND OUT OF THE AVAILS OF
A CERTAIN BOND OF RECOGNIZANCE
THEREIN MENTIONED

NOVEMBER 8TH, 1796

Whereas, it appears to this Assembly that Jacob Cooley had stolen
from Titus Watson of Ballstown, in the state of New York, and from
Reuben Stevens of Poultney, in Rutland county, two certain horses, the

---

1. State Papers of Vermont, Vol. X, *General Petitions,* 1793-1796, "For Compensation for Support of an Indigent Foreigner," 323.

2. State Papers of Vermont, Vol. X, *General Petitions,* 1793-1796, "For compensation for the Support of an Indigent Foreigner," 345.

property of the said Titus and Reuben; and that by their laudable exertions, and at their expense, the said Jacob was apprehended, and bound over in a bond of recognizance, entered into by Gideon Cooley, late of Pittsford, in said county, for the sum of two hundred pounds lawful money, before William Ward Esqr., justice of the peace for Rutland county, to appear before and abide the order of the supreme court, in said county, respecting the feloniously taking of said horses, and that the said bond has become forfeited to and is secured to be paid into the treasury of this state. And that said Titus and Reuben have respectively commenced and prosecuted their actions, and recovered judgments thereon, against said Jacob, for the sum of forty two pounds, five shillings and ten pence, and for the sum of sixty one pounds, four shillings and three pence lawful money, for the private damages which they have sustained, and the costs of their respective suits, and that they are unable to obtain satisfaction thereon. Therefore,

It is hereby Enacted by the General Assembly of the State of Vermont, That the state's attorney for the county of Rutland, upon the collection of the avails of the aforesaid bond of recognizance, be, and is hereby authorised and directed, to pay to the said Titus, or his certain attorney, the aforesaid sum of forty two pounds, five shillings, and ten pence, and to said Reuben, or his certain attorney, the aforesaid sum of sixty one pounds, four shillings and three pence, lawful money, and to take his or their receipts for the same; which receipts the treasurer of this state is hereby directed to receive, and allow the said state's attorney, as part payment of the aforesaid bond. And upon the payment of the aforesaid sums, contained in said judgments, the aforesaid judgments shall become the property of this state.[1]

AN ACT DIRECTING THE TREASURER OF THIS STATE TO CREDIT
THE TOWN OF VERSHIRE, THE SUM OF TWO POUNDS,
TWELVE SHILLINGS AND TWO PENCE

NOVEMBER 8TH, 1796

Whereas, it appears to this assembly that there was a mistake of three hundred and thirteen pounds in the grand list of 1795. Therefore,

---

1. State Papers of Vermont, Vol. X, *General Petitions,* 1793-1796, "For Compensation for Loss by Theft," 386.

It is hereby Enacted by the General Assembly of the State of Vermont, That the treasurer be, and he hereby is directed to credit the town of Vershire the sum of two pounds, twelve shillings and two pence on the two penny tax of 1795, and the interest thereon from the first day of June last.

AN ACT ASSESSING A TAX OF ONE PENNY PER ACRE ON THE LAND
IN THE TOWN OF WHITINGHAM FOR THE PURPOSE OF
MAKING AND REPAIRING ROADS AND BUILDING
BRIDGES IN SAID TOWN

NOVEMBER 8TH, 1796

It is hereby Enacted by the General Assembly of the State of Vermont, That there be, and hereby is assessed a tax of one penny per acre on all the land in the town of Whitingham for the purpose of making and repairing roads and building bridges in said town.

And it is hereby further Enacted, That James Roberts, Jabez Foster, and Samuel Day be, and hereby are appointed a committee to superintend the expenditure of said tax; and that any justice of the peace in the county of Windham is hereby empowered to issue a warrant to Samuel Parker to collect said tax. And said collector is hereby made accountable to said committee for the amount of said tax, and said committee and collector are hereby directed in the collecting, expending, and accounting for said tax, to adhere and comply in all things with the directions of an act entitled, "an act regulating the disposition of monies raised by tax on lands in the several towns, for the purpose of making and repairing roads and building bridges," passed at the October session in the year 1796.[1]

AN ACT ASSESSING A LAND TAX ON THE TOWNSHIP OF MARSHFIELD
NOVEMBER 8TH, 1796

It is hereby Enacted by the General Assembly of the State of Vermont, That there be, and hereby is assessed a tax of one penny on each acre of land in the township of Marshfield, in the county of Caledonia (public rights excepted), for the purpose of completing the

1. State Papers of Vermont, Vol. X, *General Petitions,* 1793-1796, "For a Tax on Land to Repair Roads," 275.

public roads through said town, to be expended by the order and under the direction of Jacob Davis of Montpelier, Joshua Pitkin of said Marshfield, and James Morse of Cabot, who are hereby appointed a committee to superintend the expenditure of said tax. And any justice of the peace, within the county of Caledonia, is hereby empowered to issue a warrant to David Wing, Junr., to collect said tax, and said collector is hereby made accountable to said committee for the amount of said tax. And said collector and committee are hereby directed to govern themselves in the collecting, disposing and accounting for said tax agreeably to an act passed this present session.[1]

AN ACT LAYING A TAX OF ONE CENT AND AN HALF ON EACH ACRE OF
LAND IN THE TOWNSHIP OF LUNENBURGH

NOVEMBER 8TH, 1796

It is hereby Enacted by the General Assembly of the State of Vermont, That there be, and hereby is granted a tax of one cent and an half cent on each acre of land in the township of Lunenburgh, in the county of Caledonia, public rights excepted, for the purpose of making and repairing public roads and bridges in said town, to be expended by the order and direction of Samuel Gates, Ebenezer Hartshorn, and Jonathan Grout, who are hereby appointed a committee for that purpose; and any justice of the peace within and for said county is hereby empowered to issue his warrant to Abraham Williams of said town, to collect said tax. And the said committee and collector are hereby directed to govern themselves in the collecting, expending, and accounting for said tax, agreeably to a law passed by the Legislature of this State this present session, entitled, "An act regulating the disposition of monies raised by tax on lands for the purpose of making and repairing roads and bridges."[2]

---

1. State Papers of Vermont, Vol. X, *General Petitions,* 1793-1796, "For a Tax on Land to Build and Repair Roads," 316.
2. State Papers of Vermont, Vol. X, General Petitions, 1793-1796, "For a Tax on Land to Build and Repair Roads and Bridges," 330.

AN ACT ASSESSING A TAX OF TWO PENCE PR. ACRE ON THE TOWNSHIP
OF HUNTINGTON FOR THE PURPOSE OF MAKING ROADS AND
BUILDING BRIDGES

NOVEMBER 8TH, 1796

It is hereby Enacted by the General Assembly of the State of Vermont, That there be, and hereby is assessed a tax of two pence on each acre of land in the township of Huntington, in the county of Chittenden, public rights excepted, for the purpose of making and repairing roads and building bridges in said town, to be expended by the order and under the direction of Parley Starr, Ozem Brewster, and Jehiel Johns, all of Huntington, aforesaid, who are hereby appointed a committee to superintend the expenditure of said tax; and any justice of the peace within the county of Chittenden is hereby empowered to issue a warrant to Sylvester Russell of said Huntington to collect said tax. And said collector is hereby made accountable to said committee for the amount of said tax; and said collector and committee are hereby directed to govern themselves in collecting, disposing, and accounting for monies raised by said tax agreeable to an act entitled, "An act regulating the disposition of monies raised by tax on the several towns for the purpose of making and repairing roads and building bridges," passed October session 1796.[1]

AN ACT GRANTING A TAX ON THE COUNTY OF CHITTENDEN

NOVEMBER 8TH, 1796

I *It is hereby Enacted* by the General Assembly of the State of Vermont, That there be, and hereby is granted a tax of two pence on the pound, on the list of the polls and rateable estates of the inhabitants of the former county of Chittenden, for the year one thousand seven hundred and ninety six, to be paid into the treasury of said county on or before the first day of May next, in hard money notes issued by the Treasurer of said county, or orders drawn on said treasurer by order of the county court, or hard money.

II *And it hereby further Enacted,* That the treasurer of the county of Chittenden shall have the same power in issuing warrants and extents for the collection of said tax as is by law given to the

1. State Papers of Vermont, Vol. X, *General Petitions,* 1793-1796, "For a Tax on Land to Build and Repair Roads and Bridges," 402.

treasurer of this State, in collection of State taxes, which warrants and extents shall run into the county of Franklin; and each first constable in their respective towns in the former county of Chittenden be, and they are hereby empowered to proceed in the collection of said tax, in the same manner as they are directed by law to proceed in the collection of State taxes.

III *And it is hereby further Enacted*, That all debts, dues and demands, which now are or shall be due from the former county of Chittenden on the first day of December next, shall be presented for payment to the treasurer of said county, on or before the first day of September next, or the person having such debts or demands shall be forever debarred from collecting the same, and the treasurer is hereby directed to pay said demands out of the monies arising from the aforesaid tax.

IV *And it is hereby further Enacted*, That said treasurer shall keep a fair entry of such demand as he shall pay, as aforesaid, and he shall pay no debts with the money arising from said tax, which shall not be due before the first day of December next; and when the said debt, so due as aforesaid, shall be all paid and discharged, if any of the money arising from said tax shall remain in said treasury, that then and in that case the said treasurer of the county of Franklin [shall pay?], on demand, so much of said money as shall be so remaining in proportion to the list of the counties on which said tax is assessed.

V *And it is hereby further Enacted*, That the several town clerks within the former county of Chittenden, shall within two months from the passing of this act, make returns to the treasurer of said county, of the amount of the grand list of their respective towns, proper to assess said tax by; and in case any such clerk shall refuse or neglect to make return of such list, within two months as aforesaid, he shall pay into the treasury of said county, the sum of four dollars for every month's neglect, and the state's attorney for the county of Chittenden is hereby directed and empowered to prosecute such delinquents, in the name of the treasurer of said county before any court proper to try the same; and such court is hereby directed to render judgment thereon and issue execution accordingly.

VI *And it is hereby further Enacted*, That it shall be the duty of said treasurer of the county of Chittenden, before the first day of April next, to publish the time at which the limitation for the allowance, if demanded against the aforesaid county, will expire, by inserting an advertisement for three weeks successively in the newspapers printed in Burlington, in said county.

AN ACT MAKING APPROPRIATIONS FOR THE SUPPORT OF GOVERNMENT
FOR THE PRESENT SESSION, AND FROM THENCE UNTIL THE
SESSION OF ASSEMBLY IN OCTOBER, ONE THOUSAND
SEVEN HUNDRED AND NINETY SEVEN

NOVEMBER 8TH, 1796

I *It is hereby Enacted* by the General Assembly of the State of Vermont, That there be, and hereby is appropriated for the support of government, until the session of Assembly in October, one thousand seven hundred and ninety seven, the several sums for the several purposes following, to wit: for the salary of the governor, five hundred dollars; for the salary of the treasurer, four hundred dollars; also the sum of seven thousand and thirty eight dollars and twenty four cents, for the debentures of the lieutenant-governor, Council and General Assembly, and the necessary officers attending this session, together with the auditor of accounts against this State. Also the further sum of twelve dollars to be paid for the firewood and candles for the session of Council. Also to Samuel Walker Esqr., for the firewood and candles of the clerks at his office, two dollars; and that there be allowed two dollars to Thomas Tolman Esqr. for firewood and candles found him. Also to Elisha Clark Esqr., auditor of accounts, against this State ten dollars for his services, since the last, and previous to the present session.

II *And it is hereby further Enacted,* That there be appropriated a sum not exceeding five thousand five hundred dollars for the purpose of paying the sums allowed by the auditor of accounts against this State; and the orders drawn by and under the direction of the supreme court; which several sums of money shall be paid by the treasurer, out of the monies in the treasury. And if there be not sufficient monies in the treasury, the Treasurer shall issue hard money orders for the residue of such appropriation.

AN ACT ORGANIZING THE COUNTIES OF FRANKLIN AND CALEDONIA
AND FIXING THE TIMES AND PLACES FOR HOLDING THE SUPREME
AND COUNTY COURTS IN THE SAME, AND FOR ALTERING THE
PLACE OF HOLDING THE SUPREME AND COUNTY
COURTS IN THE COUNTY OF ORANGE

NOVEMBER 8TH, 1796

I   *It is hereby Enacted* by the General Assembly of the State of Vermont, That from and after the first day of December next, the counties of Franklin and Caledonia shall be, and they are hereby considered as distinct and separate counties, with all the powers and privileges of other counties in this State, agreeably to an act passed the fifth day of November one thousand seven hundred and ninety two, entitled, "An act for dividing the counties of Orange and Chittenden into six separate and distinct counties."

II   *And it is hereby further Enacted,* That all actions of whatever name or nature now pending before the county court in the county of Chittenden, and all actions which already are or shall hereafter be commenced before the first day of December next, and made returnable to the court in the county of Chittenden, shall be heard, tried and finally determined in said court, unless when both parties shall be inhabitants and resident within the county of Franklin, and when the said parties shall agree upon a removal of any cause, in which case such cause shall be subject to be removed to the court of the last mentioned county.

Provided always, That after the next session of the county court in the counties of Orange and Chittenden, such actions as shall remain on the docket of either of said courts, where both of the parties shall live in either of the counties of Franklin or Caledonia, and there has been no trial in such action, that then and in that case such action shall be removed from said courts respectively into the county of Caledonia or Franklin, as the case may be. And the clerks of said courts respectively, are hereby directed to deliver to such person as may be authorised by the court of the county to which such removal is to be made, the files and original papers in such actions as may be removed as aforesaid, and the expense of such removal, shall be advanced by the plaintiff in such action, and shall be taxed in the bill of cost if he shall recover.

III   *And it is hereby further Enacted,* That all appeals from the

judgment of justices of the peace in the county of Chittenden, heretofore prayed out, or which shall hereafter, and before the first day of
December next, be prayed out and granted by justices of the peace as
aforesaid, such action shall be entered on the docket of the county
court of Chittenden, and be there heard and determined, subject only
to the provisions of the foregoing paragraph of this act, for the removal
of causes.

IV   *And it is hereby further Enacted,* That the Supreme court for
the County of Caledonia shall be holden at Danville within and for
said county, on the third Tuesday next following the fourth Tuesday
of August annually. And the county court for said county, shall be
holden at Danville aforesaid, on the first Monday of January, and
last Monday of June, annually.

V   *And it is hereby further Enacted,* That the supreme court
for the county of Franklin shall (for the time being), be holden at
St. Albans, within and for said county, on the fourth Tuesday after
the [fourth Tuesday?] in August annually. And the county courts
shall, for the time being, be holden at said St. Albans, within and for
said county, on the first Monday of February and September, annually.

VI   *And it is hereby further Enacted,* That the next term of the
county court to be holden within and for the county of Orange, on
the Monday next preceding the second Tuesday of December next,
shall be holden at Chelsea within said county. And from and after
that time the supreme and county courts within and for said county
shall be holden at Chelsea, at the same times at which said courts are
now by law directed to be holden in said county, and all actions, processes, informations, recognizances or indictments which now are pending before, and which have or may be made returnable to said courts,
within and for said county to be holden at Newbury, shall be heard,
tried and determined by said courts at Chelsea, in the same manner
as though the said actions, processes, informations, recognizances or
indictments, had been originally made returnable to said courts at
Chelsea.

Provided always, That if the inhabitants of the said towns of
Chelsea and Danville shall not, within two years from the passing of
this act, each for themselves respectively, build and complete a good
and sufficient courthouse and gaol in said towns, respectively, to the
satisfaction and acceptance of the judges of the county courts of Orange

and Caledonia, free of expense to said counties, the courts shall be liable to be removed to such other place or places in said counties as the Legislature shall by law direct.

VII *And it is hereby further Enacted,* That the judges of the county court of the county of Caledonia, shall meet on the first Monday of December next and appoint a clerk for such court, and all actions, processes, informations and recognizances, of what name or nature soever, and also all appeals from justices courts, which have been or shall be prayed out before the first day of December next, where both the parties reside in the county of Caledonia, such actions shall be delivered over by the clerk of the county of Orange to the clerk of the county of Caledonia, whose duty it shall be to make application therefor; which application shall be made during the first week of the sitting of the court for the said county of Orange. And the said court of the county of Caledonia is hereby authorised and directed to hear and determine to final judgment all such actions and causes, thus transfered, in the same manner as though the same had been originally made returnable unto, and cognizable before them. And the clerk of the county of Orange aforesaid, shall be allowed one shilling for each action, so by him delivered over, which sum shall be advanced by the clerk of the county of Caledonia. And such sum so by him advanced shall be paid by the plaintiff in such action to the said clerk when such action is entered in the docket of the said last mentioned court, and the clerk of the county of Caledonia, shall give his official receipt for all the papers, as he shall receive from the said clerk of the county of Orange. And the said clerk for the county of Orange, shall not make any entries of the actions where the parties reside in the counties of Caledonia as aforesaid.

VIII *And it is hereby further Enacted,* That all depositions taken in any cause which shall be removed, shall be admitted the same as if said cause were heard in the court or courts respectively, from whence such removal took place.

AN ACT REPEALING AN ACT ENTITLED, "AND ACT TO ESTABLISH THE
RESIDENCE OF THE LEGISLATURE OF THE STATE OF VERMONT,
FOR THE TERM OF EIGHT YEARS, PASSED NOVEMBER 1ST 1791"

NOVEMBER 8TH, 1796

Whereas, said act is found to be inconvenient and expensive, Therefore,

It is hereby Enacted by the General Assembly of the State of Vermont, That the act to establish the residence of the Legislature of the State for the term of eight years be, and the same is hereby repealed.

AND ACT GRANTING TO LEMUEL BRADLEY, TIMOTHY BRADLEY, AND
ETHAN BRADLEY OF SUNDERLAND AND THEIR ASSOCIATES, THE
EXCLUSIVE RIGHT OF SMITHING [SMELTING?] AND REFINING,
CERTAIN MINERALS AND ORES

NOVEMBER 8TH, 1796

Whereas, Lemuel Bradley, Timothy Bradley and Ethan Bradley of Sunderland in this State, have prefered their petition to the Legislature, for the exclusive right of smithing [smelting?] and refining of gold, silver, brass, lead and copper ores discovered by them in a mine opened by them in Sunderland in this State, some time in the year one thousand seven hundred and ninety four.

I   *It is hereby Enacted* by the General Assembly of the State of Vermont, That Lemuel Bradley, Timothy Bradley, and Ethan Bradley of Sunderland have, and they hereby have granted unto them and their associates for the term of thirty five years, the exclusive right of smithing and refining all gold, brass, lead, silver and copper ores in a mine by them discovered and opened on their lands in said Sunderland, previous to the twenty third day of October, Anno Domini one thousand seven hundred and ninety five.

II   *And it is hereby further Enacted,* That his Excellency the Governor by and with the advice of council, be, and he hereby is authorised and empowered to issue letters patent, under the seal of this State, to the said Lemuel Bradley, Timothy Bradley and Ethan Bradley and their associates and their heirs and assigns conformably to this act.[1]

AN ACT ASSESSING A TAX OF FOUR CENTS ON THE POUND ON THE LIST
OF THE POLLS AND RATEABLE ESTATE, FOR THE YEAR ONE THOUSAND
SEVEN HUNDRED AND NINETY SIX

NOVEMBER 8TH, 1796

It is hereby Enacted, by the General Assembly of the State of

---

1. State Papers of Vermont, Vol. X, *General Petitions,* 1793-1796, "For Right to Work a Lead Mine," 360.

Vermont, That there be, and hereby is assessed a tax of four cents on the pound on the list of the polls and rateable estate of the inhabitants of this State, taken in the year one thousand seven hundred and ninety six; to be paid into the treasury by the first day of June next in money, hard money orders, or orders drawn on the treasury by order of the Supreme Court.

AN ACT GRANTING THE EXCLUSIVE PRIVILEGE OF KEEPING A FERRY FROM GEORGIA TO THE NORTH PART OF SOUTH HERO, TO DAVID MAXFIELD FOR THE TERM OF EIGHT YEARS

NOVEMBER 8TH, 1796

It is hereby enacted by the General Assembly of the State of Vermont, That the exclusive right of keeping a ferry from Georgia to the north part of South-Hero, be, and the same is hereby granted to David Maxfield, his heirs and assigns, for the term of eight years from the passing of this act; on the following conditions, to wit, the said David Maxfield, his heirs or assigns shall, by the first day of June next, have, and shall thereafter keep in good repair and well manned, sufficient ferry boats for carrying passengers, horses, cattle, teams and carriages across said ferry, under such regulations as the magistrates, selectmen and constables of said towns of Georgia and South Hero shall direct, agreeable to law.

Provided nevertheless, That if the said David Maxfield, his heirs or assigns, shall refuse or neglect to carry any passengers, horses, cattle, teams or carriages across said ferry, within one hour after application is made, provided the boat is not then on the way carrying passengers, and wind and weather will permit, shall pay a fine not exceeding three dollars and thirty four cents, to the Treasury of the town where the prosecution shall be commenced, and pay all damages to the persons, injured by such delay.

Provided also, if they shall be without sufficient boats for that purpose for the space of twelve days, between the fifteenth day of April and the Twentieth Day of December annually, they shall forfeit thereafter all the rights and privileges granted by this act.

AN ACT ADOPTING THE COMMON LAW OF ENGLAND

NOVEMBER 9TH, 1796

Whereas, from the peculiar situation of this State as a new formed government it is difficult at once to provide a system of maxims and presidents [precedents,] which may in all cases be necessary as a guide and direction to the several courts of justice within this State, and for producing a uniformity of decisions in the same; and whereas the inhabitants have been accustomed to conform their manner to the laws of England:

It is hereby Enacted by the General Assembly of the State of Vermont, That so much of the common law of England as is not repugnant to the constitution, or to any act of the Legislature of this State, be, and hereby is adoped law wihin this State; and all courts are to take notice thereof, and govern themselves accordingly.

END OF ACTS PASSED OCTOBER SESSION 1796

LAWS OF 1797

ACTS AND LAWS PASSED BY THE LEGISLATURE OF THE STATE OF VERMONT AT THEIR ADJOURNED SESSION HOLDEN AT RUTLAND IN FEBRUARY 1797

AN ACT APPOINTING DAVID KNOWLES A COMMITTEE TO SUPERINTEND THE EXPENDITURE OF A TAX ON THE LANDS IN WESTFORD

FEBRUARY 18TH, 1797

Whereas, it is represented to this Legislature, That Eliphalet Smith, one of the committee for superintending the tax granted by the Legislature in October, 1795, on the lands in the town of Westford, for making and repairing public roads, is moved out of said Westfield [Westford]. Therefore,

It is hereby Enacted by the General Assembly of the State of Vermont, That David Knowles of Westford be, and he is hereby appointed a committee to act with Hiel Williams and Martin Powell in the superintendance of the expenditure of said tax, and the said David Knowles is hereby authorised to act in the same manner, and vested with the same powers, that the said Smith would have possessed had this act not been passed.[1]

AN ACT APPOINTING NEW MANAGERS TO, AND DIVERTING THE APPROPRIATION OF CONNECTICUT RIVER LOTTERY, SO CALLED, GRANTED BY THE LEGISLATURE OF THIS STATE, OCTOBER 1793

FEBRUARY 18TH, 1797

It is hereby Enacted by the General Assembly of the State of Vermont, That Oliver Gallup, Micah Barron and Lewis R. Morris, Esqr., be, and they are hereby appointed managers of Connecticut River lottery, so called, instead of the old managers; and the said new managers shall give bonds in the sum of twenty thousand dollars to the treasurer of the county of Windsor, conditioned for the faithful discharge of their said trust. The sum to be raised by said lottery, shall be the same as directed by the said act granting the same; but the said new managers may alter the scheme or schemes thereof, if they should judge necessary. And the lottery shall be drawn, on or before the first Tuesday of March, which will be in the year 1798, and the managers

1. State Papers of Vermont, Vol. X, *General Petitions*, 1793-1796, "For Adding Members to a Land Tax Committee," 401.

shall publish a list of the prizes in the newspapers printed at Rutland, Windsor, and Walpole, and all the prizes not demanded in twelve months from the drawing thereof, shall be deemed as given for the purpose of the lottery. And the new managers are hereby empowered and directed as a committee to lay out and expend the money raised by said lottery, on the county post road from the south line of this State to the north line of Newbury, directed to be surveyed and opened by an act of the Legislature, passed at their last session at Windsor, in such parts and on such places of said road as they shall judge best, and as will best equalize the expense of said road on the towns through which it will pass. And the said new managers after they have drawn the said lottery, and expended the avails, which shall be within one year after the drawing of said lottery, in labour on the road aforesaid, and shall exhibit an account of their doings and the expenditures of the money to the judges of the county court, of the county of Windsor, and the same being approved of by the judges, their aforesaid bond shall be by them cancelled; and the new managers shall be allowed as a compensation for their trouble, expense, and risk in selling and drawing said lottery, and making payments of the prizes, six per cent on the sum directed as aforesaid to be raised by the said lottery.

And it is hereby further Enacted, That the new managers shall allow from the avails of said lottery to the old managers, for the expenses which have accrued to them in obtaining the grant of said lottery, and in printing and numbering the tickets, and the labour by them already done in Connecticut River, on the credit of said lottery, the sum of fifty pounds L.M.

And it is hereby further Enacted, That the old managers shall deliver by the time mentioned in this act, for the drawing of said lottery, unto the treasurer aforesaid, all the old tickets of said lottery, as well as those which are sold, as those on hand; and nothing in this act shall prevent the possessors of said tickets from recovering of the old managers, their money paid for said tickets on taking up their obligations given for the same, which said old managers shall be accountable for the tickets they have sold.

And it is hereby further Enacted, That that part of the said act directing the avails of said lottery to be expended in clearing Connecticut River, be, and hereby is repealed.[1]

---

1. State Papers of Vermont, Vol. X, *General Petitions,* 1793-1796, "For the Diversion of Lottery Funds," 399.

AN ACT ASSESSING A TAX OF ONE PENNY PER ACRE ON THE LANDS
IN THE TOWN OF STOCKBRIDGE

FEBRUARY 18TH, 1797

It is hereby Enacted by the General Assembly of the State of Vermont, That there be, and hereby is assessed a tax of one penny per acre on all the lands in the town of Stockbridge, in the county of Windsor, public rights excepted, for the purpose of erecting a bridge over White River in said town of Stockbridge.

And it is hereby further Enacted, That Elias Keyes, David Johnson, and Daniel Gay, all of said Stockbridge, be, and they are hereby appointed a committee to superintend the expenditure of said tax, and that Jeremiah Gay of said Stockbridge be, and he is hereby appointed collector of said tax, in the discharge of the duties of which office this act is his sufficient warrant, and he is hereby made accountable to said committee; and said committee and collector in the discharge of their duties in collecting, expending, and accounting for said tax, are directed to adhere and comply in all things to the directions of the act entitled, "An act regulating the disposition of monies raised by tax on lands in the several towns for the purpose of making and repairing roads and building bridges," passed October A.D. 1796.[1]

AN ACT ASSESSING A TAX OF ONE PENNY PER ACRE ON THE LANDS
IN THE TOWN OF BARTON

FEBRUARY 18TH, 1797

It is hereby Enacted by the General Assembly of the State of Vermont, That there be, and hereby is assessed a tax of one penny per acre on all the lands in the town of Barton, in the county of Orange, public rights excepted, for the purpose of making and repairing roads and building bridges in said town.

And it is hereby further Enacted, That William Chamberlain and John Bean be, and are hereby appointed a committee to superintend the expenditure of said tax, and that any justice of the peace in the county of Orange is hereby empowered to issue a warrant to Asa Kimball to collect said tax, and said collector is hereby made accountable to

1. State Papers of Vermont, Vol. X, *General Petitions,* 1793-1796, "For a Tax on Land to Build a Bridge," 381.

said committee. And said committee and collector are hereby directed in the collecting, expending, and accounting for said tax, to adhere and comply in all things, with the directions of "An act regulating the disposition of monies raised by tax on lands in the several towns in this State, for the purpose of making and repairing roads and building bridges," passed at the General Assembly at their October session A. D. 1796.[1]

AN ACT GRANTING A TAX OF TWO PENCE ON EACH ACRE OF LAND IN THE TOWNSHIP OF BURLINGTON IN THE COUNTY OF CHITTENDEN

FEBRUARY 18TH, 1797

It is hereby Enacted by the General Assembly of the State of Vermont, That there be, and hereby is granted a tax of two pence on each acre of land in the township of Burlington, public lands excepted, for the purpose of making and repairing public roads and bridges in said town, to be expended by the order and direction of William C. Harrington and Daniel Hurlburt, who are hereby appointed a committee for that purpose; and any justice of the peace in said county is hereby empowered to issue a warrant to Stephen Pearl to collect said tax. And said collector is hereby made accountable to said committee for the amount of said tax. And said collector and committee are hereby directed to govern themselves in the collecting, disposing, and accounting for the monies raised by said tax, agreeable to an act entitled, "An act regulating the disposition of monies raised by tax on lands in the several towns for the purpose of making and repairing roads &. c.," passed October session 1796.[2]

AN ACT ASSESSING A TAX OF ONE PENNY PER ACRE ON EACH ACRE OF LAND IN THE TOWN OF COLCHESTER IN THE COUNTY OF CHITTENDEN

FEBRUARY 18TH, 1797

It is hereby Enacted by the General Assembly of the State of Vermont, That a tax of one penny per acre be granted, and the same is hereby assessed on all the lands in the town of Colchester in the county of Chittenden (public rights excepted), for the purpose of making and repairing roads and building bridges in said town.

---

1. State Papers of Vermont, Vol. X, *General Petitions,* 1793-1796, "For a Tax on Land to Repair a Road," 378.

2. Ibid., "For a Tax on Land to Build and Repair Roads and Bridges," 338.

And it is hereby further Enacted, That Simeon Hine, Aaron Brown and Joshua Stanton, Junr., be, and they are hereby appointed a committee to superintend the expenditure of said tax, and that any justice of the peace in the county of Chittenden is hereby empowered to issue a warrant to Benjamin Boardman to collect said tax. And said collector is hereby made accountable to said committee; and said committee and collector are hereby directed in the collecting, expending, and accounting for said tax, to adhere and comply in all things with the directions of an act entitled, "An act regulating the disposition of monies raised by tax on lands in the several towns for the purpose of making and repairing roads and building bridges," passed at Rutland in October session A.D. 1796.[1]

AN ACT ASSESSING A TAX OF TWO PENCE PER ACRE ON THE TOWNSHIP OF HIGHGATE FOR THE PURPOSE OF MAKING AND REPAIRING ROADS AND BUILDING BRIDGES

FEBRUARY 18TH, 1797

It is hereby Enacted by the General Assembly of the State of Vermont, That there be, and hereby is assessed a tax of two pence on each acre of land in the township of Highgate, in the county of Franklin, public rights excepted, for the purpose of making and repairing roads and building bridges in said town, to be expended by the order and under the direction of Jonathan Butterfield and John Sax, both of Highgate, aforesaid, who are hereby appointed a committee to superintend the expenditure of said tax. And any justice of the peace, within the county of Franklin, is hereby empowered to issue a warrant to Silas Hathaway, of St. Albans, to collect said tax, and said collector is hereby made accountable to said committee for the amount of said tax; and said collector and committee are hereby directed to govern themselves in collecting, disposing, and accounting for monies raised by said tax, agreeably to an act entitled, "An act regulating the disposition of monies raised by tax on the several towns, for the purpose of making and repairing roads and building bridges &. c.," passed in October session 1796.[2]

---

1. State Papers of Vermont, Vol. X, *General Petitions,* 1793-1796, "For a Tax on Land to Build and Repair Roads and Bridges," 321.
2. Ibid., "For a tax on Land to Build Roads and Bridges," 388.

AN ACT APPOINTING A COMMITTEE TO LAY OUT AND SURVEY A STAGE
OR POST ROAD FROM VERGENNES TO BURLINGTON

FEBRUARY 18TH, 1797

Whereas, Ferrisburgh, Charlotte, Shelburn[e] and Burlington, have petitioned this assembly separately for a land tax on each of the aforesaid towns, for the purpose of making a good stage or post road through said towns from Vergennes to Burlington, and the prayer of said petitions have been granted by this assembly. And whereas it appears highly necessary that an impartial committee should be appointed to lay out and establish the most convenient place for said post or stage road. Therefore,

It is hereby Enacted by the General Assembly of the State of Vermont, That Samuel Strong, William Coit, and Joseph J. Tobias be, and they are hereby appointed a committee to lay out a public highway for a permanent post or stage road from the academy in Vergennes aforesaid, to the court house in Burlington. And the said committee are hereby directed to commence a survey of said road, on or before the first day of June next, and complete the same as soon as may be. And the said committee are hereby directed to call on any county surveyor, who is hereby directed to attend said committee, and make such survey or surveys, as they shall direct, and make a survey bill of such roads according to the direction of said committee, with the points of compass, length and width, properly attested for record. And such road or roads so laid by said committee, as aforesaid, and recorded in the town clerk's office in the town where such road lies, shall not be altered by the selectmen of such town, any law or usage to the contrary notwithstanding. And said committee are hereby directed to cause such survey or surveys to be recorded in the town clerk's office, of the town through which such road is laid.

And it is hereby further Enacted, That the aforesaid committee may set over any old road, which they may think proper to that use, to the owner or owners whose land they may take for a new road. And if said committee shall find it necessary to lay a new road through any improved land where there is no such old road, which they can set over as aforesaid, and where there is no allowance land, said committee shall assess damages for any new road they shall lay out, as aforesaid, and a certificate given by such committee to the person or persons through whose land they shall lay such new road or roads, shall be sufficient voucher for the selectmen of the town where such road shall be laid, to pay the sum therein mentioned. And such selectmen are hereby directed to pay the amount thereof out of the town treasury. And should such selectmen neglect or refuse to pay the money, so certified by such committee, the person or persons holding such certificate may, after the expiration of three months from the presentment of such certificate, sue or prosecute the town where such selectmen belong, before any court proper to try the same, and such court is hereby directed to render judgment thereon, and issue execution accordingly.

And it is hereby further Enacted, That if any person or persons through whose land such road shall be laid, as aforesaid, shall neglect or refuse to open any such road so laid out, by such committee as aforesaid, such committee shall direct the person or persons so neglecting, or refusing as aforesaid, to open such road within a term of time to be set by such committee, which term of time shall not be less than one month, nor more than six. And if such person or persons shall neglect or refuse to open such road after the expiration of the time so limited for opening such road as aforesaid, such committee are hereby authorised and directed, by themselves or others, to be by them appointed, to open such road as soon as may be. And such person or persons so neglecting or refusing to open such road as aforesaid, shall pay just damages to said committee for such neglect or refusal, to be recovered by such committee before any court proper to try the same.

And it is hereby further Enacted, That such road so laid as aforesaid, shall not be altered but by the supreme court of this State, or a committee by them appointed, on application made to said court, by the selectmen of the town through which said road runs, and on a report of such committee, and its acceptance by the said supreme court, and recorded in the town clerk's office where such road lies, such road may be altered.

And it is hereby further Enacted, That the committee and surveyor by this act appointed, are authorised to lay out and survey such post road, shall make up separate accounts for laying out and surveying such post road, through each of the towns aforesaid, and present the same to the judges of the county court in the county of Addison. And the said judges are hereby directed to examine said accounts, and allow the same according to justice and equity. And the said accounts, so examined and allowed, shall be paid out of the monies arising from the several land taxes laid on the several towns aforesaid, for the purpose of making a post or stage road by the collector in each town, who is or shall be appointed to collect said tax, and a certificate from said judges or any two of them, certifying the acceptance and the allowing said accounts, shall be a sufficient voucher for said collector of each town to pay the same. And the collector, who is or shall be appointed in each of the aforesaid towns, for the collection of the aforesaid tax, is hereby directed to pay the said committee for their services, as aforesaid, out of the first monies which shall first be collected or paid on said several taxes.

AN ACT ASSESSING A TAX OF TWO PENCE ON THE ACRE ON THE TOWNSHIP OF JAMAICA FOR THE PURPOSE OF BUILDING A BRIDGE OVER WEST-RIVER IN SAID TOWN

FEBRUARY 20TH, 1797

It is hereby Enacted by the General Assembly of the State of Vermont, That there be, and hereby is assessed a tax of two pence on each acre of land in the township of Jamaica, public rights excepted, for the express purpose of building a bridge over West-River in said town, to be expended under the order and by the direction of Elisha Chase, Samuel Livermore, and Josiah Glezen, all of Jamaica aforesaid, who are hereby appointed a committee to superintend the expenditure of said tax. And any justice of the peace within and for the county of Windham is hereby empowered to issue his warrant to John A. Alden of Jamaica, to collect said tax; and said collector is hereby made accountable to said committee for the amount of said tax, and said collector and committee are hereby directed to govern themselves in collecting, disposing, and accounting for the monies raised by said tax, agreeably to an act regulating the disposition of monies raised by taxes on the several towns for the purpose of making and repairing roads and building bridges &. c., passed November 2d 1796.

Provided always, and it is hereby further enacted, That if it shall be found by the committee aforesaid, that any part of said tax shall remain unappropriated after the building said bridge is compleated, then the said committee are hereby directed to lay out such money so remaining on such other public roads and bridges in said town, as to them shall appear will best accommodate the public.[1]

---

1. State Papers of Vermont, Vol. X, *General Petitions,* 1793-1796, "For a Tax on Land to Build a Bridge," 299.

AN ACT GRANTING A LAND TAX ON THE TOWNSHIP OF WOODBURY

FEBRUARY 20TH, 1797

It is hereby Enacted by the General Assembly of the State of Vermont, That there be, and hereby is assessed a tax of one penny on each acre of land in the township of Woodbury, in the county of Caledonia (public rights excepted), for the purpose of completing a road from Calais to Hardwick, through said town, and to repair a road in said town from Cabot to Elmore, already cleared, to be expended by the order and under the direction of Timothy Stanley, Esqr., of Greensborough, who is hereby appointed a committee to superintend the expenditure of said tax. And any justice of the peace, within the county of Caledonia, is hereby empowered to issue a warrant to David Wing, Junr., to collect said tax; and said collector is hereby made accountable to said committee for the amount of said tax. And said collector and committee are hereby directed to govern themselves in the collecting, disposing, and accounting for said tax, agreeably to an act passed this present session entitled, "An act regulating the disposition of monies raised by tax on the several towns for the purpose of making and repairing roads and building bridges."[1]

AN ACT ASSESSING A TAX OF ONE PENNY PER ACRE ON THE LANDS IN CHARLOTTE IN CHITTENDEN COUNTY

FEBRUARY 20TH, 1797

It is hereby Enacted by the General Assembly of the State of Vermont, That a tax of one penny per acre be, and the same is hereby assessed on all the lands in said Charlotte (public rights excepted) for the purpose of making and repairing roads and building bridges in said town.

And it is hereby further Enacted, That Hezekiah Barnes, Isaac Webb, and Lot Newell, all of Charlotte aforesaid, be, and they are hereby appointed a committee to superintend the expenditure of said tax; and that any justice of the peace in the county of Chittenden is hereby empowered to issue his warrant to Asahel Strong, Esqr., to collect said tax, and said collector is hereby made accountable to said

---

1. State Papers of Vermont, Vol. X, *General Petitions,* 1793-1796, "For a Tax on Land to Build a Road," 376.

committee for the amount of said tax. And said committee and collector are hereby directed in the collecting, expending, and accounting for said tax, to adhere and comply in all things with the directions of an act entitled, "An act regulating the disposition of monies raised by tax on lands in the several towns, for the purpose of making and repairing roads and building bridges," passed October, A.D. 1796.

AN ACT AUTHORISING SAMUEL FLETCHER AND EPHRAIM WHEELOCK, ESQUIRES, IN THEIR CAPACITY OF SELECTMEN FOR THE TOWN OF TOWNSHEND IN THE COUNTY OF WINDHAM, TO SELL ALL THE REAL ESTATE OF THACE WATKINS, OF SAID TOWNSHEND, A *NON COMPOS MENTIS*

FEBRUARY 20TH, 1797

It is hereby Enacted by the General Assembly of the State of Vermont, That Samuel Fletcher and Ephraim Wheelock, Esquires, two of the selectmen of the town of Townshend, for the time being, be, and they are hereby fully authorised and empowered to sell all the real estate of the aforesaid Thace Watkins, lying in Townshend, aforesaid, which consisteth of about thirty acres of land, and the avails thereof, to convert, so far as may at any time be found necessary, to the support of the aforesaid Thace. Provided nevertheless, that the vendue of the estate so sold as aforesaid, if any there be at her decease, shall descend to her heirs at law. And,

It is hereby further Enacted, That the deed or deeds executed by the selectmen aforesaid, shall be valid in law and equity to convey the title of said land so by them sold, any law or usage to the contrary notwithstanding. And the said selectmen shall be made accountable to the county court for the county of Windham, for the faithful management of their trust.[1]

---

1. State Papers of Vermont, Vol. X, *General Petitions,* 1793-1796, "For the Right to Sell Real Estate," 389.

AN ACT AUTHORISING AND EMPOWERING THEODORA YOUNG TO SELL
ALL THE REAL ESTATE OF RODOLPHUS WHEELOCK
SITUATE IN THIS STATE

FEBRUARY 20TH, 1796

Whereas, Theodora Young of Hanover, in the county of Grafton, and state of New Hampshire, has by her petition to this assembly represented that some time since she was duly and legally appointed guardian to Rodolphus Wheelock of Hanover, in the county of Grafton, and state of New Hampshire, Esqr., [?] who is adjudged to be not of sound mind, in which appointment she was authorised and directed to pay all the debts of the said Rodolphus, and for that purpose had license granted her to sell all his real estate lying in said county of Grafton, which service she hath faithfully attended, and finds that after paying out the proceeds thereof, there remain debts due to a considerable amount, and still unsettled. That said Rodolphus is prossessed of several lots of land lying in this State, which if disposed of would discharge the debts of the said Rodolphus and add to his support. Therefore,

It is hereby Enacted by the General Assembly of the State of Vermont, That the said Theodora Young be, and she is hereby authorised and empowered to sell all the real estate belonging to the said Rodolphus Wheelock, situate, lying and being in this State. And,

It is hereby further Enacted, That all deeds and conveyances which the said Theordora shall execute in her capacity aforesaid, shall be as good and valid in law, to all intents and purposes as though executed under the hand and seal of the said Rodolphus. *Provided nevertheless,* That the said Theodora shall, previous to the sale of the real estate hereinbefore described, give bond in the sum of fifteen hundred dollars to the judge of probate in the county of Grafton, conditioned, that she appropriate the money arising from such sales, for the purposes mentioned in this act, and account to the said judge of probate, or his successor in office, for the over plus if any there shall be.[1]

---

1. State Papers of Vermont, Vol. X, *General Petitions,* 1793-1796, "For the Right to Sell the Property of an Incompetent," 221.

AN ACT ASSESSING A TAX OF ONE PENNY PER ACRE ON THE LANDS
IN SHELBURNE IN CHITTENDEN COUNTY

FEBRUARY 20TH, 1797

It is hereby Enacted by the General Assembly of the State of Vermont, That a tax of one penny per acre be, and the same is hereby assessed on all the lands in the town of Shelburn[e], aforesaid, (public rights excepted) for the purpose of making and repairing roads and building bridges in said town. And,

It is hereby further Enacted, That Daniel Comstock, Benjamin Harrington, and Sturgis Morehouse, all of Shelburn, aforesaid, be, and they are hereby appointed a committee to superintend the expenditure of said tax. And that any justice of the peace in the county of Chittenden is hereby empowered to issue his warrant to Nehemiah Sexton to collect said tax, and said collector is hereby made accountable to said committee for the amount of said tax. And said committee and collector are hereby directed in the collecting, expending, and accounting for said tax, to adhere & comply in all things with the directions of an act entitled, "An act regulating the disposition of monies raised by tax on lands in the several towns for the purpose of making and repairing roads and building bridges," passed October A.D. 1796.[1]

AN ACT ASSESSING A TAX OF ONE PENNY PER ACRE ON THE LANDS
IN THE TOWN OF PITTSFIELD

FEBRUARY 20TH, 1797

It is hereby Enacted by the General Assembly of the State of Vermont, That there be, and hereby is assessed a tax of one penny per acre on all the lands in the town of Pittsfield, in the county of Rutland, (public rights excepted), for the purpose of opening and making a road from the mouth of Clark's brook, to the south line of Rochester, near the mills of E. Emmerson, Esqr., and to repair the road from Daniel Bow's, leading toward Pittsford's furnace.[2] And,

---

1. State Papers of Vermont, Vol. X, *General Petitions,* 1793-1796, "For a Tax on Land to Build and Repair Roads and Bridges," 332.

2. Crockett, Walter Hill: *Vermont, The Green Mountain State,* Volume II, 514-520. A blast furnace was authorized by the legislature by act of October 15, 1788. See State Papers of Vermont, Volume XIV, 397-398.

It is hereby further Enacted, That Amas Jones, Daniel Bow, and Thomas Hodgkins, all of said Pittsfield, be, and they are hereby appointed a committee to superintend the expenditure of said tax. And that any justice in the county of Rutland is hereby empowered to issue his warrant to Jonas Stone of said Pittsfield, to collect said tax. And said collector is hereby made accountable to said committee. And said committee and collector are hereby directed in the collecting, expending, and accounting for said tax, to adhere and comply, in all things, with the directions of the act entitled, "An act regulating the disposition of monies raised by tax on lands in the several towns for the purpose of making and repairing roads and building bridges," passed this present session.[1]

AN ACT ASSESSING A TAX OF ONE PENNY HALF PENNY PER ACRE ON THE TOWNSHIP OF LITTLETON FOR THE PURPOSE OF MAKING AND REPAIRING ROADS AND BUILDING BRIDGES IN SAID TOWN

FEBRUARY 20TH, 1797

It is hereby Enacted by the General Assembly of the State of Vermont, That there be, and hereby is assessed a tax of one penny half penny on each acre of land in the township of Littleton, in the county of Caledonia, public rights excepted, for the purpose of making and repairing roads and building bridges in said town, to be expended by the order and under the direction of John Grow, Harvey Holbrook, and Levi Goss, all of Littleton, who are hereby appointed a committee to superintend the expenditure of said tax. And any justice within the county of Caledonia, is hereby empowered to issue a warrant to Nathan Pike of Littleton, to collect said tax, and said collector is hereby made accountable to said committee for the amount of said tax. And said collector and committee are hereby directed to govern themselves in collecting, disposing, and accounting for the monies raised by said tax agreeable to an act entitled, "An act regulating the disposition of monies raised by tax on the several towns for the purpose of making and repairing roads and building bridges &. c.," passed at October session A.D. 1796.[2]

---

1. State Papers of Vermont, Vol. X, *General Petitions,* 1793-1796, "For a Tax on Land to Build Roads," 354.

2. State Papers of Vermont, Vol. X, *General Petitions,* 1793-1796, "For a Tax on Land to Build and Repair Roads and Bridges," 377.

AN ACT ANNEXING PART OF THE TOWNSHIP OF MONKTON TO THE
TOWN OF STARKESBOROUGH

FEBRUARY 21ST, 1797

It is hereby Enacted by the General Assembly of the State of
Vermont, That, that part of the town of Monkton hereinafter described, to wit, beginning at the south east corner of said Monkton, thence
west on the south line thereof, so far that a line turning at right angles
and running North will strike the West line of the second tier of the
first division lots, thence, still north on said west line of the second tier
of the first division lots, 'til it intersects a line drawn east and west
through the center of the first division lot, drawn to the right, assigned
by charter to the society for propagating the gospel in foreign parts,
thence east, through the center of the last mentioned lot, to the east line
of said Monkton; thence south on the line last mentioned to the first
bound, be, and the same is hereby declared to be annexed to the town
of Starkesborough. And the inhabitants who do, or shall hereafter
inhabit the tract of land above described, shall have and enjoy all the
privileges and immunities which the inhabitants of said Starksborough
are by law entitled to have and enjoy.[1]

AN ACT TO ENABLE SAMUEL BELLOWS OF CHARLESTOWN, IN THE
COUNTY OF CHESHIRE AND STATE OF NEW HAMPSHIRE,
ADMINISTRATOR ON THE ESTATE OF PETER BELLOWS,
JUNIOR, LATE OF SAID CHARLESTOWN, DECEASED,
TO SELL CERTAIN LANDS THEREIN
MENTIONED

FEBRUARY 21ST, 1797

It is hereby Enacted by the General Assembly of the State of
Vermont, That Samuel Bellows of Charlestown, in the county of
Cheshire and state of New Hampshire, administrator on the estate of
Peter Bellows, Junior, late of said Charlestown, deceased, be, and he
hereby is empowered to sell and convey in such manner as the court
of probate, for the district of Westminster shall direct, all the lands
belonging to the estate of said Peter, lying and being in Rockingham
in the county of Windham. Which sale and conveyance, when so

---

1. State Papers of Vermont, Vol. X, *General Petitions,* 1793-1796, "For Annexation
of Part of one Town to Another," 348.

made under the direction of the said court, shall be as good and valid in law to pass the title, as if the same had been made by the said Peter in his life time.[1]

AN ACT GRANTING A TAX OF THREE CENTS ON EACH ACRE OF LAND IN THE TOWNSHIP OF FAIRLEE IN THE COUNTY OF ORANGE FOR THE PURPOSE OF MAKING AND REPAIRING ROADS AND BUILDING BRIDGES

FEBRUARY 22ND, 1797

It is hereby Enacted by the General Assembly of the State of Vermont, That a tax of three cents on each acre of land in the township of Fairlee, in the county of Orange (public rights excepted), be granted for the purpose of making and repairing roads and building bridges in said town, the one half to be laid out in the east part of said town of Fairlee, and the other half in the west parish of said Fairlee, to be expended under the direction and by the order of Ebenezer Baldwin, Calvin Morse, and Simon B. Bissell of said Fairlee, who are hereby appointed a committee to superintend the expenditure of said money. And any Justice of the peace for the county of Orange is hereby directed to issue a warrant to Israel Morey, Esqr., of said Fairlee, who is hereby appointed a collector to collect said tax. And said committee and collector are hereby commanded to govern themselves in the collection and expenditure of said money, agreeably to an act of this Assembly passed in October session A.D. 1796, directing the collection and expenditure of money raised by tax on lands for the aforesaid purposes.[2]

AN ACT EMPOWERING BENJAMIN FASSET, ESQR., GUARDIAN OF HENRY WALBRIDGE, SECOND, A MINOR, TO SELL THE REAL ESTATE OF SAID MINOR

FEBRUARY 22ND, 1797

Whereas it is represented that it is necessary to sell a part or the

---

1. State Papers of Vermont, Vol. X, *General Petitions,* 1793-1796, "For the Right to Sell Lands to Settle an Estate," 370.
2. Ibid., Vol. XI, *General Petitions,* 1797-1799, "For a Tax on Land to Build and Repair Roads and Bridges," 24.

whole of the real estate of said minor for his maintenance and support. Therefore,

It is hereby Enacted by the General Assembly of the State of Vermont, That Benjamin Fasset of Bennington, in the county of Bennington, guardian of Henry Walbridge, second, a minor, and only heir of the estate of Henry Walbridge, late of Bennington, aforesaid, deceased, be, and he hereby is empowered to sell the whole, or such part of the real estate of the said minor, as the judge of probate for the district of Bennington shall judge will best answer the purposes and interest of the said minor. And any deed or deeds executed by the said Benjamin, as guardian of the said minor, to any person or persons conveying any part, or the whole of said minor's estate, shall be good and valid in law.

Provided nevertheless, and it is hereby further enacted, That before the said Benjamin shall execute any deed of the premise, or any part thereof, he shall give a bond with sufficient surety or sureties to the judge of probate of said district, and his successors in office, in such sum as the said judge shall think reasonable, to account with his said ward, when he arrives at full age, or his heirs, executors, or administrators for the avails of the sale of such estate. And such sum or sums as the said judge shall think reasonable, shall be delivered by the said guardian to his said ward, for his support and maintenance, and the sum or sums so delivered shall be allowed in his account against his said ward, when he becomes of age, or at any other time, when he shall be called to account. And the over plus, if any there be, of such sale or sales, the said guardian shall dispose of and put to use in such manner as will best promote the interest of his said ward, and his heirs, and shall account therefor to his said ward when he arrives at age, or his heirs, executors, or administrators, as aforesaid.[1]

AN ACT ALTERING THE NAME OF THE TOWNSHIP OF SALTASH TO THAT OF PLYMOUTH

FEBRUARY 22ND, 1797

It is hereby Enacted by the General Assembly of the State of Vermont, That from and after the first day of March next, the town-

---

1. State Papers of Vermont, Vol. XI, *General Petitions,* 1797-1799, "For Authority to a Minor to Sell Real Estate," 23.

ship of Saltash, in the county of Windsor, shall be called and known by the name of Plymouth.

And it is hereby further Enacted, That in all advertisements respecting lands in said township of Saltash, for three years from the passing hereof, said township shall be called by the name of Plymouth, alias Saltash.[1]

AN ACT DIVIDING THE TOWN OF FAIRLEE INTO TWO SEPARATE TOWNS

FEBRUARY 25TH, 1797

It is hereby enacted by the General Assembly of the State of Vermont, That the said town of Fairlee be divided in the following manner, to wit: beginning on the north line of said Fairlee at the north end of the line which divides the seventh from the eighth range of hundred acre lots, from thence southwardly on said range line until it intersects the north line of lot number three; from thence eastwardly, on the north line of said lot numbered three, to Fairlee Lake; from thence southwardly through the deepest channel of said Lake to the south line of said Fairlee. And the land contained in the said town of Fairlee, laying west of the line herein before described, be, and the same is hereby erected into a town by the name of West Fairlee, with all the rights, privileges, and immunities enjoyed by any town in this State, except the privilege of electing a Representative to represent said town of West Fairlee in the General Assembly of this State, and in any State convention hereafter to be assembled. And the land lying east of the line herein described, shall continue a town by the name of Fairlee with the same, and no greater rights, privileges, and immunities than is by this act given to West Fairlee.

And it is hereby further Enacted, That the first constables of the towns of Fairlee and West Fairlee, in their respective towns in the manner prescribed by law, shall notify the freemen of said towns to attend at the usual place for holding freemen's meetings in the town of Fairlee, on the first Tuesday of September, annually. And the freemen when met as aforesaid, shall or may elect one representative to represent said town in the General Assembly of this State; and may in like manner proceed to elect a representative to represent said towns in any

---

1. State Papers of Vermont, Vol. X, *General Petitions,* 1793-1796, "For Changing the Name of a Town," 300.

state convention hereafter to be assembled, and shall or may also give in their votes for governor, lieutenant governor, treasurer and twelve councillors, and elect and give in their votes for any other officers by law to be chosen on that day. *Provided nevertheless*, and it is hereby further enacted, that when a majority of the inhabitants of said towns shall agree on any place or places for holding freemen's meetings in said towns, such meetings shall be held at such place or places so agreed on, and the first constable of the town in which such meeting shall be held shall be the presiding officer at said meeting.

And it is hereby further Enacted, That the rights, uses, and improvements of the public lands granted by charter to the town of Fairlee, shall and may be divided between said towns in such manner as they may hereafter agree. And all taxes now due from said town of Fairlee, as well as all debts due to said town, or owing therefrom, shall be collected in the same manner as if this act had not been made.

And it is hereby further Enacted, That for and during the space of three years from and after the passing of this act, in all advertisments for taxes of any kind whatever, it shall be necessary and is hereby required, that the said town of West-Fairlee should be called West Fairlee alias the west part of Fairlee.[1]

AN ACT IN ADDITION TO AND EXPLANATION OF AN ACT ENTITLED "AN ACT GRANTING TO WILLIAM PAGE, LEWIS R. MORRIS AND THEIR ASSOCIATES, THEIR HEIRS, AND ASSIGNS FOREVER, EXCLUSIVE RIGHT OF LOCKING BELLOWS FALLS ON CONNECTICUT RIVER AND FOR REPEALING AN ACT PASSED AT WINDSOR ON THE FIRST DAY OF NOVEMBER *anno domini* ONE THOUSAND SEVEN HUNDRED AND NINETY ONE, GRANTING THE SAME"

MARCH 1ST, 1797

Whereas, the Legislature of this State, at their session at Rutland in October, in the year of our Lord 1792, passed an act entitled "An act granting to William Page and Lewis R. Morris and their associates, their heirs, and assigns forever, the exclusive right of locking Bellows

---

1. State Papers of Vermont, Vol. XI, *General Petitions,* 1797-1799, "For the Division of a Town into Two Towns," 25.

Falls on Connecticut River, and for repealing an act passed on the first day of November, *anno domini,* one thousand seven hundred and ninety one, granting the same," in and by which said act, passed in October, *anno domini,* one thousand seven hundred and ninety two, the said William Page and Lewis R. Morris and their associates, were formed, constituted and made a body politic and corporate by the name of the company for rendering Connecticut River navigable by Bellows Falls. And whereas, it is found that the said act is in several respects deficient and inadequate to the attainment of the objects therein contemplated. Therefore,

1. *It is hereby Enacted* by the General Assembly of the State of Vermont, That the interest given in and by said act shall be hereafter considered as divided into eighteen shares, and that the present owners or proprietors under said grant, be considered and taken as holding a number of shares proportioned to their respective interests therein. And that in all future acts and proceedings of said company, the several owners or proprietors in said company, either by themselves or their agents or attornies, shall be allowed one vote for each share by them respectively owned. And all votes shall be by a major part of the shares owned by the members present, at any corporate meeting of said company. And the proprietors of said company shall have power, at any of their legal meetings, to ordain, establish, and put in execution such bye laws, ordinances, and regulations as shall seem necessary and convenient for the government of said company and the management of their interest, not being contrary to the laws and constitution of this state. And generally, to do and transact all and singular acts, matters, and things, which to them it shall and may appertain to do; in order to carry into effect their said grant and every part thereof.

2. *And it is hereby further Enacted,* That every meeting of said company shall be called by the owner or owners of six shares at least, published in a public newspaper, printed in the county of Windham, or Windsor, in the state of Vermont, and some paper published in the county of Cheshire in the State of New Hampshire, three weeks successively, the last of which publication shall be at least fifteen days before the time appointed for said meeting. And if there shall not be a paper published in either of the counties of Windham or Windsor in the state of Vermont, then to be published in manner aforesaid in the nearest paper in the State of Vermont. And if there shall be no paper published in the county of Cheshire, in the State of New Hampshire, then

to be published in manner aforesaid in the nearest paper printed in the State of New Hampshire. And the said company shall have power to adjourn their meetings, from time to time, and in their adjourned meetings to transact any business proper to be done by said company. *Provided*, That if said meeting shall be adjourned for more than the space of one month, at any one time, the time to which such meeting shall stand adjourned shall be notified by publication in the same manner as is herein before directed for calling meetings of said company.

Provided always, That the advertisement for calling the first meeting shall recite the regulations, relative to said meetings introduced by this act, and shall be further published in some daily newspaper printed in the city of New York, and in Russell's Centinel printed in the town of Boston, three weeks successively, the last publication of which shall be at least fifteen days before the time appointed for holding such meeting.

3. *And it is hereby further Enacted*, That said company shall have power to appoint a clerk, and the same to remove from time to time, at any of their regular meetings. And it shall be the duty of such clerk, being first sworn to the faithful discharge of his duty in that behalf, to make a fair entry in a book to be provided for that purpose, of all the doings of said company at their corporate meetings, and of all the transfers of the shares in said company, which may be by deed, in writing, and be entered by said clerk in the books of said company. And also to keep a fair docket of all such transfers.

4. *And it is hereby further Enacted*, That the said company shall have power from time to time, at their corporate meetings, to appoint a director or directors to take care of, and manage the business and interests of the company, agreeably to their bye-laws, regulations, and directions from time to time to be made.

5. *And it is hereby further Enacted*, That the right and interest of said company be considered and taken as joint stock, and that the company have a lien on the share or shares of individuals of said company, for any sum or sums of money advanced or agreed to be advanced by the said company in the prosecution of the object of their grant. And that every individual of the said company who shall have advanced any money, or rendered services for the company, under their direction, has a lien on the stock of the company for reimbursement. And the individual shares in said company shall be deemed and holden to be personal property.

6. *And it is hereby further Enacted*, That the said company shall have power and authority to fix the several sums of money which shall, from time to time, be paid by the proprietors or stockholders of said company, to compleat and support the object of their grant, to be apportioned equally to the several shares, and the time when such sums shall be paid; and public notice thereof shall be given in the same manner as is in this act before directed for calling meetings of the said company. And such publication shall be made three weeks successively, the first time whereof shall be at least sixty days before the time appointed for the payment of such assessment. And if any proprietor or stockholder shall neglect to pay his apportionment for the space of thirty days after the time appointed for paying the same, every such proprietor or stockholder shall, after the space of thirty days from and after the time so appointed for payment, in addition to the sum so apportioned, pay at the rate of six per centum per month, for every month's delay of such payment. And if the same, and the additional percentage as aforesaid, shall not be paid within three months after the same ought to have been paid, then the share or shares on which such payment shall be due, shall be forfeited to the said company, or corporation, and may be sold by said company to any person or persons who shall be willing to purchase the same, under such regulations as the company shall, from time to time, adopt.

7. *And it is hereby further Enacted*, that if any proprietor or stockholder of said company shall be in advance to said company for monies by him laid out and expended, services performed, or otherwise under the direction of said company, or the major part of them, in any legal way, any sum of money, or the amount of any sum of money, and the said company shall have neglected for the space of sixty days after demand made on said company, in their legal meeting as by a publication in the manner before directed in this act for calling a meeting of said company, to provide for, and reimburse such sum or sums as shall be justly due such proprietor, or stockholder, being so in advance, may prefer his petition in equity against said company for relief, to the judges of the supreme court, either in session in the county of Windham, or out of session, to be heard at such time and place in said county, as they or either two of them shall appoint; and said judges, or any two of them, are hereby empowered to hear and determine such petition, and award execution thereon as is hereafter directed in this act. And the manner of service shall be, that the judge to whom the petition shall be prefered, shall make out a citation, reciting

the substance of said petition and notifying the said company or the proprietors and stockholders thereof, to appear at the time and place therein to be appointed, and shew cause why the prayer of said petition should not be granted, in whole or in part, as the justice of the case may require. Which citation the petitioner shall cause to be published in the same papers as is before in this act directed, for calling meetings of said company, at least sixty days before the session of the court, or the time appointed for a hearing thereon. And the said judges, or either two of them as aforesaid, shall have power to ascertain the sum due from said company to the petitioner, if any they find, and to award such reasonable costs for or against such petitioner as they shall think just and reasonable. And after deducting the rateable proportion of such petitioner according to the share or shares, or proportion he may own in said company, shall issue a precept directed to the sheriff of the county of Windham, or his deputy, directing him to levy and collect the sum so found due, and the costs as aforesaid, on the shares of the remaining proprietors, by an equal assessment to be specified in such precept. And the officer to whom such precept shall be directed shall leave a notification with the clerk of said company, if any there be within his district, and shall cause the same to be published in the same public papers as is directed in this act for calling meetings of said company. Which notification shall set forth the substance of such precept. And that if the proprietor or proprietors, of the share or shares as therein mentioned, shall not pay and satisfy the sum or sums as apportioned to the several shares as aforesaid, and costs, before the day therein named, which day shall not be less than twenty nor more than thirty days from the time of publication, he will proceed to sell those shares which shall be delinquent, at the most public place to be therein appointed within his district, at or near said falls. And if the sums due and costs shall not have been paid on any or all of said shares, the officer shall proceed to sell at public auction, the share or shares on which payment shall not have been made, and shall return his said precept, with his doings thereon, to the clerk of the supreme court for the county of Windham, aforesaid, specifying in his said return, on what share or shares, payment had been made, and by or for whom, and the shares sold, to whom sold, and for what sums; which precept, with the officer's return thereon, shall be by said clerk recorded. And the officers shall deliver to the clerk of said company, if any there be within his district, a true and attested copy of said precept, with his return thereon, to be by such clerks entered in the books of said company. And the said officer shall make out and deliver to the purchaser or purchasers a certificate of their several purchases. And thereupon the purchaser or purchasers shall become proprietors and owners in the same manner as those whose rights or shares they shall have severally purchased. And the said officer shall, on demand, return the overplus money, if any there shall be, arising on the sale of the shares as aforesaid, to the respective owners, whose shares shall have been so sold.

8. *And it is hereby further Enacted,* That if such petition as herein before mentioned shall be brought before the said judges of the supreme court, out of session, nothing shall be allowed therefor by the state, but the wages of the said judges shall be advanced by the petitioners, and the same shall be allowed the said petitioner if he recover, in his bill of costs, either in whole or in part, as to the said judges shall seem just and reasonable. And if such petition shall be brought before the said judges out of session, they shall return their proceedings in the premises, to the clerk of the supreme court in the county of Windham aforesaid, who shall enter the same on record.

AN ACT LAYING A TAX OF TWO CENTS ON THE POUND ON THE
GRAND LIST OF THE POLLS AND RATEABLE ESTATES IN THE
COUNTY OF WINDSOR FOR THE YEAR SEVENTEEN
HUNDRED AND NINETY SIX, FOR BUILDING A
COUNTY GAOL IN SAID COUNTY

MARCH 1ST, 1797

It is hereby Enacted by the General Assembly of the State of Vermont, That there be, and hereby is granted a tax of two cents on the pound on the grand list of the polls and rateable estates of the inhabitants of the county of Windsor, for the year seventeen hundred and ninety six, for the purpose of building a county gaol in Woodstock in said county, to be collected and paid into the treasury of said county by the first day of June next, in orders drawn by the county court in the county aforesaid, on the treasurer of said county, or in dollars.

It is hereby further Enacted, that the treasurer of said county shall have the same power in issuing warrants and extents for the collection of the aforesaid tax, as is by law given to the treasurer of this State, in the collection of state's taxes. And the first constable in each of the respective towns, in the said county of Windsor, be, and they are hereby empowered to proceed in the collection of the aforesaid tax in the same manner as they are by law directed to proceed in the collection of state taxes.

Provided nevertheless, That the said treasurer be, and he is hereby required not to issue an extent against any constable or selectmen of said county, until requested thereto by at least two judges of said county court. And,

It is hereby further Enacted, That the judges of the county court, for the said county of Windsor, be, and they are hereby authorised and empowered forthwith, to take all due and necessary measures for building a county gaol as aforesaid, and to appoint an agent or contractor to superintend the said business, to make contracts, employ workmen, and to draw orders on the treasurer of said county, for the payment of contracts by him made, or workmen by him employed, in procuring materials or erecting such gaol agreeable to such plan, in such manner, and at such place in said Woodstock, as shall be directed by the aforesaid judges. And,

It is hereby further Enacted, That when the gaol shall be erected as aforesaid, the judges of the aforesaid court are hereby empowered to appoint a commissioner to sell and convey the gaol now erected in said Woodstock, together with that part of the common belonging to the aforesaid county, lying on the south side thereof, between the said gaol and the west end of the said common, of the width of the said gaol. And any deed or deeds executed by such commissioners in the name of the said county, shall be deemed good in law for conveying the property hereinbefore described, and such commissioners shall account to said judges for the money arising from such sale, which money shall by said judges be appropriated to building and finishing the gaol directed to be built by this act. And the said agent shall account to the judges as aforesaid, for all monies by him drawn from the treasury of said county, as well as all monies subscribed and paid by individuals for erecting and compleating said gaol, and the judges, aforesaid, are hereby empowered to adjust and settle the accounts of the aforesaid agent, and commissioner; and when the gaol shall be erected and finished to the acceptance of the said judges, the same shall become the gaol for the county of Windsor, and liberties shall be set out or assigned for the said prison according to law, and all prisoners then in custody of the sheriff of the said county, shall by him, under the order of said court or judges, be removed thereto. And,

It is hereby further Enacted, That the town clerk in each of the towns in the county aforesaid, shall, on or before the first day of April next, make return to the treasurer of said county of the names of the first constable in the town where such clerk may belong, and in case the said clerk shall neglect or refuse to make returns as herein before directed, he shall forfeit and pay into the treasury of said county the sum of five dollars for every month which he shall so neglect or refuse to make such return. And the state's attorney for the county of Windsor is hereby directed and empowered to prosecute such delinquent in the name of the treasurer of said county, before any court proper to try the same, and such court is hereby directed to render judgment thereon and issue execution accordingly.

AN ACT APPOINTING A COMMITTEE TO LAY OUT AND SURVEY A POST
ROAD FROM RUTLAND TO VERGENNES

MARCH 3RD, 1797

It is hereby Enacted by the General Assembly of the State of Vermont, That Jonathan Bell, John Ramsdell and Joel Linsly, Esquires, be, and they are hereby appointed a committee to lay out a public highway for a permanent post or stage road from the court house in Rutland to Vergennes, by the way of Middlebury Falls. And the said committee are hereby directed to commence a survey of said road, on or before the fifteenth day of May next, and compleat the same as soon as may be. And the said committee are hereby directed to call on any county surveyor in said counties of Rutland and Addison, who is hereby directed to attend said committee, and make such survey bills as said committee shall direct, with the points of compass, length, and width of said road, properly attested for record. And such road, so laid by said committee as aforesaid, and recorded in the town clerk's office in the town where such road lies, shall not be altered by the selectmen of such town, any law or usage to the contrary notwithstanding. And said committee are hereby directed to cause such survey or surveys to be recorded in the town clerk's office of the town through which such road is laid.

2. *And it is hereby further Enacted,* That the aforesaid committee may set over any old road, which they may think proper to shut up, to the owner or owners whose land they may take for a new road. And if said committee shall find it necessary to lay a new road through

improved land, where there is no such old road, which they can set over as aforesaid, and where there is no allowance land to make compensation, said committee shall assess damages for any new road which they shall lay out as aforesaid. And a certificate given by such committee to the person or persons through whose lands they shall lay such new road or roads, shall be a sufficient voucher for the selectmen of the town where such road shall be laid, to pay the sum therein mention. And such selectmen are hereby directed to pay the amount thereof out of the town treasury. And should such selectmen neglect or refuse to pay the money so certified by such committee, the person or persons holding such certificate may, after the expiration of six months from the presentment of such certificate, sue, or prosecute the town where such selectmen belong, before any court proper to try the same. And such court is hereby directed to render judgment thereon, and issue execution accordingly.

3. *And it is hereby further Enacted*, That if any person or persons through whose lands such road shall be laid as aforesaid, shall neglect or refuse to open said road laid out by the committee as aforesaid, such committee shall direct the person or persons so neglecting or refusing as aforesaid, to open such road within a term of time, to be set by said committee, which time shall not be less than one month, nor more than six, and if such person or persons shall neglect, or refuse, to open such road, after the expiration of the time so limited for the opening of such road, as aforesaid, such committee are hereby authorised and directed, by themselves, or others by them appointed, to open such road as soon as maybe. And such person or persons, so neglecting or refusing to open such road, as aforesaid, shall pay just damages to the said committee, for such neglect or refusal, to be recovered by such committee, before any court proper to try the same. And,

4. *It is hereby further Enacted,* That such road so laid as aforesaid, shall not be altered, but by the supreme court, or a committee by them appointed, on application made to said court by the selectmen of the town through which such road runs. And on a report of such committee, and its acceptance by the said supreme court, such road may be altered.

5. *And it is hereby further Enacted*, That the expense of laying out the aforesaid road, shall be paid by the several towns through which such road shall be laid, in such proportion on each town as the said committee shall judge equitable.

AN ACT TO ENABLE THE FREEMEN OF THE TOWN OF ATHENS,
TOGETHER WITH THE FREEMEN OF THE NORTH PART OF
BROOKLINE, TO HOLD FREEMEN'S MEETINGS IN
SAID BROOKLINE AS THEREIN DESCRIBED

MARCH 4TH, 1797

It is hereby Enacted by the General Assembly of the State of Vermont, That the freemen of the town of Athens, together with the freemen residing in that part of Brookline, heretofore called and known by the name of the south parish of Athens, be, and they are hereby fully authorised and empowered to hold freemen's meetings at the most convenient place in said north part of Brookline, such part or proportion of time as they shall mutually agree on for the purpose of transacting any kind of business for which such meeting is by law designed. And when said freemen shall so agree, the first constable of the town of Athens is hereby empowered and directed to notify or warn such meeting, and also to preside therein as directed by law.

AN ACT IN ADDITION TO AN ACT ENTITLED "AN ACT ASSESSING A
TAX OF TWO PENCE ON EACH ACRE OF LAND IN THE TOWN OF
HUNTINGTON," PASSED NOVEMBER THE SEVENTH ONE
THOUSAND SEVEN HUNDRED AND NINETY SIX

MARCH 7TH, 1797

It is hereby Enacted by the General Assembly of the State of Vermont, That said tax of two pence on each acre of land in Huntington, be laid on all the lands contained in the original charter of said town of Huntington, formerly called Newhuntington, now composing part of Richmond and Bolton (public rights excepted). And the committee appointed by the act aforesaid to superintend the expenditure of the same, are hereby directed to lay out and expend the said tax so that the inhabitants and land owners in the said towns of Richmond and Bolton, within the limits of the original charter of said New Huntington, shall be equally benefited thereby.[1]

---

1. State Papers of Vermont, Vol. XI, *General Petitions,* 1797-1799, "For a Tax on Land to Repair Roads and Bridges," 20.

AN ACT ASSESSING A TAX OF TWO PENCE PER ACRE ON THE TOWNSHIP
OF MILTON FOR THE PURPOSE OF MAKING ROADS
AND BUILDING BRIDGES

MARCH 7TH, 1797

It is hereby Enacted by the General Assembly of the State of
Vermont, That there be, and hereby is assessed a tax of two pence on
each acre of land in the township of Milton, in the county of Chittenden (public rights excepted), for the purpose of making roads and
building bridges in said town, to be expended by the order and under
the direction of John Jackson, Thomas Dewey of Milton, and Benjamin Holmes of Georgia, who are hereby appointed a committee to
superintend the expenditure of said tax. And any justice of the peace
within the county of Chittenden is hereby empowered to issue his
warrant to Enoch Ashley of said Milton to collect said tax. And said
collector is hereby made accountable to said committee for the amount
of said tax, and said collector and committee are hereby directed to
govern themselves in collecting, disposing, and accounting for monies
raised by said tax, agreeably to an act entitled, "An act regulating the
disposition of monies raised by tax on the several towns for the purpose of making and repairing roads and building bridges &.c.," passed
October session 1796.

AN ACT EMPOWERING BENJAMIN SWAN AND MOSES OSGOOD, BOTH OF
WOODSTOCK IN THE COUNTY OF WINDSOR, TO RAISE THE SUM
OF FIVE HUNDRED DOLLARS BY LOTTERY FOR THE PURPOSE
OF BUILDING A BRIDGE OVER WATER QUECHEE RIVER
SO CALLED RUNNING THROUGH WOODSTOCK IN
THE COUNTY OF WINDSOR, AFORESAID

MARCH 7TH, 1797

It is hereby Enacted by the General Assembly of the State of
Vermont, That Benjamin Swan and Moses Osgood, both of Woodstock aforesaid, be, and they are hereby empowered to raise by lottery
the sum of five hundred dollars for the purpose of erecting a bridge
over Water Quechee River in Woodstock, aforesaid, at such place as
the selectmen of said Woodstock shall appoint, not exceeding twenty
five rods from the bridge now standing on said river near the court
house. And,

It is hereby further Enacted, That the said Benjamin and Moses shall commence the drawing of said lottery within one year from the first day of March instant, and before they enter upon the execution of their said office, they shall enter into a bond with sufficient surety to the acceptance of the judges of the county court, in the county of Windsor, for the faithful performance of their trust, and shall, within one year from the drawing of said lottery, expend the avails thereof on the bridge, aforesaid.

Provided nevertheless, That no costs shall be taxed in any action that may hereafter be brought in favour of any plaintiff for the recovery of any sum or sums of money that may become due or owing for any ticket or tickets that shall be purchased by any person or persons whatever, in said lottery, unless the defendant or defendants in such action shall appeal or review said cause. And in that case if judgment be affiirmed against him, her or them, the plaintiff shall recover full costs.

AN ACT APPOINTING A COMMITTEE TO LAY OUT AND SURVEY A POST
ROAD FROM BURLINGTON ON ONION RIVER TO THE PROVINCE LINE

MARCH 8TH, 1797

It is hereby Enacted by the General Assembly of the State of Vermont, That Elisha Sheldon, Jonathan Spafford, and Joshua Stanton, Esqrs., be, and they are hereby appointed a committee to lay out a public highway for a permanent post or stage road from such place on Onion River, in the town of Colchester, as the committee shall think best, thence running through the said town of Colchester, Milton, Georgia, St. Albans, Swanton, and Highgate to the province line. And the said committee are hereby directed to commence a survey of said road on or before the first day of July next, and complete the same as soon as may be. And the committee are hereby further directed to call on any county surveyor in the county of Chittenden and Franklin, who is hereby directed to attend said committee and make such survey bill as said committee shall direct, with the points of compass, length, and breadth of said road properly attested for record. And such road, so laid by said committee, as aforesaid, and recorded in the town clerk's office in the town where such road lies, shall not be altered by the selectmen of such town, any law or usage to the contrary notwithstanding. And said committee are hereby further directed to cause such survey or surveys to be recorded in the town clerk's office of the town through which said road is laid. And,

It is hereby further Enacted, That the aforesaid committee may set over any old road which they think proper to shut up, to the owner or owners whose land they may take for a new road. And if said committee shall find it necessary to lay a new road through improved land where there is no such old road which they can set over as aforesaid, and when there is no allowance land to make compensation, said committee shall assess damages for any new road that they shall lay out as aforesaid, and a certificate given by such committee to the person or persons through whose land they shall lay such new road or roads, shall be a sufficient voucher for the selectmen of the town where such road shall be laid, to pay the sum therein mentioned. And such selectmen are hereby directed to pay the amount thereof out of the town treasury, and should such selectmen refuse or neglect to pay the money so certified by such committee, the person or persons holding such certificate may, after the expiration of three months from the presentment of such certificate, sue or prosecute the town where such selectmen belong, before any court proper to try the same. And such court is hereby directed to render judgment thereon and issue execution accordingly. And,

It is hereby further Enacted, That if any person or persons through whose land shall be laid as aforesaid, shall neglect or refuse to open said road so laid as aforesaid, shall neglect or refuse to open said road, so laid by the committee as aforesaid, such committee shall direct the person or persons so neglecting or refusing as aforesaid, to open such road with a term of time to be set by said committee, which time shall not be less than one month nor more than six. And if such person or persons shall neglect or refuse to open such road after the expiration of the time so limited for the opening of such road as aforesaid, such committee are hereby authorised and directed by themselves or others by them appointed, to open such road as soon as may be, and such person or persons so neglecting or refusing to open said road as aforesaid, shall pay just damages to the committee, aforesaid, for such neglect or refusal, to be recovered by such committee before any court proper to try the same. And,

It is hereby further Enacted, That such road so laid out as aforesaid, shall not be altered but by the supreme court, or a committee by them appointed, on application made to said court by the selectmen of the town through which said road runs, and on a report of such committee, and its acceptance by the said supreme court, such road may be altered. And,

It is hereby further Enacted, That the expenses of surveying, laying out, and repairing or making the aforesaid road, shall be paid by the several towns through which such road shall lead, and in such proportion to each town as the committee shall judge equitable. And,

It is hereby further Enacted, That the committee, aforesaid, shall have right to direct the appropriation of one half of the taxes laid on the several towns of Colchester, Milton, Georgia, St. Albans, Swanton and Highgate, as aforesaid, for making and repairing highways, and shall have the controul of the several committees appointed in those towns, and have right to direct such part of the taxes mentioned as above to be laid out upon the aforesaid road as they shall judge will be most conducive to the public interest.

AN ACT FOR THE PURPOSE OF ENABLING A COMMITTEE THEREIN
APPOINTED TO STRAIGHTEN, LAY OUT, AND REPAIR A ROAD
FROM THE SOUTH LINE OF SALISBURY TO
ONION RIVER BRIDGE

MARCH 8TH, 1797

Whereas, it appears to this General Assembly, that it will be of public utility to render the road direct and good, for the convenience and accommodation of travellers from Rutland to Onion River Bridge. And whereas, a respectable number of the inhabitants of the towns of Salisbury, Middlebury, Monkton, Hinesburgh, New Haven, St. George, Shelburn[e] and Burlington have entered into subscriptions for repairing the road on the before mentioned rout[e], formerly admeasured by Joseph Beman. Therefore,

It is hereby Enacted by the General Assembly of the State of Vermont, That Elias Kelsey and John Deming of Salisbury, Joshua Hyde [Hide] and Phillip Foot of Middlebury, Matthew Phelps and Elijah Foot, of Newhaven, Daniel Smith and Joseph Day of Monkton, Andrew Burret and Nathan Leavensworth, Junr., of Hinesburgh, Jared Isham of St. George, Elnathan Higby of Shelburn[e]; and Jason Comstock and Peter Benedict of Burlington, be, and they are hereby appointed a general committee, to superintend the repairing the road before mentioned, leading through the several towns to which they respectively belong, from the south line of Salisbury in the county of Addison, to Onion River Bridge, aforesaid, which committee, in their respective towns, in case of any difficulty arising respecting the laying out, straightening or surveying said road, may call to their advice and assistance, the committee of the next adjoining town or towns, as the case may require.

2. *And it is hereby further Enacted*, That the said committee shall have power to survey, straighten and alter the aforesaid road, in their respective towns, so as they shall judge will best accommodate the public for travelling, confining themselves however as far as may be convenient to the said road as it is now laid out and runs. And the selectmen of the several towns through which said road leads, shall not have power to obstruct or alter said road, after the said committee shall have laid out and surveyed the same.

Provided, That upon application of the selectmen of any such town, for any alteration of said road, to the county court of the county in which the town lies, whose selectmen shall make such application, such court if they see just reason therefor, may order any alteration of said road, and the same shall then be accordingly altered.

3. *And it is hereby further Enacted*, That in case any person shall be injured in his property by the said road running through his land, as the said committee shall lay out and survey the same, the said committee, for their respective towns, shall award recompence to such person or persons so injured, in the same manner and under the same restrictions as selectmen are by law directed to award recompence to persons who are in the same manner injured by the laying of new roads under the authority and direction of the selectmen. And when the said committee for a respective town shall have ascertained the sum due to any such person, they shall give such person an order on the treasurer of such town for the payment thereof, and such treasurer is hereby directed to pay the same in the same manner as though the order had been drawn by the selectmen of such town. *Provided*, That the expense of laying out, surveying and recording the survey bills of said road in the town clerk's office of the respective towns (which records such clerks are hereby directed to make on the survey bills being presented to them by said committee), shall not be paid by such towns, but shall be borne by those living on and near said road who have sub-

scribed for that purpose, in the respective towns. *Provided also,* That the expense of such labour as shall be expended under the direction of said committee in the opening and repairing of said road shall in like manner be wholly borne by such subscribers.[1]

AN ACT GRANTING TO JOHN WOOD THE LIBERTY OF RAISING THE SUM OF FIVE HUNDRED DOLLARS BY WAY OF LOTTERY

MARCH 9TH, 1797

It is hereby Enacted by the General Assembly of the State of Vermont, That the said John Wood have liberty, and authority is hereby given to the said John Wood for the raising the sum of five hundred dollars by way of lottery.

And it is hereby further Enacted, That Stephen Avery, Elias Buell and John Wood be, and they are hereby appointed managers of said lottery, who shall be sworn to a faithful discharge of their duty, and before they proceed in the business of their appointment, they shall give bonds with sufficient surety to the judges of the county court for the county of Rutland, for the faithful discharge of the duties of their said trust. *Provided,* That this state shall be no wise accountable for said lottery.

Provided nevertheless, That no costs shall be taxed in any case whatever for the plaintiff for the recovery of any sum or sums of money that shall become due or owing for any ticket or tickets, hereafter to be sold in said lottery, unless the defendant or defendants shall appeal or review from any judgment rendered against him, her or them, and the judgment of the court below be affirmed, and in that case the plaintiff or plaintiffs shall recover full costs.

AN ACT ESTABLISHING A DISTRICT SCHOOL OF PART OF THE TOWNS OF LEICESTER AND SALISBURY IN THE COUNTY OF ADDISON FOR FOUR YEARS

MARCH 9TH, 1797

Whereas, It appears to this assembly that the first school district

---

1. State Papers of Vermont, Vol. XI, *General Petitions,* 1797-1799, "For Appointment of a Committee to Lay out a Road," 3.

in the town of Leicester, as formerly known, is by the line agreed on and established by the proprietors and inhabitants of said Leicester and Salisbury, so divided by said line, dividing said towns as to leave a part of said school district, only, in the town of Leicester, and part thereof in said Salisbury. And to remedy evils and inconveniences occasioned by said district being so divided; therefore,

It is hereby Enacted by the General Assembly of the State of Vermont that said school district shall remain and continue to be the same in every view and under the same regulations as though no such division had happened by such divisional line, so agreed on by said towns as aforesaid.

And it is hereby further Enacted, That Samuel Adams of Leicester, who now lives within the limits of said district, have, and liberty is hereby given him to join with and be connected with the next adjoining district if he can be better accommodated therein.[1]

AN ACT DIRECTING THE TREASURER OF THIS STATE TO CREDIT THE TOWN OF CHESTER TWELVE DOLLARS AND TWENTY ONE CENTS ON A TAX ASSESSED ON THE GRAND LIST FOR THE YEAR 1796

MARCH 9TH, 1797

It is hereby Enacted by the General Assembly of the State of Vermont, That the Treasurer of this State be, and he is hereby directed to credit the town of Chester, in the county of Windsor, twelve dollars and twenty one cents, upon the state tax assessed on the grand list for the year one thousand seven hundred and ninety six.

AN ACT ALTERING THE NAME OF THE TOWN OF LITTLETON TO THAT OF WATERFORD

MARCH 9TH, 1797

It is hereby Enacted by the General Assembly of the State of Vermont, That the name of the town of Littleton, in he county of Caledonia be, and the same is hereby altered, and the said town shall hereafter be known and called by the name of Waterford.

---

1. State Papers of Vermont, Vol. XI, *General Petitions,* 1797-1799, "For Continuation of School District Lines After Change in Town Lines," 451.

And It is hereby further Enacted, That in all advertisements for taxes upon the lands on said town for the term of two years after passing this act, said town shall be called Waterford, heretofore known by the name of Littleton.[1]

AN ACT EMPOWERING RHODA STEVENS TO DEED A CERTAIN PIECE OF LAND THEREIN MENTIONED

MARCH 9TH, 1797

Whereas, Samuel Stevens, late of Barnet, in the county of Caledonia, deceased, did in his life time, contract with Paul Cushman of said Barnet to deed him a certain piece of land containing a mill privilege, which contract, the said Samuel died without performing. Therefore,

It is hereby Enacted by the General Assembly of the State of Vermont, That Rhoda Stevens, administratrix to the said Samuel's estate, be, and she is hereby empowered to deed the same to him, the said Paul, under the directions of the judge of probate for the district of Caledonia, and such deed so by him executed, shall be as good and valid in law as if the said Samuel had executed the same in his life time.[2]

AN ACT MAKING APPROPRIATIONS FOR THE SUPPORT OF GOVERNMENT SINCE THE LAST, AND DURING THE PRESENT SESSION OF THE LEGISLATURE

MARCH 10TH, 1797

It is hereby Enacted by the General Assembly of the State of Vermont, That there be, and hereby is appropriated, for the support of government, since the last session of the Legislature, the following sums for the several purposes following, to wit, for the lieutenant governor, council and general assembly, with the necessary officers attending the same, during the present session, together with the auditor of accounts against this State, the sum of six thousand one hundred and

1. State Papers of Vermont, Vol. X, *General Petitions,* 1793-1796, "For Changing the Name of a Town," 390.
2. Ibid., Vol. XI, *General Petitions,* 1797-1799, "For Authority to an Administratrix to Deed Land," 16.

eight dollars and ten cents; for the committee of revision, for their services in revising the laws, the sum of fifteen hundred and eighteen dollars and fifty cents; for firewood, candles &c. for the session of council, the sum of fourteen dollars; and to Thomas Tolman for firewood and candles, six dollars. Also, that there be allowed to Nathan Osgood for his services as clerk of the supreme court, the sum of thirty three dollars and thirteen cents. To Samuel Mattocks, Esqr., Treasurer, for cash paid the electors of president and vice president, forty dollars and ninety two cents. And,

It is hereby further Enacted, That there be, and hereby is appropriated a sum not exceeding one thousand dollars above the sums herein particularly specified, which several sums of money shall be paid by the treasurer out of the monies in the Treasury. And if there be not sufficient monies in the treasury, the treasurer shall issue hard money orders for the residue of such appropriation.

AN ACT SUSPENDING THE OPERATION OF CERTAIN ACTS THEREIN MENTIONED AND FOR OTHER PURPOSES

MARCH 10TH, 1797

1. *It is hereby Enacted* by the General Assembly of the State of Vermont, That the operation of the several acts passed the present session of the Legislature, which were reported by the committee of revision, be, and hereby is suspended 'til after the rising of the Legislature in October next, except the act entitled "An act relating to the office and duty of Secretary of State;" and the act entitled "An act relating to gaols and gaolers and for relief of persons imprisoned therein;" and the act entitled, "An act ascertaining the principles on which the list shall be made, and directing listers in their office and duty," which acts last mentioned shall be in force from and after the rising of this Legislature. And,

2. *It is hereby further Enacted,* That all acts and clauses of acts coming within the purview of the act before mentioned, entitled "An act relating to the office and duty of Secretary of State," and the act entitled "An act relating to gaols and gaolers, and for relief of persons imprisoned therein," shall be, and the same are hereby repealed; provided that all rights, remedies, fines, penalties and forfeitures incurred or accruing under any former act or acts, clause or clauses of acts, shall remain in the same condition as if said acts had not been made.

3. *And it is hereby further Enacted*, that the Secretary of State shall, as soon as may be, furnish the printer for this State with true and attested copies of the three last mentioned acts, and of this act, whose duty it shall be to print the same to the number of seven hundred copies for the use of the several towns within this State; and the same shall be distributed according to law.

4. *And it is hereby further Enacted,* That Samuel Hitchcock and Richard Whitney, Esquires, be, and hereby are directed to meet some time previous to the next session of the legislature and proceed in the revision of such of the laws of this State, as are yet unrevised, and report the same in proper bills to the next Legislature to be convened at Windsor. Provided always, that the said Samuel and Richard shall not be at liberty to devote a longer time than three weeks in said business, previous to the next session.

5. *Provided also,* and it is hereby further enacted, that all bills now lying before the council, for their revision, concurrence or proposals of amendment, except such as shall have remained in council five days, remain to be taken up at the session of the Legislature in October next, the same as though they were received on the second day of said session, any law, usage, or custom to the contrary notwithstanding.

AN ACT IN ADDITION TO, AND ALTERATION OF AN ACT ENTITLED
"AN ACT EMPOWERING AND DIRECTING CERTAIN PERSONS
THEREIN NAMED TO LAY OUT AND SURVEY A POST-ROAD
FROM THE MASSACHSETTS LINE, TO THE NORTH
LINE OF THE TOWN OF NEWBURY IN THE
COUNTY OF ORANGE"

MARCH 10TH, 1797

1. *It is hereby Enacted* by the General Assembly of the State of Vermont, That it shall be the duty of the several committees mentioned in said act to take proper measures to open the road in their respective counties, agreeably to the direction of said act on or before the fifteenth day of May next. And,

2. *It is hereby further Enacted,* That if any town through which said road passes, shall neglect to make such road passable, to the acceptance of said committees respectively, on or before the first day of Oc-

tober next, such town shall pay a fine of one hundred dollars, to the county treasury for every six months such town shall so neglect to open and make passable said road as aforesaid.

Provided always, That the said committees in their respective counties, shall have power on consideration of the difficulties of rendering said road passable through the several towns, to allow to such towns, in which such difficulties exist, a further time to render such road passable, not exceeding eighteen months. And, in all cases in which such further time shall be allowed by the said committees, no forfeiture shall be incurred during such time by virtue of this act. And,

3. *It is hereby further Enacted*, That the county treasurers, in their respective counties, shall pay over to the said committees, in their several counties, all fines and forfeitures, which shall be incurred by this act, And the said committee, respectively, shall lay out the monies arising from such fines and forfeitures, on the said road, in their several counties, in such places, and for such purposes, as their discretion shall direct. And,

4. *It is hereby further Enacted*, That if any treasurer shall neglect for the space of one month after the receipt of such fines and forfeitures, to pay over the monies so by him received, he shall forfeit and pay a fine of thirty dollars for every month he shall so neglect, to be recovered by the committees respectively, by action of debt brought on this statute. And,

5. *It is hereby further Enacted*, That John Bridgman and Benjamin Burt, Esquires, be, and they hereby are added to the committee for the county of Windham. And,

6. *It is hereby further Enacted*, That the selectmen of such towns, as have or may raise a land tax in pursuance of the aforesaid act, shall govern themselves in the collection and disposition of the monies raised by such tax, agreeable to an act passed at the last session of the General Assembly in October last, entitled "An act regulating the disposition of monies raised by tax on lands in the several towns for the purpose of making and repairing roads and building bridges."

AN ACT ESTABLISHING A TURNPIKE GATE OR GATES ON SUCH ROAD AS
SHALL BE MADE AT THE PLACE AND ACCORDING TO THE
PROVISIONS OF THIS ACT

MARCH 10TH, 1797

Whereas, The public road leading from the line between Clarendon and Shrewsbury, near to John Smith's dwelling house in said Shrewsbury, over Black-River-Bridge in Ludlow, is circuitous, rocky and mountainous, and there is much travelling over the same. And the expense of straightening, making and repairing a public road or highway between the line and bridge aforesaid, so that the same may be safe and convenient for travellers with horses and carriages, would be much greater than ought to be required of the towns, between the said line and bridge, under their present circumstances. Therefore,

1. *It is hereby Enacted* by the General Assembly of the State of Vermont, That Royal Crafts of Rutland, merchant, and his associates, and his and their successors, shall be a corporation by the name of the Green Mountain Turnpike Corporation; and shall by that name sue and be sued, and shall have a common seal, make bye laws, not contradictory to the constitution and laws of this State, and have and enjoy all the privileges and powers which are by law allowed to corporations, for the purpose of laying out and making a turnpike road four rods wide, from the boundary line between Clarendon and Shrewsbury, in the county of Rutland, near the now dwelling home of John Smith in said Shrewsbury, to be in such place or places, and in such direction or directions as said corporation shall, from time to time, choose and direct for the same, to the East end of the bridge aforesaid; and for keeping the same in repair. And when said turnpike road shall be sufficiently made, and shall be approved by the judges of the supreme court of this State, or by a majority of them, the said corporation shall be authorised to erect one or more turnpike gate or gates under the direction of said judges, the same to be in such manner as shall be necessary and convenient; and shall be entitled to receive from each traveller and passenger the following rates of toll, to wit: for each coach, phaeton, charriot [chariot] or other four wheeled carriages, if with steel springs and drawn by two horses, fifty cents, and if drawn by more than two horses the sum of five cents for every additional horse; and for every chaise, chair, sulkey [sulky], or other two wheeled carriage drawn by one horse, twenty five cents, if drawn by more than one horse an additional sum of five cents for each additional horse;

for every cart or waggon drawn by two oxen or two horses, thirty three cents, and if drawn by more than two oxen, or two horses, five cents for each additional ox or horse; and for every sled or sleigh drawn by two oxen or two horses, twenty five cents, and if drawn by more than two oxen or two horses, the sum of three cents for each additional ox or horse; for every man and horse, twelve and an half cents; for all horses led or driven of the number of ten or under, exclusive of those in teams or carriages, the sum of five cents each, if over the number of ten, in one drove, the sum of three cents for each additional horse over the said number of ten; for all neat cattle in droves of the number of ten or under, the sum of five cents each, if over the number of ten in one drove, the sum of three cents for each additional creature over the said number of ten; for all sheep and swine, half a cent each. And the rates of toll hereby established shall be equally apportioned on the several gates which may be erected, so that a passage through all the gates shall not cost more than the toll above specified. And,

2. *It is hereby further Enacted*, That all and every person living within the distance of eight miles of such turnpike gate or gates shall pass with his or her team, horse or any other creature free from any expense. And

3. *It is hereby further Enacted,* That said corporation may purchase and hold any lands upon which they may make said road, and compensation shall be made by said corporation to individuals whose lands they may take for such road, in the same manner and extent as is by law allowed, in the case of laying out the lands of individuals for highways. And no action of trespass or other action, petition or complaint against said corporation, in more than one instance, shall be maintainable by any one individual for compensation for lands taken by said corporation for said road, or for any part thereof. And,

4. *It is hereby further Enacted*, That if said corporation, or their toll gatherers, or any other person in their employment, shall unreasonably delay or hinder any traveller or passenger at said gate or gates, or shall demand, or receive more toll than is by this act established, the said corporation shall forfeit and pay a sum not exceeding ten dollars, nor less then one dollar, to be recovered before any court proper to try the same, where the offense shall be committed, by any person injured, delayed, or defrauded, in a special action on the case; in which action the writ shall be served on the said corporation, by leaving an attested

copy of the same, with the treasurer, or with some individual member of the corporation living within the county where the offense shall be committed, or by reading the contents thereof in the hearing of such treasurer, or individual member, at least twelve days before the day of trial. And the treasurer of said corporation, or the individual member aforesaid, shall be allowed to defend the suit in behalf of the corporation. And the said corporation shall be liable to pay damages which shall happen to any person from whom toll is, by this act demandable, for any damages which shall arise from any defect of bridges or want of repairs of the said road, and shall also be liable to presentment, by the grand jury, and to fine for not keeping said road and bridges thereon in good repair, both summer and winter. And,

5. *It is hereby further Enacted*, That if any person shall cut, break down, or destroy the said turnpike gate or gates, or shall forcibly pass, or attempt to pass the same, without having paid the legal toll at such gate, such person shall forfeit and pay a sum not exceeding forty dollars, nor less then ten dollars, to be recovered by the treasurer of the said corporation, to their use in an action of trepass, before any court proper to try the same. And if any person shall, with his carriage, team, cattle, or horse, turn out of said road, to pass the said turnpike gate or gates, on grounds adjacent thereto, with an intent to avoid the toll, due by virtue of this act, such person shall forfeit and pay treble toll, to be recovered by the treasurer of the said corporation to the use thereof, in an action on the case. And,

6. *It is hereby further Enacted*, That the shares in the said turnpike road, shall be taken, deemed and considered to be personal estate, to all intents and purposes. And,

7. *It is hereby further Enacted*, That there shall be a meeting of the said corporation held at the house of Joseph Green in Ludlow, on the third Monday of May next, for the purpose of choosing a clerk, and such other officers as may then and there be agreed upon by the said corporation, for regulating the concerns thereof. And said corporation may then and there agree upon such method of calling meetings in future as they may judge proper. And,

8. *It is hereby further Enacted*, That the books of said corporation shall, at all times, be liable and open to the inspection and examination of the judges of the supreme court. And the said corporation shall, within the term of six months, after the said road shall be com-

pleated, lodge with the chief judge of the supreme court, an account of the expense thereof. And said corporation shall annually thereafter, exhibit to the chief judge aforesaid a true account of the income or dividend arising from the said toll, together with their necessary annual disbursements on said road.

9. *And it is hereby further Enacted*, That the judges of the supreme court for the time being, after the term of twenty years from the passing of this act, may disolve said corporation, when it shall appear to them, that the income arising from the said toll shall have fully compensated the said corporation for all monies they may have expended, in purchasing, making, repairing and taking care of said road, together with an interest thereon at the rate of twelve per centum per annum. And thereupon the property of the said road shall be vested in this State and be at its disposal. And,

10. *It is hereby further Enacted*, That at the place or places where the toll directed by this act shall be taken, there shall be erected and kept constantly exposed to view, a sign or board, with the rate of toll, of all the tollable articles fairly and legibly written thereon in capital or other large letters. And,

11. *It is hereby further Enacted*, That a disinterested committee shall be appointed by the judges of the supreme court, to be under oath, to examine the two roads leading through Shrewsbury and Mount-Holly, and determine which of the two roads will be the most convenient, to answer the purposes of the said turnpike road. And if the said committee shall determine in favor of the north road, the gate or gates shall be erected in such place or places as not to intercept the travel leading from Wallingford by the now dwelling house of Stephen Clark, Esquire, to Ludlow. And,

12. *It is hereby further Enacted*, That if said corporation shall neglect to compleat the said turnpike road for the space of three whole years, from and after the passing of this act, the same shall become null and void.

AN ACT ASSESSING A LAND TAX OF THREE CENTS ON EACH ACRE OF
ALL THE LANDS IN THE TOWNSHIP OF RICHMOND, ON THAT
PART FORMERLY BELONGING TO WILLISTON IN THE
COUNTY OF CHITTENDEN AND STATE OF
VERMONT

MARCH 10TH, 1797

It is hereby Enacted by the General Assembly of the State of Vermont, That there be, and hereby is assessed a tax of three cents per acre on all the lands in that part of the township of Richmond, formerly belonging to Williston, in the county of Chittenden, public lands excepted, for the purpose of making and repairing roads and building bridges in said town. And,

It is hereby further Enacted, That Asa Brownson, Ezra Smith, Joshua Chamberlain be, and hereby are appointed a committee to superintend the expenditures of said taxes. And any justice of the peace in the county of Chittenden is hereby empowered to issue his warrants to Content C. Hallock to collect said tax. And said collector is hereby made accountable to said committee for the amount of said tax. And said committee and collector are hereby directed in the collecting, and accounting for said tax, to comply in all things with the directions of an act regulating the disposition of monies raised by tax on the several towns for the purpose of making and repairing roads and building bridges, passed in October session 1796.

AN ACT GRANTING RELIEF TO JOHN GOVE IN THE CASE
THEREIN MENTIONED

MARCH 10TH, 1797

Whereas, Nathaniel Delavan of Fredericksburgh, in the county of Dutchess and State of New York, at the term of the supreme court of the State of New York, at Albany, in April in the year one thousand seven hundred and eighty five, commenced his certain action of trespass on the case, against John Gove, now of Rutland, in the county of Rutland and State of Vermont, for the non performance of certain promises therein declared. And whereas it is represented that the said Nathaniel Delaven, by fraud, and contrary to good faith, obtained interlocutory judgment by default before the same court, at their session at New York, at their term thereof in July, in the year one thousand seven hundred and eighty five, and that afterwards at the term of said supreme court of the State of New York, holden at Albany, on the thirteenth day of December, in the year one thousand seven hundred and eighty eight, the said Delavan did, by consequence thereof, and by like fraud, obtain final judgment in said action against said John Gove for the sum of sixty one pounds, ten shillings damages, and for ten pounds and six pence for his cost, in that behalf expended. And whereas the said Delavan has commenced his certain action of debt on said judgment, against said Gove, for the recovery of said damages and cost, before the county court holden at Rutland, within and for said county of Rutland, in the State of Vermont, at their term in March in the year one thousand seven hundred and ninety, which said action last mentioned, is by appeal now pending before the supreme court within and for the county of Rutland, in the State of Vermont, now that the said Gove may have a day in court upon the merits of said original action. Therefore,

It is hereby Enacted by the General Assembly of the State of Vermont, That the said supreme court of this State, and every court of record within this state, be, and they and each of them are hereby authorised and directed in the hearing and trial of said action of debt on said judgment by default, and in the hearing & trial of any action commenced on said judgment by default, to admit the said John Gove to plead or give in evidence any matter or thing which the said John Gove could have plead or given in evidence on the hearing or trial of the merits of said original action before the said interlocutory judgment rendered by default, any law, usage, or custom to the contrary, notwithstanding.[1]

AN ACT IN ADDITION TO AN ACT GRANTING A TAX OF TWO PENCE ON EACH ACRE OF LAND IN THE TOWNSHIPS OF BRUMLEY [BROMLEY] AND LANDGROVE IN THE COUNTY OF BENNINGTON, PASSED OCTOBER THE 21ST A.D. 1788

MARCH 10TH, 1797

It it hereby Enacted by the General Assembly of the State of Vermont, That Timothy Mead, Junr., be, and he is hereby appointed

1. State Papers of Vermont, Vol. XI, *General Petitions,* 1797-1799, "For a Hearing Before the State Supreme Court," 29.

collector of said tax. And any justice of the peace in the county of Bennington is hereby authorised to issue his warrant to the said Timothy Mead to collect said tax. And said collector is hereby directed and made accountable, in the collecting and accounting for said tax, to govern himself in his duty herein by an act entitled, "An act regulating the disposition of monies raised by the tax on lands in the several towns for the purpose of making and repairing roads and building bridges," passed at the session of the General Assembly in October 1796.

AN ACT DIRECTING TIMOTHY BRADLEY OF SUNDERLAND, IN THE COUNTY
OF BENNINGTON, TO REDEED TO ELI BROWNSON, OF THE SAME PLACE,
ADMINISTRATOR ON THE ESTATE OF GIDEON BROWNSON OF SAID
SUNDERLAND, DECEASED, CERTAIN LANDS, AND ALSO
DIRECTING SAID ADMINISTRATOR TO DELIVER TO
SAID TIMOTHY BRADLEY ONE CERTAIN NOTE
EXECUTED BY SAID TIMOTHY TO SAID
GIDEON FOR AND ON ACCOUNT OF
SAID LAND

MARCH 10TH, 1797

Whereas, it appears to this Assembly that Gideon Brownson, Esqr., late of Sunderland in the county of Bennington, deceased, did, on or about the fourteenth day of December, one thousand seven hundred and ninety five, execute a deed to Timothy Bradley of said Sunderland, for about one thousand acres of land in said Sunderland, which he received in trust to dispose of, and account to the said Gideon for the avails thereof; and that the said Timothy, at the same time executed his note to the said Gideon for five hundred dollars, conditioned that the said Timothy should account for said land when sold, or to re-deed the same to the said Gideon, and in either case the said note to be given up; and the land not being sold at the death of the said Gideon Brownson, and the same not redeeded to the said Gideon, and the said note being given up to the said Timothy, renders it impossible for the said Eli in his capacity as administrator, to receive said property and administer on the same without legislative aid. Therefore,

It is hereby Enacted by the General Assembly of the State of Vermont, That Timothy Bradley of Sunderland, in the county of Bennington, be, and he hereby is directed to deed to the said Eli Brownson, in his capacity as administrator, aforesaid, when required, the whole of said land contained in said deed, save one hundred and twenty five acres, the same to be considered when deeded aforesaid, to be a part of the estate of the said Gideon, the same as though it had been deeded to the said Gideon in his life time, and that the said Eli shall cause to be delivered to the said Timothy, his note so by him executed as aforesaid, on the executing said deed as aforesaid.[1]

AN ACT APPOINTING JONAS BRIGHAM A COMMITTEEMAN OF ENOSBURGH LAND TAX IN THE PLACE OF SAMUEL LITTLE

MARCH 10TH, 1797

Whereas, the Legislature of this State in October, 1796, at Rutland, did grant a tax of two pence on the acre on all the lands in the township of Enosburgh, public rights excepted, for the purpose of making roads and building bridges in said town. And whereas, Samuel Little, one of the committee then appointed to carry said act into execution, has since that time removed out of said town of Enosburgh and declares his determination no further to attend to the business of his appointment. Therefore,

It is hereby Enacted by the General Assembly of the State of Vermont, That Jonas Brigham of Bakersfield, be, and hereby is appointed to fulfil the duties of said appointment in the room of the said Samuel Little, and the said Samuel Little is hereby discharged from any further attention to the business of the said appointment.

AN ACT IN ADDITION TO AN ACT FOR GRANTING A TAX OF ONE PENNY UPON EACH ACRE OF LAND IN THE TOWNSHIPS OF FAYSTON, STARKESBOROUGH, BUELL'S AND AVERY'S GORE, IN THE COUNTY OF CHITTENDEN PASSED OCTOBER 1793

MARCH 10TH, 1797

It is hereby Enacted by the General Assembly of the State of Vermont, That Samuel Buell, be, and he hereby is appointed a col-

---

1. State Papers of Vermont, Vol. XI, *General Petitions,* 1797-1799, "For Authority to an Administrator to Exchange a Note for a Deed," 31.

lector of said penny tax, for said Buell's and Avery's Gore, in the room of John Raymond, removed out of this State, and the said Samuel Buell is hereby vested with the same powers, and rendered accountable in the same manner as the said John Raymond was, in and by said act, empowered and made accountable.

AN ACT DIRECTING THE TREASURER TO RECEIVE A CERTAIN STATE NOTE OR ORDER

MARCH 10TH, 1797

It is hereby Enacted by the General Assembly of the State of Vermont, That the treasurer be, and is hereby directed to receive a certain note or order issued by Ira Allen, Esqr., in favor of Samuel Safford or possessor, dated February 13th, 1783, for the sum of six pounds on interest, and issue his hard money order to Paul Gates for the sum of eleven pounds one shilling and two pence in lieu thereof, provided the said note or order shall be found by the treasurer to be a true one.

AN ACT FOR MAKING AND REPAIRING A ROAD FROM THE COURT HOUSE IN RUTLAND TO SALEM IN THE STATE OF NEW YORK

MARCH 10TH, 1797

It is hereby Enacted by the General Assembly of the State of Vermont, That Isachar Reed, Benjamin Foster, Junr., and Joel Minor be, and they are hereby appointed a committee, and they or any two of them are hereby fully authorised and empowered to lay out a road or public highway from the court house in Rutland, to Salem, in the State of New York, as they shall judge will best accommodate the public; and they are hereby directed and empowered to call on some county surveyor of the county of Rutland to assist in surveying said road, who shall make an accurate survey of the same, in such place or places as shall be directed by said committee. And when so made out, said survey shall be lodged with the county clerk of the county of Rutland, whose duty it shall be to record the same, and the said road when laid, and the survey thereof recorded agreeable to this act, shall not be subject to be altered by the selectmen of the several towns through which the same may pass, or either of them. And,

It is hereby further Enacted, That if any dispute shall arise respecting damages that may accrue to any person on account of said road being laid through their land, the aforesaid committee shall have full power to assess the damages that may arise to any individual through whose land said road may be laid, and if the said committee shall find there is sufficient land allowed for highways on or adjoining the said lot or lots through which said road may be laid, of equal value of the lands so taken up by said road, in that case it shall be the duty of said committee, and they are hereby empowered to set over said allowance land to the owner or owners of such lot or lots, through which said road may run, which shall be considered as a full compensation for the land that may be so taken up by said road as aforesaid; but if said committee shall not, on hearing of the party interested, find there is any such allowance land in or adjoining such lot or lots, then it shall be the duty of said committee to assess said damages as they shall think just and reasonable, and shall make return in writing, to the town clerk of the town in which said land may lie, which said sum or sums that may be assessed by said committee shall be paid as is hereafter directed by this act. And,

It is hereby further Enacted, That Isacher Reed, George Sherman, Jonathan Griswould, Ozias Clark, Phinehas Sheldon, and William Harkness be, and they hereby are appointed a committee for the purpose of making and repairing, and superintending said road when the same shall be laid as afore directed in this act, who are hereby also empowered to receive subscriptions of any person or persons for the purpose of making or repairing said road, or to receive any that are already made, and to collect the same by suit or action, if not paid agreeable to contract, which said suit or action may be commenced in the name of said committee last mentioned; and when any sum or sums may be collected by said suit or otherwise, it shall be the duty of said committee to lay out the monies so raised on the road aforesaid, which said committee shall return a true account of all monies that they shall or may collect for the purpose of making said road, to the judges of the county court for the county of Rutland, together with the expenditure of the same, to whom said committee shall be accountable for the expenditure of the said monies. And,

It is hereby further Enacted, That if any sum or sums of money shall be assessed by the committee first above mentioned, and returned to the town clerk's office as before directed by this act, it shall be the duty of the committee last mentioned to pay the same out of the monies so raised, or to be raised by subscriptions aforesaid, within three months after said assessment shall be so lodged as aforesaid, and if the same shall not be paid within three months, the person or persons in whose favour such return of damages may be made, shall have right by action on the case to recover the same of said committee, before any court proper to try the same.

AN ACT GRANTING TO JOHN HOLBROOK, SAMUEL DICKENSON AND LEMUEL WHITNEY, ALL OF BRATTLEBOROUGH, IN THE COUNTY OF WINDHAM, THEIR HEIRS AND ASSIGNS, THE EXCLUSIVE PRIVILEGE OF RUNNING A STAGE ON THE ROUTE FROM SAID BRATTLEBOROUGH ON THE POST ROAD TO DARTMOUTH COLLEGE THROUGH THAT PART OF THE ROUTE WHICH LIES IN THIS STATE FOR THE TERM OF EIGHT YEARS

MARCH 10TH, 1797

Whereas, the said John, Samuel and Lemuel have at great expense and at considerable loss established a line of stages on said route. Therefore,

It is hereby Enacted by the General Assembly of the State of Vermont, That the said John, Samuel, and Lemuel have, and there is hereby given to them, the sole and exclusive right and privilege of running the stage on the aforesaid route, through this State, for and during the term of eight years, on the following conditions, to wit, that the said John, Samuel, and Lemuel shall not exact more or greater fare than is usually received on the different routes of the mail stage through Connecticut and Massachusetts. And,

It is hereby further Enacted, That if the mail of the United States should hereafter be continued up the river Connecticut to Newbury, the said John, Samuel, and Lemuel shall have the same privilege of extending their line of stage to Newbury, aforesaid, upon the same conditions as are heretofore mentioned in this act. *Provided* always that if the said John, Samuel, and Lemuel shall neglect to run the stage as aforesaid, for the space of two months at any time within the said term of eight years from the passing of this act, then and in that case they shall be deprived of all benefit of this act, any thing herein expressed to the contrary notwithstanding.[1]

---

1. State Papers of Vermont, Vol. X, *General Petitions*, 1793-1796, "For Exclusive Right to Run a Stage," 331.

AN ACT REGULATING THE PAY OF THE LEGISLATURE AND THEIR
SEVERAL OFFICERS DURING THE PRESENT SESSION

MARCH 15TH, 1797

It is hereby Enacted by the General Assembly of the State of Vermont, That there be, and hereby is allowed to the lieutenant governor, four dollars per day, to each member of the council, one dollar and seventy five cents, to the speaker of the house of assembly, three dollars, to the clerk for his deputy, one dollar and fifty cents per day, to the secretary for his deputy, the chaplain, each member of the House, and messenger, the sheriff and auditor of accounts against this State, one dollar and fifty cents per day, for their services during the present session. And that the secretary of council be allowed two dollars and twenty five cents per day, and to the engrossing clerk, two dollars and twenty five cents per day for their services, any law to the contrary notwithstanding.

END OF THE ACTS PASSED FEBRUARY ADJOURNED
SESSION A.D. 1797 [RUTLAND]

ACTS AND LAWS PASSED BY THE LEGISLATURE OF THE STATE OF VERMONT AT THEIR SESSION HOLDEN AT WINDSOR IN THE YEAR OF OUR LORD 1797

AN ACT DIRECTING THE TREASURER OF THIS STATE TO PAY TO ELIJAH HURLBUT THE SUM OF ONE HUNDRED AND ONE DOLLARS AND SEVENTY NINE CENTS

OCTOBER 19TH, 1797

Whereas, it is represented that Elijah Hurlbut, deputy sheriff and gaoler within and for the county of Orange, expended twenty eight dollars and ninety cents in apprehending Noah Drew for making and passing counterfeit money; and also the sum of seventy two dollars and eighty nine cents in apprehending and returning to gaol, Paine Wingate, for making counterfeit money. Therefore,

It is hereby Enacted by the General Assembly of the State of Vermont, That the treasurer of this State be, and he hereby is directed to pay to the said Elijah Hurlbut, the sum of one hundred and one dollars and seventy nine cents, it being the amount of the expenditures aforesaid.[1]

AN ACT FOR THE REVIVAL OF AND IN ADDITION TO AN ACT ENTITLED, "AN ACT ASSESSING A TAX OF ONE PENNY PER ACRE ON THE LANDS IN THE TOWN OF BROWNINGTON," PASSED NOVEMBER 8TH, 1796

OCTOBER 20TH, 1797

Whereas, The committee appointed in and by said act neglected to lay out the roads therein contemplated until the expiration of the term limited therefor by law. Therefore,

It is hereby Enacted by the General Assembly of the State of Vermont, That the act entitled "An act assessing a tax of one penny per acre on the lands in the town of Brownington," passed the eighth day of November, A.D. one thousand seven hundred and ninety six,

---

1. State Papers of Vermont, Vol. XI, *General Petitions,* 1797-1799, "For Compensation for Apprehending and Boarding State Prisoners," 149.

be, and the same is hereby revived, and its operation shall to all intents and purposes be the same as though it had passed and been enacted at the present session of the Legislature.

And it is hereby further Enacted, That in the stead of the committee and collector appointed in and by said act, Amos Porter and Asahel Strong be, and they are hereby appointed the committee to superintend the expenditure of said tax. And Samuel Sias of Danville is hereby appointed collector thereof. And the said present committee and collector are directed and become responsible in the same manner as the said former committee and collector were, in and by the act aforesaid directed and made responsible.[1]

AN ACT ANNEXING PART OF WINDHAM TO LONDONDERRY

OCTOBER 21ST, 1797

It is hereby Enacted by the General Assembly of the State of Vermont, That the dividing line between the towns of Windham and Londonderry, shall be hereafter known and established as hereafter described, to wit: beginning on the north line of Windham where middle brook, so called, crosses the same, from thence running southerly up said brook to the foot of Glebe mountain, so called, thence running a direct course to the top of said mountain; thence southerly on the height of said mountain to the ancient south line of Londonderry; any law heretofore to the contrary notwithstanding.

AN ACT LIBERATING ROGER ENOS FROM IMPRISONMENT UNDER CERTAIN CONDITIONS

OCTOBER 23RD, 1797

Whereas, it appears to this Legislature that the said Roger is now a prisoner in the common gaol in Woodstock, in the county of Windsor, and State of Vermont, and so has been for fifteen months last past, by reason of a debt due from the said Roger to the treasurer of this State. And by unavoidable misfortune the said Roger has become so far reduced in his circumstances that it is not in his power at present to pay said debt or any part thereof. And the said Roger prays that he may

---

1. State Papers of Vermont, Vol. XI, *General Petitions,* 1797-1799, "For Appointment of a New Land Tax Committee and Collector," 157.

be liberated from his aforesaid imprisonment under such conditions as this Legislature shall direct. And it being further represented by the said Roger that there is a ballance due him from this State, which, were he liberated, he thinks he could make appear.

It is hereby Enacted by the General Assembly of the State of Vermont, That the said Roger Enos be liberated from his imprisonment on a certain execution issued by the clerk of the supreme court of judicature for the county of Windsor, in the name of the treasurer of this state against the said Roger Enos, on condition that the said Roger Enos, before he be released from the aforesaid imprisonment, make and execute to the treasurer of this State, and his successor in office, a promissory note, payable on demand, for the sum of the aforesaid execution, including the lawful interest of the debts and cost, from the time the judgment was rendered, on which the said execution issued, to the time when the said Roger shall make and execute his promissory note as aforesaid, which note shall be taken by the state's attorney for the county of Windsor, who is hereby made the agent for that purpose; and the said state's attorney, certifying to the sheriff or gaoler, that such note has been duly made, and executed, the said Roger shall be immediately liberated from his imprisonment on the aforesaid execution.

And it is hereby further Enacted, That if on a settlement or investigation of the demands or amounts which the said Roger may have against this State, by any proper board appointed to determine the same, there shall appear any sum or sums of money due to the said Roger, such sum or sums, being duly ascertained and certified, shall be endorsed on the note so to be executed, or be pleadable in offsett, in part discharge of said note.[1]

AN ACT DIRECTING THE TREASURER TO CREDIT ALEXANDER PENNOCK, CONSTABLE OF STRAFFORD, THE SUM OF THIRTY THREE DOLLARS & FORTY CENTS

OCTOBER 24TH, 1797

It is hereby Enacted by the General Assembly of the State of Vermont, That the treasurer of this state be, and he hereby is directed to credit Alexander Pennock, constable of Strafford, the sum of thirty

---

1. State Papers of Vermont, Vol. XI, *General Petitions,* 1797-1799, "For Release From Gaol and Settlement of Accounts with the State," 140.

three dollars and forty cents, on the state tax of said town for the year one thousand seven hundred and ninety six, it being a sum overcharged on said town by a mistake of the list.

AN ACT APPOINTING JOSEPH LORD OF ST. JOHNSBURY COLLECTOR OF A TAX ON THE TOWNSHIP OF BURKE IN THE COUNTY OF CALEDONIA IN THE ROOM OF OLIVER GALLUP WHO DECLINES ACCEPTING THE APPOINTMENT

OCTOBER 24TH, 1797

Whereas, the Legislature of this State at their adjourned [session], holden at Bennington on the twentieth day of January, one thousand seven hundred and ninety one, granted a tax of one penny on each acre of land in the township of Burke, in the county of Caledonia, public rights excepted, for the purpose of making roads and repairing bridges &.c., and appointed Oliver Gallup, a collector of said tax, who at this time declines the aforesaid appointment of collector.

It is hereby Enacted by the General Assembly of the State of Vermont, That Joseph Lord of St. Johnsbury, in the county of Caledonia, be, and he hereby is appointed collector of the aforesaid tax with the same powers as collector, as is given to the said Oliver Gallup; and made liable to the committee for the avails of the monies collected in the same way and manner as the said Oliver Gallup is, in and by said act, granting the aforesaid tax.

AN ACT FOR PAYING CHARLES BULLIS THE SUM OF EIGHTY SEVEN DOLLARS AND FIFTY CENTS

OCTOBER 24TH, 1797

Whereas, Charles Bullis purchased two lots of land lying in Manchester, containing fifty acres each, of Jeremiah French, then of said Manchester, that he paid twenty pounds in hand to said French, and gave his note for fifty pounds, payable to said French, making seventy pounds in the whole, which were reckoned in York money. That soon after he, the said French, absconded and went over to the enemy. That in the month of April, 1777, the said Charles Bullis paid over to the Committee of Safety the contents of the above mentioned note. And it further appears to the General Assembly that the most valuable of these lots was not the property of the said French, at the time of the purchase by the said Bullis, and that the said Bullis has lost the same. Therefore,

It is hereby Enacted by the General Assembly of the State of Vermont, That the treasurer be, and he hereby is directed to pay Charles Bullis the sum of eighty seven dollars and fifty cents as a compensation of the said Bullis for the money so by him paid for s'd land.

AN ACT ASSESSING A TAX OF ONE CENT AND AN HALF CENT
ON EACH ACRE OF LAND IN MEDWAY[1] IN RUTLAND COUNTY

OCTOBER 24TH, 1797

It is hereby Enacted by the General Assembly of the State of Vermont, That there be, and hereby is assessed a tax of one cent and an half cent on each acre of land in the township of Medway in the county of Rutland, public lands excepted, for the purpose of making and repairing public roads and bridges in said town, to be expended by the order and direction of Abel Spencer and Cephas Smith, Junr., Esqrs., and Benjamin Parker, who are hereby appointed a committee for that purpose, and any justice of the peace for the county of Rutland is hereby empowered to issue a warrant to Jonathan Parker, Junr., to collect said tax. And said committee and collector are hereby directed to govern themselves in collecting, disposing, and accounting for the monies raised by said tax, agreeably to an act passed October, 1796, entitled, "An act regulating the disposition of monies raised by taxes on lands in the several towns for the purpose of making and repairing public roads and bridges."[2]

AN ACT FOR THE REVIVAL OF, AND IN ADDITION TO AN ACT ENTITLED,
"AN ACT GRANTING A TAX OF ONE PENNY HALF PENNY ON EACH
ACRE OF LAND IN THE TOWNSHIP OF SALTASH FOR THE
PURPOSE THEREIN MENTIONED," PASSED
NOVEMBER 8TH, 1796

OCTOBER 24TH, 1797

Whereas, the committee appointed in and by said act, neglected to

---

1. State Papers of Vermont, Vol. I, *Index to the Papers of the Surveyors General,* Medway, Vermont Grant, Feb. 23, 1781; name changed to Mendon, 1827.

2. Ibid., Vol. XI, *General Petitions,* 1797-1799, "For a Tax on Land to Build and Repair Roads and Bridges," 143.

advertise the opportunity for land owners to discharge their taxes by labour, until the expiration of the term by law limited for such advertisement. Therefore,

It is hereby Enacted by the General Assembly of the State of Vermont, That the act entitled, "An act granting a tax of one penny half penny on each acre of land in the township of Saltash for the purpose therein mentioned," passed the eighth day of November A.D. 1796, be, and the same is hereby revived, and its operation, shall, to all intents and purposes, be the same as though it had passed and been enacted at the present session of the Legislature. And,

It is hereby further Enacted, That in the stead of the selectmen of said Saltash for the year 1796, who were appointed the committee by Said act, and Hart Marcy, who was appointed collector, the selectmen, who shall be chosen in said town in the year one thousand seven hundred and ninety eight, be, and they hereby are appointed the committee to superintend the expenditure of said tax. And the first constable of said town, who shall be in like manner chosen in the year 1798, is hereby appointed the collector of said tax. And the said committee and collector appointed by this act, are directed in their duty, and made responsible in the same manner as the said former committee and collector were, in and by the act aforesaid directed and made responsible.

AN ACT GRANTING TO DANIEL TAYLOR AND HIS ASSOCIATES THE
PRIVILEGE OF ERECTING A TOLL BRIDGE OVER WEST RIVER IN
THE TOWN OF DUMMERSTON

OCTOBER 28TH, 1797

It is hereby Enacted by the General Assembly of the State of Vermont, That Daniel Taylor and his associates be, and they are hereby formed into, constituted and made a body politic and corporate by the name of the "Second West-River-Bridge-Company," and that he and his successors, and such other persons as shall hereafter be admitted members of said company, shall be, and continue a body politic and corporate, by the same name, one hundred years. And that the same company have the exclusive privilege of erecting and continuing a toll bridge over said West River, at the most convenient place within two miles each way of the said Daniel Taylor's now dwelling house in said Dummerston. And,

It is hereby further Enacted, That it shall and may be lawful for the said company, to demand and receive toll at the following rates for crossing said bridge, to wit: for each passenger, two cents, for each horse, three cents; for each ox, or cow or other horned creature not exceeding ten in number, three cents; if over that number, each two cents; for each chaise or sulkey [sulky], ten cents; for each loaded cart or waggon, sixteen cents; for each cart or waggon not loaded, eight cents; for each chariot, coach or phaeton, or other four-wheeled carriage of pleasure, fifty cents; for each sleigh or sled drawn by two or more horses or by two or more cattle, twelve cents; for each sleigh or cart drawn by one horse or for any unloaded sled whatever, six cents; for each sheep or swine, half cent.

It is hereby further Enacted, That at the expiration of forty years from the first day of January, which will be in the year of our Lord seventeen hundred and ninety nine, it shall be the duty of the judges of the supreme court, to examine into the accounts of the said company, for and on account of said bridge, and the proceeds thence arising, for which purpose the said judges are hereby empowered to appoint three or more persons wholly disinterested, who shall be duly sworn to the faithful performance of their trust, commissioners, to examine into the State of the accounts of the said company. And the said commissioners for the purpose aforesaid, shall have access to all books and documents of said company, and are hereby empowered to call before them, and examine under oath, such persons as they may think fit, and make out a fair statement of the cost of erecting, maintaining and attending the said bridge, and of the proceeds arising to the said company from the same, by the rates of toll aforesaid, during the said term, and make report thereon to the said judges at the stated term of the supreme court, in the county of Windham, next after their appointment. And the said commissioners shall receive from the said company, such compensation for their services as shall be allowed by the judges of the said court. And if it shall appear to the judges by the report of the commissioners made as aforesaid, that the net proceeds, during the said term of forty years, as aforesaid, shall average a larger sum than twelve per centum per annum, on all actual expenditures, it shall be the duty of the said judges to lessen the toll, to such sum as to them shall appear reasonable; provided it shall not be in the power of the said judges to reduce the toll to such sum as shall prevent the proprietors from receiving twelve per cent per annum for all actual expenditures. And,

It is hereby Enacted, That the said company are hereby made capable of suing and being sued; of prosecuting and defending suits in their corporate capacity; may have a common seal; and make bye-laws for their company concerns; and at any meeting warned for that purpose, may choose a president and four directors who shall continue in office for two years from the time of their election, and until others shall be chosen in their place, a majority of whom including the president, shall form a quorum to transact business; that at any election of officers in said company, every owner shall be entitled to as many votes as he shall own shares in said bridge; that a secretary shall be appointed by said company, whose duty it shall be to make and keep the necessary records, and make regular entries of the transfers of all shares. And no person shall be allowed to vote at any meeting upon any share unless it shall appear by the books and entries of the secretary that he has owned said share at least twenty days previous to said meeting. That the first meeting shall be warned by the said Daniel Taylor, at such time, and in such manner as he may judge expedient, and that all future meetings shall be warned by the president, unless there shall be a vacancy, in which case it may be warned by the secretary. And,

It is hereby further Enacted, That the said company shall keep the said bridge to be by them erected, and continued in manner aforesaid, in good repair, during the term of this grant, and in case of neglect shall be liable to the same penalties to which towns are by law subjected, for not keeping roads and bridges in repair. And in case they shall neglect for the space of six months after complaint be made, they shall forfeit all the rights and privileges granted by this act, unless it shall appear that said bridge was destroyed by accident, in which case they shall have eighteen months for rebuilding the same.

Provided nevertheless, that if the said company shall not, within two years after such time as the selectmen of Dummerston shall lay out and survey a road across said river, within the bounds heretofore in this act described, build said bridge and render the same passable, they shall receive no benefit by this act.[1]

---

1. State Papers of Vermont, Vol. XI, *General Petitions,* 1797-1799, "For Authority to Erect a Toll Bridge," 132.

AN ACT FOR THE REVIVAL AND ALTERATION OF "AN ACT ASSESSING A
TAX OF ONE PENNY PER ACRE ON THE LANDS IN THE TOWN OF
WOODBURY," PASSED FEBRUARY TWENTIETH, 1797

OCTOBER 28TH, 1797

Whereas, the committee appointed in and by said act neglected to advertise the opportunity for labour on said tax until the expiration of the term limited therefor by law. Therefore,

It is hereby Enacted by the General Assembly of the State of Vermont, That the act entitled, "An act granting a land tax on the township of Woodbury," passed the twentieth of February, 1797, be, and the same is hereby revived, and its operation shall, to all intents and purposes, be the same as though it had passed and been enacted at the present session of the Legislature. And,

It is hereby further Enacted, That instead of the committee appointed in and by said act, Joseph Fisher of Cabot, James Whitelaw of Ryegate, and Gideon Wheelock of Calais, be, and they are hereby appointed the committee to superintend the expenditure of said tax; to which committee the collector of said tax is hereby made accountable. And the said present committee are hereby directed and become responsible, in the same manner as the said former committee were, in and by the act aforesaid directed and made responsible.

AN ACT STAYING PROCEEDINGS AGAINST ABEL STEVENS
FOR ONE YEAR

OCTOBER 28TH, 1797

Whereas, a suit is now pending before the county court in the county of Windsor, in the name of the treasurer of this State, against Abel Stevens, on a gaol bond given in consequence of an execution issued on a bond of recognizance entered into by the said Abel Stevens and one Isaac Stevens, for and in behalf of the said Isaac. And the said Abel is wholly unable at present to pay said bond without greatly injuring his property. Therefore,

It is hereby Enacted by the General Assembly of the State of Vermont, That the clerk of Windsor County court be, and he is hereby directed to continue from term to term, for the term of one year, on the docket of said court, the aforesaid action, and when judgment is made up against the said Abel, no cost shall be taxed for the time said action is continued under this act, except fees to the clerk for continuance, and no more than six per cent interest shall be made up against the said Abel on the suit aforesaid.[1]

AN ACT ASSESSING A TAX OF THREE CENTS PER ACRE ON THAT PART OF GOSHEN LYING BETWEEN WHEELOCK AND WALDEN FOR THE PURPOSE THEREIN MENTIONED

OCTOBER 28TH, 1797

It is hereby Enacted by the General Assembly of the State of Vermont, That there be, and hereby is assessed a tax of three cents per acre on all the lands in that part of Goshen, in the county of Caledonia, which lies situated between the towns of Wheelock and Walden, public lands excepted, for the purpose of making and repairing roads and building bridges in said tract of land, under the direction of John Bean and Nehemiah Philips, both of Wheelock, who are hereby appointed a committee to superintend the expenditure of said tax. And any justice of the peace in the county of Caledonia is hereby empowered to issue his warrant to Abraham Morrill of said Wheelock, to collect said tax. And said collector is hereby made accountable to said committee for the amount of said tax. And said committee and collector are hereby directed in the collecting, disposing, and accounting for the monies raised by said tax, to conform themselves in all things to the directions of an act entitled, "An act regulating the disposition of monies raised by tax on lands in the several towns for the purpose of making and repairing roads and building bridges," passed the second day of November, 1796.[2]

AN ACT RATIFYING THE DIVISION OF THE TOWN OF BARNARD BY AND BETWEEN THE PROPRIETORS THEREOF

OCTOBER 28TH, 1798

Whereas, an early settlement of the lands in the town of Barnard, without any legal division thereof, into severalty among the proprietors,

---

1. State Papers of Vermont, Vol. XI, *General Petitions,* 1797-1799, "For a Stay of Proceedings Against a Bondsman," 162.
2. Ibid., "For a tax on Land to Build Roads and Bridges," 37.

has rendered it impracticable at this late period to make such a division of the same as will do justice to the several proprietors and at the same time be strictly agreeable to the present existing laws of this State. And whereas the proprietors of said town have made and compleated a division thereof into severalty (a small part only excepted), as nearly equal as the present situation of said town will admit, to which divisions the proprietors and inhabitants of said town have universally agreed. And they have made a plan or map thereof which has been accepted in proprietors' meeting, and they are desirous that the same may be ratified and confirmed as appears by the said proprietors' records. Therefore,

It is hereby Enacted by the General Assembly of the State of Vermont, That the said division of the lands of said town of Barnard into severalty, so made by and between the proprietors of said town as aforesaid, shall be, and the same is hereby declared to be as good and valid in law, to all intents and purposes, as though the same had been made, in every respect, agreeably to a certain statute law of this State, entitled, "An act regulating proprietors' meetings," any law, usage or custom to the contrary notwithstanding.

Provided, that the said proprietors of said town of Barnard shall deposit a true and attested copy of said plan or map made and accepted as aforesaid, in the office of the town clerk of said town of Barnard, on or before the first day of March next.[1]

AN ACT FOR THE REVIVAL AND ALTERATION OF "AN ACT ASSESSING A TAX OF ONE PENNY PER ACRE ON THE LANDS IN THE TOWN OF WOODBURY," PASSED FEBRUARY 20TH, 1797

OCTOBER 28TH, 1797

Whereas, the Committee appointed in and by said act, neglected to advertise the opportunity for labour on said tax until the expiration of the term limited therefor by law. Therefore,

I *It is hereby Enacted* by the General Assembly of the State of Vermont, That the act entitled "An act granting a land tax on the township of Woodbury, passed the twentieth day of February, one thousand seven hundred and ninety seven, be, and the same is hereby

---

1. State Papers of Vermont, Vol. XI, *General Petitions,* 1797-1799, "For Confirmation of Land Divisions Made by Proprietors," 145.

revived and its operation shall, to all intents and purposes, be the same as though it had passed and been enacted at the present session of the Legislature.

II *And it is hereby further Enacted,* That instead of the committee appointed in and by said act, Joseph Fisher of Cabot, and James Whitelaw of Ryegate and Gidson Wheelock of Calais, be, and they are hereby appointed the Committee to superintend the expenditure of said tax, to which Committee the collector of said tax is hereby made accountable. And the said present Committee are hereby directed, and become responsible, in the same manner as the former Committee were, in and by the act aforesaid directed and made responsible.

AN ACT TO AUTHORISE OLIVER KIDDER TO SELL THE REAL ESTATE OF
TYRUS PRESSON, LATE OF WEATHERSFIELD, DECEASED

OCTOBER 30TH, 1797

Whereas, it appears to this Legislature that it would be for the benefit of the heirs of Tyrus Presson, late of Weathersfield, in the county of Windsor, deceased, to sell the real estate which they inherit from their father, Tyrus Presson, late deceased, and vest the avails thereof in other property. And whereas several of said heirs are minors and incapable of making conveyance of their shares of said estate. Therefore,

It is hereby Enacted by the General Assembly of the State of Vermont, That Oliver Kidder of said Weathersfield, be, and he hereby is authorised and empowered (under the direction of the judge of probate of wills, for the District of Windsor) for and in behalf of said heirs, to sell and convey by deed the whole of the real estate which belonged to the said Tyrus at his decease, and is now inheritable by said heirs respectively. And it shall be the duty of the said Oliver Kidder to apply the avails arising from the sale of said estate, or such part thereof as he shall dispose of, to the purchase of such other property, real or personal, for the benefit of said heirs, respectively, as by the direction or approbation of said judge of probate shall be considered most beneficial to said several heirs, according to their several portions of said estate, or to pay over the money arising from such sales to the said heirs, their guardian or guardians, for the use and benefit of said heirs, taking a receipt therefor. And for the better securing the interest of said heirs, the said Oliver, before he shall make sale of any of said estate, shall become bound with good and sufficient surety or sureties, in such sum or sums, as said judge shall direct, by bond or bonds, which shall be executed to said judge of probate and to his successor or successors in said office, and lodged in the hands of the said judge for the benefit of said heirs; conditioned that the said Oliver shall faithfully execute the trust and perform the duties enjoined by this act. And all deeds executed by the said Oliver shall be of equal force and validity for the conveying of said estate as though the same were executed by said heirs, respectively, when of full age.

AN ACT ASSESSING A TAX OF THREE CENTS PER ACRE ON ALL THE
LANDS IN THE TOWNSHIPS OF GUILDHALL, EAST HAVEN, NEWARK
AND WESTMORE AND ONE CENT AND AN HALF CENT ON GRANBY,
ALL IN THE COUNTY OF CALEDONIA, FOR THE PURPOSE
OF LAYING AND OPENING A ROAD FROM THE
RIVER ROAD IN GUILDHALL TO THE
WEST LINE OF WESTMORE

OCTOBER 30TH, 1797

It is hereby Enacted by the General Assembly of the State of Vermont, That a tax of three cents per acre be, and hereby is assessed on all the lands in Guildhall, East Haven, Newark, and Westmore, and one and half cent per acre on Granby (public lands excepted) for the purpose of making roads and building bridges through said towns, and particularly on a road to be laid out through said towns, leading from the river road in Guildhall to the west line of Westmore, which said monies shall be expended in the towns aforesaid, respectively, from which by this act they are to be collected. And if any money shall remain from said tax after completing the aforesaid road, to be expended as aforesaid on the roads already laid out in said towns, and where no other road is laid out, to be disposed of by the committee appointed by this act, in each town, to which town the surplus money shall belong. And,

It is hereby further Enacted, That Eben W. Judd, David Hopkinson, and Hezekiah May, be, and they are hereby appointed a committee to lay out said road and superintend the expenditure of said tax on the towns of Guildhall, Grandby, East Haven and Newark. And that David Porter, Joseph Herrick, and Joseph Wait, be, and they are hereby appointed a committee for laying out said road, and for superintending the expenditure of said tax on the town of Westmore, any law to the contrary notwithstanding. And any justice of the peace in the county of Caledonia, is hereby authorised to issue his warrant to James Lucas of Maidstone, who is hereby appointed a collector of the said taxes on the towns aforesaid, to collect the same. And the said committees and collector, in the collection and expenditure of the aforesaid taxes, are directed to govern themselves agreeably to the directions of a law of this state entitled, "An act regulating the disposition of monies raised by tax on lands in the several towns for the purpose of making and repairing roads and building bridges," passed the second day of November, A.D. 1796.[1]

AN ACT GRANTING TO GEORGE REAB A NEW TRIAL IN A CERTAIN CASE THEREIN MENTIONED

OCTOBER 30TH, 1797

Whereas, George Reab, late of Pownall, in the county of Bennington, now residing in Schaktacook [Schaghticoke], county of Rensselaer and State of New York, has prefered his petition to this assembly setting forth that he has been greatly injured by a judgment had and rendered before county court, holden at Bennington, within and for the county of Bennington, at their December term, A.D. one thousand seven hundred and ninety four, in a cause wherein the said George Reab was plaintiff and Nathaniel Stevens and Asahel Stevens of Castleton, in the county of Rutland, defendants, in an action on note, which cause was instituted by the said George, against the said Nathaniel and Asahel, by writ bearing date the fourteenth day of May, A.D. 1794; and the said George has prayed that a new trial may be granted him in said cause; and it having appeared to this Assembly that justice so requires. Therefore,

It is hereby Enacted by the General Assembly of the State of Vermont, That a new trial be, and the same is hereby granted in said cause; and the said county court, for the county of Bennington, are hereby empowered and directed to permit the said action to be entered anew, on the docket of said court, and to proceed to hear, try,

---

1. State Papers of Vermont, Vol. XI, *General Petitions,* 1793-1796, "For a Tax on Land to Build a Road," 139.

and determine said cause between said parties in the same manner as though the same had been brought forward by the said George Reab on review.

Provided nevertheless, That is shall be the duty of the said George Reab to serve the said Asahel Stevens, the surviving joint subscriber to said note, with a true and attested copy of this act, at least twelve days before the sitting of the next county court, to be holden at Bennington, within and for the county of Bennington, on the Monday next preceding the third Tuesday of December next, and produce and deliver a like copy to the clerk of said court. And on the first day of the term of said court, to cause said action to be entered as aforesaid, in said court, which shall be deemed sufficient notice to the said Asahel Stevens to appear and prosecute the same. And also that the said George Shall procure bail to the acceptance of the said county court by way of recognizance, to the said Stevens, in the sum of one hundred dollars; that he prosecute his said action against the said Asahel to effect, and in case of failure, to answer all intervening damages. And,

It is hereby further Enacted, That the said George Reab shall not recover any costs which have already accrued in said cause, should he finally recover in said action. And,

Whereas, great inconveniencies may arise to the parties in taking the depositions anew, which have been taken in said cause;

It is hereby further Enacted, That all depositions which have been legally taken to be improved in said cause, or heretofore have been made use of in the trial of said cause, may be received by the court in the future trials of said cause, and admitted as evidence in said cause, the same as though said depositions were taken, particularly for the court before whom the said future trials shall be had.

AN ACT ASSESSING A TAX OF ONE CENT AND HALF CENT PER ACRE ON
THE LANDS OF KILLINGTON FOR THE PURPOSE THEREIN MENTIONED

OCTOBER 31ST, 1797

It is hereby Enacted by the General Assembly of the State of Vermont, That there be, and hereby is assessed a tax of one cent and an half on each acre of land in the town of Killington, in the county of Rutland (public lands excepted), for the purpose of making and repairing roads and building bridges in said town of Killington, to be distributed in the following manner, to wit, two thirds of the amount of said tax to be laid out on the road in said town leading from Woodstock to Rutland, and the other third of the amount, or net proceeds of said tax, on the road in said town leading by Killington mills (so called) to Pittsfield, and that John Anthony, William Tripp, and Jesse Williams, be, and they are hereby appointed a committee to superintend the expenditure of said tax. And any justice of the peace within the county of Rutland, is hereby authorised to issue his warrant to Albro Anthony of said Killington, who is hereby appointed a collector to collect said tax. And said committee and collector are hereby directed in the collecting, disposing, and accounting for said tax, to govern themselves in all things conformably to the directions of an act entitled, "An act regulating the disposition of monies raised by tax on lands in the several towns for the purpose of making and repairing roads and building bridges," passed the second day of November, one thousand seven hundred and ninety six.[1]

AN ACT EMPOWERING DAMARIS HARRINGTON TO DEED A CERTAIN TRACT
OF LAND IN MIDDLESEX, COUNTY OF
CHITTENDEN

OCTOBER 31ST, 1797

It is hereby Enacted by the General Assembly of the State of Vermont, That Damaris Harrington of Middlesex, in the county of Chittenden, administratrix on the estate of Jonah Harrington, late of said Middlesex, deceased, be, and she is hereby empowered to execute and deliver a deed to John Taplin, of seven acres and three rods of land, lying and being in the said town of Middlesex, and on the southwesterly corner of lot number three in the first division of said town, it being a part of the farm on which the said Jonah last lived. And the deed so to be executed by the said Damaris, administratrix as aforesaid, shall be as valid in law to pass the fee of the land mentioned as aforesaid, to the said John Taplin, as though the deed had been executed by the said Jonah in his life time, any law, usage, or custom to the contrary notwithstanding.[2]

1. State Papers of Vermont, Vol. XI, *General Petitions,* 1793-1796, "For a Tax on Land to Build and Repair Roads and Bridges," 161.
2. Ibid., "For Authority to an Administrator to Give a Deed of Land," 115.

AN ACT RESTORING AARON BARLOW TO HIS LAW IN A CERTAIN CASE
THEREIN MENTIONED

OCTOBER 31ST, 1797

Whereas, Aaron Barlow of Barnard, in the county of Windsor, hath prefered his petition to this Legislature praying relief in an action brought on note by William Burtch [Burch] of Hartford, in said county of Windsor, against him, before Benjamin Emmons, Esqr., one of the justices of the peace for said county, wherein judgment on the fifteenth day of July in the year of our Lord, one thousand seven hundred and ninety three, passed against the said Aaron, and an appeal was granted to the county court, then next to be holden in and for said county of Windsor, and Oliver Bowman became recognized to prosecute said appeal to effect, in due form of law. And the said justice being unable to make out and deliver to the said Aaron, copies of the aforesaid judgment in due season to enter the same, the said Aaron was prevented having a trial in said cause. Whereby the said William, before the supreme court holden at Woodstock, in and for the county of Windsor, on the third Tuesday of August last, recovered against the said Oliver, on the said recognizance entered as aforesaid, the sum of forty four dollars and fifty one cents, which the said Aaron will be compelled to pay unjustly, without the interposition of this Legislature. Therefore,

It is hereby Enacted by the General Assembly of the State of Vermont, That the said Aaron have liberty to enter his said appeal granted as aforesaid, before the county court, next to be holden at Woodstock, in and for the county of Windsor, at the next stated term of said court, and the judges of said court are hereby directed to receive the same, and grant a trial on the merits of said action in the same manner as if said appeal had been duly and regularly entered before the court to which the same was granted by said justice. And no further proceedings shall be had on any execution which has been or may hereafter be issued on the judgment recovered before the supreme court as aforesaid, until after final trial had in the action aforesaid. And in case judgment in said action pass in favor of the said Aaron, the said judgment rendered by the supreme court on the said recognizance as aforesaid, is hereby declared null and void, and no execution shall hereafter ever issue on the same, any law, usage, or custom to the contrary in any wise notwithstanding.[1]

---

1. State Papers of Vermont, Vol. XI, *General Petitions,* 1797-1799, "For a New Trial," 79.

AN ACT DIRECTING THE TREASURER OF THE STATE OF VERMONT TO PAY
THE STATE'S ATTORNIES AND CLERKS OF THE SUPREME COURT THE
SEVERAL SUMS THEREIN MENTIONED

OCTOBER 31ST, 1797

It is hereby Enacted by the General Assembly of the State of Vermont, That the treasurer of this State be, and is hereby directed to pay out of the treasury the following sums of money to the following persons, state's attornies for the several counties in this State:

To William Mattocks, Esqr., fifteen dollars.

To David Fay, Esqr., thirty five dollars.

To Elnathan Keyes, Esqr., two dollars.

To Daniel Farrand, Esqr., seventy four dollars, twenty two cents.

To Daniel Chipman, Esqr., thirty two dollars, sixteen cents.

To Amara Paine, Esqr., one hundred fourteen dollars, fifty nine cents.

To Abel Spencer, Esqr., ninety seven dollars, forty one cents.

To Royal Tyler, Esqr., sixty four dollars.

It is hereby further Enacted, That the treasurer pay the several sums to the following persons, clerks of the supreme court for the several counties:

To Benjamin Swan, Esqr., fifty three dollars, eighteen cents.

To Isaac Bailey, Esqr., thirty five dollars, twenty cents.

To David Dunbar, Esqr., fifteen dollars, ninety three cents.

To Seth Pomeroy, Esqr., four dollars, seventeen cents.

To Lemuel Whitney, Esqr., forty six dollars, thirty nine cents.

To Samuel Robinson, Esqr., Thirty one dollars, twenty one cents.

To John Law, Esqr., forty one dollars, eighty cents.

To Daniel Chipman, for the use of the legal representatives of Samuel Painter, late clerk of the supreme court, deceased, twenty one dollars, 17 cents.

To Nathan Osgood, Esqr., thirty five dollars, twenty three cents.

AN ACT ASSESSING A TAX OF ONE AND A HALF CENT ON EACH ACRE OF
LAND IN GLOVER, FOR THE PURPOSES THEREIN MENTIONED

NOVEMBER 1ST, 1797

It is hereby Enacted by the General Assembly of the State of
Vermont, That there be, and hereby is assessed a tax of one and a
half cents on each acre of land in the township of Glover, situate in
that part of the county of Orleans now within the jurisdiction of the
county of Caledonia, for the time being, (public lands excepted) for
the purpose of making and repairing public roads and bridges in said
town, to be expended by the order and direction of Timothy Stanley,
Esqr., Samuel Huntington, and Ralph Parker, who are hereby appointed a committee for that purpose. And any justice of the peace throughout the State is hereby empowered to issue a warrant to Ezra Hoyt to
collect said tax, who is hereby appointed a collector for that purpose.
And said committee and collector are hereby directed to govern themselves in collecting, disposing, and accounting for the monies raised by
said tax, agreeably to an act passed November second 1796, entitled
"An act regulating the disposition of monies raised by tax on lands in
the several towns for the purpose of making and repairing roads and
building bridges."[1]

AN ACT GRANTING TO ELKANAH STEVENS AND OTHERS THE
EXCLUSIVE RIGHT OF LOCKING WHITE RIVER

NOVEMBER 1ST, 1797

Whereas, Elkanah Stevens, Daniel Gilbert and Jacob Smith, all
of Royalton, in the county of Windsor, and State of Vermont, have
petitioned that the exclusive privilege of locking and continuing locks
on White River from the mouth of said river up the same as far as
Royalton meeting house, may be granted to them, their heirs and
assigns forever. Therefore,

[1.] *It is hereby Enacted* by the General Assembly of the State
of Vermont, That Elkanah Stevens, Daniel Gilbert, Jacob Smith, and
their associates, be, and they hereby are formed into, constituted and
made a body politic and corporate, by the name of *The company for
Locking White River;* and they and their successors, and such other

1. State Papers of Vermont, Vol. XI, *General Petitions,* 1797-1799, "For a Tax
on Land to Repair Roads and Bridges," 151.

persons as shall be hereafter admitted members of said company, shall be, and continue a body politic and corporate by the same name forever. And the said company shall have the exclusive privilege of erecting and continuing locks on White River, in the State of Vermont, in such places as they shall think necessary, from the mouth of said River, up said stream as far as Royalton meeting house, under the following limitations and restrictions, to wit, that the said company shall be liable to forfeit, to and for the use of this State, all right of locking said river, if they shall not, within the term of eight years from the first day of November next, have made and are making all reasonable exertions in procuring materials, labour, and other necessaries to forward the execution of said locks; or shall not have fully erected and completed the same, fit for use, within ten years from the first day of November next. And the toll for conveying loaded boats through each of said locks, shall be twenty cents per ton, and half of said sum for all empty boats according to the tons such boats will carry, and the same sum for every thousand feet of boards and timber &c., which sum shall be and remain the rate of said toll forever, excepting the same shall be diminished by the supreme court, as by this act herein after provided. And,

[2.] *It is hereby further Enacted,* That at the expiration of the term of thirty one years, from and after the compleating of said locks, it shall be the duty of the judges of the Supreme Court to examine into the state of the accounts of the said company, for and on account of the said locks, and proceeds thence arising. For which purpose the said judges are hereby empowered to appoint three or more persons wholly disinterested, who shall be duly sworn to the faithful performance of their trust, commissioners, to examine into the state of the accounts of said company. And the said commissioners for the purpose aforesaid shall have access to all books and documents of said company, and are hereby empowered to call before them and examine under oath such persons as they shall think fit, and make out a fair statement of the costs of erecting, maintaining, and attending the said locks, and of the proceeds arising to said company from the same, at the rates of toll aforesaid, during the said term, and make report thereon to the said judges, at the stated term of said supreme court in the county of Windsor, next after their appointment. And the said commissioners shall receive from said company such compensation for their services as shall be allowed by the judges of said supreme court. And if it shall appear to the said judges, by the report of the commissioners made as aforesaid, that the net proceeds during the said term of thirty one years, as aforesaid, shall average at a larger sum than twelve per cent per annum, upon all actual expenditures, it shall be the duty of said judges to lessen the toll to such sum as to them shall appear reasonable. *Provided,* that it shall not be in the power of the said judges to reduce the toll to such sum as shall prevent the proprietors from receiving twelve per cent per annum for all actual expenditures. And,

3. *It is hereby further Enacted,* That if the company shall find it necessary to erect the locks on or through any lands, the fee of which lands is not vested in the said company, they shall make application to the county court of the county of Windsor, describing the said lands by proper metes and bounds, and ascertaining the quantity of the said lands, and serve the proprietor or proprietors of said lands with a true copy of such application &c., at least twelve days before the sitting of the county court. And the said county court are hereby empowered and directed to appoint a judicious and impartial committee to examine and report to the court the real value of the lands so described as aforesaid. And on the acceptance of such report by the said court, and the company paying the sum reported by the committee as aforesaid, with the legal cost arising thereon, to the clerk of said court, a record thereof shall be made by the said clerk, and the fee of the land shall thereby pass to the said company as fully and compleatly as if deeded by the owner or owners of said lands. And,

4. *It is hereby further Enacted,* That if it shall be found necessary to fully effect the intention of this act, to erect dams on said river, and thereby flow, or otherwise injure the property of any of the good citizens of this State, such person or persons, so injured, shall, upon application to the county court for the county of Windsor, be entitled to receive from the company aforesaid, such compensation as the said county court shall adjudge to be just and equitable, for the injury which such person or persons has sustained or probably may in future sustain, by the flowing of such land or in any other way whatever. And a record being made thereof by the clerk of said court, shall be a complete bar to any future application for compensation for any injury done to the same property, whether real or personal; and an action for damages sustained by such dam or dams as aforesaid, shall be commenced in the mode prescribed by this act, and in no other way, unless the company shall have failed to pay the sum or sums assessed by the court as aforesaid, any law, usage or custom to the contrary notwithstanding.

And it shall be the duty of the clerk of the said county court, to pay over on request all sums of money by him received from the said company as aforesaid, to the persons to whom they respectively belong, taking proper receipts therefor; which receipts the said clerk shall safely keep with the files in his office, and minute the same in the records of the proceedings in each respective cause. And,

5. *It is hereby further Enacted,* That after the term of thirty one years as before mentioned, it shall be the duty of the supreme court, for the time being, on application made for that purpose, to examine at the end of every ten years in the same manner as at the end of thirty one years as aforesaid, and to reduce the toll, in the same manner as is before directed.

AN ACT DIRECTING THE TREASURER TO TAKE SECURITY OF STEPHEN JACOB AND BENJAMIN STEBBINS IN THE CASE THEREIN MENTIONED

NOVEMBER 1ST, 1797

Whereas, it appears to the Legislature that Stephen Jacob and Benjamin Stebbins were the bondsmen of William Sweetser as sheriff for the county of Windsor, and that in the years one thousand seven hundred and ninety three, four, and five, the said William, by neglect of duty, became indebted to the treasurer of this State in a large sum of money amounting to about three thousand dollars, which sum the said Stephen and Benjamin are liable to pay; and notwithstanding, the said Stephen and Benjamin have taken a conveyance of the real estate of the said William in part security for the said demand, yet from the extreme scarity of money, they have not been able to make sale of the same, and should they be immediately compelled to pay the ballance due from the said William, it would greatly distress them and their families. Which to prevent,

It is hereby Enacted by the General Assembly of the State of Vermont, That the treasurer of this State be, and he hereby is directed to take notes of hand from said Stephen and Benjamin, jointly and severally, for the ballance due to the treasury through the said delinquency of the said William, payable in three installments in hard money, hard money orders, and treasurer's notes; one third of said sum to be made payable within one year from the second Thursday of

October in the present year, and one third of said sum to be made payable within two years from the said second Thursday of October, and the residue to be made payable within three years from the second Thursday of October aforesaid. And it is hereby further declared to be the duty of the treasurer to take a mortgage or mortgages on real estate to such amount as he shall judge ample for securing the payment of the respective sums aforesaid.[1]

AN ACT ASSESSING A TAX OF TWO AND ONE HALF CENTS PER ACRE ON ALL THE LANDS IN THE TOWNSHIP OF ANDOVER (PUBLIC RIGHTS EXCEPTED) FOR THE PURPOSE THEREIN MENTIONED

NOVEMBER 1ST, 1797

It is hereby Enacted by the General Assembly of the State of Vermont, That there be, and hereby is assessed a tax of two cents and one half cent per acre on all the lands in the township of Andover, in the county of Windsor and State of Vermont (public lands excepted), for the purpose of making and repairing roads and building bridges in said town under the direction of Samuel Burton, David Spafford, Junr., and James Parker, all of Andover aforesaid, who are hereby appointed a Committee to superintend the expenditure of said tax, and any justice of the peace in the county of Windsor is hereby empowered to issue his warrant to Joel Maning [Manning] of said Andover, who is hereby authorised and empowered to collect said tax. And said collector is hereby made accountable to said committee for the amount of said tax, and said committee and collector are hereby directed in the collecting, disposing, and accounting for the monies raised by said tax, to conform themselves in all things to the directions of an act entitled, "An act regulating the disposition of monies raised by tax on lands in the several towns for the purpose of making and repairing roads and building bridges," passed the second day of November, A.D. one thousand seven hundred & ninety six.[2]

---

1. State Papers of Vermont, Vol. XI, *General Petitions,* 1797-1799, "For the Relief of Bondsmen," 159.
2. Ibid., "For a Tax on Lands to repair Roads and Build Bridges," 52.

AN ACT DIRECTING THE TREASURER OF THE STATE TO PAY LUCIUS HUB-
BARD THE SUM OF THIRTY FOUR DOLLARS AND FIFTY FOUR CENTS,
IT BEING FOR MONEY EXPENDED BY HIM IN BEHALF OF THIS
STATE, AND FOR THE PAYMENT OF WHICH NO PROVISION
HAS BEEN MADE BY LAW

NOVEMBER 1ST, 1797

It is hereby Enacted by the General Assembly of the State of
Vermont, That the treasurer of this State pay unto Lucius Hubbard
the sum of thirty four dollars and fifty four cents, it being for money
by him paid as sheriff of the county of Windsor, in conveying Apollus
Finney, John Johnson, and Nicholas Allen from Woodstock, in the
county of Windsor to Manchester gaol, in March last, and said John
Johnson to Manchester gaol, in August last, which money was necessarily expended for the support of said prisoners, and the persons by said
Hubbard employed to assist him.

AN ACT ASSESSING A TAX OF THREE CENTS PER ACRE ON THE TOWNSHIP
OF JOHNSTON [JOHNSON] FOR THE PURPOSE THEREIN MENTIONED

NOVEMBER 1ST, 1797

It is hereby Enacted by the General Assembly of the State of
Vermont, That there be, and hereby is assessed a tax of three cents on
each acre of land in the township of Johnson, in the county of Franklin,
public lands excepted, for the purpose of erecting a bridge or bridges,
in the said town over the River La Moille, under the direction of George
Gragg, George Hall, and David Erwin, all of said Johnson, who are
hereby appointed a committee to superintend the expenditure of said
tax, and the erection of said bridge or bridges. And any justice of
the peace within the county of Franklin is hereby empowered to issue
his warrant to John McConnel of the same Johnson, who is hereby
empowered to collect said tax. And the said collector is hereby made
accountable to the said committee for the amount of said tax. And
the said committee and collector are hereby directed in the collecting,
disposing, and accounting for said tax, to conform themselves in all
things to the directions of an act entitled, "An act regulating the disposition of monies raised by tax on lands in the several towns, for
the purpose of making and repairing roads and building bridges," passed the second day of November A.D. 1796.

And it is further Enacted, That if any monies should remain un-expended after the completion of one or more bridge or bridges over the river La Moille, the same shall be expended in the making or repairing roads in said town.[1]

AN ACT EMPOWERING ASA GROUT AND ELIHU GROUT TO DEED CERTAIN LANDS IN WEATHERSFIELD

NOVEMBER 2ND, 1797

Whereas, the Legislature at their session in June, Anno Domini one thousand seven hundred and eighty five, granted a tax of three pence on each acre of land in the township of Weathersfield, in the county of Windsor, for the purpose of building a meeting house in said town, and appointed Helkiah Grout collector of the same, who proceeded to sell the lands of the delinquent proprietors, some of which were not redeemed, and the purchaser entitled by law to a deed from the said Helkiah Grout, as collector, which deeds were not made and executed by the said Helkiah in his life time.

It is hereby Enacted by the General Assembly of the State of Vermont, That Asa Grout and Elihu Grout of Weathersfield, in the county of Windsor, administrator to the estate of Helkiah Grout, late of Weathersfield, deceased, be, and they hereby are empowered to execute to the purchasers of any lands sold by the said Helkiah, for the aforesaid tax, any deed or deeds which the said Helkiah, in his life time as collector of said tax, might by law give to such purchaser for the lands of any delinquent proprietor in said town of Weathers-field, and any deed given by the said Asa and Elihu, as administrators on the estate of the said Helkiah Grout, shall be as valid in law to pass the fee of the land of such delinquent proprietor, to the purchaser of any lands so sold to them by the said Helkiah, as though the deed or deeds had been executed to the purchaser by the said Helkiah in his life time, any law to the contrary notwithstanding.[2]

---

1. State Papers of Vermont, Vol. XI, *General Petitions,* 1797-1799, "For a Tax on Land to Build Bridges," 138.
2. Ibid., "For Authority of Administrators to Give Deeds of Lands," 163.

AN ACT ALLOWING THE TOWN OF BENNINGTON THE SUM OF FORTY
THREE DOLLARS AND FOURTEEN CENTS OUT OF THE TREASURY
OF THIS STATE

NOVEMBER 2ND, 1797

Whereas, it appears to this Assembly that one George Hill, and
one George Coleman, foreigners, was [were] provided for by the town
of Bennington at the expense of this State, to the amount of forty
three dollars and fourteen cents.

It is hereby Enacted by the General Assembly of the State of
Vermont, That the treasurer be, and he hereby is directed to pay the
selectmen of the town of Bennington the sum of forty three dollars and
fourteen cents for the purpose above mentioned.[1]

AN ACT APPOINTING A COMMITTEE TO LAY OUT AND SURVEY A COUNTY
ROAD FROM THE COURT HOUSE IN CHELSEA IN THE COUNTY OF
ORANGE, TO THE COURT HOUSE IN DANVILLE IN THE
COUNTY OF CALEDONIA

NOVEMBER 3RD, 1797

Whereas, there is no direct road leading from the place of holding
supreme and county courts in the county of Orange, to the place of
holding the same in the county of Caledonia, for want of which the
judges of the supreme court, when on their circuit, and the central
and north western parts of said counties, are obliged to travel about
twenty miles further than is necessary to get from one court house to
the other. Therefore,

1. *It is hereby Enacted* by the General Assembly of the State of
Vermont, That Elias Curtis and James Whitelaw, Esquires, be, and
they hereby are appointed a committee with full powers to lay out
and survey a county or post road in the most direct and convenient
course, from the court house in Chelsea to the court house in Danville;
that the said Elais Curtis and Abraham Morril, Esqrs., be a committee to lay out or continue said road from the court house in Danville
aforesaid, to the north line of said Danville, and it shall be the duty
of said committee to make a return of the road so by them laid out,

---

1. State Papers of Vermont, Vol. **XI**, *General Petitions,* 1797-1799, "For Compensation for the Support of Invalid and Indigent Foreigners," 122.

to the town clerks of the several towns through which said road shall be laid, whose duty it shall be to record the same in their respective offices; and such road so laid out and recorded shall thereafter be considered as the permanent road between the said counties. And,

2. *It is hereby further Enacted,* That the proprietors and inhabitants of the several towns, through which said road shall pass, shall be at liberty to agree upon the mode of defraying the expense of making and repairing such road, either by taxing the polls and rateable estate of the inhabitants of such towns, or by applying to the Legislature for a tax on the lands in such towns, within a proper time before the session of the Legislature in October next. And,

3. *It is hereby further Enacted,* That it shall be the duty of said committee to lay out said road some time before the first day of June next, and the expense of such survey shall be paid by the persons applying for this act, viz., Reuben Hatch, Esqr., of Chelsea, and Benjamin Sias, Esqr., of Danville. And the said committee shall give notice to the selectmen of the several towns through which said road will probably be laid, of the time they will attend to said business.

AN ACT ESTABLISHING THE DOINGS OF THE SELECTMEN OF THE TOWN OF HARTLAND IN THE COUNTY OF WINDSOR

NOVEMBER 3RD, 1797

Whereas, it is represented to this Legislature that the selectmen who have been appointed in the town of Hartland have entered upon the business required of them, and discharged the duty of selectmen, without taking the oath of office as selectmen, and that no record is made in the book of records in said town of their being sworn to that office.

It is hereby Enacted by the General Assembly of the State of Vermont, That the record of the appointment of the selectmen of the town of Hartland shall be as valid in law, and received as evidence in any court of justice in this State, the same as though a record had been made of the selectmen taking the oath of office as such. And,

It is hereby further Enacted, That all and singular the doings of said selectmen in the discharge of their office, as such, shall be as valid in law, as though said selectmen had taken the oath of office, and a record of the same had been made.

Provided nevertheless, that this act shall in no wise affect the title of any lands in said town, or make the doings of said selectmen more valid in law than they otherwise would be, where their doings have any respect to the sale of real property.

AN ACT DIRECTING THE TREASURER TO PAY ELISHA CLARK, AUDITOR OF ACCOUNTS AGAINST THIS STATE FIFTY TWO DOLLARS FOR HIS SERVICES

NOVEMBER 3RD, 1797

It is hereby Enacted by the General Assembly of the State of Vermont, That the treasurer be, and he hereby is directed to pay Elisha Clark, auditor of accounts against this State, fifty two dollars.

AN ACT ASSESSING A TAX OF THREE CENTS ON EACH ACRE OF LAND IN THE TOWNSHIP OF STAMFORD IN THE COUNTY OF BENNINGTON, FOR THE PURPOSE OF MAKING AND REPAIRING HIGHWAYS IN SAID TOWN LEADING FROM READSBOROUGH TO POWNALL

NOVEMBER 3RD, 1797

It is hereby Enacted by the General Assembly of the State of Vermont, That there be, and hereby is assessed a tax of three cents on each acre of land in the township of Stamford, public rights excepted, for the purpose of making and repairing highways in said Stamford, to be expended by the order and under the direction of David Stearnes, Sargeant Baker, and Abijah Norton, all of said Stamford, who are hereby appointed a committee to superintend the expenditure of said tax, and any justice of the peace within the county of Bennington is hereby empowered to issue a warant to Calvin Stowell of said Stamford, who is hereby appointed a collector for that purpose, to collect said tax, and said collector is hereby made accountable to said committee for the amount of said tax. And the said collector and committee aforenamed, are hereby directed to govern themselves in collecting, disposing, and accounting for the monies raised by said tax, agreeable to an act entitled, "An act regulating the disposition of monies raised by tax on the several towns, for the purpose of making and repairing roads and building bridges," passed November 2d, 1796.[1]

1. State Papers of Vermont, Vol. XI, *General Petitions,* 1797-1799, "For a Tax on Land to Build Roads and Bridges," 86.

AN ACT EMPOWERING SILAS CROSBY, ADMINISTRATOR ON THE ESTATE
OF JAREB CROSBY, LATE OF HALIFAX, IN THE COUNTY OF WINDHAM,
DECEASED, TO SELL ALL THE REAL ESTATE OF SAID
DECEASED

NOVEMBER 3RD, 1797

It is hereby Enacted by the General Assembly of the State of
Vermont, That Silas Crosby, administrator on the estate of Jareb
Crosby, late of Halifax, in the county of Windham, deceased, be, and
he hereby is empowered to sell the whole of the real estate of the
said deceased, lying in Halifax aforesaid, for the purpose of paying the
debts due from said estate, and the overplus arising from such sale,
to be laid out for the benefit of the heirs of said deceased, under the
direction of the Judge of Probate for the district of Marlborough.
And any deed or deeds executed by the said Silas Crosby of the aforesaid real estate, to any person or persons, shall be considered as a
good title to the same, any law, usage, or custom to the contrary
notwithstanding.[1]

AN ACT IN ADDITION TO AN ACT ENTITLED, "AN ACT GRANTING A TAX
OF THREE CENTS ON EACH ACRE OF LAND IN THE TOWNSHIP OF
FAIRLEE, IN THE COUNTY OF ORANGE FOR THE PURPOSE
OF MAKING AND REPAIRING ROADS AND BUILDING
BRIDGES," PASSED THE TWENTY SECOND
DAY OF FEBRUARY A.D. 1797

NOVEMBER 3RD, 1797

Whereas, the committee appointed in and by said act have not
been able to lay out the whole of the monies arising by said tax the
preceding season, agreeably to law. And whereas, it appears to this
assembly that it would be greatly beneficial to the public to have the
post road through said town completed the present year. Therefore,

It is hereby Enacted by the General Assembly of the State of
Vermont, That said committee be, and they are hereby authorised
and empowered to proceed and lay out the residue of said tax, at any
time in the present year, any thing in this or any other act or acts
of this State, to the contrary notwithstanding. And,

---

1. State Papers of Vermont, Vol. XI, *General Petitions,* 1797-1799, "For Authority
to An Administrator to Sell land," 53.

It is hereby further Enacted, That the county court of said county be, and they hereby are directed to allow the same price for labour, which shall be laid out in pursuance of this act, as is directed to be allowed in the months of November and December in and by an act of this State entitled, "An act regulating the disposition of monies raised by tax on lands in the several towns, for the purpose of making and repairing roads and building bridges," passed November 2d A.D. 1796.

AN ACT FOR QUIETING THE HEIRS OF WILLIAM UTLEY, LATE OF BRUMLEY[1][BROMLEY] (OR LANDGROVE) IN THE COUNTY OF BENNINGTON, DECEASED, AND THEIR HEIRS AND ASSIGNS IN THE POSSESSION OF CERTAIN LOTS OF LAND SITUATE IN THE SAID BRUMLEY

NOVEMBER 4TH, 1797

Whereas, it appears to this Legislature, that William Utley late of Brumley (or Landgrove), in the county of Bennington, deceased, purchased forty two rights or shares of land in said Bromley, and about the same time, laid out and surveyed, two thousand acres of land in said town, on the rights or shares so purchased as aforesaid, and at the same time removed his family and settled in said town, and made improvements on some of said pitches. And it appears the the said William, and his family, have ever since continued actually to occupy and improve some of said pitches; and that the remaining part of the proprietors have not come forward, to make an actual division of said township, until in the present year A.D. one thousand seven hundred and ninety seven. And the said proprietors, having now made an actual division and allotment of said town, and on consideration of the circumstances of the said pitches, and the acknowledgment due for the exertions and hardships through which the said William, deceased, and his family have passed, in the early settlement of said town, have consented and agreed that his heirs, and their heirs, and assigns shall be quieted and confirmed in twenty, hundred-acre lots, as herein described amounting to the aforesaid quantity of two thousand acres. *Provided,* That their title to the original rights to

1. State Papers of Vermont, Volume 1, *Index to the Papers of the Surveyors General,* Brumley, alias Bromley, N. H. grant to William Sumner and associates, Oct. 13, 1761; name changed to Peru, 1804, page 43.

which the said lots or pitches are affixed in the draught [draft] be valid, as appears by their vote, passed the twenty eighth day of October in the present year, which twenty, hundred-acre lots are described and to be known as follows, to wit, the lot lying in range fourth and tier fifth, affixed by the said proprietors in their draft to the original right of Samuel Gilbert; the lot lying in range fourth and tier sixth, affixed in manner aforesaid, to the original right of Thomas Post; the lot lying in range sixth and tier third affixed to the original right of Thomas Post, junior; the lot lying in range eighth and tier fourth, affixed to the original right of David Webster; the lot lying in range seventh and tier third affixed to the original right of Samuel Gilbert, Junior; the lot lying in range fifth and tier fifth affixed to the right of John Gillet, Junior; the lot lying in range fifth and tier fourth affixed to the right of Daniel Little; the lot lying in range seventh and tier fourth affixed to the right of James Noble; the lot number eight in the draft affixed in manner aforesaid to the right of Reuben Harriman; the lot lying in range fourth and tier seventh affixed to the right of Jonathan Kimball; the lot lying in range first and tier tenth affixed to the right of Edmund Morse; the lot lying in range fifth and tier sixth affixed to the right of Benjamin Harriman; the lot lying in range third and tier eighth affixed to the right of Aaron Wright; the lot lying in range third and tier seventh, affixed to the right of Ebenezer Root, Junior; the lot lying in range fourth and tier third, affixed to the right of Roger Loomis; the lot lying in range fourth and tier fourth affixed to the right of Ebenezer Buck; the lot lying in range fifth and tier third affixed to the right of Jonathan Sumner; the lot lying in range eighth and tier fifth affixed to the right of Isaac Ford, being lots of the first division in said town. And the lot lying in range first and tier ninth, affixed to the right of Thomas Gilbert; and the lot number thirteen in said draft affixed to the right of John Atwood, being lots of the second division in said township. Therefore,

It is hereby Enacted by the General Assembly of the State of Vermont, That the heirs of William Utley, late of Brumley, in the county of Bennington, deceased, be, and they and their heirs and assigns in behalf of themselves and the present holders of said lands, are hereby quieted and confirmed in the full and entire possession of the said twenty, hundred-acre lots above designated and described, in as full and ample a manner as though the said lots had each of them been actually settled at the time of making the division and draft aforesaid, and as though the said lots had each of them, agreeably to law, been set off by said proprietors as pitches to actual settlers and proprietors in lieu of their drafts.

Provided nevertheless, That if the said William, deceased, did not in his life time possess a legal right and title as a proprietor, in common to said [lands], either in part, or in the whole, then the benefit of this act, to his heirs, and to their heirs and assigns shall cease and become null in part, or in the whole, commensurate and not otherwise, with such default of legal title.

AN ACT ASSESSING A TAX OF TWO CENTS ON EACH ACRE OF LAND IN THAT PART OF THE TOWN OF GOSHEN WHICH LIES IN THE COUNTY OF ADDISON

NOVEMBER 4TH, 1797

It is hereby Enacted by the General Assembly of the State of Vermont, That there be, and hereby is assessed a tax of two cents on each acre of land in that part of the town of Goshen which lies within the county of Addison (public lands excepted) for the purpose of making and repairing the public roads and bridges in said Goshen, to be laid out and expended on the road leading from Middlebury to Hancock, and for the laying out and making a road through said town from Brandon to Ripton by the order and under the direction of Gamaliel Painter, Hiram Horton, and Joshua Hyde, who are hereby appointed a committee for that purpose. And any justice of the peace for the county of Addison, is hereby empowered to issue a warrant to Samuel Miller of Middlebury, in said county, to collect said tax, who is hereby appointed a collector for that purpose. And the said committee and collector are hereby directed to govern themselves in collecting, disposing, and accounting for the monies raised by said tax, agreeably to the directions of an act entitled, "An act regulating the disposition of monies raised by tax on lands in the several towns, for the purpose of making and repairing roads and building bridges," passed the second day of November A.D. 1796.[1]

---

1. State Papers of Vermont, Vol. XI, *General Petitions,* 1797-1799, "For a Tax on Land to Build and Repair Roads," 65.

AN ACT DIRECTING THE SALE OF THE REAL ESTATE OF SILAS AYLESWORTH, A MINOR

NOVEMBER 6TH, 1797

Whereas, it has been represented that one Silas Aylesworth of Pownall, a minor, is a lunatic and not able to support himself, and his guardian having petitioned for leave to sell the real estate of the said minor for his support. Therefore,

It is hereby Enacted by the General Assembly of the State of Vermont, That Benjamin G. Gardner, the guardian of said Silas Aylesworth, be, and he hereby is empowered and directed to make sale of all the real estate of the said Silas Aylesworth, and appropriate the same at his discretion to the maintenance of the said Silas. And it shall be the duty of the said Benjamin G. Gardner, before he shall proceed to sell said estate, to enter bonds with surety before the Judge of probate for said district, conditioned for his faithful discharge of said trust, which bond shall be for such sums as the said judge of probate shall appoint.

And it is hereby further Enacted, That the deed and conveyance of the said Benjamin, in his capacity as guardian as aforesaid, shall be considered as good and valid in law, for the legal transfer of said estate, and the purchaser shall thereby receive all the title which now vests [in] the said Silas, minor as aforesaid, by virture of his being an heir to such estate.[1]

AN ACT IN ADDITION TO, IN ALTERATION AND IN REVIVAL OF AN ACT, ENTITLED, "AN ACT ASSESSING A TAX OF ONE PENNY PER ACRE ON ALL THE LANDS IN THE TOWNSHIP OF COLCHESTER IN THE COUNTY OF CHITTENDEN FOR THE PURPOSE OF MAKING AND REPAIRING ROADS &C.," PASSED FEBRUARY 18TH, 1797

NOVEMBER 6TH, 1797

Whereas, a tax of one penny per acre, as granted by said act will be insufficient for making and repairing the roads &c. in said town, and for defraying other expenses to which the said tax is to be

---

1. State Papers of Vermont, Vol. XI, *General Petitions,* 1797-1799, "For Authority to a Guardian to Sell the Land of an Idiot Minor," 99.

appropriated. And whereas the collector appointed in and by said act is about to remove out of said town; and whereas the committee of superintendance have neglected to lay out the road or roads on which said tax was to be expended, and to advertise the same agreeable to law. Therefore,

It is hereby Enacted by the General Assembly of the State of Vermont, That there be, and hereby is assessed a tax of two cents per acre instead of one penny per acre as before assessed, on all the lands of the township of Colchester in the county of Chittenden, public lands excepted, for the purpose of making and repairing roads and building bridges in said town. And,

It is hereby further Enacted, That Dennis Downing be, and he is hereby appointed a collector to collect said tax. And the said collector is made accountable and is alike responsible, and under the same obligations as the former collector was, in and by said act. And,

It is hereby further Enacted, That the act entitled "an act assessing a tax of one penny per acre on all the lands in the township of Colchester for the purpose of making and repairing roads &c.," passed the eighteenth day of February A.D., one thousand seven hundred and ninety seven, except in the additions and alterations by this act made and specified, be, and the same is hereby revived, and its operation shall, to all intents and purposes, be, the same as though it had passed and been enacted at the present session of the Legislature.

AN ACT IN ADDITION TO, IN ALTERATION AND IN REVIVAL OF AN ACT
ENTITLED "AN ACT ASSESSING A TAX OF TWO PENCE PER ACRE
ON ALL THE LANDS IN THE TOWNSHIP OF HIGHGATE IN
THE COUNTY OF FRANKLIN, PUBLIC RIGHTS EX-
CEPTED, FOR THE PURPOSE OF MAKING AND
REPAIRING ROADS," WHICH WAS PASSED
THE EIGHTEENTH FEBRUARY 1797

NOVEMBER 6TH, 1797

Whereas, a tax of two pence per acre as granted by said act will be insufficient for making and repairing the roads and for defraying other expenses, to which said tax is to be appropriated. And whereas the committee of superintendance have neglected to lay out the road or roads on which said tax was to be expended, and advertise the same agreeably to an act entitled "An act regulating the disposition of monies raised by tax on lands in the several towns in this State for the purpose of repairing roads &c.," passed November second 1796. Therefore,

It is hereby Enacted by the General Assembly of the State of Vermont, That there be, and hereby is assessed a tax of three cents per acre (instead of two pence as before granted) on all the lands in the township of Highgate in Franklin county, (public rights excepted) for the purpose of making and repairing roads and building bridges in said town. And,

It is hereby further Enacted, That Ella [?] Smith be, and he hereby is appointed one of the committee, in addition to the former committee, and the said Ella Smith is made accountable and is alike responsible and under the same obligations with the other committee appointed in said act.

AN ACT IN REVIVAL AND ALTERATION OF AN ACT ENTITLED "AN ACT
ASSESSING A TAX OF ONE PENNY PER ACRE ON THE TOWNSHIP
OF GEORGIA, AND TWO PENCE PER ACRE ON THE TOWN-
SHIP OF ST. ALBANS IN THE COUNTY OF FRANKLIN
FOR THE PURPOSE OF MAKING ROADS AND
BUILDING BRIDGES IN SAID TOWN,"
PASSED THE EIGHTH DAY OF
OCTOBER, A.D. 1796

NOVEMBER 6TH, 1797

Whereas, the committees appointed by said act, to superintend the expenditure of said taxes, have neglected to lay out the roads on which said taxes were to be expended, and to advertise the same agreeably to law. Therefore,

It is hereby Enacted by the General Assembly of the State of Vermont, That the act entitled, "An act assessing a tax of one penny per acre on the township of Georgia, and two pence per acre on the township of St. Albans &c.," for the purposes therein mentioned, passed the eighth day of October A.D. one thousand seven hundred and ninety six, be, and the same is hereby revived, and its operation shall, to all intents and purposes, be the same as though it had passed and been enacted at the present session of the Legislature, excepting the alteration hereinafter made. And,

It is hereby further Enacted, That David Powers of St. Albans aforesaid, be, and he is hereby appointed a collector to collect the said tax assessed on the town of St. Albans, in the room of Alfred Hathaway, who was appointed collector of the tax last aforesaid, by the said act. And any justice of the peace within the county of Franklin is hereby authorised to issue his warrant to the said David Powers, to collect the said tax. And the said collector is made accountable, and is alike responsible, and under the same obligations as the said Alfred Hathaway was, in and by said act.

AN ACT ASSESSING A TAX OF TWO CENTS PER ACRE ON THE LANDS IN ENOSBURGH FOR THE PURPOSE THEREIN MENTIONED

NOVEMBER 6TH, 1797

It is hereby Enacted by the General Assembly of the State of Vermont, That there be, and hereby is assessed a tax of two cents per acre on all the lands in the township of Enosburgh, in the county of Franklin, public lands excepted, for the purpose of making a bridge over Missisque River, at or near the great falls in said township, and for making and repairing roads in the same under the direction of Amos Fasset and Stephen House, both of Bennington, and Jonas Brigham of Bakersfield, who are hereby appointed a committee to superintend the expenditures of said tax. And any justice of the peace in the county of Franklin is hereby empowered to issue his warrant to William Barber of said Enosburgh, who is hereby appointed a collector to collect said tax, and said collector is hereby made accountable to said committee for the amount of said tax. And said committee and collector are hereby directed in the collecting, disposing, and accounting for the monies raised by said tax to conform themselves in all things to the directions of an act entitled, "An act regulating the disposition of monies raised by tax on lands in the several towns for the purpose of making and repairing roads and building bridges," passed the second day of November A.D. 1796.

Provided nevertheless, and it is hereby further Enacted, That the collector of said tax shall have no power to sell any lands for the payment of the same until after two years from the passing this act.

And it is also further provided, That the aforesaid committee shall not be entitled to charge or receive any more pay for their services in overseeing and directing the expenditures of monies arising on said tax, than they would be entitled to receive if they lived in said township of Enosburgh.[1]

AN ACT ASSESSING A TAX OF FOUR CENTS ON EACH ACRE OF LAND IN
THE TOWNSHIP OF TOWNSHEND, IN THE COUNTY OF WINDHAM,
FOR THE PURPOSE OF BUILDING A BRIDGE OVER WEST RIVER
AND REPAIRING HIGHWAY IN S'D TOWN

NOVEMBER 6TH, 1797

It is hereby Enacted by the General Assembly of the State of Vermont, That there be, and hereby is assessed a tax of four cents on each acre of land in the township of Townshend, public rights excepted, for the purpose of building a bridge over West-River in the southerly part of said Townshend, to be expended by the order and under the direction of Benjamin Livingston, Ephraim Wheelock, and Joseph Belknap, all of Townshend aforesaid, who are hereby appointed a committee to superintend the expenditure of said tax. And any justice of the peace, within the county of Windham, is hereby empowered to issue a warrant to Willard Taft of said Townshend, who is hereby appointed a collector to collect said tax, and said collector is hereby made accountable to said committee for the amount of said tax.

And it is hereby further Enacted, That the place for erecting said bridge over said West-River, shall be agreed upon by the selectmen of said town, and the committee aforenamed; and the overplus of the monies raised as aforesaid, if any there be, after the said bridge is completed, shall be by the committee aforesaid, laid out in repairing highways in said town, in such places as the selectmen of said town shall direct. And the said collector and committee aforenamed, are hereby directed to govern themselves in collecting, disposing, and accounting for the monies raised by said tax agreeably to an act entitled, "An act regulating the disposition of monies raised by tax on the several towns, for the purpose of making and repairing roads and building bridges," passed November 2d, 1796.

---

1. State Papers of Vermont, Vol. XI, *General Petitions,* 1797-1799, "For a Tax on Land to Build Roads and Bridges," 85.

AN ACT ALLOWING CORNELIUS THORPE AND WILLIAM DUNCAN, THE
BOUNTY FOR KILLING A GROWN WOLF IN WINHALL

NOVEMBER 6TH, 1797

Whereas, it hath appeared to this Legislature, that Cornelius
Thorpe and William Duncan, did, on the fourteenth day of September,
one thousand seven hundred and ninety seven, take and kill a full
grown wolf, and through mistake carried the head of said wolf to be
cropped by an improper officer, by reason whereof they are wholly
unable to recover the bounty allowed by law to such persons as shall
kill and destroy wolves and panthers. Therefore,

It is hereby Enacted by the General Assembly of the State of
Vermont, That the treasurer of this State, be, and he hereby is directed
to pay to the said Cornelius Thorpe and William Duncan the sum of
twenty dollars as a bounty for the taking and killing of said wolf.[1]

AN ACT DIRECTING THE TREASURER TO PAY SAMUEL HITCHCOCK AND
RICHARD WHITNEY, ESQUIRES, THE SUMS THEREIN MENTIONED

NOVEMBER 6TH, 1797

It is hereby Enacted by the General Assembly of the State of
Vermont, That the treasurer be, and he hereby is directed to pay to
Samuel Hitchcock, Esquire, the sum of one hundred forty five dollars,
& eighty cents; and to Richard Whitney, Esquire, the sum of two
hundred and one dollars, it being for their services in revising the laws
of this State.

AN ACT DIRECTING CERTAIN TRUSTEES TO MAKE THE CONVEYANCE AND
TRANSFERS THEREIN MENTIONED

NOVEMBER 6TH, 1797

Whereas, in the year one thousand seven hundred and seventy
eight, the then township of Kent was confiscated as the property of
James Rogers, late of Upper Canada, deceased, and was on the
twentieth day of April, one thousand seven hundred and eighty, granted by the name of Londonderry[2], to Edward Aikin, Samuel Fletcher

---

1. State Papers of Vermont, Vol. XI, *General Petitions,* 1797-1799, "For a Bounty
   for Capturing a Wolf," 124.

2. Ibid., Vol. II, *Charters Granted by the State of Vermont,* 127.

and Joseph Tyler, Esquires, as trustees to dispose of the same for the use of this State, part of which township remains in the care of said trustees. And whereas James Rogers, son and heirs of James Rogers above mentioned, hath petitioned that said lands and the avails thereof be granted to him. Therefore,

It is hereby Enacted by the General Assembly of the State of Vermont, That Edward Aikin, Samuel Fletcher and Joseph Tyler, Esqrs., be, and they are hereby authorised and required to convey to James Rogers by deed of quit-claim all right and title to lands in Londonderry and Windham, which said trustees now hold in right of and in behalf of this State. Also to transfer to said James Rogers, all right and property, which said trustees, in their said capacity, now have to lands in Londonderry and Windham, by virtue of mortgage; also to pay and transfer to the said James Rogers all property which said trustees now have in notes of hand, or other writings obligatory which said trustees now hold as security for the payment of any sum or sums of money due for lands by said trustees, heretofore sold in their capacity aforesaid, and generally to account to said James Rogers for the avails of all lands by said trustees heretofore sold, in their aforesaid capacity, except such part of said avails as said trustees have paid into the treasury of this State.

Provided always, that at the time said trustees convey to said James Rogers all property and right which said trustees now have in their capacity aforesaid, to lands in Londonderry and Windham, and transfer the avails thereof as aforesaid, the said James Rogers shall pay said trustees the amount of all costs and charges, which hath accrued against this State, and become payable to said trustees for executing the business of said trust. And when said trustees shall convey and transfer as aforesaid, the said James Rogers shall deliver to said trustees a discharge which shall exonerate said trustees from all demands of this State, upon said trustees for the avails of the sales of lands in Londonderry and Windham, and every part thereof.

Provided Also, That said James Rogers shall not prosecute his right to any settled lands assigned by mortgage as aforesaid until the expiration of one year from the passing of this act. And,

It is hereby further Enacted, That the said James Roger be, and he is hereby fully authorised and empowered in the name and behalf of this State, to do and transact all acts and things relating to acquiring and possessing the property aforesaid, as fully and effectually as said trustees are, or ever were empowered, for the use and at the expense of said James Rogers. *Provided also,* that the said James Rogers secure to the treasury of this State, the payment of four hundred dollars within two years from the passing of this act.

AN ACT ESTABLISHING THE DIVISION OF LAND IN THE TOWN OF BETHEL

NOVEMBER 6TH, 1797

Whereas, the proprietors of the town of Bethel as appears from their books and records, before their charter issued, compleated the division of said town into severalty, and immediately after said divisions were made, the proprietors and land owners in said town made large improvements, under said division, and do now hold all their lands and improvements under the same. And the said proprietors and land owners have universally acquiesced in said divisions ever since they were made. And whereas doubts have arisen whether said divisions were made agreeably to the rules of law. Therefore,

It is hereby Enacted by the General Assembly of the State of Vermont, That the proprietors of said town of Bethel, be, and they hereby are empowered at any legal meeting warned for that purpose, to ratify and establish all or any of the divisions made in said town; and if, hereafter, at any meeting of said proprietors warned as aforesaid, said proprietors shall vote to ratify and establish all or any of the divisions, made in said town, either before or after the issuing their charter, the same shall be considered as good and valid in law; and any person concerned in the trial for any lands in said town may, and are hereby empowered to give the records of the divisions of said proprietors, so ratified and confirmed, in evidence, the same as though they were originally legally made.[1]

---

1. State Papers of Vermont, Vol. XI, *General Petitions,* 1797-1799, "For Confirmation of Land Divisions Made by Proprietors," 145.

AN ACT IN ADDITION TO AND ALTERATION OF AN ACT ENTITLED "AN ACT
EMPOWERING THE PROPRIETORS OF THE TOWNSHIP OF NEW HAVEN,
IN ADDISON COUNTY, TO PITCH THE UNDIVIDED LANDS IN
SAID TOWN, AND TO TAX THE LANDS IN SAID TOWN
FOR THE PURPOSES THEREIN MENTIONED,"
PASSED AT THE SESSION OF THE
LEGISLATURE IN OCTOBER
1796

NOVEMBER 6TH, 1797

Whereas, the proprietors and landowners of said New Haven in consequence of the said act, have began and actually done a considerable part of the resurveying of the lands in said town of New Haven. And whereas in order to make the proceeding respecting the resurveying and making a plan of said town of New Haven valid, they were obliged by said act to have the same resurveying done, and a plan of said town made by the first day of October, one thousand seven hundred and ninety seven, and as the whole is not completed, the expense already arisen must be lost, unless a remedy therefor in this way be had, which shall likewise leave the land owners in the same disagreeable situation as before said act. Therefore,

1. *It is hereby Enacted* by the General Assembly of the State of Vermont, That the time for compleating of said survey and a plan of said town, be, and hereby is prolonged to the first day of October one thousand seven hundred and ninety eight. And that the same proceeding may be had in consequence of said act, as if the time in said act had been stated as last aforesaid in this act. *Provided,* the said proprietors shall not commence the pitching of the undivided lands in said town until said plan is compleated as aforesaid. And,

2. *It is hereby further Enacted,* That the proprietors and land owners in a legal meeting warned for that purpose may grant a tax on all the lands in said town of New Haven as originally granted (public lands excepted), not to exceed three cents per acre to defray the expense of said surveying.[1]

---

1. State Papers of Vermont, Vol. XI, *General Petitions,* 1797-1799, "For Additional Time to Complete a Town Survey and for a Tax on Land to Pay the Cost Thereof," 148.

AN ACT INCORPORATING ST. ANDREWS GORE INTO A TOWNSHIP BY THE
NAME OF PLAINFIELD

NOVEMBER 6TH, 1797

It is hereby Enacted by the General Assembly of the State of
Vermont, That the tract of land now known by the name of St.
Andrews Gore, in the county of Caledonia, being a part of a grant
to Savage, Whitelaw and Company, bounded westerly by Montpelier,
Southwardly by Barre and Orange, Eastwardly by Harris's Gore, and
Northwardly by Marshfield, be, and the same is hereby incorporated
into a township by the name of Plainfield, with all the rights, privileges
and imunities enjoyed by other towns in this State.

AN ACT APPOINTING A COMMITTEE FOR THE PURPOSE OF ESTABLISHING
A PLACE FOR THE SITTING OF THE SUPREME AND COUNTY COURTS
IN THE COUNTY OF FRANKLIN, AND TO REPORT THEIR OPINION
TO THE NEXT SESSION OF THE LEGISLATURE, WHETHER
THE TOWNS OF THE NORTH HERO, ISLE [LA] MOTT AND
ALBURGH IN THE COUNTY OF FRANKLIN, AND SOUTH
HERO IN THE COUNTY OF CHITTENDEN
OUGHT TO BE SET OFF AS A
SEPARATE COUNTY

NOVEMBER 6TH, 1797

Whereas, the Shire town in the county of Franklin, hath not been
established, only for the time being, and in order to prevent any
disputes in future, and at the request of the Representatives from said
county,

It is hereby Enacted by the General Assembly of the State of
Vermont, That Israel Smith of Rutland, in the county of Rutland,
Enoch Woodbridge of Vergennes, in the county of Addison, and Lott
Hall of Westminster, in the county of Windham, Esquires, be, and
they hereby are appointed a committee to fix on and establish the
place for the holding of the supreme and county courts in said county
of Franklin, and it is hereby made the duty of the said committee,
after viewing the situation of said county, to erect a stake or other
monument at such place as they or either two of them shall agree
on for the building of a Court-House within said county, and to make
out and deliver to the judges of the county court, within and for said

county of Franklin, a certificate signed by them or either two of them, describing the place where they shall have erected the said stake or monument as aforesaid, which said certificate shall be recorded by the clerk of said county court, and the place where the said committee or either two of them shall erect the stake or monument for the building of a court-house within said County, shall be the place for holding the supreme and county courts in said county forever.

Provided nevertheless, That no alteration shall take place until a Court-House shall be built to the acceptance of the judges of the county court of said county. And,

It is hereby further Enacted, That the town so agreed on by the said Committee for the shire town in said county, shall pay the whole charge and expense of said committee for their services, and free the remaining part of said county from any expense towards building a court house in the same. And,

It is hereby further Enacted, That the said Israel Smith, Enoch Woodbridge, and Lott Hall, Esquires, be, and they hereby are appointed a committee to examine and view the situation of the said towns of North Hero, Isle [la] Mott, Alburgh and South Hero, and to report their opinion to the next session of the Legislature, whether the said towns ought to be set off as a separate county.

AN ACT GRANTING POWER TO THE ADMINISTRATORS OF DAVID JOHNSON, LATE OF CHESTER, DECEASED, TO EXECUTE THE DEED THEREIN MENTIONED

NOVEMBER 6TH, 1797

Whereas, by the petition and memorial of Edy [Edward] Johnson and John Johnson, 3d., administrators on the estate of David Johnson, late of Chester, deceased, it appears that on the third day of May A.D. 1794, the said David in his life time executed a certain bond under his hand and seal to Nathaniel Gowing, Junr., and Benjamin Gowing, conditioned that the said David, his heirs, or assigns should execute and deliver to the said Nathaniel and Benjamin their heirs, and assigns a good deed of warranty of a certain tract of land in Chester, bounded as follows, to wit: beginning at the southwest corner of John Ellison's land, from thence running north ten degrees, east eighty rods to stake and stones, from thence running west ten degrees, north one hundred rods, from thence south ten degrees, west eighty rods, from thence easterly to the first bounds; and that said David neglected to execute said deed. Therefore,

It is hereby Enacted by the General Assembly of the State of Vermont, That the said Edy Johnson and John Johnson 3d, administrators of the said David Johnson, deceased, be, and they are hereby fully authorised and empowered in the room and stead of the said deceased, to convey the land aforesaid, by deed to be by them executed, as administrators aforesaid, according to the tenor and condition of the aforesaid bond, as amply and fully as could be done by the said deceased, were he still living, any law, usage, or custom to the contrary nothwithstanding.[1]

AN ACT FOR REVIVAL AND IN ALTERATION OF AN ACT ENTITLED, "AN ACT ASSESSING A TAX OF ONE PENNY PER ACRE ON THE LANDS IN THE TOWNSHIP OF CRAFTSBURY &C.," PASSED NOVEMBER 7TH A.D. 1796

NOVEMBER 6TH, 1797

Whereas, the committee appointed in and by said act neglected to advertise the opportunity of labouring for the payment of said tax, as is by law provided, until the expiration of the term limited by law for that purpose. Therefore,

It is hereby Enacted by the General Assembly of the State of Vermont, That the act entitled, "An act assessing a tax of one penny per acre on the lands in the township of Craftsbury, for the purpose of making and repairing roads and building bridges in said town," passed the seventh day of November, A.D. 1796, be, and the same is hereby revived, and its operation shall, to all intents and purposes, be the same as though it had passed and been enacted the present session of the Legislature. And,

It is hereby further Enacted, That in the stead of the committee appointed in and by said act, Ebenezer Crafts, Ephraim Morse, and Daniel Davison, all of said Craftsbury be, and they are hereby appointed the committee to superintend the expenditure of said tax, to whom the collector of said tax is hereby made accountable. And the

---

1. State Papers of Vermont, Vol. XI, *General Petitions*, 1797-1799, "For Authority of Administrators to Give Deed of Land," 120.

said present committee are hereby directed and become responsible in the same manner as the said former committee were, in and by the act aforesaid directed, and made responsible.

AN ACT LAYING A TAX OF HALF A CENT ON THE DOLLAR ON THE LIST OF THE POLLS AND RATABLE ESTATE[S] OF THE INHABITANTS OF THE COUNTY OF WINDSOR, FOR THE PURPOSE OF COMPLETING THE GAOL IN WOODSTOCK AND OF DISCHARGING OTHER DEMANDS AGAINST SAID COUNTY

NOVEMBER 7TH, 1797

It is hereby Enacted by the General Assembly of the State of Vermont, That there be, and there hereby is granted a tax of half a cent on the dollar on the list of the polls and rateable estate[s] of the inhabitants of the county of Windsor for the year one thousand seven hundred and ninety seven, to be paid in county orders, notes issued by the treasurer of said county, or in lawful money to be collected and paid into the treasury by the first day of August next. And,

It is hereby further Enacted, That the treasurer of said county have, and he hereby has granted to him the same power in issuing warrants and extents, as are vested in the treasurer of the State in the collection of State taxes. And the first constables of the respective towns in said county are hereby empowered, and it is made their duty to proceed in the collection of said tax, and paying the same into the county treasury, in the same manner as it is made their duty by law to collect state taxes and pay them into the State treasury, and they are hereby made liable in the same manner for neglect of duty. And,

It is hereby further Enacted, That it shall be the duty of the town clerks of the respective towns in said county, to return to the county treasurer, the grand list of all the polls and rateable estates, and the name of the first constable of their respective towns, by the first day of January next, and each town clerk, neglecting his duty aforesaid, shall forfeit & pay to the treasurer of said county the sum of ten dollars, and the sum of ten dollars for every month's neglect after the said first day of January. And it shall be the duty of the state's attorney to sue for the same, in action to be brought on this statute before any court proper to try the same.

AN ACT FOR THE REVIVAL AND ALTERATION OF AN ACT ASSESSING A
TAX OF ONE PENNY PER ACRE ON ALL THE LANDS IN THE TOWNSHIP
OF HINESBURG IN THE COUNTY OF CHITTENDEN, PASSED
NOVEMBER SEVENTH, 1796

NOVEMBER 7TH, 1797

Whereas, the committee appointed in and by said act, neglecting to advertise for the labour to be done on said tax agreeable to an act passed November 2d, 1796, entitled, "An act regulating the disposition of monies raised by tax on the several towns in this State for the purpose of making roads and building bridges," And whereas Salmon Bostwick, one of the committee appointed in and by said act declining to serve. Therefore,

It is hereby Enacted by the General Assembly of the State of Vermont, That the act entitled "An act assessing a tax of one penny per acre on the township of Hinesburgh, for the purpose of making roads and building bridges," passed the 7th day of November 1796, be, and the same is hereby revived, and its operation shall, to all intents and purposes, be the same as though it had passed and been enacted at the present session of the Legislature. And,

It is hereby further Enacted, That instead of the said Salmon Bostwick, Gershom Bostwick be, and he hereby is appointed a committee with all the powers, and under the same restrictions, and responsible in the same manner as the said Salmon was, in and by the aforesaid act, directed and made responsible.

And it is hereby further Enacted, That James Cummings be, and he hereby is appointed a collector of said tax in the room of Justus Byington, and he is hereby made accountable in the same manner as the aforesaid Justus was, in and by said act, directed and made responsible.

AN ACT IN REVIVAL OF AN ACT ENTITLED "AN ACT ASSESSING A TAX OF
TWO PENCE PER ACRE ON THE LANDS IN THE TOWNSHIP OF SWANTON
FOR THE PURPOSE OF MAKING AND REPAIRING ROADS AND
BUILDING BRIDGES," PASSED THE 8TH DAY OF
NOVEMBER, 1796

NOVEMBER 7TH, 1797

Whereas, the committee appointed in and by said act to super-intend the expenditure of said tax, have neglected to lay out the road on which said tax is to be expended, and to advertise the same agreeably to an act entitled, "An act regulating the disposition of monies raised by tax on lands in the several towns in this State for the purpose of making and repairing roads and building bridges," passed the second day of November A.D. 1796. Therefore,

It is hereby Enacted by the General Assembly of the State of Vermont, That the act entitled "An act assessing a tax of two pence on each acre of land in the township of Swanton, public rights excepted, for the purposes therein mentioned," passed the 8th day of November A.D. 1796, be, and the same is hereby revived, and its operation shall, to all intents and purposes, be the same as though it had passed and been enacted at the present session of the Legislature.

AN ACT ASSESSING A TAX OF ONE CENT AND HALF PER ACRE ON ALL THE LANDS IN DANVILLE, AND IN THAT PART OF DANVILLE KNOWN BY THE NAME OF WALDEN GORE FOR THE PURPOSE THEREIN MENTIONED

NOVEMBER 7TH, 1797

It is hereby Enacted by the General Assembly of the State of Vermont, That there be, and hereby is assessed a tax of one and half cent on each acre of land in the town of Danville aforesaid, and that part of Danville known by the name of Walden Gore, public lands excepted, for the purpose of making a post or county road, directed by an act of the Legislature passed at the present session, to be layed out from the court house in Chelsea to the court house in Danville, and from thence to the north line of said Danville, by a committee appointed in and by said act for that purpose; the said tax to be expended in the said town of Danville on said road, from the south line of Wheelock to the courthouse in said Danville, and from thence to the south line of said Danville, under the direction of Samuel Chamberlain, Ephraim Magoon and Benjamin Sias, all of said Danville, who are hereby appointed a committee to superintend the expenditure of said tax. And any justice of the peace within the county of Caledonia, is hereby authorised to issue his warrant to David Dunbar of said Danville, who is hereby appointed a collector, to collect said tax; and said committee and collector are hereby directed in the collecting, disposing, and accounting for said tax, to conform themselves in all things to the direction of the statute in that case made and provided. And,

It is hereby further Enacted, That such monies raised by said tax as shall not be needed in the making of the county or post road in said Danville, shall be expended on such other roads in said town as the selectmen shall direct.

AN ACT DESCRIBING THE DIVISION LINE BETWEEN THE TOWNS OF BURLINGTON AND WILLISTON

NOVEMBER 8TH, 1797

It is hereby Enacted by the General Assembly of the State of Vermont, That the future division line between the towns of Burlington and Williston, shall begin at the middle of Muddy Brook (so called), where the same falls into Onion River, thence running along the middle of said brook, up stream, east of Post's sawmill to Shelburn[e] town line. And the tract of land which lays east of the above said line, and formerly belonged to the town of Burlington, be, and the same is hereby annexed to the town of Williston, and the several inhabitants who now reside, or hereafter shall reside, on the tract of land lying easterly of the aforesaid line, shall, for all purposes be considered, and are hereby declared to be inhabitants of the town of Williston aforesaid.

AN ACT AUTHORISING THE PROPRIETORS OF THE TOWNSHIP OF LEICESTER TO DIVIDE THEIR LANDS BY PITCHING

NOVEMBER 8TH, 1797

It is hereby Enacted by the General Assembly of the State of Vermont, That the proprietors of the township of Leicester, in the county of Addison, be, and they are hereby authorised and empowered, at any legal meeting warned for that purpose, to make a division of the undivided lands in said township, to and among the said proprietors, by pitching the same in such manner as shall be agreed upon by said proprietors in such proprietors' meeting, warned as aforesaid, any law, usage, or custom to the contrary notwithstanding.

AN ACT IN ADDITION TO AN ACT ENTITLED "AN ACT GRANTING TO ISRAEL
CONVERSE, JOSIAH EDSON, STEPHEN FISK AND TIMOTHY MITCHELL
THE EXCLUSIVE PRIVILEGE OF RUNNING A STAGE FROM
WINDSOR TO BURLINGTON FOR THE TIME
THEREIN MENTIONED"

NOVEMBER 8TH, 1797

Whereas, it is represented to the Legislature that it is very difficult
and inconvenient by reason of the badness of roads, to run a stage on
the rout[e] mentioned in said act at present. Therefore,

It is hereby Enacted by the General Assembly of the State of
Vermont, That the said Israel Converse, Josiah Edson, Stephen Fisk
and Timothy Mitchell shall be entitled to all the privileges and benefits
resulting from and appertaining to said act. *Provided,* they set up
and run said stage agreeable to said act within one year from January
next, any law or statute of this State to the contrary notwithstanding.[1]

AN ACT IN ADDITION TO AN ACT ENTITLED "AN ACT GRANTING LEAVE TO
JABEZ ROGERS OF MIDDLEBURY TO RAISE TWELVE HUNDRED POUNDS
BY LOTTERY FOR HIS BENEFIT"

NOVEMBER 8TH, 1797

Whereas, by the death and resignation of the managers of the
lottery aforesaid, appointed by the act entitled "An act granting leave
to Jabez Rogers of Middlebury to raise twelve hundred pounds by
lottery for his benefit," passed the 31st day of October, 1792, there
is not at present any proper person authorised to act as manager of
said lottery. Therefore,

It is hereby Enacted by the General Assembly of the State of
Vermont, That the judges of the county court for the county of Addison
be, and they are hereby fully authorised and empowered on application
to them made, by the said Jabez Rogers, Junr., for that purpose, to
appoint any suitable persons managers of said lottery, in the room and
stead of any managers heretofore appointed. And,

It is hereby further Enacted, That the managers so appointed by

---

1. State Papers of Vermont, Vol. XI, *General Petitions,* 1797-1799, "For Extension
of Time to Put a Stage Route into Operation," 126.

the said county court, before they proceed to take upon themselves the management of said lottery, execute bonds to the treasurer of this State, conditioned for the faithful performance of their said trust, in the same sum and manner as is directed by the aforesaid act, and in all things conform themselves to the direction of the act aforesaid, any law, usage, or custom to the contrary notwithstanding.

AN ACT LAYING OUT AND ESTABLISHING A POST ROAD THROUGH THE TOWNS OF ST. JOHNSBURY AND LYNDON IN THE COUNTY OF CALEDONIA

NOVEMBER 8TH, 1797

It is hereby Enacted by the General Assembly of the State of Vermont, That Joseph Lord, Nathaniel Edson, Nathaniel Jenks & Daniel Cahoon be, and they are hereby appointed a committee to lay out and establish a post road from the north line of Barnet, through the towns of St. Johnsbury and Lyndon, in the county of Caledonia, to the east line of Wheelock, in said county. And the aforesaid committee are hereby directed to lay out said road as near the banks of Pasumsick [Passumpsic] River as may be eligible and convenient in their opinion, to best promote travel to Lake Memphremagog, which road shall be surveyed by the surveyor general, or some person authorized by him for that purpose, who shall cause the survey thereof to be recorded in the town clerk's office of each town respectively. And the selectmen of the respective towns shall cause the said road to be made good and passable. And the selectmen of each town, respectively, are hereby empowered, with the consent of the town, to assess a tax of not more than six cents on the dollar on the polls and rateable property of the inhabitants of each town, or a tax on the lands in such town of not more than one cent and half on each acre, public lands excepted. And the selectmen aforesaid, are hereby appointed a committee to superintend the expenditure of said tax, and any justice of the peace in such town is hereby empowered to issue his warrant to the collector appointed by the authority of such town to collect State taxes, who is hereby appointed a collector for the purpose aforesaid, and such collector is hereby made accountable to the selectmen aforesaid, for the amount of said tax, and the selectmen and collector are hereby directed to govern themselves in collecting, disposing, and accounting for the monies raised by such tax, agreeable to the statute law of this State regulating the disposition of monies raised by tax for the purpose of making and repairing roads and building bridges, passed November 2d, 1796.[1]

AN ACT IN ADDITION TO AN ACT ENTITLED "AN ACT ORGANIZING THE COUNTIES OF FRANKLIN AND CALEDONIA, AND FIXING THE TIME AND PLACES FOR HOLDING THE SUPREME AND COUNTY COURTS IN THE SAME, AND FOR ALTERING THE PLACE OF HOLDING THE SUPREME AND COUNTY COURTS IN THE COUNTY OF ORANGE," PASSED THE 8TH DAY OF NOVEMBER A.D. 1796

NOVEMBER 8TH, 1797

Whereas, in the said act, it is provided, as a condition of the sitting of the supreme and county courts in the town of Chelsea, in the county of Orange, that the said town of Chelsea shall, at the expense of said town, build a Court House and Gaol in said town within two years from the passing of the said act; and it appearing to this Legislature that a longer time ought to be allowed to said town for the erecting of the said buildings. Therefore,

It is hereby Enacted by the General Assembly of the State of Vermont, That the term in and by said act affixed to the town of Chelsea for performing the forementioned condition, as far as it respects the building of a court house, be, and the same is hereby prolonged two years, the termination of which period shall be on the thirty first day of October, which will be in the year A.D., one thousand eight hundred.

AN ACT FOR THE PURPOSE OF ESTABLISHING A COUNTY GRAMMAR SCHOOL AT MIDDLEBURY IN THE COUNTY OF ADDISON

NOVEMBER 8TH, 1797

It is hereby Enacted by the General Assembly of the State of Vermont, That there be, and hereby is instituted and established a grammar school at such place in Middlebury, in the county of Addison, as the corporation herein after named shall think most convenient for that purpose, to be known and designated by the name of Addison County Grammar School. And,

---

1. State Papers of Vermont, Vol. XI, *General Petitions,* 1797-1799, "For Appointment of a Committee to Lay Out a Post Road," 164.

It is hereby further Enacted, That Messrs. Gamaliel Painter, Seth Storrs, Samuel Miller, Daniel Chipman and Darius Matthews, and such others as shall be appointed, in manner and to the number hereinafter directed, shall at all times hereafter form and constitute the board of trustees for the said institution, and be known by the name and stile [style] of the Corporation of *Addison County Grammar School.* And the said corporation and their successors in office are hereby declared, constituted, ordained and appointed a body corporate and politic to all intents and purposes in name and fact; shall have full power to take by gift, grant, purchase or devise, any estate whether real or personal for the use of said grammar school; and to take charge of, lease, rent and improve to the best advantage, all such grants as have been already made within said county of Addison, by the authority of this State, for the use and benefit of grammar schools; and also to receive and appropriate all such donations as have been or hereafter shall be made for the use of the said institution; and by themselves or their attornies, to institute, maintain and defend any suit or suits which may or shall be sued, prosecuted or impleaded, either in law or equity, for the recovery or defense of any of the rights or property of the said institution, as they shall find necessary; and also to appoint, elect, support and remove from time to time all such instructors as they shall find necessary.

It is hereby further Enacted, That when and so often as they shall find it needfull for the interest of said institution that additions should be made to the number of trustees, or to supply any vacancy occasioned by death, or otherwise, of any of the members of said corporation, it shall and may be lawful for the said corporation, at any regular stated meeting, or when specially notified to attend for that purpose, to elect by ballot such and so many as they shall think proper, so as that the whole number appointed shall not exceed twelve, and that a majority of the trustees shall be a quorum to act in all cases.

It is hereby further Enacted, That all the estate, both real and personal, sequestered for the use of said grammar school, shall be free and forever exempt from taxes, and the persons of the instructors and students belonging to said grammar school shall, during their continuance therein, be exempt from taxes and military service.

Provided always, That the inhabitants of Middlebury aforesaid, and such others as may voluntarily subscribe therefore, shall build and finish a good and sufficient house for said grammar school, of the value of one thousand dollars, by the next stated session of this Legislature, and shall forever after keep the same in good repair.[1]

AN ACT ASSESSING A TAX OF TWO CENTS PER ACRE ON ALL THE LANDS IN THE TOWNSHIP OF DERBY, PUBLIC RIGHTS EXCEPTED, FOR THE PURPOSE OF MAKING ROADS AND BUILDING BRIDGES IN SAID TOWNSHIP

NOVEMBER 8TH, 1797

It is hereby Enacted by the General Assembly of the State of Vermont, That there be, and hereby is granted a tax of two cents on each acre of land in the township of Derby, public rights excepted, for the purpose of making roads and building bridges in said township, to be expended by the order and under the direction of Ebenezer Strong, Charles Kingsbury, and Rufus Steward, all of Derby aforesaid, who are hereby appointed a committee to superintend the expenditures of said tax. And any justice of the peace in the county of Caledonia, is hereby empowered to issue his warrant to Timothy Hinman of Derby, aforesaid, who is hereby appointed a collector to collect said tax. And said collector is hereby made accountable to said committee for the amount of said tax, and said committee and collector are hereby directed to govern themselves in all things in collecting, disposing, and accounting for the monies raised by said tax agreeably to an act entitled, "An act regulating the disposition of monies raised by tax on the several towns for the purpose of making and repairing roads and building bridges," passed the second day of November, A.D. 1796.[2]

AN ACT ASSESSING A TAX OF ONE CENT ON EACH ACRE OF LAND IN HOLLAND FOR THE PURPOSE THEREIN MENTIONED

NOVEMBER 8TH, 1797

It is hereby Enacted by the General Assembly of the State of Vermont, That there be, and hereby is assessed a tax of one cent on each acre of land in the township of Holland, in the county of

---

1. State Papers of Vermont, Vol. XI, *General Petitions,* 1797-1799, "For the Location of a County Grammar School," 172.

2. Ibid., "For a Tax on Lands to Build and Repair Roads," 93.

Caledonia (public lands excepted), for the purpose of making and repairing roads and bridges in said town, to be expended by the order and direction of Ebenezer Strong, Isaac Hinman and Benjamin Hinman, who are hereby appointed a committee for that purpose; and any justice of the peace for the county of Caledonia is hereby empowered to issue a warrant to Timothy Hinman, who is hereby empowered to collect said tax; and said committee and collector are hereby directed to govern themselves in collecting, disposing, and accounting for the monies raised by said tax, agreeably to an act passed November 2d, 1796, entitled, "An act regulating the disposition of monies raised by tax on lands in the several towns for the purpose of making and repairing roads and building bridges."[1]

AN ACT ASSESSING A TAX OF THREE CENTS PER ACRE ON THE LANDS IN THE TOWN OF BARNET FOR THE PURPOSE THEREIN MENTIONED

NOVEMBER 8TH, 1797

It is hereby Enacted by the General Assembly of the State of Vermont, That there be, and hereby is assessed a tax of three cents per acre on all the lands in the town of Barnet in the county of Caledonia (public lands excepted), for the purpose of making and repairing roads and building bridges in said town. And that Alexander Harvey, Enos Stevens, and William Stevenson, be, and they are hereby appointed a committee to superintend the expenditure of said tax. And said committee are hereby authorised to examine the main road leading up Connecticut River, at and near the mouth of Passumsick [Passumpsic] River in Barnet, and to make such alterations on said road, and on other roads in said town, as to them shall appear necessary for the public convenience. And any justice of the peace, within the county of Caledonia, is hereby authorised to issue his warrant to John Rankin of said Barnet, who is hereby appointed and authorised to collect said tax. And said committee and collector are hereby directed in the collecting, disposing, and accounting for the monies raised by said tax, to govern themselves in all things, conformably to the law in that case made and provided.[2]

---

1. State Papers of Vermont, Vol. XI, *General Petitions,* 1797-1799, "For a Tax on Lands to Build and Repair Roads," 93.

2. Ibid., "For a Tax on Land to Build and Repair Roads and Bridges and Against a Post Road," 116.

AN ACT ASSESSING A TAX OF TWO CENTS PER ACRE ON THE LANDS IN
THE TOWN OF WHITING IN THE COUNTY OF ADDISON

NOVEMBER 8TH, 1797

It is hereby Enacted, by the General Assembly of the State of
Vermont, That there be, and hereby is assessed a tax of two cents on
each [acre] of land in the town of Whiting, in the county of Addison
(public lands excepted), for the purpose of making and repairing
roads and building bridges in said town, to be expended under the
direction of Ezra Allen, Stukeley Stone, and Thomas McNeil, all of
Whiting, who are hereby appointed a committee to superintend the
expenditure of said tax. And any justice of the peace for the county
of Addison is hereby authorised to issue his warrant to Ebenezer
Wheelock, Esqr., of said Whiting, who is hereby appointed a collector
to collect said tax. And the said committee and collector are hereby
directed in collecting, disposing, and accounting for the monies raised
by said tax, to govern themselves in all things by the directions of an
act entitled, "An act regulating the disposition of monies raised by tax
on lands in the several towns for the purpose of making and repairing
roads and building bridges," passed the second day of November 1796.[1]

AN ACT IN ADDITION TO "AN ACT ASSESSING A TAX OF TWO PENCE PER
ACRE ON THE TOWN OF CRAFTSBURY," PASSED OCTOBER 24TH, 1788

NOVEMBER 8TH, 1797

It is hereby Enacted, by the General Assembly of the State of
Vermont, That Nathan Cutler and Nehemiah Lyon, both of Craftsbury, in the county of Caledonia, be, and they are hereby appointed
members of the committee appointed to superintend the expenditure
of a tax of two pence per acre on the said town of Craftsbury, in and
by an act of the Legislature passed at Manchester the 24th day of
October, A.D. 1788, in the room of Jesse Leavenworth and Lyman
Hitchcock, appointed in and by said act, whose distance from said
Craftsbury renders it at this time inconvenient for them to attend
said business. And the said Nathan Cutler and Nehemiah Lyon, are
hereby directed, and made responsible and liable in the same manner
and extent as the said members of the committee before appointed,

1. State Papers of Vermont, Vol. XI, *General Petitions,* 1797-1799, "For a Tax on
Land to Build and Repair Roads and Build Bridges," 39.

whose place they supply, were in, and by the act aforesaid, and by the law directed and made responsible.

AN ACT DIRECTING THE TREASURER OF THIS STATE TO PAY THE SELECTMEN OF STOCKBRIDGE THE SUM THEREIN MENTIONED

NOVEMBER 8TH, 1797

Whereas, it appears to this Legislature that the selcetmen of Stockbridge have expended the sum of thirty dollars for the support of one Robert Thompson, a foreigner, since October 1796. Therefore,

It is hereby Enacted, by the General Assembly of the State of Vermont, That the treasurer of this State be, and he hereby is directed to pay the selectmen of Stockbridge the aforesaid sum of thirty dollars.[1]

AN ACT DIRECTING THE TREASURER OF THIS STATE TO PAY THE SELECTMEN OF NORTH HERO SIXTY SIX DOLLARS AND FIFTY NINE CENTS

NOVEMBER 8TH, 1797

It is hereby Enacted, by the General Assembly of the State of Vermont, That the treasurer be, and he is hereby directed to pay the selectmen of North Hero, in hard money orders, the sum of sixty six dollars and fifty nine cents, in the payment for the support of nursing, doctoring, and funeral charges of one Peter Wilson, a foreigner.[2]

AN ACT AUTHORISING REUBEN BRADLEY TO DEED LANDS OF BROWN JENKS, A MINOR

NOVEMBER 8TH, 1797

It is hereby Enacted, by the General Assembly of the State of Vermont, That Reuben Bradley of St. Johnsbury, in the county of Caledonia, legal guardian to Brown Jenks, a minor, be, and is hereby

---

1. State Papers of Vermont, Vol. XI, *General Petitions,* 1797-1799, "For Compensation for the Support of an Invalid Foreigner," 171.

2. Ibid., "For Compensation for the Support of a Deceased Invalid Foreigner," 102.

authorised and empowered to sell and deed so much of the lands belonging to the said Brown as will raise the sum of one hundred and thirty dollars, which monies, when raised, shall be appropriated to and for the use of paying certain debts, lying against the estate of Jonathan Jenks, Esqr., late of Winchester, in the State of New Hampshire, deceased, father to the said Brown, which was not discharged and paid before the estate was divided, for which the said Reuben is holden as guardian to said Brown to pay his proportion; and the remainder to pay a debt lying against said Brown for his schooling. And,

It is hereby further Enacted, That the said Reuben shall be responsible for his proceeding therein in the probate office where the estate of the said minor's father was settled.[1]

AN ACT EMPOWERING JOEL FOSTER AND JERUSHA WASHBURN ADMINISTRATORS ON THE ESTATE OF DANIEL WASHBURN, DECEASED, TO DEED A CERTAIN ONE HUNDRED ACRES OF LAND

NOVEMBER 8TH, 1797

Whereas, it appears to this Legislature, that Daniel Washburn, late of Whiting, in the county of Addison, deceased, did in his life time execute a bond to John Blanchard of Clarendon, for a deed of certain one hundred acres of land lying in the said town of Clarendon, in the county of Rutland, which deed, by reason of non-payment of consideration money during the life of the said Daniel, was not executed. And whereas, by the reason of the continuance of such non-payment, and by agreement between the aforesaid obligee, and Joel Foster, and Jerusha Washburn, administrators on the estate of the said deceased, said bond has been delivered up into the hands of the said administrators. And whereas the said administrators have, for the benefit of the heirs of the said deceased, bargained and sold the said land to Samuel Arnsby and George Beach, both of Clarendon, aforesaid, and have prayed that they may be enabled to execute a deed therefor to the said purchasers. Therefore,

It is hereby Enacted, by the General Assembly of the State of Vermont, That the said Joel Foster and Jerusha Washburn, adminis-

---

1. State Papers of Vermont, Vol. XI, *General Petitions,* 1797-1799, "For Authority to Sell the Real Estate of a Minor," 7.

trators as aforesaid, be, and they are hereby authorised and empowered to execute, jointly, a deed of the one hundred acres of land aforesaid, to Samuel Arnsby and George Beach, the aforesaid purchasers. And such deed when by them duly executed, in legal form, shall be as efficient and valid in law to the said purchasers, as though the same had been executed and given to them by the said deceased, in his life time.[1]

AN ACT SUSPENDING ALL PROSECUTIONS AGAINST SIMEON HAGAR, JUNR., FOR THREE YEARS

NOVEMBER 9TH, 1797

Whereas, Simeon Hagar, Junr., of Dorset, in the county of Bennington, has prefer[r]ed his petition to this Legislature, stating that by reason of sickness and unavoidable losses, he is unable to pay the demands which are against him at present. Therefore,

It is hereby Enacted by the General Assembly of the State of Vermont, That all prosecutions of a civil nature shall be, and hereby are suspended, and no process shall be had or maintained against him, the said Simeon Hagar, Junr., for any debts or demands against him, the said Simeon, for and during the term of three year from and after the passing of this act.

Provided nevertheless, and it is hereby further enacted, that the said Simeon Hagar shall take no benefit by this act until he give bond, with one or more sureties, to the acceptance of one of the judges of the county court, for Bennington county, in the sum of one thousand dollars, to his creditors generally, conditioned that the said Simeon shall not waste, embezzle, secrete or destroy any of his estate, with intent to defraud any one of his creditors, which bond shall be filed with the clerks of said county court, and each creditor on any breach of said condition shall have right of action in his own name on said bond, a copy of which, attested by the clerk of said county court, may be read in evidence on any such action, and have the same operation as if such creditors had been severally named in such bond, and the same was produced in court.[2]

---

1. State Papers of Vermont, Vol. **XI**, *General Petitions,* 1797-1799, "For Authority to Administrators to Deed Land," 152.

2. Ibid., "For Temporary Suspension of Civil Suits," 113.

AN ACT GRANTING A LAND TAX ON THE TOWNSHIP OF LINCOLN

NOVEMBER 8TH, 1797

It is hereby Enacted by the General Assembly of the State of Vermont, That there be, and hereby is assessed a tax of two cents on each acre of land in the township of Lincoln, in the county of Addison (public rights excepted), for the purpose of making and repairing roads and building bridges in said town, to be expended by the order and under the direction of Jedediah Durfry, James Verney and Loring Orvis, who are hereby appointed a committee for that purpose, and any justice of the peace in the county of Addison, is hereby empowered to issue his warrant to Jedediah Durfry, who is hereby appointed a collector to collect said tax. And said committee and collector are hereby directed to govern themselves in collecting, disposing, and accounting for the monies raised by said tax agreeable to an act passed November 2d, 1796, entitled, "An act regulating the disposition of monies raised by tax on lands in the several towns, for the purpose of making and repairing roads and building bridges."[1]

AN ACT ASSESSING A TAX OF TWO CENTS PER ACRE ON THE TOWN OF STERLING FOR THE PURPOSE THEREIN MENTIONED

NOVEMBER 8TH, 1797

It is hereby Enacted by the General Assembly of the State of Vermont, That there be, and hereby is assessed a tax of two cents per acre on all the lands in the town of Sterling, in the county of Franklin, public rights excepted, for the purpose of making and repairing roads and building bridges in said town, to be expended under the direction of Joseph Scott of Craftsbury, and John McConnel and David McConnel, both of Johnston [Johnson], who are hereby appointed a committee to superintend the expenditures of said tax. And any justice of the peace within the county of Franklin, is hereby authorised to issue his warrant to George Gragg of Johnson, who is hereby appointed a collector to collect said tax. And said committee and collector are hereby directed in the collecting, disposing, and accounting for the

---

1. State Papers of Vermont, Vol. XI, *General Petitions,* 1797-1799, "For a Tax on Land to Build Roads and Bridges," 87.

monies raised by said tax, to conform themselves, in all things, to the directions of the statute in that case made and provided.[1]

AN ACT APPOINTING A COLLECTOR OF A LAND TAX IN FLETCHER

NOVEMBER 8TH, 1797

Whereas, Benjamin Fasset, was in the year 1789, appointed a collector of a tax of two pence per acre, on the township of Fletcher, and the said Benjamin refuses and neglects to collect said tax. Therefore,

It is hereby Enacted by the General Assembly of the State of Vermont, That Lemuel Scott, of said Fletcher, be, and he hereby is appointed a collector in room of said Benjamin. And any justice of the peace in the county of Franklin, is hereby authorised to issue his warrant to the said Lemuel, to collect said tax, the same as he was directed by the act granting said tax, to issue his warrant, to the aforesaid Benjamin, and the said new collector is hereby vested with all the power and authority; and is in the same manner and respect directed and made accountable in the collecting said tax as the said Benjamin was, in and by the act aforesaid; and the said Benjamin is hereby directed to deliver over to the said Lemuel all papers he has received as collector as aforesaid.

AN ACT DIRECTING THE TREASURER OF THIS STATE TO PAY THE SELECTMEN OF SHELBURNE TWENTY FIVE DOLLARS AND FORTY FIVE CENTS

NOVEMBER 8TH, 1797

Whereas, it hath been represented and made to appear to the General Assembly, That the selectmen of Shelburne have been at expence in supporting one John Burrell, a foreigner. Therefore,

It is hereby Enacted by the General Assembly of the State of Vermont, That the treasurer be, and he is hereby directed to pay to

1. State Papers of Vermont, Vol. XI, *General Petitions,* 1797-1799, "For a tax on Land to Build Roads and Bridges," 135.

the selectmen of Shelburne twenty five dollars and forty five cents in hard money orders.[1]

AN ACT DIRECTING THE TREASURER OF THIS STATE TO PAY THE
SELECTMEN OF DUMMERSTON THE SUM OF FORTY SIX DOLLARS
AND EIGHT CENTS FOR THE SUPPORT
OF HANNAH KNOWLE

NOVEMBER 8TH, 1797

Whereas, by the petition of Jason Duncan and John S. Gates, selectmen of the town of Dummerston, it appears that the said selectmen have expended the sum of forty six dollars, eight cents for the necessary support of Hannah Knowle, a pauper, having no settlement in said Dummerston or in any part of the United States. Therefore,

It is hereby Enacted by the General Assembly of the State of Vermont, That the Treasurer of the State pay the selectmen of the town of Dummerston the sum of forty six dollars and eight cents for monies by them expended for the support of the said Hannah Knowle, since the eighth day of October 1796.[2]

AN ACT TO REPEAL A CERTAIN SECTION IN AN ACT ENTITLED, "AN ACT
DEFINING WHAT SHALL BE DEEMED AND ADJUDGED A LEGAL
SETTLEMENT, AND FOR THE SUPPORT OF THE POOR, FOR
DESIGNATING THE DUTIES AND POWERS OF THE
OVERSEERS OF THE POOR, AND FOR THE
PUNISHMENT OF IDLE AND
DISORDERLY PERSONS"

NOVEMBER 8TH, 1797

It is hereby Enacted by the General Assembly of the State of Vermont, That the tenth section of said act be, and the same is hereby repealed. And the secretary of state in furnishing the printer of this state with a copy of said act be, and he hereby is directed to omit

---

1. State Papers of Vermont, Vol. XI, *General Petitions,* 1797-1799, "For Compensation for the Support of an Invalid Foreigner," 83.

2. Ibid., "For Compensation for the Support of an Indigent Foreigner," 112.

said section, noting that it is repealed as aforesaid, but preserving the other sections as they are now numbered.

AN ACT ASSESSING THREE CENTS PER ACRE ON THE TOWNSHIP OF ORANGE FOR THE PURPOSE OF MAKING ROADS AND BUILDING BRIDGES

NOVEMBER 8TH, 1797

It is hereby Enacted by the General Assembly of the State of Vermont, That there be, and hereby is assessed a tax of three cents on each acre of land in the township of Orange, in the county of Orange, public rights excepted, for the purpose of making and repairing roads and building bridges in said town, to be expended by the order and under the direction of John Stacy, Gould Camp and Thomas S. Paine of Orange, aforesaid, who are hereby appointed a committee to superintend the expenditure of said tax, and any justice of the peace, within the county of Orange, is hereby empowered to issue a warrant to Joseph Thayer of said Orange, who is hereby appointed a collector to collect said tax, and said collector is hereby made accountable to said committee for the amount of said tax, and said committee and collector are hereby directed to govern themselves in collecting, disposing, and accounting for monies raised by said tax, agreeable to an act entitled, "An act regulating the disposition of monies raised by tax on the several towns for the purpose of making and repairing roads and building bridges &c.," passed November 2d, 1796.[1]

AN ACT APPOINTING A COLLECTOR OF A LAND TAX IN FAIRFIELD

NOVEMBER 8TH, 1797

Whereas, Levi Wakeman was, in the year 1791, appointed a collector of a tax of one penny per acre of the township of Fairfield, and the said Levi refuses and neglects to collect said tax. Therefore,

It is hereby Enacted by the General Assembly of the State of Vermont, That Joseph Bowdish of said Fairfield, be, and he hereby is appointed a collector in room of said Levi, and any justice of the

1. State Papers of Vermont, Vol. XI, *General Petitions,* 1797-1799, "For a Tax on Land to Build Roads and Bridges," 137.

peace in the county of Franklin, is hereby authorised to issue his warrant to the aforesaid Joseph, to collect said tax, the same as he was directed by the act granting said tax, to issue his warrant to the said Levi, and the said new collector is hereby vested with all the power and authority, and in the same manner and respect directed and made accountable in the collecting said tax, as the said Levi was, in and by the aforesaid act.

AN ACT ASSESSING A TAX OF THREE CENTS PER ACRE ON THE TOWN OF CONCORD FOR THE PURPOSE THEREIN MENTIONED

NOVEMBER 8TH, 1797

It is hereby Enacted by the General Assembly of the State of Vermont, That there be, and hereby is assessed a tax of three cents on each acre of land in the township of Concord, in the county of Caledonia, public rights excepted, for the purpose of building a bridge over Passumsick [Passumpsic] or Moose River (so called) and for making and repairing roads and building bridges in said township, to be expended under the direction of Samuel Wetherbe and Jonathan Woodbury of said Concord, who are hereby appointed a committee to superintend the expenditure of said tax. And any justice of the peace, within and for the county of Caledonia, is hereby authorised to issue his warrant to Samuel Wetherbe, Junr., of said Concord, who is hereby appointed a collector, to collect said tax. And the said collector is hereby made accountable for the amount of said tax. And the said committee and collector are hereby directed in collecting, disposing, and accounting for the monies raised by the aforesaid tax, to govern themselves in all things by the directions of an act entitled, "An act regulating the disposition of monies raised by tax on lands in the several towns for the purpose of making and repairing roads and building bridges," passed the second day of November A.D. 1796.[1]

---

1. State Papers of Vermont, Vol. XI, *General Petitions,* 1797-1799, "For a Tax on Land to Build and Repair Roads and Build a Bridge," 134.

AN ACT TO REMIT TO JOSEPH MARKS OF WILMINGTON IN THE COUNTY
OF WINDHAM PART OF A DEMAND DUE FROM SAID
JOSEPH TO THIS STATE

NOVEMBER 9TH, 1797

Whereas, it appears to this assembly that at a supreme court
holden at Newfane, on the first Tuesday of March, 1795, this State
recovered judgment against the said Joseph Marks for the sum of
one hundred nine pounds, nineteen shillings and four pence, and by
the direction of the attorney general, extended the execution on the
farm of the said Joseph Marks in said Wilmington, which was set
off to satisfy said execution. And the said Joseph was unable, within
the time limited by law, to redeem his lands so extended on by said
writ of execution. Therefore,

It is hereby Enacted by the General Assembly of the State of
Vermont, That if the said Joseph Marks shall, on or before the first
day of May, one thousand seven hundred and ninety eight, pay or cause
to be paid into the treasury of this state one hundred and sixty seven
dollars, with the lawful interest from the date of this act, the said
treasurer on the receipt of said sum of one hundred and sixty seven
dollars, and the interest thereon as above, is hereby empowered and
directed in his capacity of treasurer of the State of Vermont, to make,
execute, acknowledge and deliver to the said Marks, a quit claim deed
of the lands so extended on by the said writ of execution, which shall
vest in the said Marks, and his heirs and assigns, all the title the state
received by virtue of extending the said writ of execution.[1]

AN ACT ASSESSING A TAX OF ONE CENT ON EACH ACRE OF LAND IN THE
TOWNSHIP OF FAIR HAVEN AND WEST HAVEN FOR THE
PURPOSES THEREIN MENTIONED

NOVEMBER 9TH, 1797

Whereas, by the petitions of the proprietors of the towns of Fair
Haven and West Haven, it appears to this Legislature that the lands
in said towns have been heretofore surveyed and pitched in such manner as to render it doubtful whether the lands in said towns would

---

1. State Papers of Vermont, Vol. XI, *General Petitions,* 1797-1799, "For Relief
of a Bondsman," 90.

be liable to a proprietors' tax, should such tax be voted by said proprietors. And whereas said proprietors conceive it necessary to resurvey the same, for the purpose of authenticating the division of said land into severalty. Therefore,

It is hereby Enacted by the General Assembly of the State of Vermont, That there be, and hereby is granted a tax of one cent on each acre of land in the said towns of Fair Haven and West Haven (public land excepted), to be appropriated for paying the expences of such surveys and plans and other regulations of the proprietors of the towns aforesaid, as shall be agreed on by the said proprietors at any legal meeting by them duly warned and holden. And,

It is hereby further Enacted, that the said proprietors of said towns shall, at such legal meeting, as aforesaid, have power to appoint a collector, for the collection of said tax, and the said collector so to be appointed, shall be under the same regulations as are by law provided for collectors of proprietors' taxes.

AN ACT, IN ADDITION TO AN ACT ENTITLED, " AN ACT EMPOWERING AND DIRECTING CERTAIN PERSONS THEREIN NAMED TO LAY OUT AND SURVEY A POST ROAD FROM MASSACHUSETTS LINE TO THE NORTH LINE OF THE TOWN OF NEWBURY IN THE COUNTY OF ORANGE," PASSED THE 27TH OF OCTOBER A.D. 1795

NOVEMBER 9TH, 1797

Whereas, by the aforesaid act the several committees therein appointed, were directed to lay said road near the banks of Connecticut-River, as may be eligible and convenient. And whereas said road through several towns, and in many places, may be made with more convenience to the public, and with less expense and injury to towns and individuals, by diverting the course of said road from the River, which under a critical construction of the direction aforesaid, the said committee did not view themselves authorised to do. Therefore,

It is hereby Enacted, by the General Assembly of the State of Vermont, That the committee or committees, or either of them, appointed in and by said act, be, and they are hereby respectively authorised and empowered, on application of any town, through their agent or agents, or on application of any man or number of men, in writing for that purpose to divert the course of said road, from the River, by laying out and surveying the same in some other part of such town or place, mentioned in such application, if, in their opinion, the public good shall require it.

Provided always, that the expense incurred in laying out and surveying such road, shall be paid by the town, man or number of men making application as aforesaid. *Provided also, and be it further Enacted*, That the same proceeding in all things, shall and may be had, as well by the committee, as by the inhabitants, of any town or towns, or by any other person or persons, relative to the road so laid out, pursuant to such application, as is or are given, directed or provided in the above recited act, any law, usage, or custom to the contrary notwithstanding.

And it is hereby further Enacted, That two of the committee appointed in said act for the county of Windham, to wit, Samuel Cutler and Eliakim Spooner, be, and they are hereby discharged from any further service in the duties of their appointment.

And it is hereby further Enacted, That whereas in and by said act the said committee appointed therein respectively, were authorised and empowered by the second section of said act, to set over lands and assess damages in certain cases, and whereas in case any person or persons shall be dissatisfied with any lands set over, or damages assessed, pursuant to said section, no relief is granted. Therefore, if any person or persons shall be dissatisfied with any lands set over, or which hereafter may be set over, or with the damages assessed as aforesaid, such person or persons may petition the county courts in such counties for relief in the premises, who are hereby created a board to assess the damages contemplated in said petition. And their order or decree on such petition shall be final and conclusive, as to the person or persons so petitioning. And a certificate shall be given to such person or persons under the hands of either two of the judges of said court, to which such petition was prefer[r]ed, of the sum or sums so ordered or decreed by said court. And such certificate shall be a sufficient voucher to such person or persons, and the same proceedings shall be had thereon, in all things, as it relates, as well to the holder or holders of such certificates as to the selectmen of the town in which the land for which the assessment was made lies, as is provided in the aforesaid section of said act, any thing therein contained to the contrary notwithstanding.

And whereas, by the second section of an act entitled, "An act in addition to, and alteration of an act entitled 'An act empowering and directing certain persons therein named, to lay out and survey a post road from Massachusetts line to the north line of the town of Newbury, in the county of Orange,' " passed the tenth day of March A.D. 1797, it was enacted, that if any town through which said road passed, should neglect to make said road passable to the acceptance of the committees respectively, on or before the first day of October 1797, such town should be liable to a fine of one hundred dollars, to the county treasury, for every six months neglect, under certain conditions. And whereas the time limited as aforesaid, is too short for the purpose of opening and rendering such roads passable. Therefore,

It is hereby further Enacted, That the time limited as aforesaid be, and is hereby extended to the first day of October, which will be in the year one thousand seven hundred and eighty nine, any thing in the act last afore recited, to the contrary notwithstanding.[1]

AN ACT EMPOWERING SAMUEL WHEAT, ADMINISTRATOR ON THE ESTATE OF DANIEL SABIN, LATE OF PUTNEY, IN THE COUNTY OF WINDHAM, DECEASED, TO SELL ALL THE REAL ESTATE THE SAID DECEASED DIED, SEIZED AND POSSESSED OF, THE WIDOW'S DOWER, ONLY EXCEPTED

NOVEMBER 9TH, 1797

It is hereby Enacted by the General Assembly of the State of Vermont, That Samuel Wheat, administrator on the estate of Daniel Sabin, late of Putney, in the county of Windham, deceased, be, and he hereby is empowered under the direction of the judge of probate for the district of Westminster, to sell all the real estate of that the said deceased died seized and possessed of, the widow's dowry, only excepted, and the avails thereof to be appropriated for the benefit of the heirs to said estate, in such manner as the said judge of probate aforesaid, shall direct. And any deed or deeds executed as aforesaid by the said Samuel, in his capacity aforesaid, shall be considered to be good and valid, any law or usage to the contrary notwithstanding.[2]

---

1. State Papers of Vermont, Vol. XI, *General Petitions,* 1797-1799, "For Appoint-
2. Ibid., "For Authority to an Administrator to Sell Real Estate," 119.
   ment of a Committee to Lay Out a Post Road," 164.

AN ACT ASSESSING A TAX OF ONE HALF CENT ON EACH ACRE OF LAND
IN THE TOWN OF WILLISTON AGREEABLE TO THE ORIGINAL CHARTER

NOVEMBER 9TH, 1797

Whereas, the Legislature of this State at their session in one thousand seven hundred and eighty eight, assessed and doomed said town of Williston, a tax on the lands in said town amounting to eighteen pounds, seven shillings and four pence. And whereas the treasurer of this State issued his warrant to Joshua Chamberlain, then first constable of said Williston, for the collection of said tax; and whereas there has been no provision made by the persons authorised to assess said tax, whereby the said collector hath ever had power to collect the same, by reason whereof the said constable hath become accountable to the treasurer of this State, for the amount of said tax, and is liable to pay the same with the interest thereon arising. Therefore,

It is hereby Enacted by the General Assembly of the State of Vermont, That there be, and hereby is granted a tax of one half cent on each acre of land in the town of Williston, aforesaid, agreeable to the original charter of said Williston (public rights excepted) to be appropriated by, and under the direction of the selectmen of said Williston, for the purpose of paying and discharging the said warrant, so issued by the treasurer of this State to the said Joshua Chamberlain for the collection of the aforesaid sum of eighteen pounds, seven shillings, and four pence as aforesaid, together with the interest thereon arising. And,

It is hereby further Enacted, That the said Joshua Chamberlain be, and he is hereby appointed a collector for the collection of said tax. And the said collector and the selectmen of said town of Williston be, and they hereby are directed to proceed in the same manner, and be under the same obligation as is provided and directed, to and for the sheriffs and selectmen in the several towns mentioned in an act passed the present session of the Legislature entitled, "An act assessing a tax of one cent on each acre of land in this State, for the support of government during the year one thousand seven hundred & ninety seven and for other purposes."

AN ACT IN ADDITION TO, AND IN ALTERATION AND REVIVAL OF AN ACT
ENTITLED "AN ACT ASSESSING A TAX OF TWO PENCE PER ACRE ON
ALL THE LANDS IN THE TOWNSHIP OF MILTON IN THE COUNTY
OF CHITTENDEN, PUBLIC RIGHTS EXCEPTED, FOR THE
PURPOSE OF MAKING AND REPAIRING ROADS &C.,"
PASSED THE SEVENTH DAY OF MARCH 1797

NOVEMBER 9TH, 1797

Whereas, the collector appointed in and by said act hath neglected
to collect said tax. And whereas the committee of superintendence have
neglected to lay out the road or roads on which said tax was to be expended, and to advertise the same agreeable to an act entitled, "An
act regulating the disposition of monies raised by tax on lands in the
several towns in this state, for the purpose of making and repairing
roads &c.," passed November second, 1796. Therefore,

It is hereby Enacted by the General Assembly of the State of
Vermont, That there be, and hereby is assessed a tax of two cents per
acre instead of two pence per acre as before granted, on all the lands
in the township of Milton, in the county of Chittenden (public rights
excepted), for the purpose of making and repairing roads and building bridges in said town. And,

It is hereby further Enacted, That Abel Drury be, and he hereby
is appointed and authorised to collect said tax, and the said collector
is made accountable and is alike responsible and under the same obligations as the former collector was, in and by said act.

And it is hereby further Enacted, That Abel Waters be, and he
hereby is appointed one of the committee of superintendence in lieu of
Benjamin Holmes who declines serving in that capacity. And,

It is hereby further Enacted, That the act entitled, "An act assessing a tax of two pence per acre on all the lands in the township of
Milton, for the purpose therein mentioned," passed the seventh day
of March, 1797, excepting the provisions before in this act mentioned,
be, and the same is hereby revived and its operation shall, to all intents and purposes, be the same as though it had passed and been enacted at the present session of this Legislature.

AN ACT DIRECTING THE TREASURER TO PAY BENJAMIN CADY
TWELVE DOLLARS IN HARD MONEY ORDERS

NOVEMBER 9TH, 1797

It is hereby Enacted by the General Assembly of the State of
Vermont, That the treasurer of this State be, and hereby is directed
to pay Benjamin Cady twelve dollars in hard money orders, as a reward for services rendered this State in conveying intelligence to the
chief magistrate, of the appointment of a Representative to Congress
in the Eastern District of Vermont, and bringing the credentials of
said Representative, in May, 1797.

AN ACT DIRECTING THE TREASURER OF THIS STATE TO PAY TO THE
SELECTMEN OF SOUTH HERO, ONE HUNDRED AND NINE
DOLLARS AND SIXTY SIX CENTS

NOVEMBER 9TH, 1797

It is hereby Enacted by the General Assembly of the State of
Vermont, That the Treasurer of this State be, and hereby is directed
to pay to the selectmen of South-Hero in hard money orders the sum
of one hundred and nine dollars, sixty six cents in payment for the
support, nursing and doctoring one John McCoachin [McCochen],
a foreigner.[1]

AN ACT EMPOWERING AND DIRECTING THE TREASURER OF THIS STATE
TO PAY TO THE SELECTMEN OF THE TOWN OF NORWICH THE
SUM OF FIFTEEN DOLLARS AND FORTY CENTS

NOVEMBER 9TH, 1797

It is hereby Enacted by the General Assembly of the State of
Vermont, That the Treasurer of this State be, and hereby is authorised
and directed to pay unto the selectmen of the town of Norwich the
sum of fifteen dollars and forty cents, being a sum overcharged said
town by reason of a mistake of the listers in returning the sum total of
the grand list of said Norwich for the year 1795.

1. State Papers of Vermont, Vol. XI, *General Petitions,* 1797-1799, "For Compensation for the Support of an Invalid Foreigner," 124.

And it is hereby further Enacted, That the treasurer for the county of Windsor be empowered and directed to pay over to the selectmen of the town of Norwich, the sum of five dollars and twenty three cents, being a sum overcharged said town by reason of a mistake of the listers of said Norwich in returning the sum total of the grand list of said town for the year 1795.[1]

AN ACT DIRECTING THE TREASURER OF THIS STATE TO PAY UNTO HIS
HONOR PAUL BRIGHAM, ESQR., LIEUTENANT GOVERNOR, THE SUM
OF ONE HUNDRED AND THREE DOLLARS AND SIXTY SIX CENTS
FOR MONIES EXPENDED BY HIS DIRECTION FOR
EXPENSES ON ELECTION DAY

NOVEMBER 9TH, 1797

It is hereby Enacted by the General Assembly of the State of Vermont, That the treasurer of this State be, and he hereby is directed to pay unto his honor Paul Brigham, Esqr., Lieutenant Governor of this State, the sum of one hundred and three dollars and sixty six cents, for monies expended by his direction on election day.

AN ACT ASSESSING A TAX OF THREE CENTS PER ACRE ON THE TOWNS OF
IRASBURGH AND COVENTRY FOR THE PURPOSE THEREIN MENTIONED

NOVEMBER 9TH, 1797

It is hereby Enacted by the General Assembly of the State of Vermont, That there be, and hereby is assessed a tax of three cents on each acre of land in the townships of Irasburgh and Coventry, situate in that part of the county of Orleans, within the jurisdiction of the county of Franklin for the time being, public lands excepted, for the purpose of making and repairing roads and building bridges in said towns, to be expended under the direction of Samuel C. Crafts and Elijah Allen both of Craftsbury, and William Guy of Wheelock, who are hereby appointed a committee to superintend the expenditure of said tax, in and for the town of Irasburgh, and Silas Hathaway of St. Albans, Nathaniel P. Sawyer of Johnson and Abraham Morrill of Wheelock, who are hereby appointed a committee to superintend the

---

1. State Papers of Vermont, Vol. XI, *General Petitions,* 1797-1799, "For a Tax Abatement," 121.

expenditure of said tax in the town of Coventry. And any justice of the peace within the county of Franklin is hereby authorised to issue his warrant to Joseph Scott of Craftsbury, who is hereby appointed a collector to collect said tax on both of the said townships. And the said collector is hereby made accountable for the amount of the tax on both the said townships, to the committees aforesaid, respectively. And the said committees and collector are hereby directed in collecting, disposing, and accounting for the monies raised by the aforesaid tax, to govern themselves in all things, by the directions of an act entitled, "An act regulating the disposition of monies raised by tax on lands in the several towns for the purpose of making and repairing roads and building bridges," passed the 2d day of November, A.D. 1796.[1]

AN ACT GRANTING TO SAMUEL CAMPBELL A NEW TRIAL IN A CAUSE THEREIN MENTIONED

NOVEMBER 9TH, 1797

Whereas, Samuel Campbell of the Grand Isle, heretofore brought his certain action in a plea of debt on a bond against Jedediah Hide [Hyde] of Hydespark [Hyde Park], which said action was entered at the county court holden at Burlington, in the county of Chittenden, on the last Monday save one, of September 1795, and by appeal carried to the supreme court, and judgment in said cause was finally rendered by the said supreme court, holden at Burlington, in said county, on the first Tuesday of January, 1797, against the said Samuel and in favor of the said Jedediah Hyde, that he, the said Jedediah, should recover his costs in said suit against the said Samuel. Therefore,

It is hereby Enacted by the General Assembly of the State of Vermont, That said judgment so recovered by the said Jedediah, be set aside and for nought accounted, and that the said Samuel Campbell be allowed, and he is hereby allowed a new trial in said cause, and to proceed in the same manner as though said cause was now pending and undetermined in said supreme court, and said judgment so recovered shall not be allowed to be pleaded in bar of said new trial, and all proceedings upon said judgment shall be staid until final judgment had and rendered on a new trial of said cause, unless the said Samuel shall neglect to prosecute his said action anew for the space of one full year.

1. State Papers of Vermont, Vol. XI, *General Petitions,* 1797-1799, "For a Tax on Land to Build Roads and Bridges," 156.

And it is hereby further Enacted, That the clerk of the supreme court within and for the county of Chittenden be, and he hereby is authorised and directed on application of the said Samuel, at the supreme court next to be holden at Burlington, within and for the county of Chittenden, on the first Tuesday of January next, to enter said cause anew, upon the docket of said court, and the judges of said court are hereby directed to take cognizance of said cause so entered, and proceed to trial and judgment therein in the same manner as though said cause had never been tried in said supreme court, but now stood upon the docket of said court as it did when first brought into said supreme court by appeal. And on a final judgment in said cause, said court is hereby authorised and empowered in taxing the bill of costs in favor of the party recovering, to tax all the cost in the former trial and proceedings, and costs of the application for or opposing this act as in their discretion they shall judge reasonable, and to award execution accordingly. *Provided* that the said Samuel shall so enter or cause to be entered said cause at the court aforesaid, and shall cause said Jedediah to be served with a true copy of this act, twenty days before the sitting of said supreme court, which shall be deemed sufficient notice to the said Jedediah to appear and defend in said cause and notice being so given, said court may proceed to render judgment on default as in other cases, if the said Jedediah shall not appear to defend in said action.[1]

AN ACT TO ALTER AN ACT ENTITLED, "AN ACT TO APPOINT NEW
MANAGERS TO AND DIRECTING THE APPROPRIATION OF
CONNECTICUT RIVER LOTTERY, SO CALLED,"
PASSED AT RUTLAND 28TH OF
FEBRUARY, 1797

NOVEMBER 9TH, 1797

It is hereby Enacted by the General Assembly of the State of Vermont, That Eliakim Spooner of Westminster, Oliver Barrett of Windsor and Jesse Hawley of Thetford be, and they are hereby appointed new managers of Connecticut River Lottery, instead of the former managers that have been heretofore appointed. And that the said managers shall give bonds to the amount of twenty thousand dollars to the judges of the county court for the county of Windsor, be-

---

1. State Papers of Vermont, Vol. XI, *General Petitions,* 1797-1799, "For a New Trial," 60.

fore they, the said managers, enter upon the business of their appointment. That the said managers shall have power to alter the scheme of said lottery if they think it necessary; provided however, the sum to be raised by said lottery be two thousand five hundred dollars; and shall commence drawing by the last Tuesday in December in the year 1798, at the Masons' Hall in Windsor. And a list of the fortunate numbers shall be published in the public papers printed at Rutland, Windsor and Walpole immediately after the drawing. Those who do not apply for the prize drawn against their number, within six months after the drawing said lottery, it shall be deemed as given for the benefit of said lottery. And,

It is hereby further Enacted, That the said managers be, and they are hereby appointed a committee to superintend and lay out the money raised by said lottery on the great post road from the south line of this State to the north line of Newbury, directed to be surveyed and opened by an act of the Legislature, passed at Windsor, October 1795, on such parts and in such places of said road as they shall judge shall best equalize the expense of said road in the towns through which the same may pass. And,

It is hereby further Enacted, that the managers be allowed for their trouble and risque of selling tickets and drawing said lottery twelve and half per cent.

And it is hereby further Enacted, That the said managers be directed to pay to the former managers, out of the money arising from said lottery, as a compensation for getting the former grant printed and numbering the former tickets and for the work which has been by them done, on Connecticut River, on the credit of said lottery one hundred, sixty six dollars and sixty seven cents, payable at the drawing of said lottery. And,

It is hereby further Enacted, That the former managers shall, at the time of drawing this lottery, settle for and return to the treasurer of the county of Windsor all the tickets that shall be at that time unaccounted for or on hand, and the said treasurer is directed to receive the same and deliver up to them their bond, as if the lottery had been by them drawn.

And it is hereby further Enacted, That the claims of all persons holding tickets purchased from the former managers shall be suspended until the time appointed in this act for the drawing said lottery.

And it is hereby further Enacted, That after the managers shall have laid out the remainder of the money to be raised from said lottery (which has not been by this act appropriated to other purposes), in work on said road which shall be within one year from the drawing of said lottery, that they shall then exhibit their accounts of the expenditure of said money, to said judges of the county court for the county of Windsor, and the same being by them approved of, their aforesaid bond shall be by them given up.

AN ACT POINTING OUT THE MODE OF COLLECTING LAND TAXES IN SEVERAL TOWNS IN THE COUNTY OF CHITTENDEN

NOVEMBER 9TH, 1797

Whereas, it so happened that the laws already had and provided are insufficient to procure the proprietors' records of sundry towns in the county of Chittenden, to be delivered over to the town clerks, which renders it impossible for the collectors of land taxes to proceed with any degree of safety in the collection of the same. Which difficulty to remedy,

It is hereby Enacted by the General Assembly of the State of Vermont, That when it shall so happen that the proprietors' records of any town in the county of Chittenden shall not be delivered over to the town clerk of the town of which he was proprietors' clerk, it shall be the duty of the selectmen of such town to make an accurate survey of all the lands in such town and enter the same in a field book, with the metes and bounds and numbers of each lot, agreeable to the former survey, if any shall be, and the same deliver to the town clerk, whose duty it shall be to record the same; and it shall be the duty of the collector of any land taxes in any such town or towns, which are or shall be granted by the Legislature of this State, to proceed to sell by the lot, and he shall sell so much of each lot as to pay the tax and all legal cost, together with the cost of surveying each lot, and any sale so made by the lot, or part of lot, shall be good and valid in law, any law, usage, or custom to the contrary notwithstanding.

Provided always, That the collector or collectors shall proceed in all things agreeably to an act entitled, "An act regulating the disposition of monies raised on lands on all the towns in this state," passed the second day of November, 1796.

AN ACT DIRECTING PROPRIETORS' CLERKS UPON THE DISSOLUTION
OF THE PROPRIETORSHIP OF ANY TOWN TO DELIVER
OVER THE RECORDS TO THE TOWN CLERK

NOVEMBER 9TH, 1797

It is hereby Enacted by the General Assembly of the State of Vermont, That as soon as all the lands in any town in this State are divided into severalty, it shall, and hereby is made the duty of the proprietors' clerk of such town, upon application of one or more of the selectmen, to deliver over to the town clerk all records, maps & other papers belonging to said proprietors' clerk's office. And,

It is hereby further Enacted, That such towns as have been or may hereafter be divided, or parts thereof annexed to any other town, the proprietors' records of such town shall be kept within the limits of such town as retains the name by which said town was originally granted, and if said proprietors' clerk shall, for the space of one month, neglect or refuse to deliver over the records of said office, to the town clerk as aforesaid, he shall pay a fine of ten dollars, for each month's neglect as aforesaid, to be recovered by and for the use of any person who will prosecute the same to effect.

AN ACT EMPOWERING THE SELECTMEN OF THE TOWN OF BENNINGTON
AND THEIR SUCCESSORS IN OFFICE, TO APPROPRIATE CERTAIN
LANDS THEREIN MENTIONED FOR THE USE AND BENEFIT
OF PUBLIC HIGHWAYS IN SAID TOWN

NOVEMBER 10TH, 1797

Whereas, The Governor of the province of New Hampshire, by letters patent, bearing date the 3d day of January, 1749, granted to William Williams and his associates, the Township of Bennington, annexing thereto a plan of said township, subdividing the same into equal shares, among said proprietors, and by said patent it appears that a certain proportion of said land was allowed and reserved for highways, and also by the plan aforesaid, it appears that certain strips of land are left upon the heads of the lots through the town, East and West, north and south, which have from the first settlement of said town, been considered and disposed of as lands sequestered for public roads in said town. But upon examining the grant, plans and proceedings of said land owners in said town, it does not appear that said strips of land (appearing on the plan aforesaid) have been so identified as to enable the selectmen of said town to let over said lands in compensation for roads and highways in said town. To enable the selectmen,

It is hereby Enacted by the General Assembly of the State of Vermont, That the selectmen for the time being, of the town of Bennington, and their successors in office forever, be, and hereby are empowered to appropriate said land (appearing upon said plan as aforesaid, reference thereto being in all cases had) for the use and benefit of the public roads and highways in said town, the same and in the same manner as though the said lands had heretofore been duly identified for that purpose, hereby confirming whatever may have been done by said selectmen or their successors, any usage, custom, or law to the contrary notwithstanding.

Provided always, that this act is not to extend to the disturbing of any person or persons, who may have gained a legal title to the lands aforesaid, by possession, independant of such lands being let to him or them in compensation as aforesaid.[1]

AN ACT GRANTING TO AARON POST THE LIBERTY TO
RAISE THE WATERS IN FAIRLEE LAKE, SO CALLED

NOVEMBER 10TH, 1797

Whereas, it is necessary to raise the waters in Fairlee Lake, so called, in order to supply with water several mills standing on the stream which empties out of said Lake, and the supplying said mills with a sufficiency of water, would be of great public utility, especially to the inhabitants of West-Fairlee, Vershire, Strafford, Thetford, and Norwich. And whereas the raising of said waters will necessarily flow several small tracts of land belonging to sundry persons living and owning lands bordering on said lake, which will subject the said Post to many expensive law suits, if said owners are disposed to oppose the flowing of said lands. Therefore,

---

1. State Papers of Vermont, Vol. XI, *General Petitions,* 1797-1799, "For Authority to the Selectmen to Appropriate Land for Roads," 106.

It is hereby Enacted by the General Assembly of the State of Vermont, That liberty be, and hereby is granted to the said Aaron Post, his heirs and assigns, to erect and keep up a dam across the outlet of said Lake, so as to raise the waters in said lake two feet up, on a level above the rock at the south end of said Post's sawmill dam, which was anciently the bed or bottom of the stream or outlet of said lake; and to prevent unnecessary litigation by those whose lands may be flowed by raising said waters.

It is hereby further Enacted, That William Chamberlain, Esqr., of Peacham, Micah Barron of Bradford, and Elias Stevens, Esqr., of Royalton be, and they are hereby appointed commissioners to appraise the damages done, or which may at any time be done, to each and every individual whose lands, or any part thereof, may be flowed by the raising of said waters; and it shall be the duty of said commissioners, or a majority of them, to view the situation of said lake and the lands bordering thereupon, before said waters are raised by said dam upon said lands, and to take an estimate of the quantity and quality of the said lands which will probably be flowed by the raising of said waters; and the injury which may thereby be done to the several owners of said lands, upon a supposition that said lands be perpetually flowed. And after said waters are raised, and said lands flowed to the full heighth by this act allowed to be raised, said commissioners or a majority of them, shall again take a view and estimate of said lands so flowed, and shall thereupon assess the damages done to such individual by the flowing of said lands, estimating said damages as though said lands were forever to be flowed; and shall thereupon make a return in writing to the next county court holden in the county of Orange, of the damages by them assessed to each individual, whose land or any part thereof shall be flowed or covered with water by the raising the waters of said lake; the expense of which several views and returns shall be paid by the said Aaron Post. And it shall be the duty of the clerk of said county court to receive said several returns so made, and to make a record thereof in the records of said county court, together with this act, the expense of which shall also be paid by the said Post. And upon the said Post's paying or causing to be paid to the several owners of said lands, the several sums so assessed by said commissioners, and by them returned as aforesaid, said owner or owners of said land, who shall be so paid, shall forever thereafter be precluded and barred of any further suit or recovery against the said Post, his heirs, or assigns, for any damage by them, or either of them sustained by the flowing of the same lands so paid for. And in case any owner or owners of said lands, so flowed, shall refuse to receipt the sum or sums so assessed them, and in that case it shall be in the power of the said Post, his heirs or assigns, to pay into the hands of the clerk of said county court, said sum or sums so refused, whose duty it shall be to receive the same, for and in behalf of said person or persons so refusing, and to make a record of the receipt of said sum or sums accordingly, which record so made shall be a perpetual bar to any further recovery or judgment for damages in flowing the same lands so paid for.

Provided nevertheless, and it is hereby further enacted, that in case any person or persons, whose lands shall be flowed as aforesaid, shall think themselves agrieved by said assessment, and return of said commissioners, it shall be in the liberty of such person or persons at the next county court in Orange county, after said return made, to file his declaration in an action of trespass on the case against the said Post, his heirs, or assigns, or who ever flowed said lands, for the damages sustained in flowing the same, giving notice to the said Post, his heirs, or assigns or whoever flowed said lands, by leaving a copy of said declaration with the said defendant twelve days before the sitting of said court, which shall be deemed sufficient notice to appear and defend in said action; and the county court shall thereupon proceed to hear and determine said cause by a jury of the county, and render up judgment accordingly. And in case the person or persons considering him or themselves so agrieved shall recover a greater or higher sum in said cause than was assessed by said Commissioners, exclusive of costs, judgment shall be rendered for said sum, and also the cost in said suit, which judgment so recovered shall likewise be a perpetual bar to any further recovery, or judgment, for flowing the same lands; and in case the person or persons so filing his or their declaration shall recover no more than the sum or sums so assessed and returned by said Commissioners for flowing the same lands, exclusive of costs, then and in that case, judgment shall be rendered for the defendant to recover his costs in said suit against the plaintiff, and said judgment shall be a perpetual bar as aforesaid.

Provided also, and it hereby [is] further enacted, that in case the raising of said waters, they shall flow any public road legally laid out, and the selectmen of the town in which said road or roads lie shall chuse [choose] not to alter but to continue said road or roads, the said Post shall, at his own expense, causeway and repair said road or roads, so as to make said road or roads equally good as they now are, which shall also be determined by said Commissioners, and return thereof made as aforesaid, and there upon the said Post shall be exonerated from any suit on that account as aforesaid.[1]

AN ACT TO RECTIFY THE ERRORS COMMITTED IN THE RECORDS OF THE PROPRIETORS OF THE TOWN OF WESTFORD

NOVEMBER 10TH, 1797

It is hereby Enacted by the General Assembly of the State of Vermont, That whereas errors of various sorts appear to have been made in the records of the proprietors of the town of Westford, in the county of Chittenden, which cannot be rectified without legislative interference, one sixteenth part, or upwards of the proprietors of said town, may call a meeting of the proprietors thereof to be held in said town of Westford, on any day or days between the tenth day of January, and the fifteenth day of February next ensuing (Sundays excepted). *Provided always*, that due notification of the said meeting shall be published in the three public papers printed in this State, to wit, at Bennington, Rutland, and Windsor, the last of which publications shall be at least one month prior to the day on which the said meeting shall be warned to be holden.

And it is hereby further Enacted, That the notifications aforesaid, shall be signed by some person or persons, who are proprietors of above one sixteenth part of said township, and in words following: "This is to notify the proprietors of the town of Westford, in the county of Chittenden, to meet on the ———— day of ———— next, at the house of ———— ———— in said town at ten oclock in the forenoon of said day, to rectify such mistakes, and make such necessary amendments in the proprietors' records of said town respecting the divided, as well as the undivided lands therein, as they shall think proper, agreeable to the true meaning and intentions of an act of the Legislature of the State of Vermont, passed at their October session, one thousand seven hundred and ninety seven."

And it is hereby further Enacted, that the present records of the proprietors, as well as the proceedings of the said meetings, as far as

---

1. State Papers of Vermont, Vol. XI, *General Petitions,* 1797-1799, "For Authority to Erect a Dam," 73.

respects the amendment or alteration of the said records, shall be laid before the supreme court, which shall sit at Burlington in the said county of Chittenden, next after the said meeting, whose duty it shall be to hear the complaints of any proprietor or proprietors, who may think themselves injured by the votes of the majority of the said proprietors at their said meeting. And that said supreme court, after hearing the assertions and allegations of both parties, and receiving the satisfactory proof so far as the nature of the case will admit, are hereby vested with full power & authority finally to determine on the alterations which ought to take place in the said records, whose determinations are hereby declared to be equally valid and binding, to all intents and purposes, as though the same had been heretofore done and established by the proprietors, at a meeting legally warned, and having powers for that purpose, any law, usage, or custom to the contrary notwithstanding.

And it is hereby further Enacted, That it shall be the duty of the proprietors at their said meeting, to provide for the payment of all expenses which have already, or may hereafter accrue, in the settlement of the above business, and enforce the collection thereof in such manner as has been heretofore practised, pursuant to an act regulating proprietors' meetings, passed March ninth, one thousand seven hundred & eighty seven.[1]

AN ACT CONFIRMING TO JONATHAN CHASE, ESQR., AND OTHERS, PROPRIETORS OF CORNISH BRIDGE, THE EXCLUSIVE RIGHT OF BUILDING TOLL BRIDGES OVER A CERTAIN PART OF CONNECTICUT RIVER BETWEEN CORNISH & WINDSOR

NOVEMBER 10TH, 1797

It is hereby Enacted by the General Assembly of the State of Vermont, That there be, and hereby is granted to Jonathan Chase, Esquire, and others, proprietors of Cornish bridge, the sole and exclusive right and privilege of owning and keeping in repair the toll bridge over Connecticut River between Cornish and Windsor, forever; and also to build and keep in repair other toll bridges, at the place, or

---

1. State Papers of Vermont, Vol. XI, *General Petitions,* 1797-1799, "For Correction of Errors in Proprietors' Records," 110.

within one mile below, and within one mile above the place where the aforesaid bridge now stands; and also the sole and exclusive right and privilege of building such bridges, three miles above, and three miles below said bridge, for the term of thirty years from the fourteenth day of January *Anno Domini* seventeen hundred and ninety five. And,

It is hereby further Enacted, That the said proprietors of Cornish Bridge be, and they hereby are incorporated into a body politic and corporate under the name of the proprietors of Cornish Bridge, and by that name may sue and be sued to final judgment and execution, and do and suffer all matters, acts, and things which bodies politic and corporate may, and ought to do and suffer. And the said meeting of said proprietors shall be warned in such manner as they shall appoint. And,

It is hereby further Enacted, that the proprietors by a vote of the majority of those present, or represented at any legal meeting, accounting and allowing to every person holding one share and not more than two, one vote; for every two shares above two, and not exceeding ten, one vote; for every four shares above ten and not exceeding thirty, one vote; for every six shares above thirty and not exceeding sixty, one vote; for every eight shares above sixty and not exceeding one hundred, one vote; and for every ten shares above one hundred, one vote; may elect any necessary officers for the purpose of regulating and governing said corporation, and may make, pass and cause to be executed any bye laws as to them may appear necessary, which are not repugnant to the constitution and laws of this State; and all representations, at any of said meetings, shall be proved by a writing signed by the person represented, which shall be filed with the proprietors' clerk; and this act and all bye laws and regulations, and the proceedings of said corporation, shall be recorded by the clerk in a book or books to be provided and kept for that purpose. And,

It is hereby further Enacted, that the proprietors aforesaid, are hereby permitted and authorised to hold any lands already purchased, & to purchase any other lands for the accommodation of said bridge, or any bridge or bridges hereafter to be built by the said proprietors, and the same hold in fee simple. And the shares in said bridges, together with the funds belonging to said corporation shall be transferred by deed, which being duly executed, acknowledged, and recorded by the clerk of the proprietors of Cornish Bridge in book or books kept for that purpose, shall be good and sufficient in law to pass the estate. And the clerk of said proprietors shall be considered as a certifying officer, entitled to the same faith and credit as county and town clerks. And for the purpose of reimbursing said proprietors the money by them expended, or that they may hereafter expend in building and supporting said bridge or bridges, the same rates of toll, which are granted to them by the acts of the Legislature of the State of New Hampshire relating to said bridge or bridges, be, and are hereby granted and established to said proprietors. And,

It is hereby further Enacted, That the directors of said corporation, for the time being, shall have power, from time to time, to make such assessments on each share as they may judge necessary for building and repairing said bridge or bridges, and shall notify the proprietors of such assessments by advertiseing the same in the Windsor newspaper at least ten days before the time of payment of such assessment. And if the assessment shall not then be paid, the treasurer of said corporation, for the time being, shall sell each delinquent share of said bridge or bridges, together with his equal share of the lands of said corporation, at public auction, the time and place of such sale having been duly notified by him, by publishing the same in the newspaper published at Windsor, at least ten days before the day of such sale. And,

It is hereby further Enacted, That a deed given by the treasurer aforesaid, in pursuance of such sale, acknowledged, and recorded in the clerks' book as aforesaid, shall be good and valid in law to pass the estate so sold and conveyed, any law or usage to the contrary notwithstanding.

AN ACT TO CONTINUE IN FORCE THE SEVERAL ACTS REGULATING FEES UNTIL THE RISING OF THE LEGISLATURE IN OCTOBER NEXT

NOVEMBER 10TH, 1797

It is hereby Enacted by the General Assembly of the State of Vermont, That the several laws now in force regulating fees be, and they are hereby declared to be, and continue, in force until the rising of the General Assembly in October next, any law for repealing all or any of said laws passed at the present session of the Legislature notwithstanding.

AN ACT MAKING APPROPRIATIONS FOR THE SUPPORT OF GOVERNMENT
FOR THE PRESENT SESSION AND FROM THENCE TO THE SESSIONS
OF GENERAL ASSEMBLY IN OCTOBER, 1798, AND
FOR OTHER PURPOSES

NOVEMBER 10TH, 1797

It is hereby Enacted by the General Assembly of the State of
Vermont, That there be paid out of the treasury of this State for the
salary of the governor, five hundred dollars; for the salary of the
treasurer, four hundred dollars; also for the debentures of the lieutenant
governor, council and general assembly, and the necessary officers attending the same, including the auditor of accounts against this State,
eight thousand eight hundred and sixty five dollars and forty five cents.
Also to Perez Jones, eight dollars for room, candles and firewood for
the committee of revision. Also to Elijah West, fifteen dollars for candles, firewood and room for the session of the governor & council; also
to Thomas Tolman, engrossing clerk, for expense of room, firewood
& candles in his office, six dollars and fifty cents. And,

It is hereby further Enacted, That there be appropriated a sum
not exceeding fourteen thousand dollars for the purpose of paying the
demands against this State, which may be allowed by the auditor of
accounts against the State, and the orders drawn by and under the direction of the supreme court. Which several sums of money shall be
paid by the treasurer out of the monies in the treasury. And if there
shall not be sufficient monies in the treasury, the treasurer shall issue
hard money orders for the residue of such appropriation.

AN ACT ASSESSING A TAX OF ONE CENT ON EACH ACRE OF LAND IN
THIS STATE FOR THE SUPPORT OF GOVERNMENT DURING THE
YEAR 1797 AND FOR OTHER PURPOSES

NOVEMBER 10TH, 1797

[1.] *It is hereby Enacted* by the General Assembly of the State
of Vermont, That there be, and hereby is assessed a tax of one cent
on each acre of land within this State (excepting lands sequestered to
public, pious, or charitable uses) to be collected and paid into the
treasury of this State on or before the first day of June in the year of
our Lord one thousand seven hundred and ninety eight, in specie, hard

money orders, or orders issued by the judges or clerks of the supreme court of judicature. And,

2. *It is hereby further Enacted*, That the surveyor general of this State be, and he is hereby directed under his oath of office to ascertain and return to the treasurer of this State a statement of the quantity of land actually contained in each town or gore of land within this state, agreeably to their original grants or charters, on or before the first day of January next. And,

3. *It is hereby further Enacted*, That the treasurer of this State be, and he is hereby directed, between the first day of January and the first day of February next, to issue his warrants to the first constables of each and every of the towns hereinafter enumerated, directing, and requiring the said first constables, respectively, to collect the said tax on their respective towns agreeably to the aforesaid return of the surveyor general. The names of which towns are as follows, to wit, — in Bennington county: Stamford, Pownall, Bennington, Reedsboro, Woodford, Shaftsbury, Arlington, Landgate, Sunderland, Manchester, Dorset, Rupert and Winhall; in Winham county: Hinsdale, Guilford, Brattleboro, Dummerston, Putney, Westminster, Rockingham, Grafton, Athens, Townshend, Newfane, Marlboro, Halifax, Whitingham, Wilmington, Wardsboro' North District, Wardsboro' South District, Jamaica, Londonderry, Somerset & Stratton; in Rutland County: Orwell, Benson, Fair Haven, Poultney, Wells, Pawlet, Danby, Harwich [Mt. Tabor], Mount-Holly (formerly Jackson's Gore), Shrewsbury, Clarendon, Tinmouth, Ira, Castleton, Hubbardton, Pittsford, Rutland, Killington, Brandon, Pittsfield, Sudbury and Wallingford; in Windsor County: Andover, Bridgewater, Bernard, Bethel, Chester, Cavendish, Hartford, Hartland, Ludlow, Norwich, Pomfret, Reading, Rochester, Royalton, Stockbridge, Springfield, Plymouth, (late Saltash), Sharon, Windsor, Woodstock and Weathersfield; in Addison County: Middlebury, Salisbury, Leicester, Whiting, Cornwall, Weybridge, Shoreham, Bridport, Addison, Panton, Ferrisburgh, Monkton, New Haven, Bristol, Starkesboro', Hancock, and Kingston; in Orange County: Braintree, Bradford, Brookfield, Barre, Berlin, Thetford, Strafford, Tunbridge, Randolph, Fairlie [Fairlee], Vershire, Chelsea, Roxbury, Corinth, Washington, Williamstown, Northfield, Newbury, Topsham and Orange; in Chittenden County: Burlington, Shelburne, Charlotte, Hinesburgh, Williston, Huntington (late Newhuntington), Duxbury, Moretown, Waitsfield, Colchester, Essex, Jericho, Bolton, Waterbury,

Middlesex, Milton, Westford, Underhill, South-Hero, and Stowe; in Caledonia County: Ryegate, Barnet, Peacham, Danville, and that part of Danville known by the name of Walden Gore, Waterford (late Littleton), Groton, St. Johnsbury, Lyndon, Billymead, Hardwick, Walden, Cabot, Montpelier, Calais, Sheffield, Concord, Lunenburgh, Guildhall, Maidstone, Brunswick, Greensboro', Craftsbury, Derby, Plainfield (late St. Andrews Gore), and Canaan; in Franklin County: Georgia, St. Albans, Swanton, Highgate, Huntsburgh, Berkshire, Sheldon, Fairfield, Fairfax, Cambridge, Johnson, Hyde Park, Wolcott, Elmore, North Hero, Alburgh, Isle of [La] Mott and Fletcher.

4. *It is hereby further Enacted*, That each and every of the first constables of the aforesaid towns shall, within ten days next after the receipt of the above mentioned warrants, apply to the selectmen of their respective towns, who shall, within ten days after such application to them made as aforesaid, make out and deliver to such constables a rate bill, containing a list of all the lands in such towns, held in severalty (agreeably to the actual limits of their respective grants or charters), and the number of acres contained in each lot, and the division to which it was drawn or pitched, and the tax to be paid thereon; except in cases where they cannot ascertain the original proprietor or division, in those cases it shall be set in the bill to the present owner. And where there are undivided lands in such town, the said selectmen shall make out an estimate of the quantity of such undivided lands to the best of their judgment, and insert the same in said rate bill agreeably to the true intent and meaning of this act. And,

5. *It is hereby further Enacted*, that when any original proprietor or land owner shall pay his proportion of said tax, or any part thereof, it shall be the duty of said constable to make endorsement on his rate bill of the name of the person paying the same, and receipt the same if required. And all lands, on which the tax aforesaid shall be so paid, shall be thereupon discharged from said tax. And,

6. *It is hereby further Enacted*, That if the sums so assessed as aforesaid, or any part thereof, shall remain unpaid on the first day of April in the year one thousand seven hundred and ninety eight, such constable shall give notice, by posting up an advertisement at the accustomed place or places for advertiseing freemen's meetings in their respective towns, of the tenor following, to wit: "The proprietors and landowners of the town of ———— are hereby notified and warned

that unless they pay the tax of one cent on each acre of land granted by the Legislature of this State, at their October session in Windsor, A.D. 1797, to me the subscriber, on or before the ————— day of ————— next, that so much of their lands as will pay said tax and cost will be sold at public vendue at ————— in said town of ————— at ————— oclock ————— noon to the highest bidder. Dated at &c. ————— ————— Collector Which advertisement shall be posted up as aforesaid three weeks before the time therein appointed for the sale of the lands therein mentioned. And the time so to be appointed, and mentioned in said advertisement, shall be on some day between the first day of May and last day of July in the year 1798. And the said first constables are hereby authorised and directed, in pursuance of said advertisement, to proceed to sell at public vendue, so much of each delinquents' lands as will pay said tax and the costs thereon arising, and deed the same to the purchaser as is herein after directed. And,

7. *It is hereby further Enacted*, That the treasurer of this State be, and he is hereby directed to issue his warrants to the sheriffs of the several counties in this State, on or before the first day of February, 1798, authorising and directing them to collect the said tax on all the lands in the several towns or gores in their respective counties not herein before mentioned and named, upon the receipt of which warrants the said sheriffs shall immediately apply to the secretary of this State, or the Secretary of the governor and council, for the list of the names of the proprietors in each of such towns or gores, whose duty it shall be to forward the same to the said sheriffs respectively, as soon as may be. And on receiving the same the said sheriffs shall assess said tax upon the lands in such towns and gores. And upon default of the said tax being paid as is herein before directed, shall proceed to notify the proprietors and landowners of such towns and gores respectively, by publishing an advertisement in which shall be specified the names of all the several towns and gores of land upon which the tax has not been paid, of the tenor herein before directed; for a constable, three weeks successively, in the newspapers printed in Bennington, Rutland, and Windsor, the day of the last publication of which shall be at least ten days before the day therein appointed for the sale of said lands. And,

8. *It is hereby further Enacted*, That the said sheriffs shall, in pursuance of such advertisement, proceed to sell at public vendue so

much of such delinquents' lands as shall pay said tax and costs, and shall deed the same as is hereinafter directed.

Provided always, That the selectmen and sheriffs in assessing the said tax, shall allow for highways out of each proprietor or landowner's share or lot, in the proportion of five acres to each hundred acres. And,

9. *It is hereby further Enacted*, that if any person or persons shall, within twelve months from and after the day of such sale, pay or tender to the said collector such tax, together with the costs of such sale, and interest upon the same, at the rate of twelve per cent per annum, his, her, or their lands, shall thereupon be discharged and redeemed from such sale. And the said collector or collectors, in such case or cases, shall pay over to the purchaser or purchasers of such lands the monies so by him or them received for the redemption thereof as aforesaid; and all redemptions shall be made before the setting of the sun on the day on which the lands are made redeemable.

10. *And it is hereby further Enacted*, That if such lands so sold as aforesaid, shall not be redeemed and discharged from said tax within one year, from and after the day of the sale thereof, the said collector or collectors shall execute and deliver to the purchaser or purchasers, a deed or deeds of the lands so by him, her or them purchased, as aforesaid, conveying the same to the purchaser, in fee simple. Which deed being acknowledged and recorded, shall vest in the purchaser, his heirs, and assigns forever, a good title thereto. And,

11. *It is hereby further Enacted*, That the sheriff of Addison county be, and he is hereby declared to be the collector of the tax aforesaid on that tract of land called Goshen Gore, lying and being in the county of Caledonia. And,

12. *It is hereby further Enacted*, That the sheriff of Franklin county be, and he is hereby declared to be the collector of the tax aforesaid, on the tracts of land in said county, heretofore known by the name of Smithfield and Knoulton's Gore, agreeably to the original charters thereof. And,

13. *It is hereby further Enacted*, That the first constable of Newhaven [New Haven] be, and he is hereby declared to be the collector of the tax aforesaid on the tract of land, called Newhaven Gore in said county of Addison. And,

14. *It is hereby further Enacted,* That the sheriffs aforesaid, shall have right to ask and receive, each for their said services, the following fees, to wit: for trouble and postage, for inserting said advertisements in the three newspapers aforesaid, agreeably to the directions aforesaid, four dollars, in addition to the sum paid the printers for inserting said advertisements; and also two dollars to constables for their services and trouble in advertiseing the same in their respective towns, as is herein before directed; to be apportioned by said sheriffs and constables respectively, upon such lands as shall be delinquent in the payment of said tax. And also such collectors shall have right to ask and receive for every right or lot of land sold at vendue, seventeen cents, and for every deed duly executed and acknowledged to the purchaser of such vendued lands, thirty four cents, and no deed shall be executed of the lands, so sold as is herein before directed, until the time for the redemption of the same be fully expired. And,

15. *It is hereby further Enacted,* That if any of the collectors aforesaid, shall neglect or refuse to collect and pay said tax into the treasury of this State, on or before the first day of August, A.D., one thousand seven hundred and ninety eight, the said treasurer is hereby authorised and directed to issue his extents against such delinquent collector or collectors for the collection of the same, in due form of law.

16. *And it is hereby further Enacted,* That the constables and selectmen of the several towns within this State be, and they are hereby fully authorised and empowered to proceed in all things in the assessing and collecting of said tax, within the actual limits of their original grants or charters, whether the same be within the limits of their respective towns, or within the limits of any other town established by any act of this Legislature, any law, usage, or custom to the contrary notwithstanding.

17. *And it is hereby further Enacted,* That any possessor or landowner in any town in this State, shall be unable through the insufficiency of the records, or otherwise, to show what original right he holds under, it shall be the duty of such possessor or landowner to make out a survey of his land with metes and bounds, certifying the number of acres, and present the same to the said collector, together with the tax and cost, if any. And it is hereby made the duty of the said collector, to receive said tax and give a receipt, declaring that he has received the tax on such land, meted and bounded as aforesaid.

And said land shall not pass, by any sale made by said collector, any thing in this act to the contrary notwithstanding.

18. *And it is hereby further Enacted*, That the selectmen in any organized town, shall have power to grant bills of abatement in the following cases, to wit, where it shall appear to them that the collector is made accountable for the collection of said tax on any quantity of lands which may be cut off from such town by the interference of grants; and also such part of a town as may be covered by natural ponds or lakes; and shall also certify the quantity of land contained in the public rights in their respective towns; which certificate shall be in the form following, as the case may require, viz.,

"These certify that the lands sequestered for public, pious, or charitable uses in the town of ———— in the county of ———— amount in the whole to ———— acres; and, (if the case or cases shall so be) that by the interference of the charter of the town of ———— and the town of ———— there is cut off ———— acres of land from the said town. And that there is covered by natural ponds or lakes contained within the limits of the charter of said town of ———— (here insert the name or names of such waters) to the amount of ———— acres; amounting in the whole to ———— acres, which at one cent per acre is ———— dollars ———— cents, which sum we do hereby abate to ———— ———— first constable of said town on a State land tax of one cent on the acre, assessed by the Legislature of this State at their October session, A.D. one thousand seven hundred and ninety seven.

Dated at ———— 179—

Attest ———— ———— (Selectmen of said
———— ———— (town of ————

Which said bills of abatement, signed by two or more selectmen, and presented to the treasurer of this State, by such constables, shall, by the said treasurer, be placed to the credit of such constable on said tax. And said treasurer, shall also place to the credit of all the collectors, contemplated and authorised by this act, such sum respectively, as the five acres to the hundred hereinbefore allowed, as a deduction for highways will amount to, on the quantities of their warrants respectively; after a deduction on said warrants of the quantity of land contained in the aforesaid bills of abatement respectively. And,

19. *It is hereby further Enacted*, That all vendues for sales of lands under this act shall be, between the hours of nine oclock in the

morning and the setting of the sun of the same day or days on which the same may be holden, and every sale which shall not be made within the period of the day or days above described, is hereby declared to be null and void. And,

20. *It it hereby further Enacted*, That the several collectors aforesaid, shall, within thirty days next after the ending of such vendues for the sale of lands as aforesaid, lodge a true and attested copy of such sales, together with their advertisement thereof, with the several town or county clerks, as the case may be, whose duty it shall be to record the same at the expense of such collector. And,

21. *It is hereby further Enacted*, That the Secretary of this State be, and he is hereby directed immediately after the rising of this assembly to publish this act, in all the public newspapers printed within this State, at least six weeks successively.

END OF ACTS PASSED OCTOBER ADJOURNED
SESSION A.D., 1797 [Windsor]

LAWS OF 1798

ACTS AND LAWS PASSED BY THE LEGISLATURE OF THE
STATE OF VERMONT AT THEIR SESSION HOLDEN AT
VERGENNES ON THE SECOND THURSDAY OF
OCTOBER A.D. ONE THOUSAND SEVEN
HUNDRED & NINETY EIGHT

AN ACT DIRECTING THE TREASURER OF THE STATE TO PAY CEPHAS
SMITH, JUNR., A SUM OF MONEY THEREIN MENTIONED

OCTOBER 25TH, 1798

It is hereby Enacted by the General Assembly of the State of
Vermont, That Cephas Smith, Junr., be allowed for inspecting the
press while the revised laws were printing, one hundred and eighty
dollars, and the treasurer of the state is hereby directed to pay the same
to him.

Passed October 25, 1798.

A true record,

Attest, Ros. Hopkins, Sec'y.

AN ACT RESTORING SAMUEL B. SHELDON TO HIS LAW

OCTOBER 26TH, 1798

Whereas Ira Allen of Colchester, in the county of Chittenden,
recovered a judgment by default, by consideration of the county court
holden at Burlington, within and for the county of Chittenden at their
session in September, A.D. 1796, against the said Samuel B. Sheldon
for the sum of one hundred, ninety pounds, thirteen shillings, and three
pence, damages and costs, contrary to a certain agreement, made and
entered into by and between the said Ira and the said Sheldon, and
by reason of which certain other suits have been commenced to the
great damage, expense and cost of the said Sheldon. Therefore,

Sec. 1. *It is hereby Enacted* by the General Assembly of the
State of Vermont, That the action of the said Ira, against the said
Sheldon, be again entered on the docket of said court, and stand open
for a new trial, and that all judgments rendered against any person
or person in consequence of said judgment be stopped, and no further
proceedings thereon had.

Sec. 2. *And it is hereby further Enacted,* That if the said

Samuel B. Sheldon shall eventually recover in said suit against the said Ira, he shall have right to tax his legal costs, from the commencement of his said suit, and his legal costs which has arisen in all suits, which have been instituted in consequence of said judgment.[1]

Passed October 26, 1798.

A true record,

Attest, Ros. Hopkins, Sec'y.

AN ACT GRANTING TO ELIAKIM SPOONER, LEAVE TO APPEAL FROM A
CERTAIN JUDGMENT RENDERED BY THE COUNTY COURT, IN THE
COUNTY OF WINDHAM TO THE SUPREME COURT

OCTOBER 26TH, 1798

Whereas, William Horn of Dover, in the county of Stafford and State of New Hampshire, heretofore brought his certain action of trespass against Eliakim Spooner of Westminster, in the county of Windham, in this state, and caused said action to be entered at the county court, holden at Newfane, in and for the county of Windham, on the Monday next preceding the second Tuesday of November, A.D. 1797, at which court the said William recovered judgment in said cause, against the said Eliakim, in the absence of the said Eliakim, by means whereof, the evidence on the part of the said Eliakim was not produced on said trial. And whereas the council for the said Eliakim, through mistake, omitted to appeal said cause, by means whereof great injustice is said to have been done to the said Eliakim. Therefore,

Sec. 1. *It is hereby Enacted* by the General Assembly of the State of Vermont, That on application of the said Eliakim Spooner, to the county court next to be holden, within and for the county of Windham, and entering into bonds as by law directed in granting appeals, it shall be the duty of said county court, to take such bonds, and grant an appeal in said cause in the same manner as though said appeal had been moved within the time prescribed for granting an appeal in said cause. And it shall be in the power of the said Eliakim Spooner to carry said cause, so appealed, to the supreme court, next to be holden within and for the county of Windham, on the first Tuesday of August. And it shall be the duty of said supreme court

---

1. State Papers of Vermont, Vol. XI, *General Petitions,* 1797-1799, "For a New Trial," 225.

to receive said appeal, so made, and proceed to hear, try and determine said cause, in the same manner as though the judgment of the said county court had heen rendered in said cause, at the same term in which said appeal was granted.

Sec. 2. *And it is hereby further Enacted,* That from and after entering bonds as aforesaid, in said county court, all proceedings on said judgment rendered by said county court in said cause shall be stayed until final judgment be rendered in said cause, in said supreme court, as in other cases of appeal. And in case execution shall have been granted on said judgment, the same shall be void and be returned without being levied.[1]

Passed October 26, 1798.

A true record,

Attest, Ros. Hopkins, Sec'y.

AN ACT EMPOWERING ISRAEL HAY TO DEED CERTAIN LANDS

OCTOBER 26TH, 1798

Sec. 1. *It is hereby Enacted* by the General Assembly of the State of Vermont, That Israel Hay of Rupert, in the county of Bennington, under the direction and by the approbation of the judge of probate for the probate district of Manchester, in said county, be, and he is hereby authorised and empowered to make and execute a deed or deeds of two certain pieces of land herein after designated, to Pelatiah King of said Rupert.

Sec. 2. *And it is hereby further Enacted,* That the premises thus to be deeded, under the direction and by the approbation aforesaid, are two parcels of land, which were as appears to this Legislature, contracted to the said Pelatiah King, by Jonathan Hay of Rupert, deceased, of whose last will and testament, the said Israel Hay is executor, and which premises are defined and described in a certain bond for a deed, given to the said Pelatiah by the executrix of said will, Anna Hay, also deceased, bearing date the 12th day of April Anno Domini 1794, as follows, beginning at a stake and stones in the north west corner of John Nelson's land, on the line of the highway, and running thence south forty degrees east twenty six rods to a

---

1. State Papers of Vermont, Vol. XI, *General Petitions,* 1797-1799, "For Entry of an Appeal to the Court Docket," 211.

stake and stones; thence east forty five degrees north, fifty seven rods to a stake and stones; thence north forty-five degrees west, twenty rods to a stake and stones in the south line of the highway; from thence on the line of the highway to the first mentioned bounds. And the other piece, beginning at the south east corner of a piece of land, laid out to John Nelson, running thence north forty five degrees west, sixty three rods on the said Nelson's line, to a stake and stone; thence east forty five degrees north eighteen rods to a stake and stones; thence south forty five degrees east to the south west corner of Pelatiah King's land, thence on the west line of said King's land, to the north line of the highway, to a stake and stones; and from thence to the first mentioned bound; said pieces of land lying and being in Rupert & county of Bennington, aforesaid.

Sec. 3. *And it is hereby further Enacted,* That the deed or deeds made and executed under the direction and by the approbation aforesaid, and for the premises intended and described by the second section of this act, shall be to all intents as good and valid in law to the said Pelatiah, and to his heirs and assigns as if the same had been executed by the said Jonathan Hay in his life time.

Passed October 26, 1798.

A true record,

Attest, Ros. Hopkins, Sec'y.

AN ACT REGULATING FEES

OCTOBER 27TH, 1798

Sec. 1. *It is hereby Enacted* by the General Assembly of the State of Vermont, That the fees for the several officers, and other persons herein after mentioned, shall be as follows, namely:

GOVERNOR'S FEES

	Dollars	Cents
For signing a charter of land	8	—
For every other charter or grant by him signed	3	—

LIEUTENANT GOVERNOR'S FEES

	Dollars	Cents
For attendance on Council per day	4	—
Travel per mile each way		6

COUNCILLOR'S FEES

	Dollars	Cents
For attendance per day	1	50

	Dollars	Cents
Travel per mile, each way	—	6

REPRESENTATIVE'S FEES

	Dollars	Cents
For attendance per day	1	50
Travel per mile, each way		6
Speaker of the General Assembly's fees per day	2	50
Travel per mile each way		6
Clerk of the General Assembly's fees per day	2	50
Travel per mile, each way		6
Engrossing clerk's fees per day	2	50
Travel per mile, each way		6

SECRETARY OF STATE'S FEES

	Dollars	Cents
Recording laws, for every hundred words		7
Receiving & filing each petition of a private nature		11
Receiving & filing each petition for grants of land		17
For drawing, attesting and registering a charter for lands	3	34
For copies of laws, petitions and other papers, for each hundred words		7
For each citation between party & party		17
Attendance on the General Assembly per day	2	50
Travel per mile each way		6
And there shall be paid to the Secretary for the use of the treasury, on filing each petition between party and party	4	—

SECRETARY OF COUNCIL'S FEES

	Dollars	Cents
For each military commission and affixing the seal thereto, he finding blanks		25
Each commission for the judge of the supreme court		34
Each commission for the judges of the county courts and of the probate courts		34
For justices commission for each county		75
Every order of council for the benefit of particular persons		17
Affixing the State seal (Military commissions excepted)		17
Attendance on council per day	2	50
Travel per mile each way		6

SUPREME COURT'S FEES

	Dollars	Cents
Chief Judge while on the circuit per day	4	50
Each side judge while on the circuit per day	3	67
Each motion for arrest of judgment or new trial, for the benefit of the judges		67

	Dollars	Cents

For allowing and signing writs or error *audita querela,* and
   habeas corpus, & taking recognizance for the same   67

And there shall be paid into the hands of the clerk for the
   benefit of the judges, for each action tried   2   50

And for each non-suit, default or confession   1   —

COUNTY COURT'S FEES

For each action tried, there shall be paid to the clerk for the
   benefit of the judges   67

For each abatement, non-suit, default or confession   34

For each license for a tavern keeper   50

For each entry of an action for the benefit of the judges   67

The chief judges' share of the above perquisites, to be one
   quarter more than the side judges

For allowing and signing *audita querela* & *habeas corpus,*
   and taking recognizance in the same for each judge   50

For each motion in arrest of judgment & new trial   50

JUDGES OF PROBATE FEES

For granting administration   34

If the inventory exceed 166 dollars   50

Receiving and approving each will if the inventory do not
   exceed 166 dollars   34

If the inventory exceed that sum   50

Allowing accounts, settling & dividing estates   48

Every necessary order or rule   17

Appointment of persons to inventory and appraise   25

Appointing commissioner or commissioners to set off
   widows' dower   25

Appointing guardians   34

Fees for commissioners appointed on testate or intestate estates,
   per day   1   —

Travel per mile   6

Executors and administrators such sum per day as the judges
   of probate shall judge reasonable

REGISTER'S OF PROBATE FEES

Drawing & filling an administration bond   34

Drawing each letter of administration   25

Drawing probate of will, if the inventory do not exceed
   166 dollars   34

If it exceeds 166 dollars   42

	Dollars	Cents

Recording or copying a will, codicil, inventory or other
    necessary paper for each hundred words   8

For every citation   13

For every quietas or acquittance   42

Making out and registering commission to receive and examine
    the claims of creditors to insolvent estates   50

Entering an order upon the administrator to pay the debts of
    the several creditors returned by commissioners   25

Entering every other necessary order or rule   9

Drawing and filling guardian bond   34

JUSTICES' FEES

Drawing a writ   17

Signing a summons   9

Signing an attachment or summons when bond is given   13

Subpoena for each witness   6

Judgment in each action tried   50

If on verdict of jury   67

On confession or default   25

For taking deposition out of court   34

For citation to appear   17

Each continuance   17

Every warrant for criminals & bond   34

Recognizance   17

Each venire for a jury   25

For every appeal including the recognizance   25

For taking acknowledgment of deed   12

For recording execution, and officers return thereon extended
    on real estate, which the officer serving the same shall
    collect & pay   75

For issuing a citation to the adverse party on complaint of a
    prisoner to swear out of gaol   50

For making and signing certificates to prisoners & gaolers each   25

For attending court of gaol delivery   50

For travel per mile each way   5

Making rule of reference between parties   50

Rendering judgment on report of referees, so appointed   50

For every execution   25

CLERKS OF THE SUPREME AND COUNTY COURT FEES

For signing each summons   9

	Dollars	Cents
For signing each summons or attachment when bond is given		13
For attendance at the supreme court per day	1	—
Entering each judgment on abatement, non-suit default, or confession		25
Clerks of the county court for entering each judgment on demurrer or after verdict		50
Clerk of the supreme court for the same	1	—
Taking each recognizance in court		17
Filing each necessary paper		6
Every appeal or review		34
Every rule or order of court		9
Every continuance in supreme court		16
Every continuance in county court		8
Every execution including the filing		25
For recording each sheriff's deputation and oath		25
Recording execution extended on real estate with the officers return, who shall collect and pay the same	1	—
Every license to an innkeeper		17

For all copies and other services made or done by direction of the court, and not herein before numerated, such sum or sums as shall be allowed by the court respectively according to their length and difficulty.

ATTORNIES' FEES

For drawing writ and declaration on note		17

All other writs, such sum as shall be allowed by the courts respectively, according to their length and difficulty.

STATE'S ATTORNIES' FEES

	Dollars	Cents
For every indictment or information	1	—

If more than one count, such sum as shall be allowed by the court.

Term fee	2	—
For each cause tried, not exceeding	5	—

Copy of the indictment such sum as shall be allowed by the court.

SHERIFFS' CONSTABLES' & COLLECTORS' FEES

Serving every process on each defendant, by reading		6
If by a copy		17
For taking bail		17

	Dollars	Cents
For each mile's travel for the service of all writs and other processes, to be computed from the place of service to the place of return		6
For levying each execution amounting to three dollars or under		15
And for each three dollars over		4
For each day's attendance on appraisement, or sale of estate, taken in execution		34
For attending before a justice's court when required		34
For attending freeholders' courts per day	1	—
Copy of an execution, extended on lands, and the return thereof to the office for record		50
For attendance on the General Assembly, or supreme or county court, per day	1	—
Constables for the like service	1	—

Collectors of taxes, to be allowed the like fees as sheriffs, in cases of execution, when they levy on persons or estate, and one dollar out of each fifty dollars, collected and paid into the state or county treasury.

Provided, That no sheriff, constable, or other officer shall be entitled to any fee for a return of *non est inventus,* on any civil writ or process.

	Dollars	Cents
For sheriffs &c. assistants per day, for		67
For half a day		34
For appraisers of real estate on execution		67
For half a day		34

PARTIES AND WITNESSES' FEES IN THE SUPREME AND COUNTY COURTS

	Dollars	Cents
Term fee on abatement, non-suit or default in the first term	1	—
Term fee in all other cases	1	—
And the party recovering shall be allowed for his attorney or non-suite or default	1	50
For trial of issue of law or fact	3	—
Travel for plaintiff or defendant within this State per mile		5
Witnesses travel per mile		5
Attendance per day		75
In justices courts, travel for plaintiff or defendant, and witnesses, per mile		5
Attendance of plaintiff or defendant and witnesses, per day		50
For a half a day		34

GRAND JURORS' FEES

	Dollars	Cents
Travel per mile		6
For each day's attendance on supreme and county courts		75
For each complaint		50

PETIT JURORS' FEES

Panel of, for trying each cause before the supreme or county court	5	—
For trying each cause before a justice to be advanced by the party praying the same in a civil action	1	50
For trying each cause, before a freehold court, such sum as shall be allowed by the justices holding the same, according to their travel and attendance.		

TOWN CLERKS' FEES

For recording a common deed poll, including the certificate of filing, to be advanced by the party lodging the same for record		20
Copying the same		20
And in the same proportion for all other deeds.		
Recording survey bill		9
Do. marriage, birth or death		4
Do. each mark		9
Do. execution extended on real estate, with the officers' return thereon, to be collected and paid by the officer serving the same	1	—
Do. a certificate of a religious sentiment		12

PROPRIETORS' AND OTHER COLLECTORS' FEES

Travel from his dwelling house to the place of sale, to be equally divided among the delinquent proprietors or landowners, per mile		6
For drawing and conveying an advertisement, to be divided as aforesaid	1	—
For attendance and sale of each delinquent proprietor's right		34
Each deed of conveyance, including the acknowledgement		34
For each receipt for money before sale		6

GAOLERS' FEES

For commitment of a prisoner		34
For discharge of Do.		34
Diet per week for state prisoners	1	—
For bonds for the liberties of the prison		34

	Dollars	Cents
Fees for freeholders, summoned to assess damages sustained in laying out highways, per day		50
For half a day		33

SURVEYOR GENERAL'S FEES

Per day (exclusive of expenses)	1	50

COUNTY SURVEYORS

Exclusive of expenses, per day	1	—

AUDITORS OF ACCOUNTS FEES

With the treasurer, per day	2	—

AUDITOR OF ACCOUNTS AGAINST THE STATE

While attending the Legislature, Travel per mile each way		6
Attendance per day	1	50

IMPOUNDERS' FEES

For all horse kind and neat cattle per head		11
Sheep, per head		2
Swine, per head		8

Three fourths to the impounder and the other fourth to the pound keeper.

NOTARIES' PUBLIC FEES

For every protest under seal	1	—
For every certificate under seal		50
For waiting on a person to demand payment, or witness any matter and certify the same under seal.	1	—

Sec. 2. *And it is hereby further Enacted,* That the judges of the supreme court of judicature, judges of the county court, judges and registers of probate, justices of the peace, secretary of state, secretary of council, clerk of the general assembly, clerks of the supreme and county courts, town clerks, notaries public, sheriffs, and all other persons whose duty it may be by law, to record any proceedings, or give any copies, attestations or certificates, other than such for which particular fee or fees is, are, or shall be established, shall be allowed seven cents for every hundred words, and for less than an hundred words in the same proportion. And for every certificate on the copy of the whole case, seventeen cents, and for any other duty or service done or performed, such sum shall be in proportion to the fees specifi-

cally provided by this or any other act, for such officers or persons respectively.

Passed October 27, 1798.

A true record,

Attest, Ros. Hopkins, Sec'y.

AN ACT REGULATING THE CHOICE OF A COUNCIL OF CENSORS

OCTOBER 27TH, 1798

It is hereby Enacted by the General Assembly of the State of Vermont, That the first constable, in each town in this State or in case of his absence or inability, the town clerk, or one or more of the select-men, is hereby required at least twelve days before the last Wednesday of March next, to warn a meeting of the freemen in their respective towns, by notifying the same in writing, in the most public place or places in the respective towns, to be held at the places agreed upon for holding freemen's meetings in such towns on the last Wednesday of March next, at one of the clock afternoon, to give in their votes for thirteen such persons as they should chuse [choose], as a council of censors in this State, as provided by the constitution. And the presiding officers are hereby required to open the meetings, and to receive, and seal up the votes of the freemen in presence of such meeting, and write the name of the town on the outside of the paper, containing the votes and these words, "Vote for Censors," and also to certify that they were sealed up by such officer whose duty it is hereby made to deliver such votes, so sealed up, to the clerk of the county court in the county in which such votes were taken, within fourteen days from the taking of such votes; and the said clerks of the respective county courts are hereby directed to receive the said votes, and to meet at the court house in Windsor, in the county of Windsor on the Wednesday next following the first Monday of May next, at one of the clock afternoon, who when convened, shall proceed to count said votes, and shall certify to his Excellency, the governor, under their hands, the thirteen persons who have the highest number of votes, as elected censors, within six days from the time of their meeting as aforesaid; who is hereby requested at the charge of the State, to notify such persons officially of their election within twenty days.

Sec. 2. *And it is hereby further Enacted,* That in case of absence or disability of any such clerk, it shall be the duty of the presiding officers aforesaid, to deliver such votes, so sealed, to the sheriff of such county, whose duty is hereby made to perform the services in this act enjoined on the county clerks.

Sec. 3. *And it is hereby further Enacted,* That the Council of Censors shall hold their first meeting at the court house in Windsor, in the county of Windsor, on the day appointed by the constitution for that purpose, and notice from the governor of such election shall be sufficient credentials of such choice. And it is hereby made the duty of the secretary of state to cause this act, with a list of the council and house of representatives, to be printed before the rising of this assembly, and to forward an attested copy thereof, directed to the first constable, or for want thereof to the town clerk, or one of the selectmen in each organized town in this State, by the representative belonging to such town; and where there is no representative present, such copy directed as aforesaid shall be forwarded by a representative of some adjoining town, whose duty it shall be to cause the same to be delivered according to the direction previous to the first day of February next.

Sec. 4. *And it is hereby further Enacted,* That if the first constable or any other presiding officer, in any town, shall refuse or neglect to perform any of the duties enjoined by this act, and be thereof convicted, before the county court of the county where such refusal or neglect shall take place, he shall forfeit and pay to the treasury of the same county a fine of twenty dollars with costs.

Sec. 5. *And it is hereby further Enacted,* That if any county clerk or sheriff refuse or neglect to perform the duties by this act of him required, and be thereof convicted before the supreme court, he shall forfeit and pay a fine to the treasury of this State of one hundred and fifty dollars with costs.

Sec. 6. *And it is hereby further Enacted,* That the said presiding officers shall be entitled to receive for their service in returning the said votes, six cents per mile from their respective dwellings to the residence of the county clerk or sheriffs, to whom such return is by this act to be made; and the said county clerks and sheriffs shall receive six cents per mile for their travel, and one dollar and sixty seven cents per day, while attending on the business of their appointment, to be paid out of the treasury of this State. And the auditor of accounts against the

State, is hereby directed to audit their respective accounts and draw orders accordingly.

Passed October 27, 1798.

A true copy,

Attest, Ros. Hopkins, Sec'y.

AN ACT LAYING A TAX OF TWO CENTS PER ACRE ON THE TOWN OF RYEGATE FOR THE PURPOSE THEREIN MENTIONED

OCTOBER 29TH, 1798

It is hereby Enacted by the General Assembly of the State of Vermont, That there be, and hereby is laid a tax of two cents per acre on the lands in the town of Ryegate, in the county of Caledonia, public rights excepted, for the purpose of making and repairing roads and building bridges in said town, to be expended under the direction of William Nelson, Senr., Josiah Page and Jonathan Darling, who are hereby appointed a committee to superintend the expenditure of said tax. And any justice of the peace within the county of Caledonia is hereby authorised to issue his warrant to Benjamin Wright, to collect said tax, who is hereby appointed a collector of the same. And said collector is hereby made accountable to the said committee for the amount of said tax; and said committee and collector are hereby directed in the collection, expenditure, and accounting for said tax, to govern themselves in all things agreeably to the directions of the act entitled "An act regulating the disposition of monies raised by taxes on lands in the several towns for the purpose of making and repairing roads and building bridges," passed November 2d, 1796.[1]

AN ACT FOR THE REMOVAL OF PRISONERS FROM THE GAOL IN VERGENNES, TO THE GAOL IN BURLINGTON

OCTOBER 29TH, 1798

Whereas, many persons from the county of Chittenden, for the want of a gaol in said county, have been imprisoned in the gaol in Vergennes, and are there still detained, at a great distance from their

---

1. State Papers of Vermont, Vol. XI, *General Petitions,* 1797-1799, "For a Tax on Land to Build and Repair Roads and Bridges." 187.

familes, friends, and connections, notwithstanding a good and sufficient gaol is now erected at Burlington, in said county of Chittenden.
Therefore,

Sec. 1. *It is hereby Enacted* by the General Assembly of the
State of Vermont, That on application of the sheriff of the county of
Chittenden, to the keeper of the said gaol in Vergennes, for that purpose, it shall be the duty of the keeper of the said gaol in Vergennes, to
deliver over to the said sheriff of the county of Chittenden, any prisoner or prisoners belonging to the said county of Chittenden and now
imprisoned in the gaol, or the liberties thereof at Vergennes on any
process, or writ of execution issued from any authority in the said
county of Chittenden, together with the cause or warrant of such
imprisonment, and the bond or bonds executed for the liberties of said
prison, if any such shall be held by the keeper of said prison. And it
shall be the duty of the sheriff of the county of Chittenden, on application to him made, in behalf of any such prisoner or prisoners, for that
purpose, immediately to apply to the said keeper of the gaol in Vergennes, and take into his custody said prisoner or prisoners together
with the cause of his, her, or their imprisonment, and the bonds given
for the liberties of said prisoner, if any such shall be, in the custody and
keeping of said gaoler, and the said prisoner or prisoners to remove
from the said gaol in Vergennes, with the cause of commitment, to the
keeper of the gaol at Burlington, in the said county of Chittenden, and
deliver over said prisoner or prisoners, so removed, to the said keeper
of the said gaol in Burlington, in the county of Chittenden. And it shall
be the duty of the said keeper of the gaol in Burlington to receive such
prisoner or prisoners so delivered over, with the cause of their said commitment, and him, her, or them to safely keep in the same manner as
though such prisoner had been originally committed to the said gaol
in said Burlington. And all bonds given for the liberties of the said
prisoner, at Vergennes, by or on behalf of such prisoner or prisoners so
removed, shall be utterly void, except such bonds as have been or may
be forfeited, before the removal of such prisoners. And no prisoner so
removed, shall be entitled to the liberties of said prison at Burlington,
by virtue of any bonds given for the liberties of the said prison at
Vergennes, but on being admitted to the liberties of the said prison at
Burlington, shall procure new bonds, to indemnify the sheriff of the
county of Chittenden, therefor,

Sec. 2. *Provided nevertheless*, and it is hereby further Enacted,

That all fees due and payable to the keeper of the gaol in Vergennes, for keeping and dieting any such prisoner, shall be paid by such prisoner before his removal, and also the costs and expense of such removal, shall be paid by such prisoner or prisoners so removed, to the said sheriff of Chittenden county, before he, she or they shall be entitled to such removal.

Passed October 29, 1798.

A true record,

Attest, Ros. Hopkins, Sec'y.

AN ACT FOR THE SURVEYING OF A PUBLIC COUNTY ROAD, THROUGH THE COUNTY OF BENNINGTON

OCTOBER 29TH, 1798

Sec. 1. *It is hereby Enacted* by the General Assembly of the State of Vermont, That David Robinson, Asa Burnham, and Eli Brownson, all of the county of Bennington, be, and they are hereby appointed a committee of this Legislature, to lay out and survey a public county road, through the county of Bennington, from the south line of the State at Pownal to Manchester meeting house, and from thence a western road leading toward Fairhaven and Westhaven, through Pawlet, to the north line of said county, on the northline of said town of Reupert [Rupert]. And also from the said Manchester Meeting House, an eastern road leading toward Rutland through the eastern part of Dorset, to the north line thereof; and also the middle road leading through the center of said Dorset to the north line of said county, by altering the present road and roads by straightening them, and laying the same as they shall judge will best accommodate the public for travelling, having in their view as may be possible, to combine the interests of the public, as well for the future as the present day, with the accommodation of the towns through which the said roads shall pass, and individuals. And either two of said committee, with a county surveyor, under the oath of his office, are empowered to lay out and survey said roads, of which they shall make and attest one general survey bill, and lodge the same for record in the office of the clerk of the county court, in said county. And another survey bill to be made by sections as it passes through the several towns, beginning and ending at town lines, and deliver the same for record, to the several town clerks of such towns respectively. And said bills shall accurately specify the width of said roads, and all the angles thereof, describing monuments at every angle, with their true course and distance from each other. And said roads when thus laid out and surveyed, and the survey bills thereof lodged for record, as before directed, shall not be altered but by a future order from the county court, of the said county of Bennington, or the Legislature of this State.

Sec. 2. *And it is hereby further Enacted,* That the said committee in laying out the said roads shall have the same power as selectmen, by law have, in laying out roads in their respective towns, in setting over old roads in lieu of lands taken for a new road; and where there is not allowance lands, to assess damages to individuals whose lands may be taken for such new road. And a certificate from said committee in the lands of any person to whom damages shall be thus assessed, shall have the same effect and solidity against the treasurer of the town in which such damages shall be assessed, as a certificate from selectmen as aforesaid. And said new road shall be opened, cleared, and made passable, and kept in repair, by the towns through which they shall pass, in the same manner as public roads laid out and surveyed by selectmen.

Sec. 3. *And it is hereby further Enacted,* That the expenses attending the execution of this act, and also of detaining the same shall be paid out of the treasury of the said county of Bennington. And the judges of the county court of the said county of Bennington are hereby authorised and directed, on receiving the accounts of said committee, and being certified that the service directed in this act, is performed, and in the manner herein directed, to audit the same, and allow a compensation and a disbursement of expenses, which shall to them appear reasonable and just and draw orders on the treasurer of said county accordingly.[1]

Passed October 29, 1798.

A true record,

Attest, Ros. Hopkins, Sec'y.

---

1. State Papers of Vermont, Vol. XI, *General Petitions,* 1797-1799, "For Appointment of a Committee to Consider Alteration of Roads," 284.

AN ACT ANNEXING THE TOWN OF DUNCANSBOROUGH TO THE COUNTY OF CALEDONIA FOR THE TIME BEING

OCTOBER 30TH, 1798

It is hereby Enacted by the General Assembly of the State of Vermont, That the town of Duncansborough, now within the jurisdiction of the county of Franklin, be, and hereby is annexed to the jurisdiction of the county of Caledonia, for the time being, or until a future order of this Legislature.

Passed October 30, 1798.

A true record,

Attest, Ros. Hopkins, Sec'y.

AN ACT ALTERING THE TIMES FOR THE SITTING OF THE SUPREME COURT OF JUDICATURE, COURT OF CHANCERY AND COUNTY COURT IN THE COUNTY OF FRANKLIN

OCTOBER 30TH, 1798

Whereas, the times fixed by law for the sitting of the said court, in the said county of Franklin, is found inconvenient. Therefore,

Sec. 1. *It is hereby Enacted* by the General Assembly of the State of Vermont, That the next county court in the said county of Franklin, shall be holden at St. Albans, in said county, on the second Monday of March next ensuing, and forever after, on the second Monday of November and March annually, and the supreme court of judicature, and court of chancery, shall be holden at St. Albans in and for said county of Franklin, on the last Tuesday of December, which will be in the year of our Lord one thousand seven hundred and ninety nine, and thereafter on the last Tuesday of December annually.

Sec. 2. *And it is hereby further Enacted*, That all writs, processes, recognizances, or other proceedings which have been issued, commenced, had, or pending in either of said courts, or made returnable before the same at the times now fixed by law, for the sitting of the said courts, shall be had, made and returned, and the same proceedings had thereon by said courts in the same manner as though the times for the sitting of said courts had not been altered.

Sec. 3. *And it is hereby further Enacted*, That so much of the act affixing the times and places of holding the several county courts and supreme court of judicature and court of chancery, in the several counties in this State, passed March the eighth *Anno Domini* one thousand seven hundred and ninety seven, as affixes the time for holding the said courts in the county of Franklin be, and the same is hereby repealed.

Passed October 30, 1798.

A true copy,

Attest, Ros. Hopkins, Sec'y.

AN ACT ALLOWING ENDORSEES TO MAINTAIN ACTIONS IN THEIR OWN NAME

OCTOBER 30TH, 1798

Sec. 1. *It is hereby Enacted* by the General Assembly of the State of Vermont, That the endorsee or endorsees of any bill or promisory note for the payment of money, to any person or persons, his or their order, or to bearer, may maintain an action thereon, in his, her, or their own name, or names, for the recovery of the money, *Provided always*, That in all such actions, it shall be lawful for the defendant, or defandants, to plead an offset of all demands, proper to be plead in offset, which the defendant or defendants may have against the original payee, or payees, before notice of such endorsement, against the endorsee or endorsees, and may also plead or give in evidence, on trial of any such action, any matter or things which would equitably discharge the defendant or defendants in any action brought in the name of the original payee or payees.

Sec. 2. *Provided also*, and it is hereby further Enacted, That in all such cases the endorsee or endorsees, shall recover no more costs than the original payee or payees would be entitled to recover, had the suit been brought in his, her, or their own name.

Sec. 3. *And it is hereby further Enacted*, That an act entitled, "An act with respect to the negociability of notes," passed the 27th day of October A.D. 1795, be, and the same is hereby repealed.

Passed October 30, 1798.

A true record,

Attest, Ros. Hopkins, Sec'y.

AN ACT REVIVING AN ACT ENTITLED "AN ACT ASSESSING A TAX OF
THREE CENTS PER ACRE ON THE TOWNS OF IRASBURGH AND
COVENTRY FOR THE PURPOSE THEREIN MENTIONED,"
SO FAR AS IT RESPECTS THE TOWN OF IRASBURGH,
PASSED NOVEMBER 2D, 1797, AND APPOINTING
AN ADDITIONAL MEMBER OF COMMITTEE

OCTOBER 30TH, 1798

Whereas, the act aforementioned has become of no effect as it respects the town of Irasburgh, through the failure of advertiseing the opportunity for proprietors to pay their taxes by labour, as required by general statute.

It is hereby Enacted by the General Assembly of the State of Vermont, That the act entitled "An act assessing a tax of three cents per acre on the towns of Irasburgh and Coventry, for the purposes therein mentioned," passed the ninth day of November A.D. 1797, as it respects the town of Irasburgh, be, and the same is hereby revived, and shall to all intents have the same effect as if it had passed and been enacted at the present session of the Legislature. And,

It is hereby further Enacted, that Abraham Morell of Wheelock, be, and he is hereby appointed a member of the committee for superintending the expenditures of said tax, as it respects Irasburgh, in the room of William Guy.

AN ACT DIRECTING THE MODE OF SUMMONING GRAND JURORS

OCTOBER 30TH, 1798

Sec. 1. *It is hereby Enacted* by the General Assembly of the State of Vermont, That when the state's attorney of any county shall think it necessary for the grand jury to attend the supreme or county court, to be holden in such county, it shall be his duty to notify the same, to the clerk of such court, a sufficient time before the sitting of the same, who shall issue his venire, directed to the sheriff of such county, or to his deputy, requiring him to summon as many able freeholders as are mentioned in such venire, from the different towns therein mentioned, not exceeding twenty-four, nor less than thirteen, to attend on such court on the first day of the sitting of the same, at ten of the clock in the forenoon; and in order that such jury may be impartially summoned, it shall be the duty of the sheriff or his deputy, who shall receive such venire, to repair to the respective clerks of the towns, out of which he shall be directed to summon such jury; and the town clerk, with the advice of some justice of the peace, of the same county, shall agree upon three times the number of able freeholders of such town, and out of that number shall draw by lot the number required for grand jurors, who shall be summoned as aforesaid.

Sec. 2. *And it is hereby further Enacted,* That this act shall continue and be in force until the first day of April *Anno Domini* 1799 and no longer.

Passed October 30, 1798.

A true record,

Attest, Ros. Hopkins, Sec'y.

AN ACT DIRECTING THE TREASURER OF THIS STATE TO PAY
ABLE SHEPHERD FIRST CONSTABLE OF THE TOWN OF
HALIFAX FOR THE YEAR 1796, SEVEN DOLLARS
NINETY TWO CENTS

OCTOBER 30TH, 1798

It is hereby Enacted by the General Assembly of the State of Vermont, That the treasurer of this State be directed, and he is hereby directed to pay to Abel Shepherd, first constable of the town of Halifax, for the year 1796, the sum of seven dollars and ninety two cents, which sum the said Abel Shepherd has actually paid to said treasurer, over and above the sum he ought to have paid, which was by reason of a mistake made by the listers of said Halifax in the return of the grand list of said town for the year 1796.

Passed October 30, 1798.

A true copy,

Attest, Ros. Hopkins, Sec'y.

AN ACT DIRECTING THE TREASURER OF THIS STATE TO PAY
NAHOR HAYWARD [HAYWORD], FIRST CONSTABLE OF
JAMAICA FOR THE YEAR 1797, THE SUM
THEREIN MENTIONED

OCTOBER 30TH, 1798

Whereas, it appears to this Assembly that the warrant of the treasurer dircted to the first constable of Jamaica, for the year 1797, contained 300 acres more than the selectmen of said town could tax. Therefore,

It is hereby Enacted by the General Assembly of the State of Vermont, That the treasurer be, and he hereby is directed to pay unto Nahor Hayword, the sum of three dollars.

Passed October 30, 1798.

A true record,

Attest, Ros. Hopkins, Sec'y.

AN ACT GRANTING TO JOSEPH HAWKINS, LEAVE TO RAISE BY
LOTTERY, THE SUM OF TWO THOUSAND DOLLARS

OCTOBER 30TH, 1798

Sec. 1. *It is hereby Enacted* by the General Assembly of the State of Vermont, That leave be, and hereby is granted to Joseph Hawkins (late of Alburgh in said state), to raise the sum of two thousand dollars after deducting all the prizes and expenses of said lottery.

Sec. 2. *And it is hereby further Enacted,* That the said Joseph Hawkins be, and he hereby is appointed manager of said lottery with full power to appoint such assistant manager as to him shall seem proper. Provided nevertheless, That the said Joseph Hawkins, before he proceed to sell, utter or publish any ticket or tickets under color or by virtue of this act, shall make, execute and deliver to the treasurer of the State of Vermont, a bond with sufficient surety to the satisfaction of said treasurer, in the penal sum of ten thousand dollars, conditioned for the faithful performance of the trust reposed in the said Joseph Hawkins by virtue of this act.

Sec. 3. *And it is hereby further Enacted,* That the state of Vermont shall and will in no wise be accountable for said lottery.[1]

Passed October 30, 1798.

A true copy,

Attest, Ros. Hopkins, Sec'y.

AN ACT LAYING A TAX OF ONE CENT PER ACRE ON THE TOWN OF HARDWICK

OCTOBER 31ST, 1798

It is hereby Enacted by the General Assembly of the State of Vermont, That there be, and hereby is laid a tax of one cent on each acre of land in the town of Hardwick, in the county of Caledonia, public rights excepted, for the purpose of making and repairing roads and building bridges in said town, to be expended under the direction of Charles Bayley, John Bridgman and Samuel Fuller, who are hereby appointed a committee to superintend the expenditure of said tax. And any justice of the peace in the county of Caledonia, is hereby authorised to issue his warrant to Paul Spooner of said Hardwick, who is hereby appointed a collector to collect said tax. And said collector is hereby made accountable to said committee for the amount of said tax; and said committee and collector are hereby directed in the collecting, disposing, and accounting for the monies raised by said tax, to conform themselves in all things to the directions of the statute entitled "An act regulating the disposition of monies raised by taxes, in the several towns for the purpose of making and repairing roads and bridges," passed November 2d, 1796.[2]

AN ACT APPOINTING A COLLECTOR OF A LAND TAX IN JOHNSTON [JOHNSON]

OCTOBER 31ST, 1798

Whereas, by an act passed at the last session of this Legislature

---

1. State Papers of Vermont, Vol. XI, *General Petitions,* 1797-1799, "For a Lottery for the Benefit of a Blind Person," 315.
2. State Papers of Vermont, Vol. XI, *General Petitions,* 1797-1799, "For a tax on Land to Build and Repair Roads," 266.

laying a tax of three cents per acre on the lands in Johnson for the purpose of building bridges, John McConnel was appointed collector of said tax. And whereas the said collector declines to serve in the said office. Therefore,

It is hereby Enacted by the General Assembly of the State of Vermont, That John McDaniel of Hyde Park, be, and he is hereby appointed a collector of said tax in the room of the said John McConnel. And the said collector appointed by this act is in the same manner empowered and directed, and rendered responsible and accountable, as the aforesaid collector, now discharged, was in and by said act empowered, and made accountable. And,

It is hereby further Enacted, That on application of the present collector appointed in and by this act, to the said former collector, for that purpose, the said former collector shall immediately render an account of such taxes as he may have received, from the proprietors, if any, and also pay over the monies received, to said present collector, who shall give his receipt therefore. And the said former collector, shall be held in law accountable, to any person who may be injured by his neglecting or refusing to deliver over all such accounts and monies, or if an error or incorrectness in such accounting.

AN ACT ASSESSING A TAX OF THREE CENTS PER ACRE ON THE LANDS IN
THE TOWN OF LANDGROVE FOR THE PURPOSE THEREIN MENTIONED

OCTOBER 31ST, 1798

It is hereby Enacted by the General Assembly of the State of Vermont, That there be, and hereby is assessed a tax of three cents on each acre of land in the township of Landgrove in the county of Bennington (public rights excepted), for the purpose of making roads and building bridges in said town, to be expended under the direction of David Carpenter, Peabody Utley, and Daniel Tuttle, who are hereby appointed a committee to superinted the expenditure of said tax. And any justice of the peace within and for the county of Bennington is hereby authorised to issue his warrant to Oliver Utley to collect said tax, who is hereby appointed a collector of said tax; and said collector is hereby made accountable to said committee for the amount of said tax; and said committee and collector are hereby directed in the collection, expenditure and accounting for said tax, to conform themselves in all things to the directions of the statute of this State entitled

"An act regulating the disposition of monies raised by tax on lands in the several towns for the purpose of making and repairing roads and building bridges," passed November 2d, 1796.[1]

AN ACT APPOINTING A COLLECTOR OF TAX IN THE TOWN OF MILTON

OCTOBER 31ST, 1798

Whereas, by an act assessing a tax of two cents on the acre in the town of Milton, passed at the last session of the Legislature, Abel Drury of said Milton was appointed a collector, and whereas the said Drury has sold his property in, and removed from said Milton. Therefore,

It is hereby Enacted by the General Assembly of the State of Vermont, That Moses Davis of the said Milton be, and hereby is appointed collector of said tax in the room of said Abel Drury, which said new collector is vested with the same powers and is hereby made accountable in the discharge of said office, in the same manner as if he had been the original collector appointed for the collection of said tax.

AN ACT ANNEXING PART OF THE TOWN OF WELLS
TO THE TOWN OF POULTNEY

OCTOBER 31ST, 1798

Sec. 1. *It is hereby Enacted* by the General Assembly of the State of Vermont, That the Northwest part of the town of Wells, in the county of Rutland be, and the same is hereby annexed to the town of Poultney, in said county, to wit, that part of said Wells lying north of the following line, beginning at the west corner of the town of Middletown, thence west to the east line of the town of Granville in the State of New York. And the inhabitants of said northwest part of Wells, so annexed to the town of Poultney, shall be forever hereafter, entitled to the same privileges and immunities in common with the other inhabitants of said Poultney.

Sec. 2. *And it is hereby further Enacted*, That the town of Poultney be, and it is hereby declared forever hereafter, to be entitled to such part of the rents, profits, and privileges, of all the public lands

1. State Papers of Vermont, Vol. XI, *General Petitions,* 1797-1799, "For a Tax on Land to Build and Repair Roads and Build Bridges," 261.

in the town of Wells, as shall be in proportion to the quantity of lands in and by this act, annexed to the town of Poultney as aforesaid.

Passed October 31, 1798.

A true record,

Attest, Ros. Hopkins, Sec'y.

AN ACT EMPOWERING THE PROPRIETORS OF THE TOWNSHIP OF CORNWALL TO AUTHENTICATE AND CONFIRM THEIR DIVISION

OCTOBER 31ST, 1798

Whereas, in the year one thousand seven hundred and seventy eight, the proprietors records of Cornwall were wholly destroyed by fire, in consequence of which it becomes extremely difficult to prove the legality of their first proprietors' meeting, which stood adjourned at the time said records were burned, on which the whole of said division depends.

It is hereby Enacted by the General Assembly of the State of Vermont, That the proprietors of the township of Cornwall aforesaid, are hereby authorised and empowered, at a proprietors' meeting notified agreeably to the present existing laws of this State, mentioning the business to be transacted at said meeting to pass any vote or votes, ratifying and confirming the votes of said proprietors, passed at their adjourned meeting as aforesaid, and to pass any other vote or votes, ratifying and confirming their division as aforesaid, which votes shall be good and valid in law to establish their former records and division, any law to the contrary notwithstanding.

Passed October 31, 1798.

A true record,

Attest, Ros. Hopkins, Sec'y.

AN ACT TO ENABLE THE PROPRIETORS OF BROOKFIELD IN THE COUNTY OF ORANGE, IN CONJUNCTION WITH THE LANDOWNERS TO RATIFY AND ESTABLISH THE DIVISION OF LANDS IN SAID TOWN

OCTOBER 31ST, 1798

Sec. 1. *It is hereby Enacted* by the General Assembly of the

State of Vermont, That the proprietors and landowners of the said town of Brookfield be, and they are hereby authorised and empowered to call a meeting of said proprietors and landowners, in the manner prescribed for the calling of proprietors' meetings in this state, notifying the particular business to be transacted at said meeting. And said proprietors and landowners when so met, shall have the right of voting according to the interest they have in the lands in said town. *Provided nevertheless,* That there shall be accounted and recorded, but one vote to any original proprietors' right, and where there shall be a number of persons claiming under the same original right, such persons shall be allowed their vote, according to the interest they so claim; and a majority of interest so claimed shall determine the vote for said right, under which said several persons shall so claim.

Sec. 2. *And it is hereby further Enacted,* That said proprietor and landowners, proceeding in manner aforesaid, shall have the right to ratify and confirm all or any part of the former votes or proceedings of said proprietors relative to the division of their lands into severalty, and to rectify any errors or mistakes which have taken place in the records of their said proceedings, relative to said division, so as to render said votes and proceedings, conformably to the true intent and meaning of said proprietors, at their said former meetings. And the votes and proceedings of said proprietors, so ratified and confirmed; and the votes rectifying any errors or mistakes in said proceedings, heretofore had by said proprietors relative to the division of said lands, shall be received in any court in this State as evidence of a legal division in said town, in as full and ample a manner as though the same proceedings and votes, had been strictly conformably to the laws of this State, at the time the same were had and passed by said proprietors. And this act being recorded in the records of said proprietors, may at all times be given in evidence of the authority and power of said proprietors and landowners to legalize the former proceedings of said proprietors as aforesaid.[1]

Passed October 31, 1798.

A true record,

Attest, Ros. Hopkins, Sec'y.

---

1. State Papers of Vermont, Vol. XI, *General Petitions,* 1797-1799, "For Confirmation of Proprietors' Proceedings," 292.

AN ACT FOR THE PURPOSE OF ANNEXING THE TRACT OF LAND CALLED
AND KNOWN BY THE NAME OF KNIGHT'S GORE, IN THE COUNTY OF
FRANKLIN, TO THE TOWN OF BAKERSFIELD: AND A PART OF
THE TOWN OF BAKERSFIELD TO THE TOWN OF
ENOSBURGH

OCTOBER 31ST, 1798

Sec. 1. *It is hereby Enacted* by the General Assembly of the State of Vermont, That all that tract of land in the county of Franklin, called and known by the name of Knight's Gore, be, and the same is hereby annexed to and incorporated with the town of Bakersfield.

Sec. 2. *And it is hereby further Enacted,* That the tract of land hereinafter described, be, and the same is hereby annexed to, and incorporated with the town of Enosburgh, to wit, beginning at a hemlock tree, formerly marked for the north east corner of Smithfield, and running south twenty five degrees west, to the south west corner of Enosburgh, thence north eighty two degrees and twenty minutes west, to the easterly line of Fairfield, thence north twenty degrees east, to the north easterly corner thereof, thence to the first mentioned bounds.[1]

Passed October 31, 1798.

A true copy,

Attest, Ros. Hopkins, Sec'y.

AN ACT POINTING OUT THE METHOD OF ESTABLISHING THE LANDS
DIVIDED INTO SEVERALTY IN THE TOWN OF NEWHAVEN,
ACCORDING TO THE LINES THEREOF

OCTOBER 31ST, 1798

Whereas through various accidents, which have happened during the American war, the proprietors records of said town of Newhaven have been almost wholly lost and destroyed, which renders the few remaining records which were not lost, as aforesaid, totally useless. And whereas the lines of the first, second and third divisions of said towns, were by a committee appointed by said proprietors regularly run, and have never been disputed, and the original minutes of some

---

1. State Papers of Vermont, Vol. XI, *General Petitions,* 1797-1799, "For Annexation of a Gore of Land to a Town," 224.

parts of said divisions, as taken by the surveyors, are now existing, and there are people who now know the situation of the allotment of said lands which will add very much to benefit said proprietors, in proceeding to regulate the same, and were said persons not living, the title of the landowners in said town would be in a dangerous situation.

Sec. 1. *It is hereby Enacted* by the General Assembly of the State of Vermont, That the proprietors of said Newhaven, at a legal meeting warned for that purpose, shall have power to establish each division made in said town, agreeably to the respective lines of said divisions, as they were respectively laid, so as to do the least injustice, to the inhabitants of said town, and a plan of said town, made out under the direction of said proprietors, agreeably to the actual original lines of said division, and confirmed as a plan of said town, by the proprietors aforesaid, shall be deemed full and conclusive evidence of the allotment, and division of said lands, in any court in this State, by virtue of this act, the same as though said records were now regularly existing.

Sec. 2. *And it is hereby further Enacted,* That the fourth and fifth divisions in said town, shall contain respectively, the quantity of land which was voted by said proprietors, to compose said division. And that the said proprietors, together with the landowners, at a legal meeting warned for that purpose, shall have liberty to tax the lands in said town, such sum as they may consider necessary to defray the expense of resurveying and making out the plan aforesaid, not to exceed three cents per acre.

Sec. 3. *And it is hereby further Enacted,* That an act passed at the session of the Legislature of this State, in the year one thousand seven hundred and ninety seven, relative to the resurveying and making out a plan of said town, be, and hereby is repealed.

Passed October 31, 1798.

A true copy,

Attest, Ros. Hopkins, Sec'y.

AN ACT IN ALTERATION OF AN ACT, ENTITLED "AN ACT FOR DIVIDING
THE TOWN OF WESTMINSTER INTO TWO PARISHES," PASSED
OCTOBER NINETEENTH ONE THOUSAND SEVEN HUNDRED
AND EIGHTY SEVEN

OCTOBER 31ST, 1798

Whereas, the inhabitants of said town of Westminster, at their meeting holden on the fourth day of September, one thousand seven hundred and ninety eight, voted that in future the town and freemen's meeting of said town, should be holden alternately, in the western and eastern parishes in said town, and have, by their representative, requested that an act may be passed for that purpose. Therefore,

It is hereby Enacted by the General Assembly of the State of Vermont, That all the town and freemen's meetings of the inhabitants and freemen of said town, whether stated, special or adjourned, shall be holden from and after the first day of March next, until the first day of March, which will be in the year one thousand eight hundred, in such place in the western parish in said town, as the selectmen or the inhabitants thereof, in a legal meeting shall appoint. And all such meetings which shall be holden in said town, after the said first day of March next thereafter, shall be holden in the eastern parish at such place as shall be agreed upon, as aforesaid, and thus alternately, from year to year, in each of said parishes, forever thereafter.

Passed October 31, 1798.

A true copy,

Attest, Ros. Hopkins, Sec'y.

AN ACT ASSESSING A LAND TAX ON THE TOWNSHIP OF WASHINGTON,
ORANGE, HARRIS'S GORE, GROTON AND PEACHAM FOR THE
PURPOSE THEREIN MENTIONED

OCTOBER 31ST, 1798

It is hereby Enacted by the General Assembly of the State of Vermont, That there be, and hereby is assessed a tax of two cents on each acre of land in the township of Washington, and three cents on each acre of land in the township of Orange, in the county of Orange, and also three cents on each acre of land in Harris's Gore and Groton, and one cent on each acre of land in the township of

Peacnam, in the county of Caledonia, public rights excepted, for the purpose of laying out and making a county road from the court house in Chelsea in the county of Orange, through said towns to the court house in Danville, in the county of Caledonia, as surveyed by James Whitelaw and Elias Curtis, Esquires, a committee appointed for that purpose, to be expended by order and under the direction of Nathan Coggswell and Bether Bartholomew for the town of Washington, Sanborn Batcheldor, Charles C. Nelson and Joseph Thayer for the town of Orange and Harris's Gore, and Nicholas C. Buzzel, Jonathan McComber[?] and John Cameron for the town of Groton, and Ashbell Martin and David Merrill for the town of Peacham who are hereby appointed committees, respectively, in the several towns for that purpose. And any justice of the peace in said county of Orange is hereby empowered to issue his warrant to Aaron Stiles to collect said tax in the town of Washington, and also to Thomas S. Paine to collect said taxes in Orange and Harris's Gore; and any justice of the peace in the county of Caledonia is hereby empowered to issue his warrant to Benjamin Bailey, to collect said tax in the town of Groton, and also to Timothy Hall to collect said tax in the town of Peacham, who are hereby appointed collectors to collect said taxes in the several towns for which they are respectively appointed. And said collectors are hereby made accountable to said committees, respectively, for the amount of said taxes. And said collectors and committees are hereby directed to govern themselves in collecting, disposing, and accounting for the monies raised by said taxes, agreeably to an act entitled, "An act regulating the disposition of monies raised by tax on lands in the several towns for the purpose of making and repairing roads and building bridges," passed November 2d, 1796, except that part of said act which directs committees of land taxes to lay out and survey roads in the month of May.[1]

AN ACT LAYING A TAX OF TWO CENTS PER ACRE ON THE TOWNSHIP OF WARREN

OCTOBER 31ST, 1798

It is hereby Enacted by the General Assembly of the State of Vermont, That there be, and hereby is laid a tax of two cents on each acre of land in the township of Warren, in the county of Addison

---

1. State Papers of Vermont, Vol. XI, *General Petitions,* 1797-1799, "For a Tax on Land to Build a Road," 291.

(public rights excepted), for the purpose of making and repairing roads and building bridges in said town, to be expended under the direction of Benjamin Page, Samuel Lord, and Joseph Raymond, who are hereby appointed a committee to superintend the expenditures of said tax. And any justice of the peace within the county of Addison is hereby authorised to issue his warrant to Reed Sherman of said Warren, who is hereby appointed a collector to collect said tax. And said collector is hereby made accountable to said committee for the amount of said tax. And said collector and committee are hereby directed in the collecting, expending, and accounting for said tax, to govern themselves in all things by the directions of the statute of this State entitled, "An act regulating the disposition of monies raised by tax on lands in the several towns for the purpose of making and repairing roads and building bridges," passed November 2d, A.D. 1796.[1]

AN ACT LAYING THREE CENTS ON EACH ACRE OF LAND IN THE TOWN OF CRAFTSBURY, PUBLIC LANDS EXCEPTED

OCTOBER 31ST, 1798

It is hereby Enacted by the General Assembly of the State of Vermont, That there be, and hereby is assessed a tax of three cents on each acre of land in the town of Craftsbury, in the county of Caledonia, public lands excepted, for the purpose of making and repairing roads and building bridges in said town. And Ebenezer Crafts, Daniel Davison, and Robert Trumbull are hereby appointed a committee to superintend the expenditure of said tax. And any justice of the peace in the county of Caledonia is hereby empowered to issue his warrant to Joseph Scott to collect said tax, who is hereby appointed a collector to collect the same. And the said collector is hereby made accountable to the said committee for the amount of said tax; and the said committee and collector are hereby directed to govern themselves in laying out said roads and in collecting and expending said tax, agreeably to a statute law of this State regulating the expenditure of monies raised for the purpose of making roads and building bridges &c., passed November second 1796.[2]

---

1. State Papers of Vermont, Vol. XI, *General Petitions,* 1797-1799, "For a Tax on Land to Build a Road," 264.
2. State Papers of Vermont, Vol. XI, *General Petitions,* 1797-1799, "For a Tax on Land to Build and Repair Roads and Bridges," 169.

CONSTITUTING AND ESTABLISHING A COMPANY OF ARTILLERY
AN ACT IN ADDITION TO AN AMENDING AN ACT ENTITLED "AN ACT
IN THE TOWN OF RUTLAND"

OCTOBER 31ST, 1798

Whereas, by the act aforesaid, said company is annexed to the second brigade and second division of the militia of this State. And whereas the said company have prayed that they may be subject, as other companies of artillery, to be annexed to the regiment out of which they are raised. Therefore,

It is hereby Enacted by the General Assembly of the State of Vermont, That said company of artillery be, and hereby is made subject and liable to be annexed to the said regiment out of which the same is raised, in the same way and manner as other companies of artillery in this State now are, or hereafter may, from time to time, be liable by law to be annexed, any thing in said act to the contrary notwithstanding.

Passed October 31, 1798.

A true record,

Attest, Ros. Hopkins, Sec'y.

AN ACT GRANTING A NEW TRIAL IN A CERTAIN CAUSE THEREIN
MENTIONED

OCTOBER 31ST, 1798

Whereas, it has been represented to this Assembly by John Shumway of Dorset, in the county of Bennington, that Nehemiah Fuller of Fitzburgh, in the county of Worcester, in the commonwealth of Massachusetts, was an original grantee in the town of Brandon, in the county of Rutland, that on the third day of March A. D. one thousand, seven hundred and seventy four he sold and conveyed the same to Nathan Metcalf; that on the seventh day of July 1774, said Metcalf sold and conveyed the same to Abel Stevens; that on the fourteenth day of October 1774, said Stevens sold and conveyed the same to said John Shumway; that on the twenty first day of October 1774, said Shumway sold and conveyed the same to Elisha Strong, and that said Strong, or his administrators, sold and conveyed the first lot, containing one hundred and ten acres of said right, to Samuel

Kelsey who took possession of the same; that afterwards at the county court holden at Rutland, within and for the county of Rutland, on the third Tuesday of November, A. D. 1788, William Maxwell of Stow, in the State of Massachusetts, as lessor of the plaintiff, commenced his action of trespass and ejectment against the said Samuel Kelsey, to recover possession of said lot; and afterward at the term of said court in November term 1789, recovered judgment for the possession of said lot, by producing evidence of a title adverse to the title aforesaid; and that the said Kelsey did not put said cause to trial by jury or shew in evidence the title so derived as aforesaid; and that he, the said John Shumway, has had no day in court to show the same. And that an action of *scire facias* is now pending in said court, against said Kelsey for the possession of said lot. Therefore,

Sec. 1. *It is hereby Enacted* by the General Assembly of the State of Vermont, That a new trial be, and is hereby granted in said cause. And that said John Shumway be admitted, as voucher in the title to said Kelsey, of the lot aforesaid, to defend said cause. And the county court, within and for the county of Rutland, at their term in March next, are hereby empowered and directed, to cause the said action to be brought forward, and entered on the docket of said court, and to proceed therein as in other actions of a like nature. *Provided, nevertheless,* That the said John Shumway, shall pay unto the said William Maxwell, or his attorney, all legal costs that have arisen in said action of *scire facias,* before the said court shall proceed in the trial of said cause.[1]

Passed October 31, 1798.

A true copy,

Attest, Ros. Hopkins, Sec'y.

AN ACT APPOINTING A COMMITTEE TO LAY OUT, ALTER AND STRAIGHTEN
THE ROAD FROM VERGENNES THROUGH CASTLETON TO BENNINGTON

OCTOBER 31ST, 1798

Whereas, a lottery has been granted to Chancey Langdon and others to repair and amend the public road from Vergennes to Bennington and Troy, in the towns of Sudbury, Hubbardton and Castle-

---

1. State Papers of Vermont, Vol. XI, *General Petitions,* 1797-1799, "For a New Trial in An Ejectment Suit," 228.

ton, by an act of the Legislature at their session at Rutland in October A.D. one thousand seven hundred and ninety six. And by said act no authority or right is given to the managers of said lottery to turn or lay out said road; and it appears that many alterations are necessary to be made in several towns through which said road lies, to lessen the distance and accommodate the public for travelling, previous to any further sum of money raised by such lottery, being expended in said road. Therefore,

Sec. 1. *It is hereby Enacted* by the General Assembly of the State of Vermont, That Samuel Strong of Vergennes, Ebenezer Wilson of Orwell, and Groove Moore of Rupert, be, and they are hereby appointed a committee to view, survey, lay out, and alter, or turn said road from Vergennes through Waltham, Weybridge, Cornwall, Whiting, Sudbury, Hubbardton, Castleton, Poultney, Wells, and to Colonel Elisha Averill's in Pawlet. And also to lay out and survey a road from the road to be laid out and surveyed as aforesaid, beginning near Simon Francis's dwelling house in said Wells, through the western part of the town of Pawlet, to Martin Smith's, on the southern line of said Pawlet, and that the aforesaid committee or either two of them, have the same authority and power, and be governed by the same rules and regulations to lay out, survey, turn, or alter said road in the towns aforesaid, as by a certain statute law of this State, entitled, "An act reducing into one the several acts for laying out, making, repairing and clearing highways," is given to selectmen in the several towns to which they respectively belong. And said committee are hereby directed to commence the survey of said road, on or before the first day of May next.

Sec. 2. *And it is hereby further Enacted,* That such road, laid out or turned by said committee as aforesaid, shall not be any way altered, but by the supreme court, or a committee by them appointed, on application of the selectmen of the town through which such road runs, any law to the contrary notwithstanding.

Passed October 31, 1798.

A true record,

Attest, Ros. Hopkins, Sec'y.

AN ACT ASSESSING A TAX OF TWO CENTS ON EACH ACRE OF LAND IN
THE TOWNSHIP OF DUXBURY FOR THE PURPOSE THEREIN
MENTIONED

NOVEMBER 1ST, 1798

It is hereby Enacted by the General Assembly of the State of
Vermont, That there be, and hereby is assessed a tax of two cents on
each acre of land in the township of Duxbury, in the county of Chittenden, public rights excepted, for the purpose of making and repairing roads and building bridges in said town, to be expended under
the direction of Benjamin Davis, Joseph Nash and Eleazer Wells, all of
said Duxbury, who are hereby appointed a committee to superintend
the expenditure of said tax. And any justice of the peace, within
the county of Chittenden is hereby empowered to issue his warrant to
Moses Heaton of said Duxbury, who is hereby appointed a collector,
to collect said tax; and said collector is hereby made accountable to
said committee for the amount of said tax. And said collector and
committee are hereby directed in the collecting, expending, and accounting for the monies raised by said tax, to govern themselves in
all things agreeably to the statute of this State, entitled, "An act
regulating the disposition of monies raised by tax on lands in the
several towns for the purpose of making and repairing roads & building
bridges," passed November 2d, 1796.[1]

AN ACT ASSESSING A TAX OF TWO CENTS PER ACRE ON THE TOWNSHIP
OF MONTGOMERY FOR THE PURPOSE THEREIN MENTIONED

NOVEMBER 1ST, 1798

It is hereby Enacted by the General Assembly of the State of
Vermont, That there be and hereby is assessed a tax of two cents on
each acre of land in the township of Montgomery, in the county of
Franklin, public rights excepted, for the purpose of making and repairing roads and building bridges in said town, to be expended under
the direction of Joshua Clap, Thomas Byrd and Russell S. Richards,
who are hereby appointed a committee to superintend the expenditure
of said tax. And any justice of the peace within the said county of
Franklin is hereby authorised to issue his warrant to Samuel Barnard

---

1. State Papers of Vermont, Vol. XI, *General Petitions,* 1797-1799, "For a Tax on
Land to Build and Repair Roads and Bridges," 280.

of said Montgomery, who is hereby appointed a collector to collect said tax. And said collector is hereby made accountable to said committee for the amount of said tax; and said committee and collector are hereby directed in the expending, collecting, and accounting for the monies raised by said tax, to govern themselves in all things agreeably to the directions of the statute of this state entitled, "An act regulating the disposition of monies raised by tax on lands in the several towns for the purpose of making and repairing roads and building bridges," passed November 2d, 1796.[1]

AN ACT ASSESSING A TAX OF THREE CENTS PER ACRE ON THE TOWNSHIP OF BERKSHIRE FOR THE PURPOSE THEREIN MENTIONED

NOVEMBER 1ST, 1798

It is hereby Enacted by the General Assembly of the State of Vermont, That there be, and hereby is assessed a tax of three cents on each acre of land in the township of Berkshire in the county of Franklin, public rights excepted, for the purpose of making and repairing roads, and building bridges in said town, to be expended under the direction of Elisha Sheldon, Stephen Royce, and Abraham Hard, who are hereby appointed a committee to superintend the expenditure of said tax. And any justice of the peace within said county of Franklin is hereby directed to issue his warrant to Timothy R. Barker, to collect said tax, who is hereby appointed a collector of said tax; and said collector is hereby made accountable to said committee for the amount of said tax. And said committee are hereby directed in the collection, expenditure, and accounting for said tax, to conform themselves in all things to the direction of the statute of this State entitled, "An act regulating the disposition of monies raised by tax on lands in the several towns, for the purpose of making and repairing roads and building bridges," passed November 2d, 1796.

AN ACT LAYING THREE CENTS ON EACH ACRE OF LAND IN THE TOWNSHIP OF BILLYMEAD, PUBLIC RIGHTS EXCEPTED

NOVEMBER 1ST, 1798

It is hereby Enacted by the General Assembly of the State of

---

1. State Papers of Vermont, Vol. XI, *General Petitions,* 1797-1799, "For a Tax on Land to Build and Repair Roads and Build Bridges," 307.

Vermont, That there be, and hereby is asesssed a tax of three cents on each acre of land in the township of Billymead, in the county of Caledonia, public rights excepted, for the purpose of making roads and building bridges, in and through said town. And Enoch Blake, Samuel Cahoon, and Peter Atwood are hereby appointed a committee to superintend the expenditure of said tax; and any justice of the peace in the county of Caledonia is hereby empowered to issue his warrant to James Cahoon to collect said tax, who is hereby appointed a collector to collect the same. And the said collector is hereby made accountable to the said committee for the amount of said tax; and the said committee and collector, are herby directed to govern themselves in laying out said roads, and in collecting and expending said tax, agreeably to the statute law of this State regulating the expenditure of monies raised for the purpose of making roads, and building bridges &c., passed November 2d, 1796.[1]

AN ACT ASSESSING A TAX OF TWO CENTS PER ACRE ON ALL THE LANDS IN THE TOWNSHIP OF BURKE AND THREE CENTS PER ACRE ON ALL THE LANDS IN THE TOWNSHIP OF WESTMORE (PUBLIC RIGHTS EXCEPTED) FOR THE PURPOSE OF MAKING AND REPAIRING ROADS AND BUILDING BRIDGES

NOVEMBER 1ST, 1798

It is hereby Enacted by the General Assembly of the State of Vermont, That a tax of two cents per acre be, and hereby is assessed on all the lands in the township of Burke, and three cents per acre on all the lands in the township of Westmore (public rights excepted), in the county of Caledonia, for the purpose of making and repairing roads and building bridges in said towns, and the said monies shall be expended in the aforesaid towns respectively, from which by this act they are to be collected, and on such roads and bridges as the committee appointed by this act shall see fit to direct. And,

It is hereby further Enacted, That David Porter, William Woodruff, and John Anthony, Junr., be, and they are hereby appointed a committee to lay out said roads, and superintend the expenditure of said taxes. And any justice of the peace for the county of Caledonia

---

1. State Papers of Vermont, Vol. XI, *General Petitions,* 1797-1799, "For a Tax on Land to Build Roads," 194.

is hereby authorised to issue his warrant to John Woodruff of Burke, who is hereby appointed a collector to collect said taxes, and is hereby made accountable to the committee for the same. And the committee and collector, in the collection and expenditure of the above taxes, are hereby directed to govern themselves agreeably to the statute of this State regulating the disposition of monies raised by taxes on lands for the purpose of making & repairing roads & building bridges, passed November 2d, 1796.[1]

AN ACT LAYING A TAX OF THREE MILLS ON THE DOLLAR, ON THE POLLS AND RATEABLE ESTATES OF THE INHABITANTS IN THE COUNTY OF ORANGE

NOVEMBER 1ST, 1798

Whereas, for the purpose of discharging the debts due from said county it appears necessary to lay a tax on said county. Therefore,

Sec. 1. *It is hereby Enacted* by the General Assembly of the State of Vermont, That there be, and hereby is granted a tax of three mills on the dollar on the list of the polls and rateable estate of the inhabitants of the county of Orange, for the year one thousand seven hundred and ninety eight, to be paid in county orders, notes issued by the treasurer of said county, or in lawful money to be collected and paid into the treasury, by the first day of July, one thousand seven hundred and ninety nine.

Sec. 2. *And it is hereby further Enacted,* That the treasurer of said county have, and he hereby has granted to him, the same power in issuing warrants and extents as are vested in the treasurer of the State in collecting state taxes, and the first constables of the respective towns in said county, are hereby empowered, and it is hereby made their duty, to proceed in the collection of said tax, and paying the same into the county treasury, in the same manner as it is made their duty by law, to collect state taxes, and pay them into the state treasury; and they are hereby liable in the same manner for neglect of duty.

Passed November 1, 1798.

A true record,

Attest, Ros. Hopkins, Sec'y.

---

1. State Papers of Vermont, Vol. XI, *General Petitions,* 1797-1799, "For a Tax on Land to Build Roads and Bridges," 240.

AN ACT GRANTING AN APPEAL TO SYLVANUS LEARNED IN THE CASE
THEREIN MENTIONED

NOVEMBER 1ST, 1798

Whereas, it appears to this Assembly that Moses Chaplin of Rowley, in the county of Essex and Commonwealth of Massachusetts, on the 27th day of January, A.D. 1798, prayed out a writ of attachment in an action in his favor against Sylvanus Learned, signed by and returnable before David Hopkinson, justice of the peace for the county of Caledonia, at his, the said David's dwelling house in Guildhall, in said county of Caledonia, on the 5th day of February A.D. 1798, at one oclock before noon. And whereas it appears that by unfair practices, the said Moses obtained a judgment on default against the said Sylvanus Learned, for the sum of thirty three dollars and twenty cents debts or damages, and costs of suit taxed by said justice at one dollar ninety three cents, so that the said Sylvanus hath not had a fair opportunity to have the said cause heard and determined on the merits of the same. To the end, therefore, that justice may be done in the premises;

It is hereby Enacted by the General Assembly of the State of Vermont, That the said David Hopkins, justice of the peace as aforesaid, may and he is hereby directed to grant an appeal to the said Sylvanus in the aforesaid cause, to the next stated term of the county court in the county of Caledonia, upon the said Sylvanus producing good and sufficient bonds for prosecuting the same to effect. And the said county court, for said county of Calendonia are hereby authorised and directed to receive and enter said appeal, and to hear and determine said cause in the same manner as though judgment had been rendered by said justice on the merits of said cause, and the said appeal had been prayed for and entered in due time.[1]

Passed November 1, 1798.

A true record,

Attest, Ros. Hopkins, Sec'y.

---

1. State Papers of Vermont, Vol. **XI**, *General Petitions,* 1797-1799, "For Voiding a Judgment at Law," 191.

AN ACT GRANTING RELIEF TO SETH WETMORE

NOVEMBER 1ST, 1798

Whereas, it has been represented by Seth Wetmore of Middlebury in the county of Addison, that by a train of misfortunes, equally impossible to be by him foreseen as prevented, he is rendered unable to pay his just debts, and this assembly are fully satisfied as to the truth of this representation. Therefore,

Sec. 1. *It is hereby Enacted* by the General Assembly of the State of Vermont, That Samuel Mattocks, John Chipman, and Roswell Hopkins, Esquires, be, and hereby are appointed commissioners to receive the estate of the said Seth Wetmore, into their custody for the purpose of discharging the debts due by the said Seth Wetmore to his respective creditors. And they are hereby fully empowered to sue for and recover, in their own names, as commissioners, all debts, dues, and demands, which the said Seth shall or may have against any person or persons whatever, and on payment being made, their discharges to grant, in as full and ample a manner, as he the said Seth could have done, before the passing of this act. Provided always that each of the said commissioners, before entering upon any part of the duties by this act assigned to them, shall take the following oath, before a judge of the supreme court of this State, or a judge of the county court of the county of Addison, to wit, "You, being appointed by an act of the Legislature of this State entitled, 'An act granting relief to Seth Wetmore', one of the commissioners to receive the estate of said Seth Wetmore, for the purpose of discharging his debts, do solemnly swear, that without partiality to the said Seth Wetmore, and with due regard to all and each creditor, you will receive and distribute his estate, real and personal as the same shall come into your hands, amongst his respective creditors in manner and form as directed by said act. And you do further solemnly swear that you will not give your consent to grant to him, the said Seth Wetmore, the certificate hereinafter mentioned, as proof of his discharge from all his debts until you are clearly convinced that he, the said Seth Wetmore, has well and truly done and performed every matter and thing expected from, and enjoined on him by this act. And that he has not fraudulently or intentionally, directly or indirectly, in any manner, way or form whatever, disposed of any part of his estate real or personal with an intent to defraud or deceive all or any of his said creditors, so help you God."

Sec. 2. *And it is hereby further Enacted,* That the said commissioners being first duly sworn as aforesaid, are hereby fully authorised and empowered to call upon the said Seth Wetmore, to deliver all his estate, real and personal, to them or either of them, whose duty it shall then be, to notify the creditors of the said Seth Wetmore, to assemble at such time and place as they shall think proper (provided always, that the place shall be within the county of Addison aforesaid), at which time and place it shall be the duty of the Commissioners aforesaid, and they are hereby directed and empowered to make distribution into and amongst the said creditors in proportion to the claims and demands which shall then be exhibited to the said Commissioners, and appear to them to be really and justly due.

Sec. 3. *And it is hereby further Enacted,* That it shall be the duty of the aforesaid commissioners to notify the creditors above mentioned, by a publication made for that purpose in the newspapers printed within this State in the towns of Bennnigton, Rutland, Vergennes, and Windsor; in the Massachusetts Mercury in Boston, the Connecticut Courant at Hartford, and the Spectator in the City of New York, which publication shall be continued in each of the said papers for at least the space of three months successively, the last of which publications shall be at least nine months previous to the time which shall be affixed by such publication of the said commissioners, for the creditors of the said Seth to exhitit their claims against him.

Sec. 4. *And it is hereby further Enacted,* That the said Commissioners be, and they are hereby directed in making the distribution of his, the said Seth Wetmore estate, amongst his creditors, to retain and deliver to him, the said Seth, for his sole use & benefit forever, all such cloathing as they shall deem proper.

Sec. 5. *And it is hereby further Enacted,* That if said Commissioners shall at any time discover any estate, real or personal, belonging to the said Seth Wetmore, directly or indirectly, and which it shall appear to them he wished to conceal from their view, they the said commissioners are hereby authorised to sue for, recover, take into their possession and dispose thereof, in like manner, as if the same had been actually delivered to them by the said Seth.

Sec. 6. *And it is hereby further Enacted,* That the said Seth Wetmore, previous to his obtainment of the certificate from the said commissioners as already mentioned, shall lodge with them full and sufficient proof, under the hand of one of the judges of the supreme court of this state, or under the hand of the first judge of the county court, of the county of Addison that he has taken the following oath: "You, Seth Wetmore, do solemnly swear, by the name of the ever living [God], that you have delivered over to the commissioners, by a law of this state directed to take charge thereof, without evasion, equivocation, or mental reservation, all your estate real and personal; and that you have, at no time heretofore, directly or indirectly disposed of any part thereof, in any manner or way whatever, with intent to defraud or deceive any of your just creditors, so help you God."

Sec. 7. *And* for the purpose of rendering to the creditors of the said Seth Wetmore every advantage to which they are legally entitled in his present situation,

It is hereby further Enacted, That if the said Seth Wetmore, shall at any time hereafter be convicted of having taken the above oath, with insidious and designing views, knowing that any fact thereof, at the time he took the same was false, he the said Seth, shall not only be liable to all the pains and penalties of wilful and corrupt perjury, but shall be forever excluded from any benefit rendered or intended to be rendered to him by this act, any thing therein to the contrary notwithstanding.

Sec. 8. *And it is hereby further Enacted,* That when the said commissioners shall judge that agreeably to the true meaning and intention of this act, he the said Seth Wetmore has in every respect, conformed himself thereto, having as they firmly believe, delivered up to them the whole of his estate, real and personal, for the purposes therein mentioned, they shall then grant to him the certificate contemplated in this act.

Sec. 9. *And it is hereby further Enacted,* That a summary of of the settlement made by the said commissioners with the said Seth Wetmore, with a copy of their certificate, contemplated by this act, to be given by them to him, being returned into and registered in the probate office, of the district of Addison, the said Seth Wetmore be, and he hereby is fully and finally released and discharged forever from all debts and demands of his said creditors, from all contracts entered into, and from all debts and demands of whatever name or nature they may be, which they, his said creditors, or any one of them may have against him at the time of passing this act. And that he the said Seth, his heirs, executors, and administrators, or either of them, shall never be liable to a prosecution in law, in any wise whatever, for the recovery of any debt or debts now due from him.

Sec. 10. *And it is hereby further Enacted,* That in all things to be done by said commissioners as in this act mentioned, the act of the majority shall be binding on the whole, and be in every respect held good and valid in law, except as to the certificate to be granted by them, to him the said Seth, which certificate shall not be valid in law until signed by all of them, except one of the said commissioners shall be deceased, before it is signed by the other two, in which case the signature of the two surviving commissioners shall be in every respect equally binding and conclusive, as if it had been signed by three.[1]

Passed November 1, 1798.

A true copy,

Attest, Ros. Hopkins, Sec'y.

AN ACT DIRECTING THE ISSUING OF A NEW CHARTER TO THE GRANTEES OF GOSHEN

NOVEMBER 1ST, 1798

Whereas, the Legislature of this State, on the 23.d day of February A.D. 1782, granted to certain persons, in said grant named, a tract of land equal to six miles square, bounded south on Philadelphia and west on the lands granted by the government of New Hampshire. And whereas a charter issued from the governor of this State, dated the second day of February, A.D. 1792, to the grantees therein mentioned, describing the following tracts of land, to wit, beginning at the southeasterly corner of Middlebury and running south nine degrees west, six miles and sixteen chains in the easterly line of Salisbury, to the southeasterly corner thereof, being a hard maple tree, marked "Salisbury corner, April 14th 1786," thence north sixty three degrees twenty two minutes east, two miles and seventeen chains to the southwesterly corner of Hancock, which is a little beach [beech] seventeen links south thirty degrees west from a large beach tree, marked "Hancock corner June 28, 1787;" thence North 33.d east in the westerly line of Hancock 'til it intercepts the south line of Ripton, thence North

---

1. State Papers of Vermont, Vol. XI, *General Petitions,* 1797-1799, "For an Act of Insolvency," 195.

81.d west in said southerly line of Ripton, to the bounds began at, containing about ten thousand acres. Also another tract, beginning at a stake eight links east from a beach tree marked "Walden corner 1786," and running north 54.d west in the north line of Walden, six miles to the northerly corner thereof, being a fir tree marked "No. 24 Greensboro' corner 1786," thence north 36.d east two miles, thirty three chains seventy eight links in the easterly line of Greensboro' to a little beach tree marked "Wheelock corner July 1788;" thence north 43.d 8m. east six miles and four chains in the southerly line of Wheelock to a spruce tree marked for the westerly corner of Danville, thence south 36.d west one mile and thirty two chains in the west line of Danville to the bounds began at containing 7,339 acres. Also another tract beginning at a spruce tree, in a swamp, in the north line of Orange marked "S. W. corner 1788," and running north thirty six degrees east three miles and seventeen chains to a beach tree, in the south line of Marshfield, marked "St. Andrews Gore August 12, 1788." Thence south 54.d east one mile thirty two chains and sixty seven links to a little spruce, 17 links north east from a beach tree marked "Part of Goshen, August 13, 1788;" thence south 36.d west three miles and five chains to a spruce tree in the north line of Orange marked "part of Goshen 1788." Thence north 57d. west in said north line of Orange to the bounds began at containing 2,828 acres. And whereas that tract of land above described, situate in the county of Addison, was by a mistake of the surveyor general bounded and described in said charter, differently from the original grant, whereby the said proprietors, altho' they obtained a grant and duly paid the granting fees, for a tract of land six miles square, did not by said charter acquire the evidence of their said grant agreeably to the true intent and meaning of the same, the same charter being at this time unrecorded. And Whereas Samuel Williams, Gideon Olin and Jonathan Parker, Junr., Esquires, have since the grant aforesaid, incautiously obtained a new grant of part of the land included in the said tract, on which last mentioned grant there have been no fees paid unto or assessed by the government of this State. And whereas by the interfering of the grants aforesaid, it becomes necessary that the Legislature should direct to whom the lands aforesaid should be chartered. Therefore,

Sec. 1. *It is hereby Enacted* by the General Assembly of the State of Vermont, That his Excellency the Governor of this State, be, and he is hereby authorised and requested, to receive a surrendery of the charter before mentioned, and to issue in due form of law a charter, to the same original grantees, agreeably to the original grant, bounding and describing the lands in said charter as follows, viz, beginning at the southeasterly corner of Salisbury and running north 9ᵈ. east six miles and sixteen chains, in the easterly line of said Salisbury, to the north east corner thereof; thence south 81ᵈ. east in the southwardly line of Ripton to the westerly line of Hancock, thence south thirty degrees west in the westerly line of said Hancock to the southwest corner thereof, thence easterly in the south line of said Hancock to the point where said line intersects the north line of Philadelphia; thence westerly in the northerly line of Philadelphia to the northwesterly corner thereof; thence northerly in the east line of Leicester to the bounds began at containing about thirteen thousand acres. And another tract beginning at a stake eight links east from beech tree marked "Walden corner 1786," and running north 54ᵈ. west in the north line of Walden six miles, to the northwesterly corner thereof, being a fir tree marked "No. 24 Greensboro' corner 1786," thence north 36ᵈ. east two miles thirty three chains and seventy eight links in the easterly line of Greensboro', to a little beech tree marked "Wheelock corner July 17, 1788," thence south 43ᵈ. 8m. east six miles and four chains in the southerly line of Wheelock to a spruce tree marked for the northwesterly corner of Danville; thence south 36ᵈ. west one mile and thirty two chains, in the west line of Danville to the bounds began at, containing 7,339 acres. And another tract beginning at a spruce tree in a swamp in the north line of Orange marked "S. W. corner 1788," and running north 36ᵈ. east three miles and seventeen chains to a beech tree, in the south line of Marshfield, marked "St. Andrews Gore August 12, 1788," thence south 54ᵈ. east one mile thirty two chains and sixty seven links to a little spruce, seventeen links north east from a beech tree marked "part of Goshen August 13, 1788;" thence south 36ᵈ. west three miles and five chains to a spruce tree in the north line of Orange marked "part of Goshen 1788;" thence north 57ᵈ. west in said north line of Orange to the bounds began at, containing two thousand & twenty eight acres.

Sec. 2. *And it is hereby further Enacted,* That the surrendery of the charter aforesaid, shall not affect, or be construed to affect the right of any person or persons, concerned in the sales of lands by virtue of a title derived from the charter so surrendered, and delivered up as aforesaid, but all sales, proprietors' meetings, and other transactions both for and against said proprietors, shall, in all courts and causes of justice, meet with the same construction, although the charter contemplated and directed to be issued by his act, should bear date with the day of making the original grant aforesaid, to wit, the twenty third day of February one thousand seven hundred and eighty two, any law usage or custom to the contrary notwithstanding.

Passed November 1, 1798.

A true record,

Attest, Ros. Hopkins, Sec'y.

AN ACT IN ADDITION TO AN ACT ENTITLED "AN ACT IN ADDITION TO AN ACT GRANTING TO ISRAEL CONVERSE, JOSIAH EDSON, STEPHEN FISK, AND TIMOTHY MITCHEL THE EXCLUSIVE PRIVILEGE OF RUNNING A STAGE FROM WINDSOR TO BURLINGTON FOR THE TIME THEREIN MENTIONED"

NOVEMBER 1ST, 1798

Whereas, it is represented to this Legislature, That it is very difficult and inconvenient, by the reason of the badness of roads to run a stage on the route mentioned in said act at present. Therefore,

It is hereby Enacted by the General Assembly of the State of Vermont, That said Israel Converse, Josiah Edson, Stephen Fisk and Timothy Mitchell, shall be entitled to all the privileges and benefits resulting from and appertaining to said act. *Provided,* they set up and run said stage agreeably to said act, within two years from January next, any law or statute of this state, to the contrary notwithstanding.

Passed November 1, 1798.

A true record,

Attest, Ros. Hopkins, Sec'y.

AN ACT GRANTING TO JOSEPH MUNN AN APPEAL IN A CERTAIN CAUSE THEREIN MENTIONED

NOVEMBER 1ST, 1798

Whereas, Joseph Munn, late of Rutland, in the county of Rutland, now of Sunderland, in the county of Bennington, has prefered his petition to this Assembly, setting forth that he has been greatly injured by a judgment had and rendered by the county court, holden at Rutland, in and for the county of Rutland, on the Monday next preceding the third Tuesday of March, A.D. one thousand seven hundred and ninety eight, in favor of one Gideon Horten, Junr., of Brandon, in said county of Rutland, against him the said Joseph Munn, for the sum of one thousand and thirty two dollars and thirty eight cents damages; and for the sum of thirty seven dollars ninety cents costs of suit; and said Joseph has prayed that an appeal may be granted him in said cause, from said judgment, to the supreme court. And it having been made to appear to this Assembly that justice so requires. Therefore,

Sec. 1 *It is hereby Enacted* by the General Assembly of the State of Vermont, That the county court in and for the county of Rutland, at their term which shall commence on the third Monday of November, one thousand seven hundred and ninety eight, be empowered, and said court is hereby empowered and directed, on motion of the said Joseph Munn, to grant him an appeal from said judgment, to the supreme court, to be holden at Rutland within and for said county of Rutland on the Tuesday next following the fourth Tuesday of January A.D. one thousand seven hundred and ninety nine; he, the said Joseph, procuring and entering bail for the prosecution of said appeal as the law requires in like cases. And the said supreme court are hereby authorised and directed to proceed to hear, try and determine said cause, so coming to said court, by appeal as aforesaid, in the same manner as though the appeal had been entered in said cause, in the common course of judicial proceedings, and to render judgment thereon, and award execution accordingly.

Sec. 2. *And it is hereby further Enacted,* That no further proceedings shall be had on said judgment, so rendered by said county court, as aforesaid, until the term of said court in November next, nor thereafter, provided said Joseph shall enter his appeal as aforesaid at said term of said supreme court.[1]

Passed November 1, 1798.

A true record,

Attest, Ros. Hopkins, Sec'y.

---

1. State Papers of Vermont, Vol. XI, *General Petitions,* 1797-1799, "For the Right to Enter an Appeal in a Court Case," 176.

AN ACT DIRECTING THE TREASURER OF THIS STATE TO CREDIT THE TOWN OF WEYBRIDGE, IN THE COUNTY OF ADDISON, THE SUM OF ELEVEN DOLLARS AND FIFTY SEVEN CENTS ON THE CENT TAX

NOVEMBER 1ST, 1798

Whereas, the treasurer warrant directed to the first constable of the town of Weybridge, directing the first constable of said town to collect one cent per acre on 8761 acres of land in said Weybridge; whereas, there is no more then 7557 acres of land in said town. Therefore,

It is hereby Enacted by the General Assembly of the State of Vermont, That the treasurer of this State be, and he hereby is directed to credit the first constable of said town of Weybridge, the sum of eleven dollars and fifty seven cents.

Passed November 1, 1798.

A true record,

Attest, Ros. Hopkins, Sec'y.

AN ACT DIRECTING THE TREASURER OF THIS STATE TO PAY THE SUM OF FOUR DOLLARS AND SEVENTY FIVE CENTS TO THE SELECTMEN OF DUMMERSTON

NOVEMBER 1ST, 1798

It is hereby Enacted by the General Assembly of the State of Vermont, That the treasurer of this state be, and he hereby is directed to pay to the selectmen of Dummerston, the sum of four dollars and seventy five cents for supporting Hannah Knowle, from the ninth day of October 1797, to the tenth day of November, 1797, agreeably to a law of this State making provision for the support of foreigners, and which was repealed on the tenth day of November last, aforesaid.[1]

Passed November 1, 1798.

A true record,

Attest, Roswell Hopkins, Sec'y.

---

1. State Papers of Vermont, Vol. XI, *General Petitions,* 1797-1799, "For Compensation for the support of an Indigent Foreigner," 263.

AN ACT DIRECTING THE TREASURER OF THIS STATE TO PAY JOSEPH
CHAMBERLAIN TWENTY DOLLARS

NOVEMBER 1ST, 1798

Whereas, it appears to this assembly that Joseph Chamberlain killed a grown wolf in this State, and by some mistake in taking a certificate thereof he failed of procuring the bounty by law allowed in such case. Therefore,

It is hereby Enacted by the General Assembly of the State of Vermont, That the treasurer be, and he is hereby directed to pay the said Joseph Chamberlain twenty dollars.[1]

Passed November 1st, 1798.

A true record,

Attest, Ros. Hopkins, Sec'y.

AN ACT DIRECTING THE TREASURER TO PAY JACOB FOWLER TWENTY
DOLLARS

NOVEMBER 1ST, 1798

Whereas, it appears to this assembly that Jacob Fowler killed a grown wolf in this state, and by some mistake in taking a certificate thereof he failed of procuring the bounty by law allowed in such case. Therefore,

It is hereby Enacted by the General Assembly of the State of Vermont, That the treasurer be, and is hereby directed to pay the said Jacob Fowler twenty dollars.[2]

Passed November 1, 1798.

A true record,

Attest, Ros. Hopkins, Sec'y.

1. State Papers of Vermont, Vol. XI, *General Petitions,* 1797-1799, "For a Bounty for Killing a Wolf," 255.
2. Ibid., "For a Bounty for Killing a Wolf," 250.

AN ACT DIRECTING THE MODE OF OBTAINING LICENSES, REGULATING INNS, AND HOUSES OF PUBLIC ENTERTAINMENT

NOVEMBER 2ND, 1798

Sec. 1. *It is hereby Enacted* by the General Assembly of the State of Vermont, That the justices of the peace, selectmen, constables, and grand jurors, of the respective towns in this State, or a major part of them, assembled for that purpose, shall some time at or within fifteen days after their annual town meeting in March, nominate such person or persons as they or a major part of them, shall judge fit and suitable, to keep inns or houses of public entertainment, in their respective towns for the year ensuing; which nomination being presented to the next county court in such county, such court may grant licenses to such person or persons or to such of them as such court shall see fit, in their discretion to license, to keep an house or houses of public entertainment for one whole year from the rising of such court; and such court shall grant license to no other person or persons, where such nomination shall have been made and presented to such court as aforesaid.

Sec. 2. *Provided nevertheless,* and it is hereby further Enacted, That if no nomination shall be made as aforesaid, in any town or precinct, in any county in this State, and presented to such court as aforesaid, such court may in their discretion, at any sitting of said court, grant license or licenses to such person as such court shall judge will best accommodate the public, with houses of public entertainment, in such town, place or precinct as aforesaid. Which license so granted as last aforesaid, shall be in force, until the expiration of one whole year, from and after the rising of the county court, in such county, to which the aforementioned nominations are directed to be presented as aforesaid.

Sec. 3. *And it is hereby further Enacted,* That it shall be the duty of the several county courts in this State, in their respective counties, in their discretion, according to the profits of the several tavern keepers, by them licensed, in their respective counties, to assess them, severally, in such sum or sums as they shall judge just and equitable, not less than one dollar, nor more than thirty dollars in any one instance. And such sum so assessed, shall be paid to the clerk of said county court in order drawn on the treasurer of said county, or in due bills issued by such treasurer, or in money, before any license shall be granted as aforesaid. And such clerk shall receive seventeen cents, and the judges of said court thirty four cents, for each license so granted, and no more, any law, custom or usage to the contrary notwithstanding. For which sums so assessed and received, as aforesaid, such clerks respectively, are made accountable to the treasurers of their respective counties, and shall pay the same to such treasurer, within thirty days next ensuing the rising of the court, at which any assessment shall be so made. And it shall be the duty of the several clerks of the county courts in this State, to transmit to the clerk of the General Assembly, at each stated session thereof, a fair statement of all the licenses granted as aforesaid, and the assessments thereon, and monies by him received and paid over to the treasurer of the county as aforesaid, for the year preceding, which statement shall be kept by the clerk of the General assembly, for the use and inspection of the members.

Sec. 4. *And it is hereby further Enacted,* That every person licensed as aforesaid, shall at all times be furnished with suitable refreshments, provisions and accommodations for travellers, their cattle and horses, on penalty of forfeiting the sum of three dollars to the use of any person who may sue for the same, and may, on complaint to the county court of the same county, and just cause shewn, be deprived of his or her license.

Sec. 5. *And it is hereby further Enacted,* That every person who shall keep an inn, or house of public entertainment, shall, within thirty days after his or her license, put up a proper sign, upon or near the front of his or her house, with his or her name thereon, and keep up such sign during the time he or she shall keep such house of entertainment, under penalty of forfeiting and paying two dollars for every month's neglect. And shall also erect and keep in good repair, a good and sufficient shed, or covering for horses, near his or her house, with a suitable trough or manger, convenient for the accommodation of travellers' horses, under penalty of forfeiting and paying the sum of five dollars for every sixty days' neglect, one moiety of either of the aforesaid penalties to the use of the town in which such person lives, and the other moiety to the person who shall sue for and prosecute the same to effect, in any court having cognizance thereof.

Sec. 6. *And it is hereby further Enacted,* That all grand jurors and other informing officers, in their respective towns and precincts, shall make presentment of all persons who keep inns or houses of entertainment, who shall not keep a regular and orderly house, and duly keep and observe all the laws of this State, relative to inns or houses of public entertainment, and for the regulation of the same, to the county court of the same county. And such court shall cause the person so presented forthwith to appear before them, and to answer to said presentment. And if upon trial the person shall be found guilty, the court shall render judgment against such person, for such sum or sums as in this act before directed, and may deprive him or her of his or her license for the remainder of the year.

Sec. 7. *And it is hereby further Enacted,* That if any person or persons not having a license to keep an inn, or house of public entertainment, as is before directed in this act shall presume to become a common innkeeper or keeper of a house of public entertainment, or shall publickly or privately, sell any wine, rum, brandy, or any other strong liquors or by a less quantity than one gallon of metheglin, strong beer, ale, or cyder, by a less quantity than one quart of wine, rum, brandy, or other strong liquors, or by a less quantity than one gallon of metheglin, strong beer, ale, or cyder, he, she or they shall forfeit and pay for the first offense a fine of ten dollars to the treasury of the county in which the offense is committed, on indictment, or information, with costs of prosecution, and so double for every breach of this act, of which he, she or they shall thereafter be convicted.

Sec. 8. *And it is hereby further Enacted,* That the civil authority and selectmen of any town shall have power to license any person or persons to mix and sell any of the liquors aforesaid, in any quantities, on days of general muster, and other public and proper occasions, which license shall be signed by such authority and selectmen, and be dated, and mention the time such person is authorised to mix and sell liquors, as aforesaid, which time shall in no instance exceed three days. And if any person shall mix and sell any liquors, after the time for which he or she was licensed, has terminated, the person so offending shall forfeit and pay a fine as is directed in the last preceding section.

Passed November 2, 1798.

A true copy,

Attest, Ros. Hopkins, Sec'y.

AN ACT GIVING RELIEF TO THE PROPRIETORS OF SALEM ON THE CENT TAX

NOVEMBER 2ND, 1798

Whereas, the proprietors of the township of Salem, have paid the cent tax laid by the Legislature, at their last session, for the support of government, upon the full quantity of a township of six miles square, or twenty three thousand and forty acres. And whereas five thousand seven hundred and ten acres of said township are cut off from the same, by the interference of Derby; and also whereas three thousand five hundred and three acres of said township are cut off by the waters of Lake Memphremagog, making in the whole the deficiency of nine thousand two hundred and thirteen acres. Therefore,

It is hereby Enacted by the General Assembly of the State of Vermont, That the treasurer of this State be, and he is hereby directed to pay James Whitelaw, the lawful agent of the proprietors and land-owners of the township of Salem aforesaid, ninety two dollars and thirteen cents out of the treasury, it being the sum received at the treasury over the tax, for the actual lands of said township.[1]

Passed November 2, 1798.

A true copy,

Attest, Ros. Hopkins, Sec'y.

AN ACT LAYING A TAX OF TWO CENTS PER ACRE ON THE TOWNSHIP OF WAITSFIELD

NOVEMBER 2ND, 1798

It is hereby Enacted by the General Assembly of the State of Vermont, That there be, and hereby is laid a tax of two cents on each acre of land in the township of Waistfield, in the county of Chittenden, public rights excepted, for the purpose of making and repairing roads and building bridges in said town, to be expended under the direction of Benjamin Wait, James Easton, and Stephen Pearce, who are hereby appointed a committee to superintend the expenditure of said tax. And any justice of the peace within the county of Chittenden is hereby authorised to issue his warrant to Ezra Wait, of said Waitsfield, who

---

1. State Papers of Vermont, Vol. XI, *General Petitions,* 1797-1799, "For a Tax Abatement and a Partial Restitution of Granting Fees," 296.

is hereby appointed a collector to collect said tax. And said collector is hereby made accountable to said committee for the amount of said tax; and said collector and committee are hereby directed in the collecting, expending, and accounting for said tax, to govern themselves in all things by the directions of the statute of this State entitled, "An act regulating the disposition of monies raised by tax on lands in the several towns for the purpose of making and repairing roads and building bridges," passed November 2d, 1796.[1]

AN ACT ASSESSING A TAX OF HALF A CENT PER ACRE ON ALL THE LANDS IN THE TOWN OF KELLYVALE

NOVEMBER 2ND, 1798

It is hereby Enacted by the General Assembly of the State of Vermont, That there be, and hereby is assessed a tax of half a cent on each acre of land in the township of Kellyvale in the county of Franklin, public lands excepted, for the purpose of repairing the roads and building bridges in said town. And Udney Hay, Royal Corbin, and Samuel C. Crafts are hereby appointed a committee to superintend the expenditure of said tax. And any justice of the peace in the county of Franklin is hereby empowered to issue his warrant to James Paddock to collect said tax, who is hereby appointed a collector to collect the same; and the said collector is hereby made accountable to the said committee for the amount of said tax. And the said committee and collector are hereby directed to govern themselves in laying out said roads and in collecting and expending said tax agreeable to a statute law of this State regulating the expenditure of monies raised for the purpose of making roads and building bridges &c. passed November 2d, 1796.

AN ACT RESTORING DANIEL FARRINGTON TO HIS LAW

NOVEMBER 2ND, 1798

Whereas, by the representation of Daniel Farrington of Brandon, in the county of Rutland, it appears that Joel Woodworth of Burlington, in the county of Chittenden, commenced and brought his action against the said Daniel Farrington, before the county court holden

---

1. State Papers of Vermont, Vol. XI, *General Petitions,* 1797-1799, "For a Tax on Land to Build a Road," 264.

at Burlington, within and for said county of Chittenden, on the last Monday save two in September, 1798, at which term of said Court, a judgment was by mistake rendered on the action aforesaid, by default, against the said Daniel, for the sum of one hundred and forty two dollars and seventy five cents, in the whole, and execution prayed out by the said Joel against the said Daniel for the aforesaid sum. And whereas the said Daniel has not had a day in court to make his defence in said action. Therefore,

It is hereby Enacted by the General Assembly of the State of Vermont, That said judgment be, and hereby is declared to be null and void, and all proceedings thereon be staied [stayed]; and the clerk of the said county court be, and hereby is directed to enter said action on the docket of said court, which is to be holden on the last Monday save one in February next, which said Court is hereby authorised and required to hear, try and determine the said cause, in the same manner as though said judgment had not thereon been rendered, and said court is hereby empowered and directed to tax the former costs in said suit as shall be considered just and equitable.[1]

Passed November 2, 1798.

A true record,

Attest, Ros. Hopkins, Sec'y.

AN ACT APPROPRIATING THE MONIES RAISED BY TAX IN THE TOWN OF SWANTON TO DEFRAYING THE EXPENSE OF BUILDING A BRIDGE OVER MISSISQUE RIVER

NOVEMBER 2ND, 1798

Whereas, the inhabitants of the town of Swanton, in the county of Franklin, agreeable to an act of the legislature of this State, passed November 8, 1796, enabling all the organized towns in this State to tax themselves to raise money for the purpose of becoming stockholders in the company, called and known by the name of the president, directors, and company of the northern inland lock navigation, did levy a tax of three pence on each acre of land in said town (public lands excepted), to raise money for the purpose aforesaid; and by said act the monies so raised by said tax will become forfeit to the

---

1. State Papers of Vermont, Vol. XI, *General Petitions,* 1797-1799, "For Stay of an Execution and Entry of an Action to a Court Docket," 309.

treasury of the county of Franklin, unless the same be laid out for the purpose aforesaid, in the purchase of a share or shares in the stock of the company aforesaid. And whereas certain embarrassments have prevented the pursuit and completion of said inland lock navigation, and in a degree destroyed the object contemplated by said act. Therefore,

Sec. 1. *It is hereby Enacted* by the General Assembly of the State of Vermont, That the said tax be, and the same is hereby appropriated towards defraying the expense of building a bridge over Missisque River in said town, where the stage road crosses the same, and repairing said road.

Sec. 2. *And it is hereby further Enacted,* That John Pratt, Orange Smith, and Silas Hathaway be, and hereby are appointed a committee to superintend the expenditure of said tax, and the collector of said tax is hereby made accountable to said committee for the amount of said tax, and said committee are hereby directed to govern themselves in disposing and accounting for said tax, agreeably to an act passed the second day of November, 1796, entitled, "An act regulating the disposition of monies raised by tax on lands, for the purpose of making and repairing roads and bridges," any thing to the contrary contained in the aforesaid act notwithstanding.[1]

Passed November 2, 1798.

A true record,

Attest, Ros. Hopkins, Sec'y.

AN ACT GRANTING RELIEF TO EPHRAIM STEVENS, LATE OF PITTSFORD, NOW OF PLATTSBURGH IN THE STATE OF NEW YORK

NOVEMBER 3RD, 1798

Whereas, it has been represented to this Assembly, and satisfactorily proved, that Ephraim Stevens was a soldier in the militia of this State, and was taken prisoner in the year 1777, and carried to Canada, and there imprisoned for the term of seven months, which greatly injured his constitution, and he has remained to this day in a weakly habit, and unable to labour for a livelyhood, for which he has not had any compensation. Therefore,

---

1. State Papers of Vermont, Vol. XI, *General Petitions,* 1797-1799, "For Authority to Use Tax Money to Build a Bridge," 298.

It is hereby Enacted by the General Assembly of the State of Vermont, That the treasurer of this State be, and he is hereby directed to pay to the said Ephraim Stevens, the sum of forty six dollars and seventy five cents, as a compensation for his said imprisonment in Canada, and for other services rendered as aforesaid.

Passed November 3, 1798.

A true record,

Attest, Ros. Hopkins, Sec'y.

AN ACT EMPOWERING THE SELECTMEN IN THE SEVERAL TOWNS IN THIS STATE TO TAKE CHARGE OF AND LEASE OUT THE LANDS GRANTED TO THE FIRST SETTLED MINISTER, AND TO THE USE OF THE MINISTRY

NOVEMBER 3RD, 1798

Sec. 1. *It is hereby Enacted* by the General Assembly of the State of Vermont, That the selectmen of the several towns in this State be, and they are hereby duly authorised and empowered to take care of, and lease out for the term of five years, or until a minister shall be settled in any town, all the lands lying in such town, granted to the first settled minister, in such way and manner as such selectmen shall judge will most enhance the value of such lands.

Sec. 2. *And it is hereby further Enacted,* That the said selectmen take care of, and lease out all the lands in their respective towns, granted to the use of the ministry, or the social worship of God, and still remaining to such use, and the avails of such lands shall be applied to the use of the ministry, in such towns respectively; and if there be more than one settled minister in any such town, the avails thereof shall be applied to the use of such ministers in proportion to the numbers of their several congregations in said towns respectively. And if there be no settled minister in any such town, the same shall be applied to the use of such town to hire preaching for the time being.

Provided nevertheless, That the aforesaid selectmen shall not lease out said lands for a term exceeding fifteen years, at one and the same time.

Sec. 3. *And whereas,* individuals have, and may hereafter without a right take possession of, or trespass on such lands:

It is hereby further Enacted, That the selectmen in any town in which such land may be situate be, and they are hereby fully authorised and empowered to demand of any person or persons, who shall be in possession of, or trespass on such lands, restitution in damages and peaceable possession of the same, and on refusal, such selectmen are hereby authorised & empowered to institute in their names, actions of ejectment, trespass, or other possessory action, against any such person or persons, so in possession of, or trespassing on such lands as aforesaid, and by themselves or successors in office, to prosecute such action to final judgment and execution.

Passed November 3, 1798.

A true record,

Attest, Ros. Hopkins, Sec'y.

AN ACT LAYING A TAX OF ONE CENT PER ACRE ON THE TOWNSHIP OF KINGSTON

NOVEMBER 5TH, 1798

It is hereby Enacted by the General Assembly of the State of Vermont, That there be, and hereby is laid a tax of one cent on each acre of land in the township of Kingston, in the county of Addison, public rights excepted, for the purpose of making and repairing roads and building bridges in said town, to be expended under the direction of Joseph Patrick, Peter Thatcher, and Elijah Moulton, who are hereby appointed a committee to superintend the expenditure of said tax. And any justice of the peace within the county of Addison is hereby authorised to issue his warrant to Asa Wood of said Kingston, who is hereby appointed a collector to collect said tax. And said collector is hereby made accountable to said committee for the amount of said tax; and said collector and committee are hereby directed in the collecting, expending, and accounting for said tax, to govern themselves in all things by the directions of the statute of this State entitled, "An act regulating the disposition of monies raised by tax on lands in the several towns for the purpose of making and repairing roads and building bridges," passed November 2d, 1796.

AN ACT LAYING A TAX OF TWO CENTS AND HALF PER ACRE ON THE
TOWN OF MORETOWN, FOR THE PURPOSE THEREIN MENTIONED

NOVEMBER 5TH, 1798

It is hereby Enacted by the General Assembly of the State of
Vermont, That there be, and hereby is laid a tax of two cents and an
half per acre on all the lands in the township of Moretown, in the
county of Chittenden, public lands excepted, for the purpose of building a bridge over Mad-River near its mouth, and of making and
repairing roads and building bridges in said town, one cent and an
half cent to be expended in building bridges and repairing roads on
or near Onion-River, and one cent to be laid out in making a road
leading from Onion River through said town to Waitsfield, to be
expended under the direction of Wright Spaulding, Reuben Hawks
and Seth Munson, who are hereby appointed a committee to superintend the expenditure of said tax. And any justice of the peace of the
county of Chittenden is hereby authorised to issue his warrant to
Joseph Hazeltine, who is hereby appointed a collector to collect said
tax. And said collector is hereby made accountable to said committee
for the amount of said tax. And said committee and collector are hereby directed in the expending, collecting, and accounting for the monies
raised by said tax, to conform themselves in all things to the directions
of the statute of this State entitled, "An act regulating the disposition
of monies raised by tax on lands in the several towns for the purpose
of making and repairing roads and building bridges," passed the 2d
day of November A.D. 1796.[1]

AN ACT APPOINTING A NEW COLLECTOR OF A LAND TAX IN THE TOWN OF
ISLE OF [LA] MOTT

NOVEMBER 5TH, 1798

Whereas, the collectors heretofore appointed by the Legislature of
this State, of a land tax of two pence per acre on the township of Isle
of Mott, assessed by an act of the Legislature, passed the third day of
November A.D. 1791, refuse to discharge the duties of said office.
Therefore,

It is hereby Enacted by the General Assembly of the State of

---

1. State Papers of Vermont, Vol. XI, *General Petitions,* 1797-1799, "For a Tax
on Land to Build Roads and Bridges," 282.

Vermont, That any justice of the peace in the county of Franklin is hereby authorised to issue his warrant to Samuel Fisk, who is hereby appointed a collector to collect said tax. And said collector is hereby made accountable to the committee, who superintend the expenditure thereof for the amount of said tax.

Provided nevertheless, That if any former collector has collected any part of said tax, he is hereby made accountable to said committee for the monies thus collected. And the collector appointed in and by this act shall be credited for the amount of monies thus already collected on said tax by said committee. And,

It is hereby further Enacted, That all acts or clauses of acts relating to the appointment of a collector of said tax, be, and they hereby are repealed. *Provided nevertheless,* That any former collector or collectors are considered and held accountable as provided in the first section of this act.

AN ACT SUPPLEMENTARY TO AN ACT ENTITLED "AN ACT FOR THE PROBATE OF WILLS AND THE SETTLEMENT OF TESTATE AND INTESTATE ESTATES"

NOVEMBER 5TH, 1798

Sec. 1. *It is hereby Enacted* by the General Assembly of the State of Vermont, That the several judges of probate in this State, in their several districts, are hereby authorised and empowered, on application being made to them, by the executor or administrator, or executors or administrators, on the estate of any person or persons deceased, for liberty to deed any lands, said deceased person or persons were under contract to deed in his, her or their life time, in the discretion of such judges, to grant liberty and authority to such executor or executors, administrator or administrators, to deed all such lands in the same manner as such deceased person or persons could do were they living, which deeds duly executed, acknowledged and recorded, shall be as good and valid in law, to pass the fee of such land, as if the same had been executed by such deceased person or persons in his, her or their life time.

Sec. 2. *Provided nevertheless,* and it is hereby further Enacted, That no executor or administrator shall be authorised to make such conveyance, unless notice of application for such authority be given, by publishing the same, not less than twenty days, in such manner as the judge shall direct, requiring all persons interested to appear and show cause, if any there be why such authority should not be granted, nor unless on a hearing after notice as aforesaid, it shall appear to the satisfaction of such judge that no creditor, heir, or legatee of such deceased person or persons, will be thereby prevented from recovering the whole or any part of his, her or their just demands against the estate of such deceased person or persons.

Sec. 3. *And it is hereby further Enacted,* That it shall be the duty of executors and administrators to estates, represented insolvent, to exhibit to the commissioners appointed to receive and examine the claims against such estates, an inventory of the claims in favor of such estate. And in case of mutual claims, the said commissioners shall adjust the same, and report the balance, which shall be the rule to the judge of probate, in ascertaining the dividends to be made of such estates.

Passed November 5, 1798.

A true copy,

Attest, Ros. Hopkins, Sec'y.

AN ACT EMPOWERING THE PROPRIETORS OF THE TOWNSHIP OF WILLIAMSTOWN IN THE COUNTY OF ORANGE, TO LAY OUT THEIR UNDIVIDED LANDS BY PITCHING

NOVEMBER 5TH, 1798

Whereas, the proprietors of Williamstown have heretofore divided all their lands into severalty, except about eight acres to each right, which still remains undivided. *Therefore,* to prevent the great expense of a division in the common mode by law;

It is hereby Enacted by the General Assembly of the State of Vermont, That the proprietors of the town of Williamstown be, and they are hereby authorised and empowered at any legal meeting warned and holden for that purpose, to make a division of the undivided land in said town, to and among said proprietors, by pitching the same, they first making a draft for the days on which the proprietors shall make their pitches, in such manner as shall be agreed upon by said proprietors, in such proprietors' meetings warned as aforesaid, any law, usage, or custom to the contrary notwithstanding.

Passed November 5, 1798.

A true record,

Attest, Ros. Hopkins, Sec'y.

AN ACT RESPECTING A CLAIM MADE BY SOME OF THE CHIEFS OF THE SEVEN INDIAN NATIONS, OF THE PROVINCE OF LOWER CANADA, IN BEHALF OF THE RESPECTIVE NATIONS, OF LANDS WITHIN THIS STATE

NOVEMBER 5TH, 1798

Whereas, a claim is made by the Indians above mentioned, to a tract of land within this State, contained within the following bounds, viz., beginning on the east side of Ticonderoga, from thence to the falls of Otter Creek, continuing the same course to the height of land that divides the streams between Lake Champlain and the River-Connecticut, from thence along the heighth of land opposite to Missisque, and then down to the bay. And whereas This assembly feel a strong desire to maintain perfect peace and good understanding with the nations above mentioned, although this claim stands entirely unsupported by any legal or equitable proofs hitherto exhibited to this assembly; and whereas the state of New York have lately held a treaty with the said Indians on a claim for lands of a similar nature, to that which is now made by them on this state. Therefore,

Sec. 1. *It is hereby Enacted* by the General Assembly of the State of Vermont, That his Excellency the Governor be, and he hereby is desired to pursue such mode as he shall think proper for obtaining a full, complete, and official information from the proper department of the state of New York, aforesaid, with respect to the nature of the claim made by the aforesaid Indians for lands within that state, and termination of the treaty held between the said state and the said Indians, in consequence of that claim.

Sec. 2. *And it is hereby further Enacted,* That if his Excellency the Governor shall receive information, through the channel above described, that the claims of the said Indians was not allowed by the said state, or should be convinced that their claims on this State, ought not to be admitted, his Excellency is hereby authorised and empowered to appoint a commissioner, to go to one or more of said Indian nations, and under the direction of his Excellency, to assign to them proper reasons why their claims for lands within this state cannot be admitted. And to transmit, at the same time, by the said Commissioners, to the said nation or nations, some token of friendship not exceeding in value the sum of one hundred dollars.

Sec. 3. *And it is hereby further Enacted,* That his Excellency the Governor be, and he hereby is requested, to cause to be presented to the Indians aforesaid, now in the City of Vergennes, and in such manner and form as to his Excellency shall seem best adapted for answering the purpose intended, a present of affection not exceeding the value of one hundred dollars; and shall at the same time cause their maintainance, while they remain within the City of Vergennes, as aforesaid, to be regularly paid.

Sec. 4. *And it is hereby further Enacted,* That his Excellency the Governor be, and he is hereby authorised to draw on the treasurer of this State, for the purpose of defraying the whole of the expense of this negociation, such sum or sums, from time to time, as the same shall become necessary, to be paid, not exceeding in the whole, five hundred dollars. And the treasurer is hereby authorised and required to pay the same out of any monies which may be in the treasury, not appropriated for other purposes.

Passed November 5, 1798.

A true Record,

Attest, Ros. Hopkins, Sec'y.

AN ACT IN ALTERATION OF AN ACT ENTITLED "AN ACT GRANTING RELIEF TO TWO NATIVE INDIANS, PASSED NOVEMBER SEVENTH A.D., 1792

NOVEMBER 5TH, 1798

It is hereby Enacted by the General Assembly of the State of Vermont, That Timothy Hinman of Derby be, and he is hereby appointed to provide for the said Indians, and to receive the annual allowance made by this state for them, in and by the act aforesaid, in the room of John McDaniel of Hydes Park.

Passed November 5, 1798.

A true record,

Attest, Ros. Hopkins, Sec'y.

AN ACT LAYING A TAX OF TWO CENTS PER ACRE ON THE TOWN OF GLOVER FOR THE PURPOSE THEREIN MENTIONED

NOVEMBER 5TH, 1798

It is hereby Enacted by the General Assembly of the State of Vermont, That there be, and hereby is laid a tax of two cents per acre on all the lands in the township of Glover, in the territory of Orleans, in the jurisdiction of the county of Caledonia, public lands excepted, for the purpose of making and repairing roads and building bridges in said town, to be expended under the direction of Ralph Parker, Samuel Huntington and Timothy Stanley, who are hereby appointed a committee to superintend the expenditure of said tax; and any justice of the peace of the county of Caledonia, is hereby authorised to issue his warrant to Andrew Moore of Glover, who is hereby appointed a collector to collect said tax, and the said collector is hereby made accountable to the said committee for the amount of said tax. And said committee and collector, are hereby directed, in the expending, collecting, and accounting for the monies raised by said tax to conform themselves in all things to the direction of the statute of this State entitled "An act regulating the disposition of monies raised by tax on lands in the several towns for the purpose of making and repairing roads and building bridges," passed the 2d day of November, A.D., 1796.[1]

AN ACT APPOINTING A COMMITTEE TO LAY OUT AND SURVEY A COUNTY ROAD FROM MONTPELIER TO DANVILLE

NOVEMBER 5TH, 1798

Sec. 1. *It is hereby Enacted* by the General Assembly of the

---

1. State Papers of Vermont, Vol. XI, *General Petitions,* 1797-1799, "For a Tax on Land to Repair Roads and Bridges," 151.

State of Vermont, That Charles Bulkley and Samuel Chamberlain, Esquires, be, and they hereby are appointed a committee with full power to lay out, open and survey a county road in the most direct and convenient course from Onion River Bridge in Montpelier, to the Court-House in Danville. And it shall be the duty of said committee to make a return of the road so by them laid out, to the town clerks of the several towns through which said road shall be laid, whose duty it shall be to record the same in their respective offices; and such road, so laid out and recorded, shall not be altered by a future order from the county court of the said county of Caledonia, or the Legislature of this State.

Sec. 2. *And it is hereby further Enacted,* That the proprietors and inhabitants of the several towns through which said road shall pass, shall be at liberty to agree upon the mode of defraying the expense of making and repairing such road, either by taxing the polls and rateable estate of the inhabitants of said towns, or by applying to the Legislature for a tax on the lands in such towns, within a proper time before the session of the Legislature in October next.

Sec. 3. *And it is hereby further Enacted,* That it shall be the duty of said committee to lay out said road some time before the first day of July next, and said committee shall give proper notice to the selectmen of the several towns through which said road will probably be laid, of the time they will attend to said business.[1]

Passed November 5, 1798.

A true copy,

Attest, Ros. Hopkins, Sec'y.

AN ACT ESTABLISHING A COMPANY OF CAVALRY

NOVEMBER 5TH, 1798

Whereas, the company of Cavalry now under the command of Abner Perry, by the militia law now in force, must be disbanded unless provided for by law. Therefore,

It is hereby Enacted by the General Assembly of the State of Vermont, That the company of Cavalry aforesaid, be, and hereby is

1. State Papers of Vermont, Vol. **XI**, *General Petitions,* 1797-1799, "For Appointment of a Committee to Lay Out a Road," 278.

established as a company of Cavalry within the first brigade of the first division of the militia of this State, and are to be annexed to such regiment in the said Brigade as the commanding officer of said brigade shall direct, any law, usage, or custom to the contrary notwithstanding.

Passed November 5, 1798.

A true record,

Attest, Ros. Hopkins, Sec'y.

AN ACT AUTHORISING JOSEPH CHURCHILL TO SELL THE REAL ESTATE OF BENJAMIN DIMMICK, DECEASED

NOVEMBER 5TH, 1798

It is hereby Enacted by the General Assembly of the State of Vermont, That Joseph Churchill, administrator on the estate of Benjamin Dimmick, late of Woodstock, in the county of Windsor, deceased, be, and he hereby is fully authorised and empowered to sell all the real estate belonging to the said Benjamin in his life time. *Provided*, The said Joseph shall not sell said real estate, until he shall have given sufficient bonds to the judge of probate for the district of Hartford, for the faithful performance of his trust. And that he will put out at interest the monies arising from the sales of such lands, for the benefit of the heirs to such estate, taking sufficient security for the same, or vest the same in lands for the benefit of such heirs.

Passed November 5, 1798.

A true record,

Attest, Ros. Hopkins, Sec'y.

AN ACT EMPOWERING ASA TILDEN, ADMINISTRATOR TO THE ESTATE OF BENJAMIN FOLLET, LATE OF HARTFORD, DECEASED, TO SELL ALL THE REAL ESTATE OF THE SAID BENJAMIN

NOVEMBER 5TH, 1798

It is hereby Enacted by the General Assembly of the State of Vermont, That Asa Tilden, administrator of the estate of Benjamin Follet, late of Hartford, deceased, be, and he is hereby empowered to sell and dispose of all the real estate of the said Benjamin. And a deed of conveyance from the said administrator, shall be good and valid in law, to convey to the purchaser, all the title to the said property which was vested in the said Benjamin at the time of his decease. *Provided,* That this act shall not take effect until the said administrator shall give bonds, with sufficent sureties, to the acceptance of the judge of probate of the district of Hartford, conditioned, that he will put the monies arising from the sale of the estate aforesaid to use, and take good security therefor, for the benefit of the heirs of the said Benjamin.[1]

Passed November 5, 1798.

A true record,

Attest, Ros. Hopkins, Sec'y.

AN ACT FOR THE RELIEF OF JONATHAN FASSET IN A CERTAIN SUIT

NOVEMBER 5TH, 1798

Whereas, an execution has been issued in the name of the treasurer of this State against the aforesaid Jonathan Fasset. And whereas the said Jonathan Fasset claims a demand against this State, which has been repeatedly examined by commissioners or auditors appointed by the State, and has also had an opportunity to plead said demand in offset, before a court and jury in the county of Bennington, without being able to substantiate the same; and yet remains dissatisfied with the determination of the said commissioners and the said court. Therefore,

Sec. 1. *It is hereby Enacted* by the General Assembly of the State of Vermont, That Cephas Smith, Junr., Esqr. be, and he hereby is appointed a commissioner, with full powers (at the charge and expense of the said Jonathan Fasset) to examine into the claims of the said Jonathan, who shall, before he enter on such examination, procure the necessary documents and statements made by the commissioners or auditors, heretofore appointed to settle and adjust all demands between this State and the said Jonathan. And if on such examination he shall find any sum justly due to the said Jonathan, he shall give certificate thereof to the said Jonathan to the amount of the

---

1. State Papers of Vermont, Vol. XI, *General Petitions,* 1797-1799, "For Authority of Administrators to Give Deeds of Land," 163.

whole of said execution, if such sum be due. And the treasurer of this State is hereby directed to receive such certificate and endorse the sum so certified, to be due on the execution aforesaid, and such certificate with this act, shall be good and sufficient voucher for said treasurer on the settlement of his accounts with this State.

Sec. 2. *And it is hereby further Enacted,* That if the said Jonathan Fasset, shall choose to pay the cost of suit, due on said execution, and will make and execute to the said treasurer a receipt or discharge of all demands against this State, the said treasurer is thereby fully authorised and empowered to execute and deliver a full and ample discharge to the said Jonathan of all demands due from him to this State.[1]

Passed November 5, 1798.

A true record,

Attest, Ros. Hopkins, Sec'y.

AN ACT DETERMINING A PARTICULAR REGULATION RELATIVE TO THE PROPRIETORS AND LANDOWNERS OF GOSHEN AND WARREN

NOVEMBER 5TH, 1798

Whereas, the township of Goshen and Warren in this State, are composed of several tracts lying in the different counties of Addison and Caledonia, of which the largest is situate in the county of Addison.

Sec. 1. *It is hereby Enacted* by the General Assembly of the State of Vermont, That in future, and until otherwise ordered by the Legislature of this State, all meetings of the proprietors of said townships, and proceedings relative to the propriety thereof, whether of recording of deeds, authentication of titles of lands, or other matters relative to said proprietors, as also the collection of all taxes, of whatever name or description, may and shall be held, done and performed in the county of Addison. And all such proceedings, acts, and doings shall, and are hereby declared to be good and valid in law as to their locality, the same as though the whole of said township were situate

---

1. State Papers of Vermont, Vol. XI, *General Petitions,* 1797-1799, "For Appointment of a Committee to Examine Commissary-General Accounts," 272.

in the said county of Addison, any law or usage to the contrary notwithstanding.

Passed November 5, 1798.

A true copy,

Attest, Ros. Hopkins, Sec'y.

AN ACT LAYING A TAX OF TWO CENTS PER ACRE ON THE TOWN OF BRAINTREE FOR THE PURPOSE THEREIN MENTIONED

NOVEMBER 5TH, 1798

It is hereby Enacted by the General Assembly of the State of Vermont, That there be, and hereby is laid a tax of two cents per acre on all the lands in the township of Braintree, in the county of Orange, (public rights excepted), for the purpose of making and repairing roads, and building bridges in said town, one third part of the monies arising from said tax to be expended on the road in the west part of the town, commonly called the "Branch road;" one third on a road leading through the middle of said town to Roxbury, and the other third on a road leading through the north east part of said town near a stream commonly called Ayers Brook; to be expended under the direction of William Ford, John French, and John Hutchinson, who are hereby appointed a committee for that purpose. And any justice of the peace of the county of Orange is hereby authorised to issue his warrant to Sampson Nichols, who is hereby appointed a collector, to collect said tax. And said collector is hereby made accountable to said committee for the amount of said tax; and said committee and collector are hereby directed in the expending, collecting and accounting for the monies raised by said tax, to govern themselves in all things, conformably to the directions of the statute of this State entitled, "An act regulating the disposition of monies raised by tax on lands in the several towns, for the purpose of making and repairing roads and building bridges," passed the 2d day of November, A.D. 1796.

AN ACT TO REVIVE AN ACT ENTITLED "AN ACT ASSESSING A TAX OF ONE CENT ON EACH ACRE OF LAND IN HOLLAND, FOR THE PURPOSES THEREIN MENTIONED"

NOVEMBER 6TH, 1798

Whereas, the statutes of this State make it necessary that advertisements from committees on land taxes, giving an opportunity for proprietors to pay their taxes in labour, shall be published previous to a certain time. And whereas a failure happened to that effect, in the case of the tax above alluded to. Therefore,

It is hereby Enacted by the General Assembly of the State of Vermont, That the act entitled "An act assessing a tax of one cent on each acre of land in Holland for the purposes therein mentioned," passed at the last session of this Legislature, be, and the same is hereby revived and shall have and take the same validity and effect, as though it had been passed at the present session.

AN ACT REVIVING AN ACT ENTITLED "AN ACT FOR LAYING OUT AND ESTABLISHING A POST ROAD THROUGH THE TOWNS OF ST. JOHNSBURY AND LYNDON IN THE COUNTY OF CALEDONIA"

NOVEMBER 6TH, 1798

Whereas, an act passed by the Legislature of this State, the eighth day of November, A.D. 1797, for laying out and establishing a post road, through the towns of St. Johnsbury and Lyndon, failed of being carried into effect, by reason of not being duly advertised as the law directs. Therefore,

It is hereby Enacted by the General Assembly of the State of Vermont, That the aforesaid act in all its parts be, and the same is hereby revived, and put into full effect. And the committee, selectmen, and collectors are hereby authorised & empowered to advertise and carry the same into effect, in the year ensuing, in the same manner as was contemplated in and by said act, to have been done in the year past.[1]

---

1. State Papers of Vermont, Vol. XI, *General Petitions,* 1797-1799, "For Revival of An act Granting a Land Tax," 313.

AN ACT DIRECTING THE PUBLISHING OF ADVERTISEMENTS IN THE
NEWSPAPERS THEREIN MENTIONED

NOVEMBER 6TH, 1798

Sec. 1. *It is hereby Enacted* by the General Assembly of the State of Vermont, That from and after the first day of February next, all advertisements of the following descriptions, shall be published in manner following, to wit: all advertisements for warning proprietors' meetings, and for the sale of lands by proprietors' collectors; and all other collectors of land taxes, and of committees for notifying landowners to work out road taxes, and of giving notice to landowners, that application will be made to the legislature for road taxes, shall be published in the Rutland Herald, printed at Rutland and in the Vermont Journal, printed at Windsor.

Sec. 2. *And it is hereby further Enacted,* That all advertisements of the foregoing description, made necessary by any act of the Legislature, at their present session, shall be published as is directed in this act. And all advertisements, of the above description published as aforesaid, shall be deemed legal and sufficient notice, any law, usage, or custom to the contrary notwithstanding. *Provided nevertheless,* That if the Vermont Journal published at Windsor shall cease to be published, said advertisements shall be published in the Rutland Herald, printed at Rutland, and in the Green Mountain Patriot, printed at Peacham. And if the Rutland Herald printed in Rutland shall cease to be published, then said advertisements shall be published in the Vermont Journal printed at Windsor, and the Vergennes Gazette printed at Vergennes during the cessation of such papers respectively, or in such other papers as shall be printed at said Peacham and Vergennes respectively.

Passed November 6, 1798.

A true copy,

Attest, Ros. Hopkins, Sec'y.

AN ACT DIRECTING THE TIME WHEN NATHAN TYLER SHALL DRAW OFF
THE WATERS TO ITS NATURAL LEVEL, FROM A MILL POND BY HIM
RAISED ON MUDDY BROOK IN SHELBURNE IN THE COUNTY OF
CHITTENDEN, AND FOR WHAT LENGTH OF TIME THE SAID
NATHAN TYLER OR ANY OTHER PERSON OR PERSONS,
WHO HEREAFTER MAY OWN SAID MILLS, NOW
STANDING NEAR SAID POND, SHALL KEEP
OPEN A PASSAGE SUFFICIENT FOR
THE ABOVE PURPOSE

NOVEMBER 6TH, 1798

Whereas, it appears to this Legislature that in consequence of a mill dam's being erected by Nathan Tyler, on Muddy Brook, in Shelburne, in the county of Chittenden, a large quantity of land is flowed, and the stream raised considerably above its natural level, which has occasioned great sickness among the inhabitants of said Shelburne, to prevent which evil,

Sec. 1. *It is hereby Enacted* by the General Assembly of the State of Vermont, That the said Nathan Tyler, or any other person or persons who may hold or claim said mill, with its privileges under him or them, on the first day of May next, shall open a passage in said dam, sufficient to draw off the water in said pond to its natural level, and so continue said passage open as aforesaid, until the tenth day of September then next following, and so from year to year thereafter as long as the said Nathan, or any other person or persons shall continue said dam erected across said stream as aforesaid.

Sec. 2. *And it is hereby further Enacted,* That in case the said Nathan, by himself or some other person by him directed, or those who shall hold or claim under him, shall neglect or refuse to open and continue open, in said mill dam, a passage as aforesaid, and sufficient for the purposes aforesaid, it may and shall be lawful for any person or persons to open a passage in said dam, and continue the same open for the time, and sufficient for all the purposes as is above directed in this act.

Passed November 6, 1798.

A true copy,

Attest, Ros. Hopkins, Sec'y.

AN ACT AUTHORISING THE COMMITTEES APPOINTED TO SUPERINTEND
THE COLLECTION OF CERTAIN LAND TAXES TO PROCEED IN THE
COLLECTION THEREOF

NOVEMBER 6TH, 1798

Whereas, by the law of this State, it became necessary that the committees appointed to superintend the expenditure of monies, raised by land taxes, for the purpose of making roads and building bridges, in the towns on which such taxes were granted, should notify the landowners of such town, by advertising the same in the months of March and April, and also lay out the roads in May next following the time of granting such taxes. And whereas it appears to this assembly that such committees have, in sundry instances, neglected to advertise and lay out such roads at the times required by law, by means whereof the beneficial purposes intended in the granting of said taxes have been frustrated. To remedy which,

Sec. 1. *It is hereby Enacted* by the General Assembly of the State of Vermont, That in all cases where the committees appointed to superintend the expenditure of monies to be raised by taxes which have been granted, on any of the towns in this state, for the purpose of making and repairing roads and building bridges, in such towns, have neglected advertising according to law, such committee or committees are hereby authorised and required to notify the landowners of all such towns, in the manner directed by law, in the months of March and April next ensuing, and lay out such roads in May next ensuing, and proceed in all things, in the collection and expenditure of the monies to be raised by such taxes in manner as is directed by the act entitled, "An act regulating the disposition of monies raised by tax on land in the several towns, for the purpose of making and repairing roads and building bridges," passed the second day of November, A.D. one thousand seven hundred and ninety six.

Passed November 6, 1798.

A true record,

Attest, Ros. Hopkins, Sec'y.

AN ACT ASSESSING A TAX OF ONE CENT PER ACRE ON THE TOWNSHIP
OF MANSFIELD FOR THE PURPOSE THEREIN MENTIONED

NOVEMBER 6TH, 1798

It is hereby Enacted by the General Assembly of the State of
Vermont, That there be, and hereby is laid a tax of one cent on each
acre of land in the township of Mansfield, in the county of Chittenden
(public rights excepted), for the purpose of making roads and building
bridges in said town, to be expended under the direction of William
Utley, Ebenezer Wakefield, and George Kennan, who are hereby
appointed a committee to superintend the expenditures of said tax.
And any justice of the peace within the county of Chittenden is hereby
authorised to issue his warrant to Joshua Chamberlain of Richmond
to collect said tax, who is hereby appointed a collector of the same.
And the said collector is hereby made accountable to said committee
for the amount of said [tax]; and said committee and collector are
hereby directed in the collecting, disposing, and accounting for the
monies raised by said tax, to conform themselves in all things to the
directions of the statute entitled, "An act regulating the disposition of
monies raised by taxes on lands in the several towns for the purpose
of making & repairing roads & building bridges," passed November
2d, 1796.[1]

AN ACT LAYING A TAX OF ONE CENT PER ACRE ON THE TOWN OF
ROXBURY FOR THE PURPOSE THEREIN MENTIONED

NOVEMBER 6TH, 1798

It is hereby Enacted by the General Assembly of the State of
Vermont, That there be, and hereby is laid a tax of one cent per acre
on all lands in the township of Roxbury in the county of Orange, public
lands excepted, for the purpose of making and repairing roads and
building bridges in said town, the one half of said sum to be laid out
on a road leading from Braintree through said town to Waitsfield, and
the other half of said sum upon a road leading from Northfield, through
the east part of said Roxbury to the west part of Brookfield, to be
expended under the direction of Isaac Lewis and Samuel Richardson,
who are hereby appointed a committee to superintend the expenditure

1. State Papers of Vermont, Vol. XI, *General Petitions,* 1797-1799, "For a Tax
on land to Build a Road and Bridges," 305.

of said tax. And any justice of the peace of the county of Orange is hereby authorised to issue his warrant to David Cram of said Roxbury, who is hereby appointed a collector to collect said tax, and said collector is hereby made accountable to said committee for the amount of said tax. And said committee and collector are hereby directed in the expending, collecting, and accounting for the monies raised by said tax, to conform themselves in all things to the directions of the statute of this State, passed the 2d day of November, A.D. 1796, entitled, "An act regulating the disposition of monies raised by tax on lands in the several towns for the purpose of making and repairing roads and building bridges,"[1]

AN ACT LAYING A TAX OF ONE CENT PER ACRE ON THE TOWNSHIP OF BROWNINGTON AND NAVY,[2] FOR THE PURPOSE THEREIN MENTIONED

NOVEMBER 6TH, 1798

It is hereby Enacted by the General Assembly of the State of Vermont, That a tax of one cent on each acre of land in the townships of Brownington and Navy, in the county of Caledonia, public lands excepted, be, and hereby is laid and assessed, for the purpose of making and repairing roads and building bridges in said towns; to be expended, an equal sum on each town, under the direction of Elijah Strong, Amos Porter and Timothy Hinman, who are hereby appointed a committee to superintend the expenditure of said taxes. And any justice of the peace, within the county of Caledonia, is hereby authorised to issue his warrant to Asahel Strong of Brownington, who is hereby appointed a collector to collect said taxes. And said collector is hereby made accountable to said committee for the amount of said taxes; and said committee and collector are hereby directed in the expenditure, collection, and accounting for the monies raised by said taxes, to govern themselves in all things by the directions of the statute of this State entitled, "An act regulating the disposition of monies raised

---

1. State Papers of Vermont, Vol. XI, *General Petitions,* 1797-1799, "For a Tax on Land to Build and Repair Roads," 233.

2. State Papers of Vermont, *Index to the Papers of the Surveyors General,* Vol. I: Navy, Vt. Grant to Abraham Whipple, Esq., and associates, Nov. 10, 1780; alias 32; name changed to Charleston, Nov. 16, 1825, 107.

by tax on lands in the several towns for the purpose of making and repairing roads and building bridges &c., passed November 2d, 1796.[1]

AN ACT ASSESSING A TAX OF ONE CENT ON THE DOLLAR, ON THE LIST OF ONE THOUSAND SEVEN HUNDRED AND NINETY EIGHT

NOVEMBER 6TH, 1798

It is hereby Enacted by the General Assembly of the State of Vermont, That there be, and hereby is assessed a tax of one cent on the dollar, on the list of the polls and rateable estate of the inhabitants of this State, taken in the year one thousand seven hundred and niney eight, to be paid into the treasury by the first day of June next, to be paid in hard money, state orders, and orders drawn by the clerks of the supreme court.

Passed November 6, 1798.

A true record,

Attest, Ros. Hopkins, Sec'y.

AN ACT CONFIRMING A RATE BILL MADE BY THE SELECTMEN OF THE TOWN OF WINHALL

NOVEMBER 6TH, 1798

Whereas, in and by the fourth section of the act entitled, "An act assessing a tax of one cent on each acre of land in this State for the support of government during the year 1797, and for other purposes," it is enacted that in the making out of a rate bill for a constable, the selectmen, where they cannot ascertain the original proprietor or division, the tax shall be set in the bill to the present owner. And whereas by reason of the particular circumstances of the propriety of the town of Winhall, and of the divisions and records thereof, the selectmen of said town were not able to specify in their bill, the names of either the proprietors or present owners, but designated the lands by lots with the numbers and ranges, without names of proprietors or present owners. Therefore,

It is hereby Enacted by the General Assembly of the State of

1. State Papers of Vermont, Vol. XI, *General Petitions,* 1797-1799, "For a Tax on Land to Build Roads and Bridges," 251.

Vermont, That the bills of said tax, thus made out by the selectmen of the lands in Winhill by lots, designated by numbers and ranges, but without names of proprietors or present owners, shall be, and hereby are declared to be valid and good in law as though the names of proprietors or present owners had been inserted in said bills, and the sales of lands which may have been made thereon, or shall be made hereafter, are hereby declared to be valid and good in law as though the lands in such bill had been set to the proprietors or landowners in said town. *Provided,* That this act shall be published in the Rutland Herald, printed at Rutland, the Vermont Journal, printed at Windsor, and in the Vermont Gazette, printed at Bennington, three weeks successively before the first day of February next, any law, usage, or custom to the contrary notwithstanding.[1]

Passed November 6, 1798.

A true record,

Attest, Ros. Hopkins, Sec'y.

AN ACT DIRECTING THE TREASURER OF THIS STATE TO PAY CERTAIN SUMS OF MONEY TO THE SEVERAL PERSONS THEREIN MENTIONED

NOVEMBER 6TH, 1798

It is hereby Enacted by the General Assembly of the State of Vermont, That the treasurer of this State be, and he hereby is directed to pay the state's attornies and clerks of the supreme court, in the several counties in this state, the following sums viz., To David Dunbar, Esqr., clerk of Caledonia, the sum of $43.23 cents; To Isaac Bayley, Esqr., clerk of Orange county, the sum of $49.87 cents; To Nathan Osgood, Esqr., clerk of Rutland County, the sum of $53.47 cents; To Darius Matthews, Esqr., clerk of Addison county, the sum of $40.96 cents; To Samuel Robinson 2d, Esqr., clerk of Bennington county, the sum of $41.63 cents; To John Law, Esqr., clerk of Chittenden county, the sum of $40.37 cents; To Lemuel Whitney, Esqr., clerk of Windham county, the sum of $49.89 cents; To Seth Pomeroy, Esqr., clerk of Franklin county, the sum of $8.67 cents; To Benjamin Swan, Esqr., clerk of Windsor county, the sum of $26.15 cents; To

1. State Papers of Vermont, Vol. XI, *General Petitions,* 1797-1799, "For Ratification of a Tax Rate Bill on Undivided Land," 245.

Loyal Case, Esqr., late clerk of Addison county, the sum of $6.00 cents; To David Fay, Esqr., state's attorney of Bennington county, the sum of $51.58 cents; To William Mattocks, Esqr., state's attorney of Caledonia county, the sum of $63.00 cents; To Levi House, Esqr., state's attorney of Franklin county, the sum of $17.50 cents; To Jedidiah P. Buckingham, Esqr., state's attorney of Orange county, the sum of $38.24 cents; To Abel Spencer, Esqr., state's attorney of Rutland county, the sum of $95.50 cents; To Daniel Chipman, Esqr., state's attorney of Addison county, the sum of $29.83 cents; To Royal Tyler,[1] Esqr., state's attorney of Windham county, the sum of $36.00 cents; To Amasa Paine, Esqr., state's attorney for Windsor county, the sum of $85.44 cents; To Elnathan Keyes, state's attorney for Chittenden county, the sum of $18.00 cents.

Passed November 6, 1798.

A true record,

Attest, Ros. Hopkins, Sec'y.

AN ACT FOR SUSPENDING PROSECUTIONS AGAINST TIMOTHY CLEMENT
FOR THE SPACE OF FIVE YEARS

NOVEMBER 6TH, 1798

It is hereby Enacted by the General Assembly of the State of Vermont, That all prosecutions, processes and writs of whatever name, of a civil nature, now pending, or which might hereafter be commenced against Timothy Clement of Rochester, in Windsor County, now a prisoner in the gaol at Woodstock, are and shall be from and after the rising of this assembly, suspended, and be, and remain suspended, for the term of five years, from the passing of this act. And the keeper of the gaol in Woodstock is hereby directed, on receiving his lawful fees, and after the said Timothy shall have executed a bond with sureties to the acceptance of one of the judges of the county court, of the county of Windsor, payable to clerk of said court, for the security of his creditors, conditioned, that in the said term of five years, he will not waste, embezzle or transfer any of his property, to the injury of his

---

1. Crockett, Walter Hill: *Vermont the Green Mountain State,* Vol. V, *The Vermont Bench and Bar,* Royal Tyler, 1757-1826, pages 71-75; *ibid, Vermont Authors,* pages 538-540. (Author of first distinctively American play to be acted on an American stage; supreme court judge, 1801-1812).

creditors, or either of them, to liberate and discharge the said Timothy from said prison, and for which this act shall be his sufficient warrant. And any judge of the county court aforesaid, is authorised to take and receive the bond aforesaid, and is directed to lodge the same in the office of the clerk of the court of said county, to be by said clerk preserved in the files of his office.[1]

Passed November 6, 1798.

A true record,

Attest, Ros. Hopkins, Sec'y.

AN ACT AUTHORISING THE PROPRIETORS OF MIDDLEBURY, TO CONFIRM AND COMPLETE THE DIVISION OF THEIR LANDS

NOVEMBER 6TH, 1798

Whereas, the proprietors of the township of Middlebury in the county of Addison, have formerly, in proprietors' meetings, voted several divisions of their lands into severalty, and have settled, and at this time hold their lands by virtue of such division. And whereas, through the loss of papers, and the inaccurate manner in which the proceedings of the proprietors have been recorded, disputes may hereafter arise respecting the several divisions of the lands, pitched and laid out in said town. Which evil to prevent,

Sec. 1. *It is hereby Enacted* by the General Assembly of the State of Vermont, That the proprietors of said town of Middlebury be, and they are hereby authorised and empowered, at any legal meeting by them already warned or to be warned hereafter for the purpose, to confirm any prior or former division or divisions of the lands in said Middlebury, to and among the said proprietors, and to pass any vote for completing any division or divisions of said lands already begun, any law, usage, or custom to the contrary, notwithstanding.

Sec. 2. *And whereas,* the lands which yet remain common and undivided in said Middlebury, cannot conveniently be divided in the mode prescribed by the existing laws of this State. Therefore, *It is hereby further Enacted,* That the said proprietors of said Middlebury be, and they are hereby fully authorised and empowered, at any legal

---

1. State Papers of Vermont, Vol. XI, *General Petitions,* 1797-1799, "For Release from Gaol and Suspension of Civil Prosecutions," 217.

meeting already warned or to be warned, and holden for the purpose, to complete the division of such common and undivided lands by pitching the same.

Passed November 6, 1798.

A true record,

Attest, Ros. Hopkins, Sec'y.

AN ACT ASSESSING A TAX OF THREE CENTS PER ACRE ON THE TOWN OF FAYSTON, FOR THE PURPOSE THEREIN MENTIONED

NOVEMBER 7TH, 1798

It is hereby Enacted by the General Assembly of the State of Vermont, That there be, and hereby is laid and assessed a tax of three cents per acre on all the lands in the township of Fayston, in the county of Chittenden (public rights excepted), for the purpose of making and repairing roads and building bridges in said town, to be expended under the direction of Thomas G. Wait and Benjamin Wait, Junr., who are hereby appointed a committee to superintend the expenditure of said tax. And any justice of the peace in the county of Chittenden is hereby authorised to issue his warrant to Lynde Wait who is hereby appointed a collector to collect said tax. And the said collector is hereby made accountable to said committee for the amount of said tax; and said committee and collector are hereby directed in the expending, collecting, and accounting for said tax to govern themselves in all things agreeably to the statute of this State entitled "An act regulating the disposition of monies raised by tax on lands in the several towns for the purpose of making and repairing roads and building bridges," passed November 2d, 1796.[1]

AN ACT LAYING A TAX OF ONE CENT PER ACRE ON THE TOWNSHIP OF WORCESTER FOR THE PURPOSE THEREIN MENTIONED

NOVEMBER 7TH, 1798

It is hereby Enacted by the General Assembly of the State of Vermont, That there be, and hereby is assessed and laid a tax of one

---

1. State Papers of Vermont, Vol. XI, *General Petitions,* 1797-1799, "For a Tax on Land to Build Roads and Bridges," 262.

cent per acre on all the lands in the township of Worcester, in the county of Chittenden (public lands excepted) for the purpose of making roads and building bridges in said town, to be expended under the direction of Job Gibbs, John Hastings, and Zadock Whitney, who are hereby appointed a committee to superintend the expenditure of said tax. And any justice of the peace of the county of Chittenden is hereby authorised to issue his warrant to Jesse Elmore, who is hereby appointed a collector to collect said tax. And said collector is hereby made accountable to said committee for the amount of said tax. And said committee and collector are hereby directed in the expending, collecting, and accounting for the monies raised by said tax, to conform themselves in all things to the directions of the statute of this State entitled "An act regulating the disposition of monies raised by tax on lands in the several towns for the purpose of making and repairing roads and building bridges," passed the 2d day of November, A.D. one thousand seven hundred and ninety six.[1]

AN ACT ASSESSING A TAX OF TWO CENTS PER ACRE ON THE TOWNSHIP OF WESTFIELD FOR THE PURPOSE THEREIN MENTIONED

NOVEMBER 7TH, 1798

It is hereby Enacted by the General Assembly of the State of Vermont, That there be, and hereby is assessed a tax of two cents on each acre of land in the township of Westfield, in the county of Orleans, publick lands excepted, for the purpose of making and repairing roads and building bridges in said town, for the time being, is annexed to the county of Franklin, to be expended under the direction of Jesse Olds, Samuel French and Asa Kimball, who are hereby appointed a committee to superintend the expenditure of said tax. And any justice of the peace within the county of Franklin is hereby authorised to issue his warrant to Joseph Scott, who is hereby appointed a collector, to collect said tax. And said collector is hereby made accountable to said committee for the amount of said tax; and said committee and collector are hereby directed in the collection, expenditure, and accounting for said tax to conform themselves in all things to the directions of the statute of this State entitled "An act regulaing the disposition of monies raised by tax on lands in the several towns for the purpose of making

---

1. State Papers of Vermont, Vol. XI, *General Petitions,* 1797-1799, "For a Tax on Land to Build and Repair Roads," 206.

and repairing roads and building bridges," passed November 2d, A.D. 1796.[1]

AN ACT ASSESSING A TAX OF ONE AND AN HALF CENT PER ACRE ON THE TOWN OF ELMORE, FOR THE PURPOSE THEREIN MENTIONED

NOVEMBER 7TH, 1798

It is hereby Enacted by the General Assembly of the State of Vermont, That there be, and hereby is laid a tax of one and an half cent per acre on all the lands in the township of Elmore, in the county of Franklin, public lands excepted, for the purpose of making & repairing roads and building bridges in said town, to be expended under the direction of Martin Elmore, Jesse Elmore, and Seth Olmstead, who are hereby appointed a committee to superintend the expenditure of said tax. And any justice of the peace of the county of Franklin is hereby authorised to issue his warrent to Martin Elmore, who is hereby appointed a collector to collect said tax; and said collector is hereby made accountable to said committe for the amount of said tax. And said committee and collector are hereby directed in the expending, collecting, and accounting for the monies raised by said tax, to conform themselves in all things to the directions of the statute of this State entitled "An act regulating the disposition of monies raised by tax on lands in the several towns, for the purpose of making and repairing roads and building bridges," passed the second day of November, A.D. 1796.[2]

AN ACT APPOINTING ELISHA W. BINGHAM A COMMITTEE MAN IN ADDITION TO A COMMITTEE APPOINTED ON A ROAD TAX GRANTED BY THE LEGISLATURE OF THE STATE OF VERMONT, ON THE TOWNSHIP OF CONCORD, IN THE COUNTY OF CALEDONIA AT THEIR OCTOBER SESSION 1797

NOVEMBER 7TH, 1798

Whereas, Samuel Wetherbe and Jonathan Woodbury were appointed a committee to superintend the expenditure of the monies

---

1. State Papers of Vermont, Vol. XI, *General Petitions,* 1797-1799, "For a Tax on Land to Build and Repair Roads," 308.
2. Ibid., "For a Tax on Land to Build and Repair Roads," 78.

raised by the above said tax, and it being expedient that Elisha W. Bingham be added thereto. Therefore,

It is hereby Enacted by the General Assembly of the State of Vermont, That Elisha W. Bingham be, and he is hereby appointed a committeeman in addition to the above said committee, and is hereby authorised and empowered to proceed in all things agreeable to the act assessing said tax.

AN ACT LAYING A TAX OF ONE AND AN HALF CENT PER ACRE ON THE TOWN OF BRIDGWATER, FOR THE PURPOSE THEREIN MENTIONED

NOVEMBER 7TH, 1798

It is hereby Enacted by the General Assembly of the State of Vermont, That there be, and hereby is laid a tax of one and an half cent per acre on all the lands in the township of Bridgwater in the county of Windsor, public rights excepted, for the purpose of making and repairing the great road, leading from Woodstock to Rutland, through said Bridgwater, and for building and repairing the bridges on said road, to be expended under the direction of the present selectmen of said town of Bridgwater, who are hereby appointed a committee to superintend the expenditure of said tax. And any justice of the peace, within the said county of Windsor, is hereby authorised to issue his warrant to Joseph Hawkins of said Bridgwater, who is hereby appointed a collector to collect said tax; and said collector is hereby made accountable to said committee for the amount of said tax. And said committee and collector are hereby directed in the expending, collecting, and accounting for the monies raised by said tax, to govern themselves, in all things by the direction of the statute of this State entitled, "An act regulating the disposition of monies raised by tax on lands in the several towns, for the purpose of making and repairing roads and building bridges," passed November 2d, 1796.[1]

AN ACT ASSESSING A TAX OF ONE CENT PER ACRE ON THE TOWNSHIP OF CALDERSBURGH FOR THE PURPOSE THEREIN MENTIONED

NOVEMBER 7TH, 1798

It is hereby Enacted by the General Assembly of the State of

---

1. State Papers of Vermont, Vol. XI, *General Petitions,* 1797-1799, "For a Tax on Land to Build and Repair Roads and Build Bridges," 184.

Vermont, That there be, and hereby is assessed a tax of one cent on each acre of land in the township of Caldersburgh, in the county of Caledonia (public rights excepted), for the purpose of making and repairing roads and building bridges in said town, to be expended under the direction of David Hide, Joseph Wait, and Joseph Cowell, who are hereby appointed a committee to superintend the expenditure of said tax, and any justice of the peace within said county of Caledonia is hereby authorised to issue his warrant to Timothy Hinman of Derby in said county of Caledonia, who is hereby appointed a collector to collect said tax, and said collector is hereby made accountable to said committee for the amount of said tax, and said committee and collector are hereby directed in the expenditure, collecting, and accounting for the monies raised by said tax, to govern themselves in all things agreeably to the direction of the statute of this State, entitled "An act regulating the disposition of monies raised by tax on lands in the several towns for the purpose of making and repairing roads and building bridges," passed November 2d, 1796.[1]

AN ACT DIVIDING THE SOUTH HERO INTO TWO SEPARATE TOWNS

NOVEMBER 7TH, 1798

Sec. 1. *It is hereby Enacted* by the General Assembly of the State of Vermont, That the town of South-Hero, in the county of Chittenden, be, and the same is hereby divided into two separate and distinct towns, by a line running east and west across said township, from the north line of the lot laid to the right for the support of the ministry in said town; and that, that part of said township, which is situate north of the line aforesaid, shall forever hereafter be called, known and designated by the name of the Middle Hero. And the inhabitants thereof shall be entitled to all the town privileges which other towns in this State have and enjoy, except the privilege of electing and sending a representative to the Legislature and to state convention. And the public lands and the rents and profits thereof, which of right belonged to the inhabitants of said township of South Hero, before the passing of this act, shall be forever hereafter equally divided between said towns.

---

1. State Papers of Vermont, Vol. XI, *General Petitions,* 1797-1799, "For a Tax on Land to Build Roads and Bridges," 252.

Sec. 2.   And it is hereby further Enacted, That the freemen of said town of Middle-Hero and South-Hero, shall meet at their next freemen's meeting in said town of South-Hero, as existing before the passing of this act, and thereafter at such place or places, as the freemen in their meeting shall appoint, and jointly elect a representative to represent said town in the General Assembly, and State convention. And such freemen's meetings shall be warned by the first constable or other officer by law directed to warn freemen's meetings of each respective town, and the first constable of the town in which the meeting shall be holden shall preside in such meeting, if present; if not the first constable of the other town, shall preside, if present; if both should be absent the town clerk or one of the selectmen of the town in which the meeting is holden shall preside.

Passed November 7, 1798.

A true record,

Attest, Ros. Hopkins, Sec'y.

AN ACT ASSESSING A TAX OF TWO CENTS PER ACRE ON THE TOWN OF HANCOCK FOR THE PURPOSE THEREIN MENTIONED

NOVEMBER 7TH, 1798

It is hereby Enacted by the General Assembly of the State of Vermont, That there be, and hereby is assessed a tax of two cents per acre on all the lands in the township of Hancock, in the county of Addison (public lands excepted), for the purpose of making and repairing roads and building bridges in said town, to be expended under the direction of Zenas Robbins, Nathan Dolbear, and Levi Darling of said Hancock, who are hereby appointed a committee to superintend the expenditure of said tax. And any justice of the peace of the county of Addison is hereby authorised to issue his warrant to William Cummings of said Hancock, who is hereby appointed a collector to collect said tax, and said collector is hereby made accountable to said committee for the amount of said tax. And said committee and collector are hereby directed in the expenditure, collection, and accounting for the monies raised by said tax, to govern themselves in all things by the direction of the statute of this State, entitled "An act regulating the disposition of monies raised by tax on lands in the several towns for the purpose of making roads and building bridges," passed the 2d day of November 1796.[1]

AN ACT LAYING ONE AND HALF CENT ON EACH ACRE OF LAND IN THE TOWNSHIP OF MINEHEAD, PUBLIC LANDS EXCEPTED

NOVEMBER 7TH, 1798

It is hereby Enacted by the General Assembly of the State of Vermont, That there be, and hereby is assessed a tax of one cent and an half cent on each acre of land in the township of Minehead, in the county of Caledonia, public lands excepted, for the purpose of making a road through said town, and James Lucas, Nathaniel Wait, and James Chamberlain are hereby appointed a committee to superintend the expenditure of said tax; any justice of the peace in the county of Caledonia is hereby empowered to issue his warrant to Mills DeForest to collect said tax, who is hereby appointed a collector to collect the same, and the said collector is hereby made accountable to the said committee for the amount of said tax. And the said committee and collector are hereby directed to govern themselves in laying out said road, and in collecting and expending said tax agreeable to a statute law of this State regulating the expenditure of monies raised for the purpose of making roads, building bridges, &c., passed November 2d, 1796.

AN ACT ASSESSING A TAX OF ONE CENT PER ACRE ON THE TOWNSHIP OF MORRISTOWN FOR THE PURPOSE THEREIN MENTIONED

NOVEMBER 7TH, 1798

It is hereby Enacted by the General Assembly of the State of Vermont, That there be, and hereby is assessed a tax of one cent on each acre of land in the township of Morristown, in the county of Orleans, public lands excepted, for the purpose of making and repairing roads and building bridges in said town, to be expended under the direction of Elisha Boardman, Micajah Dunham, and Cyril Goodale, who are hereby appointed a committee to superintend the expenditure of said tax, and any justice of the peace within the county of Franklin,

1. State Papers of Vermont, Vol. XI, *General Petitions*, 1797-1798, "For a Tax on Land to Build and Repair Roads and Build Bridges," 287.

is hereby authorised to issue his warrant to Comfort Olds, Junr., who is hereby appointed a collector to collect said tax, and said collector is hereby made accountable to said committee for the amount of said tax; and said committee and collector are hereby directed in the collection, expenditure, and accounting for said tax, to conform themselves, in all things to the directions of the statute of this State, entitled "An act regulating the disposition of monies raised by tax on lands in the several towns for the purpose of making and repairing roads and building bridges," passed November 2d A.D., 1796.[1]

AN ACT ASSESSING A TAX OF TWO CENTS PER ACRE ON THE TOWN OF PLAINFIELD, LATE ST. ANDREWS GORE, FOR THE PURPOSE THEREIN MENTIONED

NOVEMBER 7TH, 1798

It is hereby Enacted by the General Assembly of the State of Vermont, That there be, and hereby is laid a tax of two cents per acre on all the lands in the township of Plainfield, late St. Andrews Gore, in the county of Caledonia, public lands excepted, for the purpose of making roads and building bridges in said town, to be expended under the direction of Jacob Davis, Thomas Vincent, and James Boutwell, who are hereby appointed a committee to superintend the expenditure of said tax. And any justice of the peace of the county of Caledonia, is hereby authorised to issue his warrant to Seth Freeman of .... who is hereby appointed a collector to collect said tax. And said collector is hereby made accountable to said committee for the amount of said tax; and said committee and collector are hereby directed, in the expending, collecting, and accounting for the monies raised by said tax, to conform themselves in all things to the directions of the statute of this State entitled "An act regulating the disposition of monies raised by tax on lands in the several towns for the purpose of making and repairing roads and building bridges," passed the 2d day of November, A.D. 1796.[2]

---

1. State Papers of Vermont, Vol. XI, *General Petitions,* 1797-1799, "For a Tax on Land to Build and Repair Roads and Bridges," 220.

2. Ibid., "For a Tax on Land to Build and Repair Roads and Bridges," 200.

AN ACT ASSESSING A TAX OF ONE CENT PER ACRE ON THE TOWNSHIP OF JAY FOR THE PURPOSE THEREIN MENTIONED

NOVEMBER 7TH, 1798

It is hereby Enacted by the General Assembly of the State of Vermont, That there be, and hereby is assessed a tax of one cent on each acre of land in the township of Jay, in the territory of Orleans county (public rights excepted), for the purpose of making and repairing roads and building bridges in said town, to be expended under the direction of Ephraim Morse, Josiah Elkins, and Noah Chittenden, who are hereby appointed a committee to superintend the expenditure of said tax. And any justice of the peace within the county of Caledonia, is hereby authorised to issue his warrant to Thomas Tolman of Greensboro' to collect said tax. And said collector is hereby made accountable to said committee for the amount of said tax; and said committee and collector are hereby directed in the expending, collecting and accounting for the monies raised by said tax, to conform themselves in all things to the statute of this state entitled, "An act regulating the disposition of monies raised by tax on lands, in the several towns for the purpose of making and repairing roads and building bridges," passed November 2d, 1796.

AN ACT ASSESSING A TAX OF TWO CENTS PER ACRE ON THE TOWN OF COLCHESTER FOR THE PURPOSE THEREIN MENTIONED

NOVEMBER 7TH, 1798

It is hereby Enacted by the General Assembly of the State of Vermont, That there be, and hereby is assessed and laid a tax of two cents per acre on all the lands in the township of Colchester, in the county of Chittenden, public rights excepted, for the purpose of making and repairing roads and building bridges in said town, to be expended under the direction of Simeon Hine, Aaron Brownell, and Joshua Stanton, Junr., who are hereby appointed a committee to superintend the expenditure of said tax. And any justice of the peace, within the county of Chittenden, is hereby authorised to issue his warrant to Dennis Downing of said Colchester, who is hereby appointed a collector to collect said tax. And said collector is hereby made accountable to said committee for the amount of said tax. And said committee and collector are hereby directed, in the expending, collecting, and accounting for the monies raised by said tax, to govern themselves in all things by the statute of this State entitled "An act regulating the disposition of monies raised by tax on lands in the several towns for the purpose of making and repairing roads and building bridges," passed November 2d, 1796.

AN ACT GRANTING TO ISACHAR REED THE EXCLUSIVE RIGHT AND PRIVILEGE OF RUNNING A STAGE FROM RUTLAND TO THE LINE OF THIS STATE ON THE ROAD FROM RUT- LAND TO SALEM IN THE STATE OF NEW YORK

NOVEMBER 7TH, 1798

Sec. 1. *It is hereby Enacted* by the General Assembly of the State of Vermont, That Isachar Reed of Rutland, in our county of Rutland, have, and there is hereby granted to the said Isachar Reed, the sole and exclusive right and privilege of running a stage or stages, from Rutland post office, through Ira, Middletown, Pawlet and Rupert, to the boundary line between this state and the State of New York, and on any rout[e] on which the mail of the United States, may from time to time, be carried from Rutland aforesaid, to said Salem, for and during the term of eight years, from and after the passing hereof.

Provided always, that the said Isachar, provide, use and employ on the road and route aforesaid, good, able, sufficient and convenient carriages and horses, during said term, and also that the said Isachar demand and receive no greater sum, by the mile, for the carriage on said road and route, of any passenger or baggage that shall, from time to time, be demanded and received by the carriers of the mail, from Rutland aforesaid to Albany in the said state of New York. *And provided also,* That said Isachar from after the first day of January, which will be in the year of our Lord one thousand eight hundred, to the full end of the term aforesaid, shall run said stage or stages on the route aforesaid, at least once every week from Rutland aforesaid, to said Salem, and return in the same week, from said Salem to said Rutland, saving, nevertheless, from the provision last aforesaid, that the said Isachar may suspend the running of said stage or stages, during three weeks in each fall, and in each spring, for and during the term aforesaid. *And provided also,* That nothing herein contained, shall be construed to affect, or shall contravene any laws of the United States, or regulations of the postmaster general thereof, which now are or at any time during the term aforesaid, may be made or passed, anything herein contained to the contrary thereof, in any wise notwithstanding.[1]

Passed November 7, 1798.

A true copy,

Attest, Ros. Hopkins, Sec'y.

AN ACT DISCHARGING JONATHAN NICHOLS, JUNR., FROM PAYMENT OF A CERTAIN NOTE THEREIN MENTIONED

NOVEMBER 7TH, 1798

Whereas, Jonathan Nichols, Junr., of Middlebury in the county of Addison, has heretofore executed his note of hand to the treasurer of this State for the sum of forty five dollars and twenty seven cents, for costs assessed by the supreme court, holden at Middlebury in the county of Addison, in January, A.D. one thousand seven hundred and ninety six, against George W. Andrews, for which costs the said George was committed to gaol. And whereas it appears to said Legislature, that the said Jonathan executed the note aforesaid, to redeem the said George out of prison, with the expectation of receiving a compensation in the labour of the said George, and that the said George made his escape without making compensation to the said Jonathan. Therefore,

It is hereby Enacted by the General Assembly of the State of Vermont, That the said Jonathan Nichols, Junr., be, and he is hereby discharged from the payment of the aforesaid note. And the treasurer of this State, and the state's attorney for the county of Addison, are directed to deliver over to the said Jonathan Nichols, the aforesaid note, and for their so doing this act shall be sufficient evidence to discharge them from being accountable to the State for the money due thereupon.[2]

Passed November 7, 1798.

A true record,

Attest, Ros. Hopkins, Sec'y.

---

1. State Papers of Vermont, Vol. XI, *General Petitions,* 1797-1799, "For The Right to Run a Stage," 286.

2. Ibid., "For Cancellation of a Promissory Note to the State," 279.

AN ACT GRANTING LEAVE TO RAISE VOLUNTEER COMPANIES FROM
EXEMPTS, AND INCORPORATING THEM INTO THE SEVERAL
REGIMENTS OF THE MILITIA OF THIS STATE

NOVEMBER 7TH, 1798

Sec. 1. *It is hereby Enacted* by the General Assembly of the State of Vermont, That where there shall be a sufficient number of able bodied effective men, in one or more towns, adjacent to each other, who by law are not subject to do military duty; and who shall voluntarily enlist themselves into a company for the purpose of doing military duty, to the number of sixty four, and shall make application to the colonel, or commanding officer of the regiment, within whose limits they are so formed, that it shall be the duty of such colonel or commanding officer of such regiment to give an order appointing time and place for such new company to meet, for the purpose of electing their officers, giving at least ten days notice for that purpose, and by himself, or some meet person for the purpose, by his order, when such company shall be so convened, to cause a muster roll, to be made out from the enlistment; and shall then proceed to lead them to the choice of such commissioned and noncommissioned officers as the several companies of infantry in this state are by law entitled. And such presiding officer shall, within twenty days from any such election, make out or duplicate from such muster roll, with his returns of the election of officers inserted thereon, to the Brigadier General within whose limits such company is formed. And the original muster roll, made out as aforesaid, shall be delivered by such presiding officer, to the captain elected to the command of any such company for the use thereof.

Sec. 2. *And it is hereby further Enacted,* That it shall be the duty of the Brigadier-General, to whom any such returns shall be made, to commission the officers chosen as aforesaid. And all such companies shall be considered as constituting a part of the regiment, within whose limits they are so raised, and shall take rank in the regiment to which they belong according to the day of the date of their organization.

Sec. 3. *And it is hereby further Enacted,* That all such volunteer companies, formed as aforesaid, shall at their own expense, arm and equip themselves with all such arms and equipments as are required by law for the several companies of infantry within this State.

And they shall be subject to the same duties, penalties and forfeitures, as are enjoined by the law regulating the militia of this State, passed the fourth day of March A.D., one thousand seven hundred and ninety seven.

Sec. 4. *And it is hereby further Enacted,* That such volunteer companies shall have the privilege to enlist, from time to time, to keep such companies full, from the exempts within the limits of any such company, which limits shall be set out by the commanding officer of the regiment to which they respectively belong.

Sec. 5. *And it is hereby further Enacted,* That it shall be the duty of every commanding officer, of any such volunteer company, some time in the month of May, annually, to make out a true and attested copy of duplicate of his muster roll, to the colonel or commanding officer of the regiment to which they respectively belong. And no commission[ed] officer or soldier belonging to any such volunteer company shall be discharged therefrom unless by the special permission of such colonel or commanding officer, except he shall have arrived at the age of forty five years.[1]

Passed November 7, 1798.

A true copy,

Attest, Ros. Hopkins, Sec'y.

AN ACT TO ENABLE THE PROPRIETORS AND LANDOWNERS OF THE TOWN OF JERICHO, TO DIVIDE THE LANDS INTO SEVERALTY

NOVEMBER 7TH, 1798

Whereas, the proprietors of Jericho, in the county of Chittenden, formerly attempted to make a division of the lands in said township, by the mode of pitching, in consequence of which, many of said proprietors made pitches and surveys of lots in said township, and many settlements and large improvements, have been made thereon, and it appears that said divisions so attempted to be made, were not made conformably to any existing law of this State, and the records of said proprietors relating thereto, are either lost or withheld, and concealed by the former proprietors' clerks. And whereas it is impossible, under the present circumstances of said proprietors and

---

1. State Papers of Vermont, Vol. XI, *General Petitions,* 1797-1799, "For Formation of a Militia Company," 207.

settlers, to make a just and equitable division of the lands in said township, agreeably to the existing laws of this State. Therefore,

It is hereby Enacted by the General Assembly of the State of Vermont, That the proprietors and landowners of the township of Jericho, shall be, and they are hereby empowered, to warn a meeting of said proprietors and landowners, and in the warning to notify the former proprietors' clerk or clerks, to deliver over all the proprietors' records, files, or papers, belonging to their said offices, respectively, on or before the day of said meeting, to the present proprietors' clerk in said town, which warning shall be published at least six months previous to the day of said proprietors' meeting. And if the former proprietors' clerks, their heirs, or assigns, do refuse or neglect to deliver over said records and files, to the clerk as aforesaid, at the time aforesaid, they shall forever thereafter, be debarred from producing them, as evidence of any division or allotment of said proprietors whatever; and in case of such neglect or refusal, the proprietors and landowners of said township are hereby empowered, at any meeting legally warned and holden for that purpose, to agree upon such mode of dividing the lands in said township into severalty, as to them shall appear most just and equitable, having regard as circumstances will admit, to the lots as the same have been already surveyed, and to the settlements and improvements made thereon; and the said proprietors and landowners having made or caused to be made an accurate survey, plan, and allotment of the lands in said townships accordingly, shall have power at said meeting, to accept thereof and establish the same as a legal division of said township, and the same shall forever thereafter, be deemed a good and valid division in law, to all intents and purposes whatever. *Provided nevertheless,* That each landowner shall have a voice in the vote, according to the quantity of land he owns, on the original right, and that the owners of the major part of a right shall carry the vote on such right.

Passed November 7, 1798.

A true record,

Attest, Ros. Hopkins, Sec'y.

AN ACT AUTHORISING THE PROPRIETORS OF THE TOWNSHIP OF
SALISBURY, TO ESTABLISH THEIR DIVISIONS ALREADY MADE,
AND ALSO TO DIVIDE THE REMAINDER OF THEIR LANDS
BY PITCHING

NOVEMBER 7TH, 1798

Whereas, the proprietors of the township of Salisbury, in the county of Addison, have voted, and made two divisions of one hundred acres each, to each original proprietors' right by pitching, called the second and third hundred acre divisions. And whereas, some doubts have arisen with respect to the legality of said divisions. Therefore,

Sec. 1. *It is hereby Enacted* by the General Assembly of the State of Vermont, That the proprietors of the township of Salisbury, in the county of Addison, be, and they are hereby authorised and empowered at any legal meeting warned for that purpose, to establish their divisions heretofore made, and also to make divisions of the undivided lands in said township, to, and among the said proprietors, by pitching the same.

Provided always, That in case it shall so happen that a survey made on the second hundred acre division, and a survey made on the third hundred acre division, shall cover the same tract of land, that it shall not be in the power of the proprietors, so to establish the third hundred acre division, as to take away the right of the second.

Passed November 7, 1798.

A true record,

Attest, Ros. Hopkins, Sec'y.

AN ACT TO SUSPEND PROSECUTIONS AGAINST THOMAS ARCHIBALD FOR
THE TERM OF FIVE YEARS

NOVEMBER 7TH, 1798

It is hereby Enacted by the General Assembly of the State of Vermont, That all prosecutions, processes and writs of whatever name of a civil nature, now pending, or which might hereafter be commenced on any contract heretofore made against Thomas Archibald of Middlebury, in the county of Addison, now a prisoner in the gaol in said Middlebury, on an execution in favor of John Curtis of said Middlebury, are and shall be, from and after the rising of this assembly, suspended and remain suspended for the term of five years from the passing of this act; and the keeper of the said gaol in Middlebury, is hereby directed on receiving his lawful fees for the commitment of the said Thomas, and after the said Thomas shall have executed a bond with sufficient surety to the acceptance of the keeper of the said gaol, which bond is hereby made assignable to the said John Curtis, in the same manner as bail bonds for the liberty of gaol yards are assignable; conditioned, that in case the debt due on said execution, be not paid in the term of the said five years, the said Thomas shall be at Middlebury, aforesaid, ready to be delivered up on the said execution, which shall then be in full force against him, as if it had never been levied, to liberate and discharge the said Thomas from prison on said execution, for which this act shall be his sufficient warrant. *Provided nevertheless,* That this act shall not extend to secure the said Thomas in the possession or enjoyment of any real estate heretofore mortgaged by him to certain of his creditors, any thing therein contained to the contrary notwithstanding.[1]

Passed November 7, 1798.

A true copy,

Attest, Ros. Hopkins, Sec'y.

AN ACT IN ALTERATION OF AN ACT ENTITLED "AN ACT GRANTING TO WILLAIM PAGE AND LEWIS R. MORRIS, THEIR HEIRS AND ASSIGNS FOREVER, THE EXCLUSIVE RIGHT OF LOCKING BELLOWS FALLS OF CONNECTICUT RIVER," AND FOR REPEALING AN ACT PASSED THE FIRST DAY OF NOVEMBER *ANNO DOMINI* 1791 GRANTING THE SAME: AND ALSO IN ALTERATION OF AN ACT PASSED ON THE SEVENTEENTH DAY OF OCTOBER 1795, FOR INCREASING THE TOLL ON ALL KINDS OF LUMBER

NOVEMBER 7TH, 1798

Whereas, the said William Page, in behalf of said company, hath petitioned the General Assembly of the State of Vermont, setting

---

1. State Papers of Vermont, Vol. XI, *General Petitions,* 1797-1799, "For Entry of an Appeal to the Court Docket," 211.

forth that the rates of toll are inadequate considering the expense of locking said falls, and praying for liberty to take higher rates of toll than are mentioned in said act, which appearing reasonable. Therefore,

It is hereby Enacted by the General Assembly of the State of Vermont, That the said company may be allowed, for the term of five years from and after the passing of this act, to take fifty cents per ton for conveying loaded boats through said locks and canals, and twenty five cents per ton for all empty boats, according to the tons said boat will carry, and the sum of fifty cents for every ton of lumber, except on square timber and logs, which shall be twelve cents per ton only for conveying through said locks and canals, any thing in the afore mentioned acts to the contrary notwithstanding. *Provided,* The said company shall in no wise obstruct or hinder the carting of lumber and other loading by said falls as has been heretofore practised. *Provided also,* That the company shall take no benefit from this act, unless the said locks shall be so far compleated, that boats and rafts may pass with safety, within one year from the passing of this act.

Passed November 7, 1798.

A true copy,

Attest, Ros. Hopkins, Sec'y.

AN ACT DIRECTING THE TREASURER OF THE COUNTY OF ORANGE TO PAY JOSEPH NORTON THE SUM THEREIN MENTIONED

NOVEMBER 7TH, 1798

Whereas, it appears that the general list of the town of Strafford for the year 1796, was returned to the county treasurer of said county, eight hundred pounds too large, by which means the said Joseph Norton, the first constable of Strafford, was obliged to pay said treasurer five dollars and fifty cents more than he ought to have done. Therefore,

It is hereby Enacted by the General Assembly of the State of Vermont, That the treasurer of said county be, and hereby is directed to pay to the said Joseph Norton the sum of five dollars and fifty cents.

[Passed November 7, 1798.]

[A true copy,]

[Attest, Ros. Hopkins, Sec'y.]

AN ACT GRANTING TO CHARLES RICH TWELVE DOLLARS AND NINETY
FIVE CENTS FOR THE PURPOSE THEREIN MENTIONED

NOVEMBER 7TH, 1798

Whereas, it appears to this Legislature that Charles Rich, collector of the cent tax in Shoreham, is made accountable to the treasurer of this State for the sum of $12.95 cents more then he is enabled to collect by the rate bill delivered to him by the selectmen of said Shoreham. Therefore,

It is hereby Enacted by the General Assembly of the State of Vermont, That the treasurer of this State be, and he hereby is directed to pay to Charles Rich, collector of the cent land tax in Shoreham, granted by the Legislature of this state at their session held at Windsor, A.D. 1797, twelve dollars, ninety five cents.

Passed November 7, 1798.

A true record,

Attest, Ros. Hopkins, Sec'y.

AN ACT DIRECTING THE TREASURER TO PAY THE EXPENSES INCURRED
ON THE DAY OF ELECTION

NOVEMBER 7TH, 1798

It is hereby Enacted by the General Assembly of the State of Vermont, That the treasurer be, and he hereby is directed to pay to his Excellency the Governor, the sum of one hundred forty six dollars for the expenses of a dinner for the clergy, and other contingent expenses, on the day of the general election.

Passed November 7, 1798.

A true record,

Attest, Ros. Hopkins, Sec'y.

AN ACT DIRECTING THE TREASURER TO PAY SETH STORRS, AUDITOR,
THE SUM THEREIN MENTIONED

NOVEMBER 7TH, 1798

It is hereby Enacted by the General Assembly of the State of Vermont, That the treasurer of this State be, and he hereby is directed to pay Seth Storrs thirty two dollars and seventy five cents for his services as auditor of accounts, for the year past.

Passed November 7, 1798.

A true record,

Attest, Ros. Hopkins, Sec'y.

AN ACT ASSESSING A TAX OF TWO PENCE PER ACRE ON THE TOWNSHIP OF HUNTINGTON FOR THE PURPOSE OF MAKING ROADS AND BUILDING BRIDGES

NOVEMBER 8TH, 1798

It is hereby Enacted by the General Assembly of the State of Vermont, That there be, and hereby is assessed a tax of two pence on each acre of land in the township of Huntington, in the county of Chittenden (public rights excepted), for the purpose of making and repairing roads and building bridges in said town, to be expended by the order and under the direction of Parley Star, Ozer Brewster, and Jehiel Johns, all of Huntington aforesaid, who are hereby appointed a committee to superintend the expenditure of said tax; and any justice of the peace within the county of Chittenden is hereby empowered to issue a warrant to Sylvester Russell of said Huntington, to collect said tax, and said collector is hereby made accountable to said committee for the amount of said tax, and said collector and committee are hereby directed to govern themselves in collecting, disposing, and accounting for monies raised by said tax agreeable to an act entitled, "An act regulating the disposition of monies raised by tax on the several towns for the purpose of making and repairing roads and building bridges," passed October Session 1796.

AN ACT APPOINTING A COLLECTOR OF A LAND TAX IN STOWE

NOVEMBER 8TH, 1798

Whereas, Thomas Kennan of Waterbury, in the county of Chittenden was, in the year 1794, appointed the collector of a land tax of one penny per acre on the township of Stowe, in and by the act assessing said tax; and whereas the said Thomas declines collecting said tax.

It is hereby Enacted by the General Assembly of the State of Vermont, That William Utley of said Stowe be, and he is hereby appointed the collector of said tax in the room of the said Thomas Kennan. And any justice of the peace, within the county of Chittenden, is hereby authorised to issue his warrant to the said William Utley to collect said tax. And the said new collector is hereby vested with all the authority, and is directed and made accountable in the collection of said tax, in the same manner and extent as the said former collector was authorised, directed and made accountable.

AN ACT TO PREVENT UNNECESSARY LAW SUITS, AND TO REGULATE THE TAXING OF COSTS IN CERTAIN CASES THEREIN MENTIONED

NOVEMBER 8TH, 1798

Sec. 1. *It is hereby Enacted* by the General Assembly of the State of Vermont, That if more than one action shall hereafter be commenced, on any one joint and several contract, or on different notes or bonds, between the same parties, and be pending in any court at the same time, such court may, in their discretion, whether judgment in such suit or suits shall be rendered for plaintiff or defendant, tax and allow such costs, and such only, for the plaintiff or defendant, or for the plaintiff and defendant, as the case may be, as such court shall judge just and equitable, and render judgment for the balance accordingly.

Sec. 2. *And it is hereby further Enacted,* That in all cases when a mortgagee or mortgagees shall commence an action or actions of ejectment, on a mortgage deed, and an action, or actions on the contract mentioned in the conditions of such deed, and such actions shall be pending at the same time, such mortgagee shall recover no more costs, than if he had commenced one of such actions only.

Sec. 3. *And it is hereby further Enacted,* That in all actions that are now pending, or that shall hereafter be commenced, in any court in this State, in which there are or shall be more than one plaintiff, no travelling fees shall be taxed or allowed in favor of the plaintiffs in such action, but from that plaintiff's place of abode, residing nearest the place of holding such court, except in case of actual travel and attendance of the other or others of the plaintiffs, for the purpose of attending to such actions, and in all such cases, such court may allow such further sum for traveling fees as shall be judged just & equitable.

Passed November 8, 1798.

A true record,

Attest, Ros. Hopkins, Sec'y.

AN ACT IN ADDITION TO AND EXPLANATION OF AN ACT ENTITLED, "AN ACT ASSESSING A TAX OF ONE CENT ON EACH ACRE OF LAND IN THIS STATE FOR THE SUPPORT OF GOVERNMENT, DURING THE YEAR ONE THOUSAND SEVEN HUNDRED AND NINETY SEVEN AND FOR OTHER PURPOSES"

NOVEMBER 8TH, 1798

Whereas, many constables in this State have not been able to collect the aforesaid tax by the sale of the lands in their respective towns or otherwise. Therefore,

Sec. 1. *It is hereby Enacted* by the General Assembly of the State of Vermont, That the several collectors of the aforesaid tax, be, and they are hereby authorised and empowered to proceed in the collection of the aforesaid tax, in as full and ample a manner as though the time by said act prescribed for the collection of the same, had not expired, pursuing in all things the direction of said statute, except as to the day of sale to be mentioned in their advertisement; and when any such collector shall duly advertise and open any vendue for the sale of lands, such collector shall have power to adjourn or continue such vendue until he shall have collected the whole of the tax committed to him for collection. And the proprietors and landowners whose lands shall be sold by such collector, at such vendue, shall have the same time to redeem the same after the day of such sale, as is given by the aforesaid act, except that such proprietor or landowner shall pay interest on the purchase money, at the rate of twenty five per cent per annum. And the said collectors are hereby authorised to add the legal cost of advertising and holding their former vendues to the cost of the vendues which they are authorised to hold by this act, and to charge the delinquent landowners or proprietors their respective proportion of the same.

Sec. 2. *And it is hereby further Enacted,* That the treasurer of this State be, and he is hereby directed to stay all further proceeding against the delinquent collectors of said tax, until the first day of July next. And it is hereby declared to be the duty of the treasurer to write as soon as may be to the several sheriffs, to whom he may have sent extents against delinquent collectors of said tax, to stay all further proceedings on such extents, and in case any sheriff shall have levied such extent, on the property or body of such delinquent collector, it shall be the duty of such sheriff forthwith to release the body or property of such collector so levied on as aforesaid, on such collector paying to such sheriff his legal fees, which shall have accrued on such extent, and such sheriff shall, without delay, return such extent to the treasurer, with his doings thereon, together with a particular account of his fees, which he shall have so taken as aforesaid. And if such collector as last aforesaid, shall make it appear to the satisfaction of the treasurer, that such delinquency was occasioned by his not having been able to make sale of lands, or otherwise to collect said tax, and not by any default of his, in such case the treasurer shall allow him the legal cost, which he shall have so paid the sheriff as aforesaid. *Provided,* such release of the body or property of such collector as aforesaid, shall not be construed to discharge such collector from any extent which the treasurer may hereafter issue against such collector.

Passed November 8, 1798.

A true record,

Attest, Ros. Hopkins, Sec'y.

AN ACT SUPPLEMENTARY TO AN ACT ENTITLED, "AN ACT DIVIDING THE STATE INTO DISTRICTS FOR ELECTING REPRESENTATIVES TO THE CONGRESS OF THE UNITED STATES, AND DIRECTING THE MODE OF THEIR ELECTION"

NOVEMBER 8TH, 1798

Whereas, no mode is pointed out by law, to fill any vacancy which may happen in the representation of this State in the Congress of the United States. Therefore,

Sec. 1. *It is hereby Enacted* by the General Assembly of the State of Vermont, That when any vacancy shall happen, the governor of this State, for the time being, be and he hereby is authorised, empowered, or directed to issue writs of election to fill such vacancy, as soon as may be, directed to the first constables, or in their absence to the town clerks, or in the absence of both, to the selectmen of the several towns, within such districts, in which such vacency shall happen, requiring, or commanding said constables, or others, as the case may be, to warn the freemen of the several towns to meet at the usual place of holding freemen's meetings, in such towns, on such day and time as the governor for the time being shall prescribe, in said writs of election, which warning shall be posted, at least twelve days previous to such meeting. And the governor for the time being, shall cause such writs to be delivered to the respective sheriffs of the several counties within such district in due time, whose duty it is hereby expressly declared to be, to deliver the said writs to the said first constables, or in their absence to the town clerks, or in the absence of both to one of the selectmen of the respective towns, seasonably for such warning to be posted as aforesaid.

Sec. 2. *And it is hereby further Enacted,* That the said meeting shall be governed, the ballots taken, sorted, counted, certified, and a record thereof made in all things in the same manner, and the same shall be delivered to the several county clerks, or in their absence to the several sheriffs in said district, as is or are directed in the aforesaid act. And the said clerks, and sheriffs shall meet at such times and places as is or are prescribed by the fifth and sixth sections of the aforesaid act, and proceed to open, sort and count the same, and to declare the person having a majority of all the votes to be elected a representative to represent this State in the Congress of the United States; of which election they shall notify the governor, for the time being, within ten days from such meeting. And in case no person shall have a majority of all the votes, that then the said clerks and sheriffs shall return to the governor within ten days as aforesaid, the name of all the candidates, with a statement of the votes for each of them.

Sec. 3. *And it hereby further Enacted,* That it shall be the duty of the governor, on notice as aforesaid, to issue writs of election anew, in the same manner as before directed by this act, and so from time to time until an election shall be declared, according to the tenor and effect of this act, and the governor for the time being shall make out and deliver to the representative so chosen, proper and sufficient credentials of his election.

Sec. 4. *And it is hereby further Enacted,* That the said constables, clerks, sheriffs, and all others on whom any duty is imposed, or of whom any act or thing is required to be done, or shall be done, under this act, shall be liable to all and singular such fines, forfeitures, liabilities and disabilities, and entitled to receive all and singular such compensation and fees for their services respectively, as is or are directed, given or provided in and by the act to which this is a supplement.

Passed November 8, 1798.

A true copy,

Attest, Ros. Hopkins, Sec'y.

AN ACT LAYING A TAX OF ONE CENT PER ACRE ON THE TOWN OF STOWE FOR THE PURPOSE THEREIN MENTIONED

NOVEMBER 8TH, 1798

It is hereby Enacted by the General Assembly of the State of Vermont, That there be, and hereby is laid a tax of one cent per acre on all the lands in the township of Stowe, in the county of Chittenden (public rights excepted), for the purpose of making roads and building bridges in said town, to be expended under the direction of Londen [Louden] Case, Josiah Hurlbut, and Elijah Hayden, who are hereby appointed a committee to superintend the expenditure of said tax. And any justice of the peace of the county of Chittenden is hereby authorised to issue his warrant to William Utley of said Stowe, who is hereby appointed a collector to collect said tax. And said collector is hereby made accountable to said committee for the amount of said tax. And said committee and collector are hereby directed in the expending, collecting, and accounting for the monies raised by said tax, to govern themselves in all things by the directions of the statute of this State entitled "An act regulating the disposition of monies raised by tax on lands in the several towns for the purpose of making and repairing roads and building bridges," passed the 2d day of November, A.D. 1796.[1]

AN ACT IN ADDITION TO AN ACT APPOINTING A COLLECTOR OF A LAND TAX IN FLETCHER, PASSED NOVEMBER 8TH, 1797

NOVEMBER 8TH, 1798

Whereas, Lemuel Scott was by said act appointed collector of a

---

1. State Papers of Vermont, Vol. XI, *General Petitions,* 1797-1799, "For a Tax on Land to Build Roads and Bridges," 178.

tax of two pence per acre, on the township of Fletcher, in the room of Benjamin Fassett, who had refused and neglected to collect said tax, and whereas the said Benjamin Fassett was in and by said act directed to deliver over to the said Lemuel, all papers he had received as collector of said tax, and hath refused to do the same, whereby the purposes for which the said tax was granted cannot be effected. Therefore,

It is hereby Enacted by the General Assembly of the State of Vermont, That the said Lemuel be, and he is hereby directed and empowered to demand of the said Benjamin all and every paper, he has received as collector of the tax aforesaid, and also a statement of the proceedings had by the said Benjamin as collector of said tax, and of the monies received by him in payment thereof, and in case the said Benjamin shall refuse or neglect to make out and render to the said Lemuel such statement as aforesaid, or refuse to pay over to him, the said Lemuel, all or any part of the monies he already has or may hereafter receive as collector aforesaid, then he, the said Lemuel, shall and may institute, in his own name, an action against the said Benjamin Fassett, and recover the sum so retained with costs before any court within this State having jurisdiction of the same, and the said Lemuel shall dispose of the monies so collected, as by statute law of this State directing collectors of such taxes as aforesaid, is already provided for.[1]

AN ACT GRANTING RELIEF IN A CERTAIN CASE TO THE PROPRIETORS
OF THE TOWN OF WESTFORD, AND DECLARING THAT PROPRIETORS
IN CERTAIN CASES SHALL PAY THE SUPREME COURT
A REASONABLE COMPENSATION

NOVEMBER 8TH, 1798

Whereas, by the third section of an act entitled, "An act to rectify the errors committed in the records of the proprietors of the town of Westford," passed the tenth day of November, one thousand seven hundred and ninety seven, it was enacted "that the present records of the said proprietors, as well as the proceedings of the said meeting, as far as respects the amendment, or alteration of the said records, shall

---

1. State Papers of Vermont, Vol. XI, *General Petitions,* 1797-1799, "For a New Collector for a Land Tax," 131.

be laid before the supreme court, which shall sit at Burlington in the county of Chittenden, next after the said meeting," (meaning a meeting of the proprietors by the aforesaid act, authorised to be held) and whereas by the absence of some of the committee appointed by the proprietors, for the purpose aforesaid, that part of the act above recited, was not complied with.

[Sec. 1.] *It is hereby Enacted* by the General Assembly of the State of Vermont, That it shall be lawful for the committee appointed as aforesaid, or anyone of them, to lay the records of said proprietors, with the amendments thereon, before the supreme court which shall sit at Burlington, next after the passing of this act, and the doings of the said supreme court, with respect to the records aforesaid, shall be as binding and valid in law, and equity as if they had been laid before the said supreme court, at the time ordered by the act of the tenth of November, one thousand seven hundred and ninety seven, above refered to.

Sec. 2. *And it is hereby further Enacted,* That in all cases of the nature above recited, which already have or hereafter may arise, on which the judges of the supreme court shall be authorised or required to give their final assent, or determination, the said judges shall be entitled to a reasonable compensation, from the proprietors, whose records have been, or shall be laid before them, in manner above mentioned, proportioned to the time they shall expend, and the trouble they shall be at in the examination thereof, any law to the contrary notwithstanding.

Passed November 8, 1798.

A true record,

Attest, Ros. Hopkins, Sec'y.

AN ACT APPOINTING A COMMITTEE TO LAY OUT AND SURVEY A ROAD
FROM GREENSBOROUGH AND HARDWICK, TO THE COURT-HOUSE
IN DANVILLE, AND LAYING A TAX OF ONE CENT PER ACRE
ON THE TOWNSHIP OF WALDEN

NOVEMBER 8TH, 1798

Sec. 1. *It is hereby Enacted* by the General Assembly of the

State of Vermont, That Horace Beardsley, Aaron Shepperd, and Timothy Hinman, be, and they are hereby appointed a committee with full power to lay out and survey a county road, in the most direct and convenient course from Ashbell Shepherd's in Greensborough, through Walden to the Court-House in Danville, and from Hardwick, to join said road in Walden. And it shall be the duty of said committee to make a return of the road so by them laid out, to the town clerks of the several towns through which the said road shall be laid, whose duty it shall be, to record the same in their respective offices. And such road so laid out, shall be considered the permanent road between said towns.

Sec. 2. *And it is hereby further Enacted*, That the several towns through which said road shall be thus laid out, shall be at liberty to agree upon the mode of defraying the expense of making and repairing said road, either by taxing the polls and rateable estate of the inhabitants of said towns, or applying to the Legislature for a land tax in October next, except the town of Walden.

Sec. 3. *And it is hereby further Enacted*, That it shall be the duty of said committee to lay out said road some time before the first day of July next. And the expense of such survey shall be paid by the committee appointed on the expenditure of the tax on Walden, so far as it respects that town, and the remainder by the several towns through which the road may be laid.

Sec. 4. *And it is hereby further Enacted*, That there be, and hereby is assessed a tax of one cent on each acre of land, in the township of Walden, in the county ofCaledonia, public rights excepted, for the purpose of making the county road aforesaid, through said Walden, to be expended under the direction of Jesse Levenworth, [Leavenworth], Horace Beardsley, and David Gilman, who are hereby appointed a committee to superintend the expenditure of said tax. And any justice of the peace for the county of Caledonia, is hereby authorised to issue his warrant to Benjamin Keate of said Walden, who is hereby authorised to collect said tax. And said collector is hereby made accountable to said committee for the amount of said tax. And said committee and collector are hereby directed in the expenditure, collection, and accounting for said tax, to conform themselves in all things, to the directions of the statute of this State entitled, "An act regulating the disposition of monies raised by tax on lands in the several towns for the purpose of making and repairing roads and building bridges," passed November second, one thousand seven hundred and ninety six.

Passed November 8, 1798.

A true copy,

Attest, Ros. Hopkins, Sec'y.

AN ACT GRANTING TO BENJAMIN BELL OF SOUTH-HERO, THE EXCLUSIVE RIGHT OF KEEPING A FERRY FROM SOUTH HERO TO CUMBERLAND HEAD, IN THE STATE OF NEW YORK

NOVEMBER 8TH, 1798

Sec. 1. *It is hereby Enacted* by the General Assembly of the State of Vermont, That the exclusive right of keeping a ferry from the South-Hero, to Cumberland Head, in the State of New York, be, and the same is hereby granted to Benjamin Bell, of said South Hero, his heirs, or assigns, for the term of ten years from the first day of January next.

Sec. 2. *Provided nevertheless*, and it is hereby further Enacted, That if the said Benjamin Bell, his heirs, or assigns, shall not have in good repair, and well manned, sufficient ferry boats, for carrying passengers, horses, cattle, teams, or carriages across said ferry, on or before the first day of June next, to the satisfaction and approbation of the selectmen of said town of South Hero, or shall at any time thereafter, for the space of fifteen days, at any one time, between the tenth day of April and tenth day of December, annually, during said term, be unprovided with good and sufficient boats, well manned, for carrying passengers, horses, cattle, teams, or carriages as aforesaid, the said Benjamin shall forfeit all the privileges granted by this act.

Sec. 3. *And it is hereby further Enacted*, That the selectmen and authority of the said town of South Hero, shall regulate the prices for ferriage across the said ferry agreeably to law. And they shall also establish rules and regulations for said ferry; which rules and regulations shall be posted up at said ferry, and recorded in the town clerk's office of the town of South Hero. And if the said Benjamin shall take greater fees for ferrying across said ferry, any person, horse, creature, team or carriage, than is established by the selectmen and authority as aforesaid, or shall neglect to carry any person, team, horse, creature or carriage across, agreeably to such regulations, the said Benjamin Bell, his heirs, or assigns, shall forfeit and pay a fine of seven dollars, and costs of prosecution, one moiety of which fine shall belong to the person who shall prosecute the same to effect, and the other moiety to the treasury of the town where the prosecution shall be had.[1]

Passed November 8, 1798.

A true record,

Attest, Ros. Hopkins, Sec'y.

AN ACT DIRECTING THE SHERIFF OF THE COUNTY OF CALEDONIA TO COLLECT THE CENT TAX ON THE TOWN OF CONCORD

NOVEMBER 8TH, 1798

Whereas, it appears to this Legislature, That the warrant issued by the treasurer of this state to the first constable of the town of Concord for the year 1797, for the collection of the cent tax granted by the Legislature at their session in October, 1797, was not delivered to said Constable, who has now removed from said town, and that said warrant, by the evil designs of some large landowners in said town, was withheld and kept back from said constable until his office expired, by means of which there is now no person authorised by law to collect said tax. Therefore,

Sec. 1. *It is hereby Enacted* by the General Assembly of the state of Vermont, That the treasurer be, and hereby is directed to issue his warrant to John Rankins, Esqr., sheriff of the county of Caledonia, for the collection of said tax; and the said sheriff is hereby authorised and directed to proceed in all things in the collection of said tax, in the same manner as the said sheriff was by law directed to collect said tax, on the unorganized towns in said county of Caledonia, and pay the same into the treasury, on or before the first day of May next.

Sec. 2. *And it is hereby further Enacted,* That it shall be the duty of the said sheriff to publish this act in the newspapers immediately preceding his advertisement for the sale of the lands in said town. And all sales of land made by said sheriff under the authority of this act shall be good and valid in law to convey the title of the land so sold to the purchaser, if not redeemed within one year from the day of

---

1. State Papers of Vermont, Vol. XI, *General Petitions,* 1797-1799, "For Authority to Operate a Ferry," 98.

such sale, and the purchaser of such lands shall be entitled to interest on the purchase money at the rate of twenty five per cent per annum, on all lands which shall be redeemed in said town, any law, usage, or custom to the contrary notwithstanding.[1]

Passed November 8, 1798.

A true record,

Attest, Ros. Hopkins, Sec'y.

AN ACT MAKING APPROPRIATIONS FOR THE SUPPORT OF GOVERNMENT FOR THE PRESENT SESSION, AND FROM THENCE UNTIL THE SESSION OF ASSEMBLY IN OCTOBER, 1799

NOVEMBER 8TH, 1798

It is hereby Enacted by the General Assembly of the State of Vermont, That there be, and hereby is appropriated, for the support of government until the session of assembly in October, 1799, the several sums for the several purposes following, to wit, for the salary of the governor, $500; for the salary of the treasurer, $400; also the sum of $8,666.04 cents being the amount of the debenture of the House of Representatives, their officers and contingent charges. And also the sum of $924.08 cents being the amount of the debenture of the lieutenant governor, members of council and their officers. Also the further sum of six dollars to Amos Marsh for firewood and candles for the engrossing clerk. Also, four dollars to John Chipman for stow, firewood &c. for the governor and council. Also the sum of ten dollars to Samuel Foot, deputy sheriff, for attendance on this house, and the sum of five dollars to Asa Strong for candles and extra services.

Sec. 2. *And it is hereby further Enacted,* That there be appropriated a sum not exceeding six thousand dollars for the purpose of paying the sums allowed by the auditor of accounts against this State, and the orders drawn by and under the direction of the supreme court, which several sums of money shall be paid by the treasurer out of the monies in the treasury of this state. And if there be not sufficient monies in the treasury, the treasurer shall issue state orders for the residue of such appropriation.

---

1. State Papers of Vermont, Vol. **XI**, *General Petitions,* 1797-1799, "For Appointment of a New Constable as Tax Collector," 249.

Sec. 3. *And it is hereby further Enacted*, That the treasurer be, and hereby is directed, under the direction of his Excellency the Governor of this State, to cause to be paid to the proper board in the state of New York, who shall be duly authorised to receive the same, such sum of money as is now due to the said State of New York, on the contract for extinguishing the claims of said State, taking a full discharge therefore, out of the monies which shall remain in the treasury after the rising of this Assembly, or which shall come into the Treasury on the cent tax of one thousand seven hundred and ninety seven, not exceeding the sum of seven thousand dollars.

Passed November 8, 1798.

A true record,

Attest, Ros. Hopkins, Sec'y.

AN ACT ALLOWING TO ABNER HAWLEY SEVEN DOLLARS FOR THE SERVICES THEREIN MENTIONED

NOVEMBER 8TH, 1798

It is hereby Enacted by the General Assembly of the State of Vermont, That the treasurer be, and hereby is directed to pay to Abner Hawley, the sum of seven dollars for services rendered this Legislature in the present session.

Passed November 8, 1798.

A true copy,

Attest, Ros. Hopkins, Sec'y.

END OF ACTS PASSED AT VERGENNES, 1798

LAWS OF VERMONT

1799

ACTS PASSED BY THE LEGISLATURE OF THE STATE OF
VERMONT AT THEIR STATED SESSION HOLDEN
AT WINDSOR ON THE SECOND THURSDAY
OF OCTOBER A. D. ONE THOUSAND
SEVEN HUNDRED AND NINETY
NINE
1799

AN ACT TO ENABLE THE PROPRIETORS AND LANDOWNERS OF THE TOWN
OF ATHENS, IN THE COUNTY OF WINDHAM, TO RATIFY AND
ESTABLISH THEIR FIRST DIVISION LOTS IN SAID TOWN

OCTOBER 22ND, 1799

Whereas, it appears to this Assembly that meetings of the proprietors of the town of Athens were holden at an early day for the division of said town into severalty, and at which votes were passed giving leave to each proprietor to pitch one hundred acres of his right, with the allowance of four acres for highways, soon after which their clerk removed out of this state with all the records of said proprietors, by reason whereof they have been prevented the necessary access to said records, which said records have also been but imperfectly kept. Therefore,

It is hereby Enacted by the General Assembly of the State of Vermont, That the said landowners and proprietors of the said town of Athens, be, and they are hereby authorised and empowered at any meeting which now is, or hereafter shall be legally warned, for the purpose of accepting a plan of the first division lots in said town, agreeable to the original intent and meaning of said proprietors at their former meetings, and designate the lots on said plan, by adding thereto the name of the original proprietor, to whose right such lot was pitched. And said proprietors and land owners, when so met, shall have the right of voting according to the interest they shall have in the lands in said town, as in other proprietors' meetings.

Sec. 2. *And it is hereby further Enacted,* That said proprietors and landowners, proceeding in manner aforesaid, shall have the right to ratify and confirm all or any part of the former votes or proceedings of the said proprietors, relative to the first division of their lands into severalty, containing one hundred acres each lot, with the allowance of four acres for highways, as aforesaid, agreeable to the original intent and meaning of said proprietors, at their former meetings. And the votes and proceedings of said proprietors, so ratified and confirmed, and the votes ratifying any errors or mistakes in said proceedings heretofore had by said proprietors, relative to the said first division of lands, shall be received in any court of law in this state as evidence of a legal division of said first division lots in said town, in as full and ample manner as though the same proceedings and votes had been strictly conformable to the laws of this State at the time the same were had and passed by said proprietors.

Provided nevertheless, That nothing herein contained shall be construed to authorize said proprietors and landowners to alter or remove any first division lot as originally located, without the consent of the owner or owners.[1]

Passed October 22, 1799.

A true record,

Attest, Ros. Hopkins, Sec'y.

AN ACT AUTHORISING THE JUDGES OF THE COUNTY OF CALEDONIA, TO ACCEPT THE COURT-HOUSE IN DANVILLE

OCTOBER 22ND, 1799

Whereas, by an act passed the Legislature of the State of Vermont, the 8th day of March A. D. 1797, it was enacted, That the town of Danville should, at their own expense, build and complete the court house and gaol in said Danville to the acceptance of the judges of the county court, of the county of Caledonia, within two years from the 8th day of November A. D. 1796.

And the said gaol having been completed and accepted by the said Judges within the time limited as aforesaid, but the said court house not having been completed, and the said judges considering that they are not authorised to accept said court house at an after period without a special act for that purpose. Therefore,

It is hereby Enacted by the General Assembly of the State of Vermont, That the judges of the county court of the county of Caledonia are hereby authorised and empowered to accept the court house built

---

1. State Papers of Vermont, Vol. XI, *General Petitions,* 1797-1799, "For Confirmation of Proprietor's Proceedings," 363.

by the inhabitants of Danville, in said Danville, at any time before the last day of January, which will be in the year 1801, any law to the contrary notwithstanding.

Passed October 22, 1799.

A true record,

Attest, Ros. Hopkins, Sec'y.

AN ACT DIRECTING THE TREASURER OF THIS STATE
TO GIVE UP A CERTAIN BOND

OCTOBER 23RD, 1799

Whereas, it hath been made to appear to this Assembly, That James Rogers, formerly of Londonderry, now deceased, was in his life time seized in fee of the town of Londonderry, alias Kent, in this State. And that during the late war between Great Britain and America, the said James joined the British government, and that afterwards, to wit, in the year 1780, a committee of trust was appointed by the Legislature of this State, to sell lands for the use of this State. And that some part of said lands remaining unsold in the year 1795, the said James Rogers being then dead, James Rogers, son of the said James, deceased, petitioned, on behalf of himself and the other heirs of the said James, deceased, that the lands which then remained unsold in the said Londonderry by the commissioners aforesaid, might be restored to them agreeably to the treaty of peace between his Britannic Majesty and the United States, which the Legislature granted upon condition that the said James would pay the sum of one thousand dollars to the treasury of this state, with which the said James complied. And whereas, it further appears that the said James petitioned the General Assembly in the year 1797 that he might be enabled to make a settlement with said committee of trust, and that an act passed for that purpose, conditioned that the said James should pay said commissioner for attending to the sales in said town, which it was then supposed would not exceed four or five hundred dollars. And that the said James gave his bond with surety for the payment of $400. to the treasurer of this state, payable the tenth day of November A. D. 1799, and that upon a settlement with said committee of their accounts against this State for their services in the sale of said lands, their accounts amounted to one thousand dollars, which the said James hath actually advanced to them on behalf of this State; and the said James, for the reason aforesaid, having prayed to this assembly to release to him the payment of the said sum of $400. Therefore,

It is hereby Enacted by the General Assembly of the State of Vermont, That the treasurer of this State be, and he is hereby directed to give up to James Rogers to be cancelled a bond executed by James Rogers and George Sexton for the penal sum of $800 conditioned for the payment of four hundred dollars by the sixth day of November, A. D. 1799.

Passed October 23, 1799.

A true record,

Attest, Ros. Hopkins, Sec'y.

AN ACT IN ADDITION TO AND IN ALTERATION OF AN ACT ENTITLED "AN ACT ESTABLISHING THE COUNTY GRAMMAR SCHOOL IN THE COUNTY OF CALEDONIA IN THE TOWN OF PEACHAM," PASSED OCTOBER 27, 1795

OCTOBER 23RD, 1799

Whereas, by the second section of said act, the time fixed for holding the annual meeting of the trustees of said corporation for the election of officers &c., was the third Tuesday of November, annually, which has been found very inconvenient. Therefore,

It is hereby Enacted by the General Assembly of the State of Vermont, That in future the annual meeting of the trustees of Caledonia County Grammar School for the election of officers &c., shall be holden at such time as the said trustees shall, by a vote, at any of their annual meetings direct, and the same to alter from time to time, as they shall judge most convenient, any thing in said act to the contrary notwithstanding.

Passed October 23, 1799.

A true record,

Attest, Ros. Hopkins, Sec'y.

AN ACT GIVING CERTAIN POWERS TO ZERUBBABEL EAGER

OCTOBER 23RD, 1799

It is hereby Enacted by the General Assembly of the State of Vermont, That Zerubbabel Eager of Lunenburgh, in the county of Essex, member of the committee of superintendance of a land tax assessed on said Lunenburgh in the year 1789, for the purpose of making roads and building bridges, of which Amasa Grout of the same Lunenburgh was appointed collector, be, and he, the said Zerubbabel Eager, is hereby authorised and empowered to ask, demand, and by law in his own name as committee aforesaid, to compel a full and complete settlement of said tax from Amasa Grout, the collector aforesaid, and the same in all and every respect, to do and perform with as full and ample power, as the whole, or a major part of said committee, might or could by law have done, in the compelling and effecting of such settlement.[1]

AN ACT DIRECTING THE TREASURER OF THIS STATE TO CREDIT THE TOWN OF WESTMINSTER THE SUM THEREIN MENTIONED

OCTOBER 25TH, 1799

It is hereby Enacted by the General Assembly of the State of Vermont, That the treasurer of this State be, and he hereby is directed to credit the town of Westminster the aforesaid sum of thirteen dollars and ninety six cents, on the state tax of one cent on the dollar on the list of the year 1798.

Passed October 25, 1799.

A true record,

Attest, Ros. Hopkins, Sec'y.

AN ACT DIRECTING THE TREASURER TO PAY TO SETH STORRS, AUDITOR, THE SUM THEREIN MENTIONED

OCTOBER 25TH, 1799

It is hereby Enacted by the General Assembly of the State of Vermont, That the treasurer of this State be, and he is hereby directed to

1. State Papers of Vermont, Vol. XI, *General Petitions,* 1797-1799, "For Appointment of a Collector of a Land Tax," 442.

pay to Seth Storrs, seventy four dollars for his services and expenditures as auditor for the year past.

Passed October 25, 1799.

A true record,

Attest, Ros. Hopkins, Sec'y.

AN ACT ASSESSING A TAX OF THREE CENTS PER ACRE ON THE TOWN OF BROMLEY

OCTOBER 25TH, 1799

It is hereby Enacted by the General Assembly of the State of Vermont, That there be, and hereby is assessed a tax of three cents per acre on all the lands in the town of Bromley, in the county of Bennington (public rights excepted), for the purpose of making and repairing roads and building bridges in said town, to be expended under the direction of Jonathan Butterfield and Aaron Killam, both of said Bromley, and Daniel Tuthill of Landgrove, who are hereby appointed a committee to superintend the expenditure of said tax. And any justice of the peace within the county of Bennington is hereby authorised to issue his warrant to Reuben Bigelow of said Bromley who is hereby appointed a collector to collect said tax. And the said committee and collector are hereby directed to govern themselves in all things in the collecting, expending, and accounting for the monies raised by said tax, agreeably to the statute of this State passed the second day of November, A. D. 1796, entitled "An act regulating the disposition of monies raised by tax on lands in the several towns for the purpose of making and repairing roads and building bridges."[1]

AN ACT DIVIDING THE TOWN OF ANDOVER AND CONSTITUTING A NEW TOWN BY THE NAME OF WESTON

OCTOBER 26TH, 1799

Sec. 1. *It is hereby Enacted* by the General Assembly of the State of Vermont, That that part of Andover in the county of Windsor, which is situate westerly of the line hereafter described, together with

1. State Papers of Vermont, Vol. XI, *General Petitions,* 1797-1799, "For a Tax on Land to Build and Repair Roads and Build Bridges," 349.

the tract of land called Benton's Gore, be, and hereby is constituted and made a separate town by the name of Weston. And the inhabitants which do or shall hereafter inhabit the said part of the town of Andover and Benton's Gore hereby constituted into a separate town as aforesaid, shall have and exercise and enjoy all the rights, privileges and immunities which the inhabitants of other towns within this State do, or ought by the constitution and laws of this State, to exercise and enjoy.

Sec. 2. *Provided nevertheless, and it is hereby further Enacted,* That but one member to the General Assembly, or to State conventions, shall be chosen by the freemen of both the towns of Andover and the said Weston. And for the purpose of such elections, the people of both the said towns shall assemble at the usual place of holding freemen's or town meetings in each of the said towns alternately, and the first meeting for such election shall be holden in the town of Andover. And it shall be the duty of the advertising officer of the town in which the meeting is to be had to post the notifications thereof, which notifications shall be legally posted, as to the time previous to such meeting, and in the same number, and at the same places in the other town as in that in which the meeting shall be holden.

Sec. 3. *And it is hereby further Enacted,* That the following be the line which shall divide the said towns of Andover and Weston, to wit, beginning on the present Andover north town line, at the intersection of the line dividing the eighth and ninth ranges of lots, thence southerly in said dividing line to the northwest corner of lot number six in the eighth range, thence easterly on the north line of said lot number six to the north east corner thereof, thence southerly in the line dividing the seventh and eighth ranges of lots to the south line.[1]

Passed October 26, 1799.

A true record,

Attest, Ros. Hopkins, Sec'y.

AN ACT ANNEXING A PART OF COITS GORE TO THE TOWN OF
BAKERSFIELD

OCTOBER 26TH, 1799

It is hereby Enacted by the General Assembly of the State of Ver-

---

1. State Papers of Vermont, Vol. XI, *General Petitions,* 1797-1799, "For a Division of a Town into Two Towns," 374.

mont, That that part of Coits Gore in the county of Franklin, lying north of the following line, to wit, beginning at the northeasterly corner of Fletcher, thence south seventy degrees east, until it intersects the west line of Belvidere, be, and the same is hereby annexed to the town of Bakersfield. And the inhabitants who do or shall hereafter inhabit said part of said Gore hereby annexed to said Bakersfield, shall have, enjoy and exercise all the rights, privileges and immunities which the other inhabitants of the said Bakersfield, can or ought by the constitution and laws of this State to have, exercise and enjoy.

Passed October 26, 1799

A true Record,

Attest, Ros. Hopkins, Sec'y.

AN ACT ASSESSING A TAX OF TWO CENTS PER ACRE ON THE TOWN OF WESTFORD

OCTOBER 26TH, 1799

It is hereby Enacted by the General Assembly of the State of Vermont, That there be, and hereby is assessed a tax of two cents per acre on all lands in the town of Westford, in the county of Chittenden, public rights excepted, for the purpose of making and repairing roads and building bridges in said town, to be expended under direction of Thaddeus Tuttle of Burlington, and David Gale, and Isaac Chase, both of said Westford, who are hereby appointed a committee to superintend the expenditure of said tax. And any justice of the peace within the county of Chittenden is hereby authorised to issue his warrant to John Seeley, Junr., of said Westford, who is hereby appointed a collector to collect said tax; and said committee and collector are hereby directed, in the collecting, expending, and accounting for said tax, to govern themselves in all things by the directions of the statute of this State in that case made and provided.[1]

---

1. State Papers of Vermont, Vol. XI, *General Petitions,* 1797-1799, "For a Tax on Land to Build and Repair Roads," 345.

AN ACT DIRECTING THE TREASURER OF THIS STATE TO CREDIT THE
CONSTABLE OF THE TOWN OF CAVENDISH THE SUM THEREIN
MENTIONED

OCTOBER 26TH, 1799

It is hereby Enacted by the General Assembly of the State of Vermont, That the treasurer of this State be, and hereby is directed to credit or pay to the first constable of the town of Cavendish in this State the sum of $4.73 cents which the said constable has paid into the treasury on the tax of one cent on the dollar, granted by the Legislature at their last session, on an error of surplusage in the list of the said town of Cavendish.

Passed October 26, 1799.

A true record,

Attest, Ros. Hopkins, Sec'y.

AN ACT DIRECTING THE TREASURER OF THIS STATE TO PAY
JOHN FOSTER, ESQR., $47.52

OCTOBER 26TH, 1799

It is hereby Enacted by the General Assembly of the State of Vermont, That the treasurer of this State pay to John Foster, Esqr., of Barnard, in the county of Windsor, the sum of $47.52 cents. *Provided,* That the said John Foster execute to the treasurer of this State a bond in the penal sum of one hundred dollars, conditions that if a certain hard money order issued by the treasurer of this State in the month of November, A.D. 1797, for the payment of $42.64 cents with interest, shall be presented to the treasurer, or by him paid, that the said John Foster shall pay the same to the treasurer on demand.

Passed October 26, 1799.

A true record,

Attest, Ros. Hopkins, Sec'y.

AN ACT LAYING A TAX OF TWO CENTS PER ACRE ON THE TOWN OF
STARKESBOROUGH

OCTOBER 26TH, 1799

It is hereby Enacted by the General Assembly of the State of Vermont, That there be, and hereby is assessed a tax of two cents per acre on all the lands in the town of Starkesboro', in the county of Addison (public rights excepted), for the purpose of making and repairing roads and building bridges in said town, to be expended under the direction of Samuel Hill, James Heading, and Solomon Holcomb, all of said Starkesboro', who are hereby appointed a committee to superintend the expenditure of said tax. And any justice of the peace within and for the county of Addison is hereby authorised to issue his warrant to Enos Parsons of the same Starkesboro' who is hereby appointed a collector to collect said tax, and said committee and collector are hereby directed in the collecting, expending, & accounting for the monies raised by said tax, to conform themselves in all things to the directions of the statute of this State, in that case made and provided.[1]

AN ACT ASSESSING A TAX OF THREE CENTS PER ACRE ON AVERY'S GORE, SITUATE IN THE COUNTY OF ORLEANS

OCTOBER 26TH, 1799

It is hereby Enacted by the General Assembly of the State of Vermont, That there be, and hereby is assessed a tax of three cents per acre on all the lands in Avery's Gore situate in that part of the county of Orleans, annexed for the time being to the county of Franklin, for the purpose of making roads & building bridges in said Gore, to be expended under the direction of Joseph Cowell of Derby, in the county of Caledonia, and Josiah Elkins of said Avery's Gore, who are hereby appointed a committee to superintend the expenditure of said tax. And any justice of the peace within the said county of Franklin is hereby authorised to issue his warrant to Jesse Olds of Westfield, who is hereby appointed a collector to collect said tax. And said committee and collector are hereby directed in the collecting, expending and accounting for the monies raised by said tax, to conform themselves in all things to the directions of the statute of this State in that case made and provided.[2]

1. State Papers of Vermont, Vol. XI, *General Petitions,* 1797-1799, "For a Tax on Land to Build Roads and Bridges," 370.
2. Ibid., "For a Tax on Land to Build Roads," 339.

AN ACT ASSESSING A TAX OF TWO CENTS ON EACH ACRE OF LAND IN THE
TOWN OF CABOT

OCTOBER 28TH, 1799

It is hereby Enacted by the General Assembly of the State of Vermont, That there be, and hereby is assessed a tax of two cents on each acre of land in the town of Cabot, in the county of Caledonia, public rights excepted, for the purpose of making and repairing roads and building bridges in said town, to be expended under the direction of John Edgerton, Reuben Atkins, and Lyman Hitchcock, who are hereby appointed a committee to superintend the expenditure of said tax. And any justice of the peace is hereby authorised to issue his warrant to Fifield Lyford of said Cabot, who is hereby authorised to collect said tax, and said collector is hereby made accountable to said committee for the amount of said tax, and said committee and collector are hereby directed in the expenditure, collection, and accounting for said tax, to conform themselves in all things to the directions of the statute of this State entitled "An act regulating the disposition of monies raised by tax on lands in the several towns for the purpose of making and repairing roads and building bridges," passed November 2d, 1796.[1]

AN ACT INCORPORATING CERTAIN PERSONS THEREIN NAMED INTO A
SOCIETY BY THE NAME OF FAIRHAVEN LIBRARY SOCIETY

OCTOBER 28TH, 1799

Whereas, a number of persons, inhabitants of Fairhaven, in the county of Rutland, and State of Vermont, influenced by a conviction of the many advantages which have arisen from social compact and literary institutions, have associated themselves under the name and title of Fairhaven Library Society. And whereas the said society, desirous to promote useful knowledge for their own entertainment, and the good of the public at large, have prayed the Legislature, that the members of said society may be created a body corporate and politic forever, under the name of Fairhaven Library Society, with such powers, privileges and immunities as may best answer the laudable purposes which the members have in view. Therefore, to assist and

---

1. State Papers of Vermont, Vol. XI, *General Petitions,* 1797-1799, "For a Tax on Land to Build and Repair Roads and Build Bridges," 369.

encourage said society in the prosecution and advancement of useful knowledge for the benefit of mankind;

Sec. 1. *It is hereby Enacted* by the General Assembly of the State of Vermont, That the members of said society, that is, Ethan Whipple, Michael Marriet, Philip Priest, John Brown, Nathaniel Dickenson, Jonathan Orms, Timothy Goodrich, Isaac Cutler, and Charles McArthur and others, their associates, be, and they are and shall be a body corporate and politic in deed and name, by the name and stile [style] of Fairhaven Library Society. And by the same name, they and their successors are hereby constituted and confirmed one body corporate and politic in law, to have perpetual succession, and to be able and capable to have, hold and enjoy any goods, chattels, tenements, hereditaments, gifts, and bequests of what nature soever, in fee simple or for term of years, life or lives or otherwise. And also to grant, sell, aliene, assign, or let the same lands, tenements, hereditaments and premises, according to the nature of the respective grants and bequests made to said corporation, and of the estate of said corporation therein. *Provided,* the amount of the clear yearly income of such real estate exceeds not the sum of five hundred dollars current money of the United States.

Sec. 2. *And it is hereby further Enacted,* That the said corporation be, and shall forever hereafter be able and capable in law to sue and be sued, to plead and be impleaded, answer and be answered unto, defend and be defended, in all or any courts of justice and other places in all manner of suits, actions, complaints, pleas, causes, and matters, of what nature or kind soverer

Sec. 3. *And it is hereby further Enacted,* That the said corporation shall have full power to make their own bye laws, and regulations such as appointing the time and place of holding their future meetings, drawing books out of said library and returning them to the same; regulating the mode of electing their officers, determining the authority and duty of each officer; establishing the mode of admitting members into said society, and regulaing all other interests and concerns of said corporation. *Provided,* such bye laws and regulations shall not be repugnant of the constitution and laws of this State.

Sec. 4. *Provided also,* and it is hereby further Enacted, That no bye laws or regulations of said corporation hereafter made, shall be binding upon officers or members unless the same shall be proposed at one regular meeting of said corporation, and received and enacted at another, after the intervention of at least thirty days. And that no sale, alienation or lease of above three years of any part of the real estate of said corporation, shall be valid unless the time and nature of such sale or lease be proposed at a previous meeting of said corporation.

Sec. 5. *And it is hereby further Enacted,* That Ethan Whipple, Esqr., be, and he is hereby authorised to warn the first meeting of said society, and duly notify the members of the time and place.[1]

Passed October 28, 1799.

A true record,

Attest, Ros. Hopkins, Sec'y.

AN ACT INCORPORATING CERTAIN PERSONS THEREIN NAMED INTO A SOCIETY BY THE NAME OF ROCKINGHAM LIBRARY SOCIETY

OCTOBER 28TH, 1799

Whereas, a number of persons, inhabitants of the town of Rockingham, in the county of Windham, and State of Vermont, influenced by a conviction of the many advantages which have arisen from social compact and literary institutions, have associated themselves under the name and title of Rockingham Library Society. And whereas the said society, desirous to promote useful knowledge for their own entertainment and the good of the public at large, have prayed the Legislature, that the members of said society may be created a body corporate and politic forever, under the name of Rockingham Library Society, with such powers, privileges, and immunities as may best answer the laudable purposes, which the members have in view. Therefore, to assist and encourage said society in the prosecution and advancement of useful knowledge for the benefit of mankind;

It is hereby Enacted by the General Assembly of the State of Vermont, That the members of said society, that is to say, Samuel Whiting,

---

1. State Papers of Vermont, Vol. XI, *General Petitions,* 1797-1799, "For the Incorporation of a Library Society," 385.

Levi Sabin, Jonathan Burt, Eliphalet Felt, Samuel Emery, James Walter, Jonathan Barron, Jehiel Webb, Junr., and others, their associates, be, and they are and shall be a body corporate and politic in deed and name by the name and stile [style] of Rockingham Library Society, and by the same name, they and their successors are hereby constituted and confirmed one body corporate & politic in law, to have perpetual succession, and to be able and capable to have, hold and enjoy any goods, chattels, tenements, hereditaments, gifts and bequests of whatever nature soever in fee simple or for term of years, life or lives, or otherwise. And also to grant, sell, aliene, assign, or let the same lands, tenements, hereditaments, and premises, according to the nature of the respective grants, and bequests, made to said corporation, and of the estate of said corporation therein. *Provided,* the amount of the clear yearly income of such real estate exceed not the sum of five hundred dollars current money of the United States.

Sec. 2. *And it is hereby further Enacted,* That the said corporation be, and shall forever hereafter be able and capable in law to sue and be sued, plead and be impleaded, answer and be answered unto, defend, and be defended in all or any courts of justice and other places in all manner of suits, actions, complaints, pleas, causes and matters of whatever nature or kind soever.

Sec. 3. *And it is hereby further Enacted,* That the said corporation shall have full power to make their own bye laws and regulations, such as appointing the time and place of holding their meetings, drawing books out of said library and returning them to the same, regulating the mode of electing their officers, determining the authority and duty of each officer; establishing the mode of admitting members into said society, and regulating all other interests and concerns of said corporation. *Provided,* such bye laws and regulations shall not be repugnant to the constitution and laws of this State.

Sec. 4. *Provided also,* and it is hereby further Enacted, That no bye laws or regulations of said corporation hereafter made shall be binding upon officers or members, unless the same shall be proposed at one regular meeting of said corporation and received and enacted at another, after the intervention of at least thirty days. And that no sale, alienation or lease of above three years of any part of the real estate of said corporation shall be valid, unless the time and nature of such sale or lease be proposed at a previous meeting of said corporation.

Sec. 5. *And it is hereby further Enacted,* That Jehiel Webb,

Junr., be, and he hereby is authorised to warn the first meeting of said society, and duly notify the members of the time and place.[1]

Passed October 28, 1799.

A true record,

Attest, Ros. Hopkins, Sec'y.

AN ACT APPOINTING A COMMITTEE TO LAY OUT AND SURVEY A COUNTY ROAD FROM MONTPELIER AND CALAIS TO DANVILLE

OCTOBER 28TH, 1799

Sec. 1. *It is hereby Enacted* by the General Assembly of the State of Vermont, That David Dunbar, Charles Bulkley and Aaron Shepherd, Esquires, be, and they are hereby appointed a committee with full powers to lay out, open, and survey a county road from Onion River Bridge, in Montpelier, in the most direct and convenient course, to the Court House in Danville, and from Calais in the most direct and convenient course to Danville Court House, until it joins the road first mentioned. And it shall be the duty of said committee to make a return of the roads, so by them laid out, to the town clerks of the several towns, through which said road shall pass, whose duty it shall be to record the same in their respective offices. And such road, so laid out and recorded, shall not be altered but by a future order of the Legislature of this State.

Sec. 2. *And it is hereby further Enacted,* That the proprietors and inhabitants of the several towns through which said road shall pass, shall be at liberty to agree upon the mode of defraying the expense of the committee for laying out and surveying and making and repairing the same, either by taxing the polls and rateable estate of the inhabitants of said town; or by applying to the Legislature for a tax on the lands in such towns, in the manner provided by law.

Sec. 3. *And it is hereby further Enacted,* That it shall be the duty of the said committee, to lay out said roads some time before the first day of July next. And said committee shall give proper notice to

1. State Papers of Vermont, Vol. XI, *General Petitions,* 1797-1799, "For the Incorporation of a Library Society," 338.

the selectmen of the several towns through which the said road will probably be laid, of the time they will attend to said business.

Passed October 28, 1799.

A true record,

Attest, Ros. Hopkins, Sec'y.

AN ACT ANNEXING A TRACT OF LAND CALLED STRATTON GORE IN THE COUNTY OF WINDHAM TO STRATTON

OCTOBER 28TH, 1799

It is hereby Enacted by the General Assembly of the State of Vermont, That the tract of land called Stratton Gore, lying between the south line of Stratton and the north line of Somerset, be, and hereby is annexed to the town of Stratton for the time being. And the inhabitants residing on said Gore are hereby entitled to all the privileges which the other inhabitants of Stratton are by law entitled to for the time being as aforesaid.

Passed October 28, 1799.

A true record,

Attest, Ros. Hopkins, Sec'y.

AN ACT GRANTING THE RIGHT OF MAKING A TURNPIKE ROAD FROM BROOKFIELD TO ONION RIVER TO ELIJAH PAINE, HIS HEIRS, AND ASSIGNS

OCTOBER 28TH, 1799

Whereas, the highway leading from Brookfield through Williamstown, Northfield, and Berlin, in the County of Orange, to Onion River, is mountainous; and the expense of making and repairing the same so that it may be conveniently travelled with horses and teams is greater than reasonably ought to be required of said towns.

Sec. 1. *It is hereby Enacted* by the General Assembly of the State of Vermont, that Elijah Paine of said Williamstown, his heirs, and assigns be, and they are hereby authorized and empowered to make a turnpike road where the road is now laid out, leading from Experience Fisk's in said Brookfield, through Williamstown, Northfield, and Berlin to the north side of Onion River, which road shall not be less than sixty feet wide, and the path to be travelled in not less than eighteen feet wide in any place. And when said turnpike shall be sufficiently made and approved by a committee to be appointed by the county court of the county of Orange for that purpose, then the said Elijah, his heirs, or assigns, shall be authorized to erect three turnpike gates, one of which shall be between the said Fisk's and Micajah Ingraham's at the foot of the hill near said Fisk's, in said Brookfield; another between Cornelius Lynde's in Williamstown, and the north line of Northfield; and the other on or near the bridge across Onion River, in such manner as said Elijah, his heirs, or assigns may judge proper for collecting the toll; and shall be entitled to receive at each of said gates, for every coach, chariot, phaeton, or other four wheeled pleasure carriage, drawn by two horses, thirty one cents & three mills, and if drawn by more than two horses, an additional sum of four cents for each additional horse; for every cart or waggon drawn by two horses or oxen, sixteen cents, and if drawn by more than two oxen or horses, an additional sum of three cents for each additional horse or ox; for every curricle or other two wheeled pleasure carriage, if drawn by more than one horse, eighteen cents, seven mills; for every chaise, or chair or other pleasure carriage drawn by one horse, ten cents; for every man and horse, five cents; for every sled or sleigh drawn by two oxen or horses, nine cents, if drawn by more than two oxen or horses, three cents for each additional ox or horse; for every sled or sleigh drawn by one horse, six cents; for all horses, mules, oxen, or neat cattle led or driven beside those in teams and carriages, one cent each; for all sheep or swine, three cents per dozen. *Provided,* That the said Elijah, his heirs, or assigns may, if they see fit, commute the rate of toll with any person by taking of him a certain sum monthly or annually to be agreed upon in lieu of the toll aforesaid.

Sec. 2. *And it is hereby further Enacted,* That the said Elijah Paine, his heirs, or assigns, may if they shall judge it necessary in any place, alter said road, by turning it from the place where it is now laid out. And they shall be liable to pay all damage which shall arise to any person by taking his land by such alteration of said road, where the same cannot be obtained by voluntary agreement, to be estimated by a committee to be appointed by the county court of the county of Orange.

Sec. 3. *And it is hereby further Enacted,* That if said Elijah, his heirs, or assigns or their toll gatherer, or others in their employ, shall unreasonably delay or hinder any traveller or passenger at either of said gates, or shall demand or receive more toll than is by this act allowed, the person so offending shall forfeit and pay a sum not exceeding ten dollars, nor less than two dollars to be recovered before any justice of the peace, for the county of Orange by any person injured, delayed, or defrauded in a special action of the case. And the said Elijah, his heirs, and assigns, shall be liable to pay all damages which shall happen to any person from whom the toll is demandable which shall arise from any default of a bridge or want of repair in said road, and shall also be liable to presentment by the grand jury for not keeping said road in repair.

Sec. 4. *Provided always,* and it is hereby further Enacted, That said Elijah, his heirs, or assigns, shall not be liable to pay any damages arising from the obstructions of snow in said road, but the surveyors of highways in the several towns through which the said road shall pass shall remove such obstruction, anything in this act to the contrary notwithstanding.

Sec. 5. *And it is hereby further Enacted,* That if any person shall cut or break down, or in any way destroy either of said gates, or shall dig up or carry away any earth of said road, or wantonly, or maliciously damage the same, or shall forcibly pass or attempt to pass by force either of said gates without having first paid the legal toll at such gate, such person shall forfeit and pay a fine not exceeding fifty dollars nor less then five dollars, to be recovered by an action of trespass, to the use of the said Elijah, his heirs, or assigns. And if any person with his team, cattle, horse, mule, sheep or swine shall turn out of said road with intent to evade the toll due by virtue of this act, such person shall forfeit and pay three times so much as the legal toll would have been to be recovered to the use of the said Elijah, his heirs, or assigns, in an action on the case. *Provided,* That nothing in the act shall extend to entitle the said Elijah, his heirs, or assigns, to demand or receive toll of any person who shall pass with his horse or carriage, to or from public worship, or with his horse, team, or cattle to or from his common labour on his farm, or to or from any grist mill or on the common and ordinary business of family concerns, or from any person passing on mititia duty.

Sec. 6. *And it is hereby further Enacted,* That the said Elijah, his heirs, or assigns, shall, within six months after the road shall be completed, exhibit an account of the expenses thereof, to the judges of the county court, for the county of Orange, who are hereby appointed a committee to examine and allow the same, and the account so examined and allowed, shall, within six months after such allowance, be lodged by said Elijah, his heirs, or assigns, in the secretary of state's office. And the said Elijah or his heirs or assigns shall keep an account of the annual income arising from said toll; and the necessary annual disbursements on said road, which they shall render to the Governor and council when thereto required.

Sec. 7. *And it is hereby further Enacted,* That the said Elijah, his heirs, and assigns, shall at each of the places where toll shall be collected, erect and keep constantly exposed to view a sign or board with the rates of toll established by this act legibly written thereon in large or capital characters.

Sec. 8. *And it is hereby further Enacted,* That said Elijah, his heirs, and assigns be, and they are hereby authorised to erect one other turnpike gate across said road near the aforesaid gate, on or near said bridge over Onion River and shall be entitled to receive of every person passing the same, one half of the toll such person would be liable to pay at either of said gates. *Provided always,* That when the said gate shall be so erected as last aforesaid, said Elijah, his heirs, and assigns, shall be entitled to receive of persons passing the gate on or near said bridge, only one half of the toll herein by this act before provided.

Sec. 9. *And it is hereby further Enacted,* That the Legislature may, at any time after thirty years, repeal this act, and all the privileges herein granted, if it shall appear to their satisfaction, that the income arising from the said toll shall have fully compensated the said Elijah, his heirs, or assigns for all monies by them disbursed in purchasing, repairing and taking care of said road, together with an interest of twelve per cent per annum. And thereupon the property of said road shall be vested in this State, and at the disposition thereof. *Provided,* That if the said Elijah, his heirs, or assigns shall neglect to complete said turnpike road for the space of four years from the passing of this act, the same shall be void and of no effect.[1]

Passed October 28, 1799.

A true record,

Attest, Ros. Hopkins, Sec'y.

---

1. State Papers of Vermont, Vol. XI, *General Petitions,* 1797-1799, "For Authority to Build a Turnpike Road," 431.

AN ACT TO SUSPEND THE OPERATION OF AN EXECUTION IN FAVOR OF
SAMUEL MATTOCKS, TREASURER OF THE STATE AGAINST
ABEL STEVENS AND JOHN C. WALLER

OCTOBER 28TH, 1799

It is hereby Enacted by the General Assembly of the State of Vermont, That the operation of an execution in favor of Samuel Mattocks, treasurer of the State of Vermont, against Abel Stevens, and John C. Waller, both of Royalton, in the county of Windsor, issued by the county court of said county of Windsor, at their September term, A.D. 1799, be, and is hereby suspended for and during the term of one year.

Passed October 28, 1799.

A true record,

Attest, Ros. Hopkins, Sec'y.

AN ACT DIRECTING THE TREASURER OF THIS STATE TO CREDIT THE
TOWN OF ROYALTON THE SUM THEREIN MENTIONED

OCTOBER 28TH, 1799

It is hereby Enacted by the General Assembly of the State of Vermont, That the treasurer of this State be, and he is directed to credit the town of Royalton the sum of $17.33 cents on the state tax of one cent on the dollar, granted by the Legislature of this State, at Vergennes, at their last session.

Passed October 28, 1799.

A true record,

Attest, Ros. Hopkins, Sec'y.

AN ACT ASSESSING A TAX OF TWO CENTS PER ACRE ON THE
TOWNSHIP OF GREENSBOROUGH

OCTOBER 28TH, 1799

It is hereby Enacted by the General Assembly of the State of Vermont, That there be, and hereby is assessed a tax of two cents per acre on all the lands in the town of Greensboro', in the county of Orleans (public rights excepted), for the purpose of making and repairing roads and building bridges in said town, to be expended under the direction of John Ellsworth, Timothy Stanley & Samuel Huntington, all of said Greensboro', who are hereby appointed a committee to superintend the expenditure of said tax. And any justice of the peace within the county of Caledonia, is hereby empowered to issue his warrant to Thomas Tolman of said Greensboro', who is hereby appointed a collector to collect said tax; and said committee and collector are hereby directed in the collecting, expending, and accounting for said tax, to govern themselves in all things by the directions of the statute of this State, in that case made and provided.[1]

AN ACT EMPOWERING DANIEL RICE TO SELL LANDS IN THE
CASE THEREIN MENTIONED

OCTOBER 29TH, 1799

Whereas, the selectmen of Somerset, in the county of Windham, made a list or rate bill, of one cent on each acre of land in said town, agreeably to an act of the General Assembly of the State of Vermont entitled, "An act assessing a tax of one cent on each acre of land in this State for the support of government during the year 1797 and for other purposes," and by reason of their not being any person legally authorised, as constable of said town for the year 1797, said selectmen delivered the same to Daniel Rice, first constable of said town for the year 1798, to collect. And whereas, part of said tax still remains to be collected; and doubts have arisen whether the said Daniel can legally sell the lands of delinquent proprietors and landowners for the payment of said tax.

It is hereby Enacted by the General Assembly of the State of Vermont, That the said Daniel Rice be, and he is hereby authorised and empowered to proceed in the collection of said tax, pursuing in all things the directions given in the act aforesaid; and in act entitled "An act in addition to and explanation of said act," passed the eighth day of November, A.D. 1798, excepting, the time of advertising said lands for sale shall be on or before the first day of January next. And the time of redemption is hereby given, as is given in and by said acts; and after one year from the day of sale, the said Daniel is hereby empowered, in his capacity of collector of said tax, to execute to the purchasers, deeds of such lands so sold, and not redeemed as aforesaid,

---

1. State Papers of Vermont, Vol. XI, *General Petitions,* 1797-1799, "For a Tax on Land to Build and Repair Roads and Build Bridges," 347.

and such deeds, so executed as aforesaid, shall be good and valid in law, to all intents and purposes, in the same manner as if the said Daniel had been the legal constable for said town for the year 1797.

Sec. 2. *And it is hereby further Enacted,* That the said Daniel collect and pay said tax into the treasury on or before the first day of July next; and the treasurer and sheriff of Windham County are hereby requested to stay any further proceedings against the said Daniel for the collection of said tax, until the first day of July next.

Passed October 29, 1799.

A true record,

Attest, Ros. Hopkins, Sec'y.

AN ACT ASSESSING A TAX OF SIX CENTS ON EACH ACRE OF LAND IN THE TOWNSHIP OF CHELSEA, IN THE COUNTY OF ORANGE, FOR THE PURPOSE THEREIN MENTIONED

OCTOBER 29TH, 1799

It is hereby Enacted by the General Assembly of the State of Vermont, That there be, and hereby is assessed a tax of six cents on each acre of land in the town of Chelsea, in the county of Orange, public lands excepted, to be paid into the treasury of said town, on or before the first day of November, 1800, for the express purpose of erecting a court house in said town; which monies shall be under the order and direction of the selectmen of said Chelsea for the time being. Said monies to be collected by Abraham Brigham of said Chelsea, who is hereby appointed a collector to collect said tax and pay it into the treasury of said town.

Sec. 2. *And it is hereby further Enacted,* That it shall be the duty of any justice of the peace within the county of Orange, on application, to issue his warrant to the said Abraham Brigham for the collection of said tax. Which collector shall immediately after receiving such warrant, proceed to advertise said tax agreeably to the directions given to collectors of taxes in and by an act entitled, "An act regulating the disposition of monies raised by tax on lands for the purpose of making and repairing roads and building bridges," passed the 2d day of November, A.D. 1796. Nevertheless, said lands shall not be liable to be sold til the first day of October, 1800.

Sec. 3. *And it is hereby further Enacted,* That if said tax is not paid to said collector by the first day of October, 1800, said collector shall then proceed to sell the lands of delinquents of said tax sufficient to pay the tax due thereon, with the legal costs, as is directed in the aforesaid act. And the said collector shall be accountable to the treasurer of said town in the same way and manner as collectors of such land taxes are, by said act, accountable to the committees appointed for the expenditures of such land taxes. And the owner or owners of any lands, which shall be sold for said tax by virtue of this act, shall have the same power to redeem their lands, so sold, by paying the sum or sums for which their lands were sold, with twelve per cent interest, as is given in and by said act to persons who may have their lands sold for such road taxes. And said collectors shall also be accountable for all monies to the purchasers which he shall receive for the redemption of such lands.[1]

Passed October 29, 1799.

A true record,

Attest, Ros. Hopkins, Sec'y.

AN ACT FOR THE RELIEF OF JONATHAN EGGLESTON OF MEDWAY

OCTOBER 30TH, 1799

It is hereby Enacted by the General Assembly of the State of Vermont, That relief be given to Jonathan Eggleston, a person in indigent and necessitous circumstances, of Medway, in the county of Rutland, in the following manner. The selectmen, for the time being, of the town of Rutland, shall on application of the said Jonathan, administer relief and support to him in money, or otherwise, according to his necessities and those of his family, in the discretion and judgment of said selectmen to an amount not exceeding the sum of fifty dollars. And upon an attested account, by a majority of said selectmen, of money or other articles at money value, having been in fact disbursed and delivered to the said Jonathan, presented to the auditor of accounts against this State, the said auditor being satisfied of the justice of the account respecting the price of other articles than money, he shall pass

---

1. State Papers of Vermont, Vol. XI, *General Petitions,* 1797-1799, "For a Tax on Land to Build a Courthouse," 398.

the same with an order upon the treasurer of the State, who is hereby directed to reimburse and pay the same out of the treasury of this State.

Passed October 30, 1799.

A true record,

Attest, Ros. Hopkins, Sec'y.

AN ACT TO DEFRAY THE EXPENSES OF A COURT OF ENQUIRY ON THE
CASE OF THE DEATH OF JOHN GRIGGS HELD IN THE MONTH
OF MAY A.D. 1799 AT ALBURGH

OCTOBER 30TH, 1799

It is hereby Enacted by the General Assembly of the State of Vermont, That the treasurer of this state be, and he is hereby directed to pay to the persons herein after named, the several sums annexed to their names respectively, to wit: to Ebenezer Marvin, $60.; to Samuel Barnard, $60.; to Levi House, $45.; to Enos Wood, $14.; and also to Levi House, state's attorney of the county of Franklin, $17.51 cents for the use of witnesses; and said House is hereby made accountable to the witnesses attending said court, for the same.

Passed October 30, 1799.

A true record,

Attest, Ros. Hopkins, Sec'y.

AN ACT DIRECTING THE TREASURER OF THE STATE OF VERMONT TO
PAY THE SUMS THEREIN MENTIONED

OCTOBER 30TH, 1799

It is hereby Enacted by the General Assembly of the State of Vermont, That the treasurer of this State be, and he is hereby directed to pay to the council of censors the sums of money herein after mentioned, and to Stephen Savage the sum hereinafter mentioned for the use of his room, candles and other expenditures for the use of the said Council of Censors:

To Moses Robinson	$56.40	To Elijah Dewey	$56.40
To Jonathan Hunt	$49.44	To Samuel Knight	$48.24
To Lot Hall	$43.20	To John Leverett	$36.00
To Nathaniel Niles	$45.12	To John White	$65.28

To Noah Chittenden $58.66   To Elias Buel $60.00
To John Willard $64.00   To Benjamin Emmons $33.40
To David Fay $41.70   To Stephen Savage for
   the purpose aforesaid $10.00

Passed October 30, 1799.

A true record,

Attest, Ros. Hopkins, Sec'y.

AN ACT DIRECTING THE TREASURER OF THE STATE OF VERMONT TO
PAY THE SEVERAL SUMS OF MONEY THEREIN MENTIONED

OCTOBER 30TH, 1799

It is hereby Enacted by the General Assembly of the State of Vermont, That the treasurer of this State be, and he hereby is directed to pay out of the treasury the following sums of money to the following persons, state's attornies and clerks of the Supreme Court for the several counties in this State:

To Truman Squier, state's attorney for Bennington County $47.00

To Samuel Robinson, 2d, clerk of Supreme Court for
   Bennington County $51.09

To Abel Spencer, state's attorney for Rutland County $69.00

To Nathan Osgood, clerk of Supreme Court for Rutland
   County $66.28

To Daniel Chipman, state's attorney for Addison County $31.60

To Darius Matthews, clerk of Supreme Court for Addison
   County $33.59

To William C. Harrington, state's attorney for Chittenden
   County $47.36

To John Law, clerk of Supreme Court for Chittenden
   County $28.13

To Royal Tyler, state's attorney for Windham County $59.48

To Lemuel Whitney, clerk of Supreme Court Windham
   County $50.45

To Amasa Paine, state's attorney for Windsor County $116.76

To Benjamin Swan, clerk of Supreme Court of Windsor
   County $56.29

To Daniel Farrand, state's attorney for Orange County　$53.00

To Isaac Bayley, clerk of Supreme Court for Orange
County　$50.57

To William Mattocks, state's attorney for Caledonia
County　$60.41

To David Dunbar, clerk of Supreme Court Caledonia
County　$46.60

Being $867.67 cents; said sums to be paid on application.

[Passed October 30, 1799.]

　　　[A true record.]

　　　　　[Attest, Ros. Hopkins, Sec'y.]

AN ACT GRANTING TO HORATIO KNIGHT LEAVE TO RAISE BY LOTTERY THE SUM OF 1000 DOLLARS

OCTOBER 31ST, 1799

[Sec. 1.]　*It is hereby Enacted* by the General Assembly of the State of Vermont, That leave be, and it is hereby granted to Horatio Knight of Brattleboro, in the county of Windham, and state aforesaid, or his assigns, to raise the sum of one thousand dollars by lottery after deducting all the prizes and expenses of the same.

[Sec. 2.]　*And it is hereby further Enacted*, That Lemuel Whitney, Esqr., be appointed manager of said lottery, with full power to appoint such assistant managers as to him shall seem meet and proper. *Provided nevertheless*, That the said manager, before he proceed to sell, utter or publish any ticket or tickets by virtue of this act, shall execute and deliver to the treasurer of the county of Windham and state aforesaid, a bond with sufficient surety to the satisfaction of said treasurer, in the penal sum of 5,000 dollars, conditioned for the faithful performance of the trust reposed in said managers by virtue of this act.

Sec. 3.　*And it is hereby further Enacted,* That the State of Vermont shall and will in no wise be accountable for said lottery.

Passed October 31, 1799.

　　　A true record,

　　　　　Attest, Ros. Hopkins, Sec'y.

AN ACT IN ADDITION TO AN ACT PASSED OCTOBER 17TH, 1783,
ENTITLED, "AN ACT DIVIDING THE TOWN OF WINDSOR
INTO TWO DISTINCT SOCIETIES"

OCTOBER 31ST, 1799

Whereas, an act passed October 17th, 1783, dividing the town of Windsor into two distinct societies appears to be incompetent to the purposes intended in said act. Therefore,

It is hereby Enacted by the General Assembly of the State of Vermont, That the town of Windsor, in the county of Windsor, be, and hereby is divided into two distinct parishes by a line drawn through the center of the seventh range of hundred acre lots. And that part of said town being east of said line shall hereafter be known by the name of the East-Parish of Windsor; and that part of said town being west of said line, shall hereafter be known by the name of the West-Parish of Windsor; and that the said parishes be made bodies politic and corporate, and vested with all the privileges of parishes of this State, and with all the powers that towns are vested with, to enable them to organize and carry the purposes of said bodies politic into effect.

Sec. 2. *And it is hereby further Enacted,* That the said parishes respectively, be, and they hereby are empowered, at any legal meeting warned for the purpose, to ratify and confirm their former proceedings so far as they were conformable to the laws regulating parish and society proceedings.

Passed October 31, 1799.

A true record,

Attest, Ros. Hopkins, Sec'y.

AN ACT APPOINTING A COLLECTOR TO COMPLETE THE SETTLEMENT
OF THE CENT TAX IN BRUNSWICK

OCTOBER 31ST, 1799

Whereas, the first constable of the town of Brunswick, in the county of Caledonia, for the year 1797, on whom devolved the collection of the state cent tax of said year, is deceased, and some part of the duties of said office remain unfinished,

It is hereby Enacted by the General Assembly of the State of Vermont, That Benjamin Wait of the same Brunswick be, and he is hereby appointed in the room of the said deceased, to possess every power of the said deceased. And all sales or deeds of sales from the said Benjamin shall have the same power & validity in law as if they had been done and executed by the said deceased.

Passed October 31, 1799.

A true record,

Attest, Ros. Hopkins, Sec'y.

AN ACT DIRECTING THE TREASURER OF THIS STATE TO PAY TO JOHN VANCE THE SUM OF $23

OCTOBER 31ST, 1799

It is hereby Enacted by the General Assembly of the State of Vermont, That the treasurer of this State be, and hereby is directed to pay to John Vance of Topsham, the sum of $23. for the expense and damage sustained by the said Vance on his delinquency of making payment of the cent tax to the treasurer of this State, of which tax the said Vance was collector in the said town of Topsham.

Passed October 31, 1799.

A true record,

Attest, Ros. Hopkins, Sec'y.

AN ACT REVIVING AN ACT LAYING A LAND TAX ON IRASBURGH AND MAKING AN ALTERATION IN THE COMMITTEE OF SUPERINTENDANCE

OCTOBER 31ST, 1799

It is hereby Enacted by the General Assembly of the State of Vermont, That the act laying a tax of three cents per acre on the towns of Irasburgh and Coventry for the purpose of making and repairing roads and building bridges, passed the 9th day of November, 1797, and revived by an act passed at the last session of the Legislature, be again, so far as respects the said Irasburgh, and the same is hereby revived and declared to be in force and effect, the same as if it had passed and been enacted at the present session of the Legislature. And,

It is hereby further Enacted, That Roger Enos, Junr., of Colchester, Samuel C. Crafts of Craftsbury, and Ralph Parker of Glover, be, and they are hereby appointed a committee to superintend the expenditure of said tax in the room of the committee heretofore appointed, which said former committee are hereby discharged from said service.

AN ACT ASSESSING A TAX OF TWO CENTS PER ACRE ON THE TOWN OF HYDES PARK [HYDE PARK]

OCTOBER 31ST, 1799

It is hereby Enacted by the General Assembly of the State of Vermont, That there be, and hereby is assessed a tax of two cents per acre on all the lands in the town of Hyde Park, in the county of Franklin, public rights excepted, for the purpose of making and repairing roads and building bridges in said town, to be expended under the direction of John McDonald, Timothy Hastings, and Porter Martin, all of Hyde Park, who are hereby appointed a committee to superintend the expenditure of said tax. And any justice of the peace within the county of Franklin is hereby empowered to issue his warrant to Gamaliel Taylor of said Hyde Park, who is hereby appointed a collector, to collect said tax. And said collector and committee are hereby directed, in the collecting, expending, and accounting for the monies raised by said tax, to conform themselves in all things to the directions of the statute of this State, in that case made and provided.

AN ACT DIRECTING THE LAYING OUT AND MAKING OF A COUNTY ROAD

FROM THE SOUTH LINE OF WHEELOCK, IN THE COUNTY OF CALEDONIA, TO THE SOUTH LINE OF STANSTEAD IN CANADA AND TAXING SUNDRY TOWNS THROUGH WHICH THE SAME WILL PASS

OCTOBER 31ST, 1799

It is hereby Enacted by the General Assembly of the State of Vermont, That Timothy Hinman, John Bean, and Timothy Stanley, Esquires, be, and they are hereby appointed a committee to lay out and survey a county road from the south line of Wheelock, county of Caledonia; beginning where the county road already laid terminates, to the south line of Stanstead, in the province of lower Canada, to be laid through the towns of Wheelock, Sheffield, Barton, Brownington, Salem, and Derby, by straightening and altering the present road through said towns, as they shall judge will best accommodate the public. And said committee, in cases which may require it, shall have the same power as selectmen in laying out new roads. And when the said road is surveyed, the surveys thereof shall, by the said committee, be transmitted to the town clerks of the respective organized towns through which the roads shall pass, and in the unorganized towns to the county clerks, and be, by the said clerks recorded. And such road shall not be altered but by a future order of the Legislature of this State. And the said committee shall be paid a reasonable compensation for the said service from the avails of the taxes herein after assessed by the committees superintending said taxes in the several towns, in proportion to the time they shall expend in each of said towns on said service. And said road shall be laid out and surveyed some time before the first day of June next.

Sec. 2. *And it is hereby further Enacted,* That the following taxes on the towns following, be, and hereby are assessed for the purpose [of] making and repairing roads, and building bridges in the said towns, especially to be expended on the county road aforesaid, in the towns of Sheffield, Brownington, and Salem under the direction and at the discretion of the committee herein after appointed. On the town of Sheffield, the sum of two cents per acre on all the lands (public rights excepted), for the superintendance of the expenditure of which John Bean of Wheelock and Reuben Miles of Sheffield, is hereby appointed a committee, and Joseph Bean of Wheelock the collector. On the town of Barton, the sum of two cents per acre on all the lands (public rights excepted), for the superintendance of the expenditure of which David Pillsbury, Asa Kimball, and Jonathan Allen, all of said Barton, are hereby appointed a committee, and Abner Allen of said Barton, the collector. On the town of Brownington, the sum of one cent per acre on all the lands (public rights excepted), for the superintendance of the expenditure of which Elijah Strong and Amos Porter, both of Brownington, are hereby appointed a committee, and Luke Gilbert of said Brownington, the collector. And on the town of Salem, the sum of one cent per acre on all the lands (public rights excepted), for the superintendance of which Timothy Hinman of Derby in this State, and Ebenezer Strong of Glastenbury, in the State of Connecticut, are appointed a committee, and Jonathan Allen of Barton, the collector. And any justice of the peace within the county of Caledonia is hereby empowered to issue his warrant to the said collectors to collect said taxes respectively. And the several committees and collectors appointed, in and by this act, are hereby directed in the collecting, expending, and accounting for the monies to be raised by said taxes, to govern themselves in all things by the directions of the statute of this State, in that case made & provided.

Passed October 31, 1799.

A true record,

Attest, Ros. Hopkins, Sec'y.

AN ACT DIRECTING THE ORGANIZATION OF THE COUNTY OF ORLEANS

OCTOBER 31ST, 1799

Whereas, it is inconvenient for the inhabitants of the county of Orleans to attend the courts of jurisprudence in the counties of Caledonia and Franklin, and the population of said county having become sufficiently numerous for the transaction of county business therein, Therefore,

Sec. 1. *It is hereby Enacted* by the General Assembly of the State of Vermont, That the county of Orleans in this State, from and after the thirtieth day of November in the present year, shall, and is hereby declared to be organized for the transaction of all legal public business as a county. And all actions, causes and suits of whatever name or nature, which shall commence or be instituted from and after the said 30th day of November, within and [for] the said county of Orleans, shall be entered, tried and determined to final judgment and execution in the said county of Orleans, excepting that the supreme court of judicature shall not perform its circuit into the said county of Orleans until the same shall be directed by a future act of the Legislature; but during such period all causes proper to come before the said supreme court, which already have, or which shall hereafter originate by original entry, or otherwise within the said county of Orleans, shall be entered, tried & determined before said supreme court at their session in Danville, within the county of Caledonia.

Sec. 2. And it is hereby further Enacted, That the Judges of the county court of the said county of Orleans, hereafter to be appointed may, at any time after their own appointment, and shall on or before the said thirtieth day of November, appoint a clerk of the county court for the said county of Orleans, and cause him to be duly qualified to that office.

Sec. 3. *And it is hereby further Enacted,* That during the present session of this Legislature, the judges, sheriff and high bailiff of said county of Orleans shall be elected in the same manner as county officers have been heretofore elected.

Sec. 4. *Provided nevertheless, and it is hereby further Enacted,* That no permanent place be established for the county building, to be erected in said county until five years from the passing of this act.

Sec. 5. *And it is hereby further Enacted,* That the places for holding the county courts in said county for the time being, shall be Craftsbury and Brownington. And that the times for holding said courts, shall be on the fourth Mondays of November and March annually, to be alternately holden in the said towns. The first session to be in Craftsbury in the month of March, A.D. 1800.

Sec. 6. *And it is hereby further Enacted,* That the Secretary of State be, and he is hereby directed, immediately to publish this act in all the newspapers printed in this State.

Passed October 31, 1799.

A true record,

Attest, Ros. Hopkins, Sec'y.

AN ACT ASSESSING A TAX OF TWO CENTS PER ACRE ON THE
TOWN OF BAKERSFIELD

OCTOBER 31ST, 1799

It is hereby Enacted by the General Assembly of the State of Vermont, That there be, and hereby is assessed a tax of two cents per acre on all the lands in the town of Bakersfield, in the county of Franklin, public rights excepted, for the purpose of making and repairing roads and building bridges in said town. To be expended under the direction of Joseph Baker and Jonas Brigham of Bakersfield, and Hubbard Barlow of Fairfield, in said county, who are hereby appointed a committee to superintend the expenditure of said tax. And any justice of the peace within the county of Franklin is hereby empowered to issue his warrant to Stephen Maynard of Bakersfield, who is hereby appointed a collector to collect said tax. And said committee and collector are hereby directed to govern themselves, in all things, by the directions of the statute of this State in that case made & provided.

And it is hereby further Enacted, That so much of the avails of said tax as shall be found necessary for that purpose shall be expended in the cutting and clearing out of a county road, so called, leading through said Bakersfield to Fairfield, and the remainder shall be expended on the other roads in said Bakersfield.[1]

AN ACT APPOINTING A NEW COLLECTOR ON A LAND TAX IN WALDEN GORE

OCTOBER 31ST, 1799

It is hereby Enacted by the General Assembly of the State of Vermont, That David Dunbar of Danville, in the county of Caledonia, be, and he is hereby appointed a collector of a tax of one penny per acre assessed by the Legislature of Vermont at their October Session, A.D. 1794, on Walden Gore, for making and repairing roads &c., in the room of Aaron Hartshorn of said Danville, deceased, for the completion of the duties and business of the said deceased, in the said office of collector of said tax. And every act, whether of conveyance by deed of lands sold at vendue and not redeemed as by law provided, or any other act or thing in the premises which the said Aaron, in his life time, might lawfully have done, shall be as valid and good in law, to all intents, when done and performed by the said David.

AN ACT ASSESSING A TAX OF ONE CENT PER ACRE ON THE TOWN OF STOW[E]

OCTOBER 31ST, 1799

It is hereby Enacted by the General Assembly of the State of Vermont, That there be, and hereby is assessed a tax of one cent per acre, on all the lands in the town of Stowe, in the county of Chittenden, public rights excepted, for the purpose of making and repairing roads and building bridges in said town, to be expended under the direction of William Utley, Clemont Moody, and Noah Churchill, who are hereby appointed a committee to superintend the expenditure of said tax.

---

1. State Papers of Vermont, Vol. XI, *General Petitions,* 1797-1799, "For a Tax on Land to Build and Repair Roads," 346.

And any justice of the peace within the county of Chittenden is hereby authorised to issue his warrant to Nathan Robinson of the same Stowe, who is hereby appointed a collector to collect said tax. And the said committee and collector are hereby directed in the collecting, expending, and accounting for the monies raised by said tax, to govern themselves in all things, by the directions of the statute of this State, in that case made and provided.[1]

AN ACT REVIVING AN ACT LAYING A TAX ON THE TOWN OF MORRISTOWN

OCTOBER 31ST, 1799

It is hereby Enacted by the General Assembly of the State of Vermont, That an act laying a land tax of one cent per acre on the town of Morristown, in the county of Franklin, for the purpose of making and repairing roads and building bridges, passed the last session of this Legislature, be, and the same is hereby revived in all and every part and respect, and declared to be in force and virtue, the same as if it had passed at the present session of the Legislature.[2]

AN ACT ASSESSING A TAX OF TWO CENTS PER ACRE ON THE TOWN OF RICHFORD

OCTOBER 31ST, 1799

It is hereby Enacted by the General Assembly of the State of Vermont, That there be, and hereby is assessed a tax of two cents per acre on all the lands in the town of Richford, in the county of Franklin, public rights excepted, for the purpose of making and repairing roads and building bridges in said town, to be expended under the direction of Jonathan James, Theophilus Hastings, and Joseph Stanhope, all of said Richford, who are hereby appointed a committee to superintend the expenditure of said tax. And any justice of the peace within the county of Franklin is hereby authorised to issue his warrant to Chester Wells of said Richford, who is hereby appointed a collector, to collect said tax. And said committee and collector are hereby directed in the

1. State Papers of Vermont, Vol. XI, *General Petitions,* 1797-1799, "For a Tax on Land to Build and Repair Roads and Build Bridges," 391.
2. Ibid., "For Revival of an Act Granting a Land Tax and Against a Tax on Land to Build a Bridge," 343.

collecting, expending and accounting for the monies to be raised by said tax, to govern themselves in all things by the directions of the statute of this State, in that case made and provided.[1]

AN ACT ASSESSING A TAX OF TWO CENTS PER ACRE ON THE TOWN OF BOLTON

OCTOBER 31ST, 1799

It is hereby Enacted by the General Assembly of the State of Vermont, That there be, and hereby is assessed a tax of two cents per acre on all lands in the town of Bolton (according to its Charter), in the county of Chittenden (public rights excepted), for the purpose of making and repairing roads and building bridges in said town, to be expended under the direction of John Fay of Burlington, Jabez Jones and Robert Canada of Bolton, who are hereby appointed a committee to superintend the expenditure of said tax. And any justice of the peace within the county of Chittenden is hereby empowered to issue his warrant to Robert Stinson of Bolton, who is hereby appointed a collector to collect said tax; and said committee and collector are hereby directed in the collecting, expending, and accounting for the monies raised by said tax, to govern themselves in all things by the directions of the statute of this State in that case made and provided.[2]

AN ACT INCORPORATING CERTAIN PERSONS INTO A SOCIETY BY THE NAME OF HARTFORD LIRRARY SOCIETY

NOVEMBER 1ST, 1799

Whereas, it appears to this assembly that a number of persons, inhabitants of the town of Hartford, in the county of Windsor, under the conviction of the utility of literary social institutions, have agreed and formed themselves into a library company and desire from this Legislature a grant of an act of incorporation under the Hartford Library Society. Therefore,

Sec. 1. *It is hereby Enacted* by the General Assembly of the

---

1. State Papers of Vermont, Vol. XI, *General Petitions,* 1797-1799, "For a Tax on Land to Build Roads and Bridges," 434.

2. Ibid., "For a Tax on Land to Build and Repair Roads and Bridges," 392.

State of Vermont that the members of said Library company, to wit, Abel Barron, Daniel Marsh, Freegrace Leveritt, Oliver Udall and William Perry, Junr., and their associates and successors, be, and they are hereby made and constituted a society, corporate and politic, under the stile [style] and designation of Hartford Library Society; which society shall be capable to have, hold and enjoy any goods, chattels, tenements, hereditaments, gifts and bequests of whatever nature, in fee simple or for term of years, life or lives, or otherwise; and also to grant, sell, aliene, assign or let the same lands, tenements, hereditaments, and premises, according to the nature of the respective grants and bequests, made of said corporation, and the estate of said corporation therein. *Provided,* That the amount of the clear yearly income of such real estate shall not exceed the sum of five hundred dollars, money of the United States.

Sec. 2. *And it is hereby further Enacted,* That the said corporation shall ever hereafter, be able in law, to sue and be sued, plead & be impleaded, to answer and to be answered unto, defend and be defended in all or any courts of justice and other places, in all manner of suits, actions, complaints, pleas, causes and matters of whatever nature or kind; and have and keep a common seal of said corporation.

Sec. 3. *And it is hereby further Enacted,* That the said corporation shall have power to appoint the time and places of their meetings, regulate the mode of electing their officers, determine the authority & duty of their officers; establish the mode of admitting members; regulate the drawing of books from and returning them to the library; and lay and collect taxes on the members; and in general make and execute their own bye laws for the good government and regularity of their society. *Provided,* That no such bye law or regulation be repugnant to the constitution and laws of this State. *Provided also,* That no such bye laws or regulations of said society hereafter to be made shall be binding on officers or members, unless the same shall have been proposed, at one regular meeting of said corporation and received and enacted at another, after the intervention of at least thirty days.

Sec. 4. *And it is hereby further Enacted,* That no sale, alienation, or lease of above three years, of any part of the real estate of said corporation, shall be valid unless the time and nature of such sale or lease be proposed at a previous meeting of said corporation.

Sec. 5. *And it is hereby further Enacted,* That Abel Barron, a senior member of said corporation, be, and he is hereby authorised to warn the first meeting of said society and duly notify the members of the time and place.

Passed November 1, 1799.

A true record,

Attest, Ros. Hopkins, Sec'y.

AN ACT TO ENABLE THE INHABITANTS OF TINMOUTH TO DRAW THE WATERS OF THE FURNACE POND IN SAID TINMOUTH TO THEIR ANCIENT AND NATURAL LEVEL AT CERTAIN SEASONS OF THE YEAR

NOVEMBER 1ST, 1799

Whereas, it appears to this Assembly that the raising of the waters in the pond called the Furnace Pond in the summer season is greatly prejudicial to the health of the inhabitants of said Tinmouth, which evil to prevent,

It is hereby Enacted by the General Assembly of the State of Vermont, That the inhabitants of the town of Tinmouth shall yearly and every year hereafter, as long as said dam shall continue, have full power and lawful authority to draw the gates in said Furnace Dam; and also at their own cost and expense to erect such floom [flume] and sluice way in said dam as may be necessary and convenient to draw the waters of said pond to their ancient and natural level; and to open and keep open the gates and floom of said dam, from the first day of June annually, forever hereafter, until the first day of September.

Sec. 2. *And it is hereby further Enacted,* That if said Furnace shall not be in blast, on the first day of May annually, or about to be put in blast on the first day of May in any year hereafter, the inhabitants of said Tinmouth shall have full power and authority to open the gates and floom to said dam on the first day of May, in any year that said furnace may not be in blast, or about to be put in blast as aforesaid, on the first day of May as aforesaid, and keep the same open until the first day of September. And they shall also have right to open the said gates and floom at any time between the first day of

May and first day of June, when the owners of said furnace shall have finished their spring blast.[1]

Passed November 1, 1799.

A true record,

Attest, Ros. Hopkins, Sec'y.

AN ACT STAYING ALL PROSECUTIONS AND SUITS OF A CIVIL NATURE AGAINST ISAIAH PARMETER FOR THE SPACE OF TEN YEARS

NOVEMBER 1ST, 1799

It is hereby Enacted by the General Assembly of the State of Vermont, That all prosecutions and suits of a civil nature be, and they are hereby declared to be suspended against Isaiah Parmeter, late of Oakham, in the county of Worcester and Commonwealth of Massachusetts, but now of Stockbridge, in the county of Windsor in this state, be, staid [stayed] for the space of ten years.[2]

Passed November 1, 1799.

A true record,

Attest, Ros. Hopkins, Sec'y.

AN ACT FOR THE RELIEF OF THOMAS LEVERETT

NOVEMBER 1ST, 1799

Whereas, Thomas Leverett of Windsor, in the county of Windsor, by losses in trade is reduced to indigent circumstances, is embarrassed with heavy demands, thereby prevented from entering upon any mesne business, and which is not in his power to discharge without some temporary relief. Therefore,

It is hereby Enacted by the General [Assembly] of the State of Vermont, That all actions and suits for the recovery of any civil demand against the said Thomas Leveret, be, and they hereby are suspended for the term of three years from and after the passing of this act. That

1. State Papers of Vermont, Vol. XI, *General Petitions,* 1797-1799, "For Seasonal Lowering of the Water Level in a Mill Pond," 350.
2. Ibid., "For an Act of Insolvency," 432.

all such actions, already commenced against the said Thomas, shall cease to be prosecuted, and all proceedings therein shall be staied [stayed] during said term of three years, without any additional costs to the said Thomas which has not already accrued. And no such action shall hereafter be commenced and maintained against the said Thomas during said term, and this act may be plead in bar thereof.

Sec. 2. *And it is hereby further Enacted,* That the said Thomas Leverett, together with one or more sureties, shall, previous to his taking any benefit of this act, execute to the creditors of the said Thomas their bond in the penal sum of ten thousand dollars; conditioned, that the said Thomas Leverett shall not, during said term of three years, embezzle or dispose of any of his property to defraud any of his said creditors; and shall, at the end of said term, place the same in as eligible a situation for the benefit of his said creditors as what the same now is. Which bonds shall be lodged with the clerk of Windsor county court, and be by him kept for the benefit of his said creditors. And in case the condition of said bond shall be broken, the creditors of the said Thomas, or any of them, shall be, and they are hereby empowered to maintain action or actions thereon against the signers of said bond in the same manner as though said bond had been executed and delivered to them, or any of them personally and by name.[1]

Passed November 1, 1799.

A true record,

Attest, Ros. Hopkins, Sec'y.

AN ACT ESTABLISHING A CORPORATION BY THE NAME OF WINDHAM TURNPIKE COMPANY

NOVEMBER 1ST, 1799

Whereas, the road from Bennington to Brattleborough in this State is exceedingly rocky and mountainous, and the expense of straightening, making, and repairing a highway across said mountain so that the same may be safe and convenient for travellers with horses and carriages, would be much greater than ought to be required of the

---

1. State Papers of Vermont, Vol. XI, *General Petitions,* 1797-1799, "For an Act of Insolvency," 415.

towns through which the same would pass under their present circumstances. Therefore,

It is hereby Enacted by the General Assembly of the State of Vermont, That Samuel Safford, Luke Knoulton, Royal Tyler, Jonas Whitney, Samuel Thompson, David Taylor, Samuel Whitney, David Weeks, Joseph Hartwell, Oliver Perry, John Steward and Samuel Mixer, and all such persons as shall be associated with them, and their successors, be, and they hereby are constituted a corporation by the name of the Windham Turnpike Company; and shall by that name sue and be sued, and shall have a common seal and enjoy all the privileges and powers which are by law incident to corporations, for the purpose of laying out and making a turnpike road, from the dwelling house of David Weeks in said Bennington to the dwelling house of General John Steward in said Brattleborough, in such place or places as the said corporation shall choose for the same. And when the said Turnpike shall be sufficiently made, and shall be allowed and approved by the judges of the county court, in Windham county, or a committee by them appointed, said corporation shall be allowed to erect five gates on the same as follows, to wit, one near the east line of said Bennington, one in the town of Reedsborough, one near Deerfield River in Wilmington; one in the west part of Marlborough, and one in the west part of said Brattleborough. And they shall be, and they are hereby entitled to receive from each traveller or passenger, the following rates of toll, to wit, for every coach, phaeton, chariot or other four wheeled pleasure carriage drawn by two horses, at each of the two eastern gates, that is, the two gates in Brattleborough and Marlborough, fifty cents; at each of the other gates, sixty seven cents; and if drawn by more than two horses, an additional sum of six cents for each additional horse; for every cart or waggon drawn by two horses or oxen, at each of said eastern gates, seventeen cents; and at each of the other gates twenty five cents; and if drawn by more than two oxen or horses, an additional sum of three cents for each additional oxen or horse; for every sled or slay [sleigh] drawn by two oxen or horses at each of said eastern gates, twelve and half cents, at each of the other three gates, seventeen cents, if drawn by more han two oxen or horses, the additional sum of two cents for each additional oxen or horse; for every chaise, chair, or other pleasure carriage drawn by one horse, the same as a waggon with two horses; for every man and horse at each of said eastern gates, eight cents, at each of the other three gates twelve cents; for all horses, mules, or oxen led or driven beside those in teams and carriages, at each gate, one cent; for all sheep or swine, at each gate, after the rate of six cents per dozen; for every foot passenger, four cents, at Deerfield river bridge in Wilmington. *Provided* That the said corporation may, if they see fit, commute the rate of toll with any person or persons by taking of him or them a certain sum monthly or annually to be mutually agreed upon in lieu of the toll aforesaid. Provided, however, That if the said corporation shall not see fit to keep said toll gate in said Reedsborough, they may discontinue the same and put one moiety of the several tolls heretofore provided to be taken at said gate, on the tolls according to their several rates to be collected at the toll gate near Bennington line, and the other moiety on the tolls to be collected at the toll gate in said Wilmington.

Sec. 2. *And it is hereby further Enacted,* That the said corporation, or a committee by them appointed, be, and they are hereby authorised to lay out, and make, and alter said road through any lands where it shall be necessary or convenient, under the same regulations and instructions which the selectmen in the several towns within this State are under, in laying out and allotting highways, which roads shall be laid out four rods in width. *Provided,* That no pay shall be allowed to any landowner for laying out or altering said road through his lands, where the lands shall not be improved at the time of such alteration, or for extending said road to the width of four rods in any place where the highway is now laid.

Sec. 3. *And it is hereby further Enacted,* That if said corporation or their toll gatherers, or any other person in their employ, shall unreasonably delay or hinder any traveller, or passenger at either of said gates, or shall demand or receive more toll than is by this act established, the corporation shall forfeit and pay a sum not exceeding ten dollars, nor less than one dollar, to be recovered before any court proper to try the same. And the said corporation shall be liable to pay all damages which may happen to any person from whom the toll is demandable for any damage which shall arise from neglect of any bridge or want of repairs in said road; and shall be liable to presentment by the grand jury for not keeping the same in good repair. Provided, That the inhabitants of the several towns through which the said road shall pass shall be obliged to clear the said turnpike from drifts or large bodies of snow in the same manner as they are obliged by law to do on other roads within their respective towns.

Sec. 4. *And it is hereby further Enacted,* That if any person or persons shall act, break down, or otherwise destroy any of said turnpike gates, or shall dig up or carry away earth from said road to the damage of the same, or shall forcible[y] pass, or attempt to pass by force the gates or any of them, without having first paid the legal toll at such gate, such person shall pay all damage which said corporation shall thereby sustain; and shall forfeit and pay a fine not exceeding fifty dollars, nor less than one dollar, to be recovered by the treasurer of said corporation to their use in an action of trespass on the case. And if the person with his carriage, cattle, or horse shall turn out of said road to pass any of the turnpike gates, and again enter the said road with intent to evade the toll due by virtue of this act, such person shall forfeit and pay three times so much as the legal toll would have been, to be recovered in manner aforesaid, to the use of said corporation. *Provided,* That nothing in this act shall extend to entitle the said corporation to demand and receive toll of any person who shall be passing with his horse or carriage to or from public worship, or on militia duty, or with his horse, team or cattle, to or from his common labour on his farm or to or from any grist mill or other ordinary business of family concerns.

Sec. 5. *And it is hereby further Enacted,* That the shares in the said turnpike road, shall be taken, deemed and considered personal estate to all intents and purposes, and shall and may be transferable in such manner as the corporation may by their bye-laws establish. And when any share shall be attached on mesne process, an attested copy of such process shall, at the time of the attachment, be left with the clerk of the corporation; otherwise the attachment shall be void. And such shares may be sold on execution in the same manner as is or may be, by law provided, for making sale of personal property on execution, the creditor leaving a copy of the execution, and the officers return thereon, with the clerk of said corporation, within fourteen days after such sale, and paying for recording the same. And such share or shares, so sold as aforesaid, shall to all intents and purposes vest in the purchaser.

Sec. 6. *And it is hereby further Enacted,* That there shall be a meeting of said corporation held at the house of Jonas Whitney, Esqr., in said Marlborough, on the first day of January next at ten oclock in the forenoon, for the purpose of choosing a clerk and such other officers as may be considered necessary by the said corporation. And said corporation may then establish such rules and regulations as the said corporation may judge necessary for regulating the concerns thereof. *Provided,* the same shall not be repugnant to the laws of this State. And the said corporation may, from time to time, establish such method of calling meetings as they shall judge proper.

Sec. 7. *And it is hereby further Enacted,* That when any proprietor shall neglect or refuse to pay any tax duly assessed by said corporation to their treasurer within sixty days after the time appointed for the payment thereof, the treasurer is hereby authorised to sell at public vendue the share or shares of such delinquent proprietor, under such regulations as the said corporation may by their bye laws direct. And such purchaser on producing a certificate of such sale from the treasurer to the clerk of said corporation, in the name of such purchaser, with the number of the shares so sold, shall be by the clerk entered on the books of said corporation. And such purchaser shall thereupon be considered to all intents and purposes the proprietor thereof. And the overplus, if any there be, shall be paid on demand by the treasurer to the person whose share or shares shall have been so sold as aforesaid.

Sec. 8. *And it is hereby further Enacted,* That the said corporation shall, at all places where the said toll shall be collected, erect and keep constantly exposed to view, a sign or board with the rates of toll of all the tollable articles fairly and legibly written thereon in large or capital letters.

Sec. 9. *And it is hereby further Enacted,* That after the expiration of fifty years from the completion of said road, the judges of the supreme court, for the time being, shall have power to examine the books and accounts of the said corporation. And if they shall find that the toll received during the said term of fifty years shall average at a larger sum than twelve per cent per annum, upon all actual expenditures, in laying out, making, repairing, and taking care of said road, and the expenses incident thereto, it shall be the duty of said judges to lessen the toll to such sum as to them shall appear reasonable. *Provided,* it shall not be in the power of said judges to reduce the toll to such sum as shall prevent said corporations from receiving twelve per cent per annum. And the said corporation shall, within one year after said road is completed, make out a correct statement of all the expenses thereof and present the same to the judges of Windham county court, to be by them approved; after which the same shall immediately be lodged in the office of the Secretary of State.

Sec. 10. *And it is hereby further Enacted,* That if the said corporation shall not complete said turnpike road to the acceptance of the judges of said Windham county court, within the term of five years from and after the passing of this act, the same shall be null and void. *Provided however,* That when said corporation shall, at any time within said five years, have completed not less than seven miles of said road, lying together to the acceptance of the judges aforesaid, said corporation may erect such toll gates as are heretofore contemplated by this act, to be erected on such part of said road, and may receive at such gate or gates the same toll as is by this act provided to be received at such gate or gates.

Passed November 1, 1799.

A true record,

Attest, Ros. Hopkins, Sec'y.

AN ACT APPOINTING A COMMITTEE TO LAY OUT AND SURVEY A COUNTY ROAD FROM WINDHAM IN THE COUNTY OF WINDHAM TO RUTLAND IN THE COUNTY OF RUTLAND

NOVEMBER 1ST, 1799

It is hereby Enacted by the General Assembly of the State of Vermont, That John Woodburn, Joseph Axtill, and John B. Wheeler, be, and hereby are appointed a committee, with full power to lay out, open, and survey a county road in the most direct and convenient course from Edward Aikin, Esquire, in Windham, in the county of Windham, to Rutland, until it intersects the road that leads from Rockingham, in the county of Windham, to Rutland court house. And it shall be the duty of said committee to make a return of the road so by them laid out to the town clerks of the several towns through which said road shall be laid, whose duty it shall be to record the same in their respective offices. And such road so laid out and recorded shall not be altered but by the supreme court, or a committee by them appointed, on application made to said court by the selectmen of the towns through which said road shall pass. And on report of such committee, and its acceptance by the said supreme court such road may be altered.

Sec. 2. *And it is hereby further Enacted,* That the proprietors and inhabitants of the several towns through which said road shall pass, shall be at liberty to agree upon the mode of defraying the expense of making and repairing such road either by taxing the polls and rateable estate of the inhabitants of said towns, or by applying to the Legislature for a tax on the lands in such towns within a proper time before the session of the Legislature in October next.

Sec. 3. *And it is hereby further Enacted,* That it shall be the duty of the committee to lay out said road some time before the first day of July next, and said committee shall give proper notice to the selectmen of the several towns through which said road is to be laid of the time they will attend to the business.

Sec. 4. *And it is hereby further Enacted,* That the expense of laying out the aforesaid road, shall be paid by the several towns through which the same shall be laid, in such proportion on each town as the committee shall judge equitable.

Passed November 1, 1799.

A true record,

Attest, Ros. Hopkins, Sec'y.

AN ACT REVIVING AN ACT LAYING A TAX ON THE LANDS IN THE TOWN OF JOHNSTON [JOHNSON]

NOVEMBER 1ST, 1799

It is hereby Enacted by the General Assembly of the State of Vermont, That an act laying a tax of one penny per acre on the lands in the town of Johnson, in the county of Franklin, for the purpose of making and repairing roads and building bridges in said town, passed by the Legislature of this State, at their October session A.D. 1796 at Rutland, be, and the same is hereby revived and declared to be in full force and virtue in every part and respect, excepting as hereinafter altered, the same as if the said act had passed at the present session of the Legislature.

And it is hereby further Enacted, That John McConnell of said Johnson be, and he is hereby appointed a member of the committee for the superintendance of the expenditure of said tax, in the room of William Coit appointed in and by the act aforesaid, and the said new member of committee is hereby directed and rendered accountable in the same manner and extent as if he had been nominated and appointed in the act aforesaid.

AN ACT FOR THE PURPOSE OF DISCHARGING THE TOWN, AND THE
SELECTMEN OF THE TOWN OF ARLINGTON FROM THE ARREARAGE
DUE ON A CERTAIN TAX WHICH OUGHT TO HAVE BEEN
COLLECTED IN OR ABOUT THE YEAR
1784 BY IRA HAWLEY

NOVEMBER 2ND, 1799

It is hereby Enacted by the General Assembly of the State of Vermont, That the town of Arlington, and the selectmen thereof, be, and are hereby discharged from the payment of the arrearage of a certain tax, which ought to have been collected by the said Ira Hawley.

Provided always, That the said town and selectmen thereof, do first relinquish all right, title, and claim, which they now have against Solomon Butler of Addison in Addison county, as bail for the widow of Ira Hawley, deceased, who was the collector of said tax, except such legal expenses as they may have been at in prosecuting any suit or suits against the said Solomon Butler as bail aforesaid.[1]

Passed November 2, 1799.

A true record,

Attest, Ros. Hopkins, Sec'y.

AN ACT TO ENABLE THE PROPRIETORS OF THE TOWN OF GEORGIA
TO DIVIDE THE LANDS OF SAID TOWN INTO SEVERALTY

NOVEMBER 2ND, 1799

Whereas, the proprietors of the town of Georgia, in the county of Franklin, formerly attempted to make a division of the lands in said township by the mode of pitching or otherwise, that each proprietor should have the liberty of laying out and surveying his own land in said town, in consequence of which many of the proprietors made pitches and surveys of lots and tracts of land in said township, and

---

1. State Papers of Vermont, Vol. XI, *General Petitions,* 1797-1799, "For a Tax Abatement," 419.

many settlements and large improvements have been made thereon; and it appears that said divisions so attempted to be made of said lands were not conformable to the existing laws of this State, and the records of said proprietors relating thereto are either lost or withheld and concealed by former clerks. And whereas it is impossible under the present existing circumstances of said proprietors, to make just and equitable division of the lands in said township conformable to the existing laws of this state. Therefore,

It is hereby Enacted by the General Assembly of the State of Vermont, That the proprietors of the township of Georgia aforesaid, shall be, and they are hereby empowered to warn a meeting of said proprietors, and in such warning to notify the former proprietors' clerk or clerks, and their successors in office, and all other person or persons whatever, that may have in their possession the records, files or papers appertaining or belonging to the said proprietors' office, or who shall have in his or their possession any bill of survey that may have been made of lands in said town, to deliver the same to the town clerk of the said town of Georgia for the time being, on or before the day of said meeting, which warning shall be published at least six months previous to the day of said meeting. And in case the person or persons so notified as aforesaid, shall neglect or refuse to deliver over the records, files, and papers as aforesaid, to said town clerk, within the time aforesaid, they shall forever thereafter be debarred from producing them as evidence, in any division or allotment made heretofore by said proprietors in said town whatever. And in case of such neglect or refusal, the proprietors of the said township of Georgia are hereby fully authorised and empowered at any meeting legally warned and holden for that purpose, to agree upon such mode of dividing the lands in said township into severalty as to them shall appear most just and equitable, having regard as nearly as circumstances will admit, to the lots as the same have been already surveyed, and to the settlements and improvement made therein. And the said proprietors having made, or caused to be made, an accurate survey allotment or plan of the lands in said township, accordingly shall have power at said meeting to accept thereof, and establish the same as a legal division of said township, and the same shall forever thereafter be deemed a good and valid division in law to all intents and purposes whatever.

Sec. 2. *And it is hereby further Enacted,* That the proprietors of said Georgia shall have the right to tax the lands in said town, legally laid out as aforesaid, in such sum as may be necessary to defray the expenses of altering the same, not exceeding three dollars thirty four cents for each hundred acres so surveyed.

Sec. 3. *And it is hereby further Enacted,* That every occupant on lands shall be considered in the dividend of the lands as aforesaid, as far the rightful owner thereof, that the same shall be set in said allotment to the original right (so far as the case will admit), to which such occupant surveyed the same, anything in this act to the contrary notwithstanding.

Passed November 2, 1799.

A true record,

Attest, Ros. Hopkins, Sec'y.

AN ACT DIRECTING THE TREASURER OF THIS STATE TO CALL ON THE SHERIFFS OF THE SEVERAL COUNTIES, TO ACCOUNT WITH HIM FOR THE VOLUMES OF REVISED LAWS WHICH THEY HAVE RECEIVED FOR SALE

NOVEMBER 2ND, 1799

It is hereby Enacted by the General Assembly of the State of Vermont, That the treasurer of this State be, and he hereby is directed to call on the sheriffs of the several counties in this State by the first day of January, A.D. 1800, to render an account to him by the first day of June in the same year, of their sales of the volumes of the revised laws belonging to this state, which they have received for sale, and of the number of volumes on hand. And if any sheriff shall neglect or refuse to render to the said treasurer a satisfactory account as aforesaid, and pay to said treasurer all the monies which he shall have received on account of such sales by the said first day of June, A.D. 1800, the said treasurer is hereby directed to lodge in the hands of the state's attorney of the same county the receipt given by such sheriff for such volumes of said revised laws. And the several state's attornies are hereby directed on the receipt of such receipts as aforesaid, to prosecute the same without delay.

Passed November 2, 1799.

A true record,

Attest, Ros. Hopkins, Sec'y.

AN ACT ASSESSING A TAX OF ONE CENT ON THE DOLLAR ON THE LIST OF
1799

NOVEMBER 2ND, 1799

It is hereby Enacted by the General Assembly of the State of Vermont, That there be, and hereby is assessed a tax of one cent on the dollar on the list of the polls and rateable estate of the inhabitants of this State, taken in the year 1799, to be paid into the treasury by the first day of June next; to be paid in hard money, state orders, and orders drawn by the clerks of the supreme court.

Passed November 2, 1799.

A true record,

Attest, Ros. Hopkins, Sec'y.

AN ACT DIRECTING THE TREASURER OF THIS STATE TO CREDIT THE
TOWN OF WESTMINSTER THE SUM THEREIN MENTIONED

NOVEMBER 2ND, 1799

It is hereby Enacted by the General Assembly of the State of Vermont, That the treasurer of this State be, and hereby is directed to credit the town of Westminster on the state tax of one cent on each acre of land granted in the year 1797, the sum of $19.83 cents.

Passed November 2, 1799.

A true record,

Attest, Ros. Hopkins, Sec'y.

AN ACT DIRECTING THE TREASURER TO CREDIT ISAAC WING, COLLECTOR
OF THE CENT LAND TAX IN ROCHESTER THE SUM THEREIN
MENTIONED

NOVEMBER 2ND, 1799

It is hereby Enacted by the General Assembly of the State of Vermont, That the treasurer of this State be, and he is hereby directed to give the credit of the sum of $11.90 cents to Isaac Wing, collector of the cent land tax of the year 1797, for the town of Rochester, in the county of Windsor, in the State, it being the sum of the difference against the said collector, between the sum directed to be collected by the treasurer's warrant, and the sum directed by the tax bill of the selectmen of said town.

Passed November 2, 1799.

A true record,

Attest, Ros. Hopkins, Sec'y.

AN ACT RESTRAINING SWINE FROM GOING AT LARGE

NOVEMBER 2ND, 1799

Sec. 1. *It is hereby Enacted* by the General Assembly of the State of Vermont, That no swine shall be allowed to run at large on the highways or commons in this State. And if any person or persons shall suffer his or their swine to run at large on the highways or commons aforesaid, it shall be the duty of the Haywards (and lawful for any other person) to impound such swine, and the owners of such swine shall pay the poundage by law allowed before they are released out of said pound. *Always Provided,* that every town in this State shall have liberty at their annual March meeting, provided there is an article in the warning for that purpose, to permit such swine to be at large within the limits of such town.

Passed November 2, 1799.

A true record,

Attest, Ros. Hopkins, Sec'y.

AN ACT DIRECTING THE SECRETARY OF STATE TO RECORD THE COMMISSIONS OR WARRANTS GIVEN BY THE LATE COURT OF CONFISCATION IN THIS STATE TO EBENEZER CURTIS AND THOMAS CHANDLER, JUNIOR, AS COMMISSIONERS OF SALES OF CONFISCATED ESTATES

NOVEMBER 2ND, 1799

Whereas, the commissions or warrants given by the late court of confication to Ebenezer Curtis and Thomas Chandler, Junior, were not recorded in the records of said court. And whereas, in disputes respecting the trial of titles of land, sold by said commissioners, it is deemed necessary to have said commissioners produced in court. And whereas, they are now much worn and damaged and are liable to be entirely lost or destroyed, which would be of great damage to a number of persons who have purchased confiscated lands. Therefore,

It is hereby Enacted by the General Assembly of the State of Vermont, That the secretary of state be, and hereby is directed to record said commissions or warrants in the book of records of the court of confiscation, with a list of the names inserted on the back of the same. And attested copies of such warrants or commissions, made by the secretary of state, shall hereafter be received as evidence in all courts of law and equity in this State, the same as if the said original warrants or commissions were produced in any such court.

Passed November 2, 1799.

A true record,

Attest, Ros. Hopkins, Sec'y.

AN ACT LAYING A TAX OF THREE MILLS ON THE DOLLAR ON THE POLLS AND RATEABLE ESTATE OF THE INHABITANTS OF THE COUNTY OF WINDHAM

NOVEMBER 2ND, 1799

Whereas, for the purposes of discharging the debts due from said county;

It is hereby Enacted by the General Assembly of the State of Vermont, That there be, and hereby is granted a tax of three mills on the dollar on the list of the polls and rateable estate of the inhabitants of the county of Windham, for the year 1799, to be paid in county orders, notes issued by the treasurer of said county, or in gold and silver money, to be collected and paid into the treasury by the first day of June 1800.

Sec. 2. *And it is hereby further Enacted,* That the treasurer of said county have and he hereby has granted unto him the same power in issuing warrants and extents as are vested in the treasurer of the state in collecting state taxes. And the first constables of the respective towns in said county are hereby empowered, and it is hereby made their duty to proceed in the collection of said tax, and paying the same into the county treasury in the same manner as it is made their duty, by law, to collect state taxes, and pay them into the state treasury, and they are hereby liable in the same manner for neglect of duty.

Passed November 2, 1799.

A true record,

Attest, Ros. Hopkins, Sec'y.

AN ACT DIRECTING THE TREASURER OF THIS STATE TO CREDIT THE TOWN OF BURLINGTON IN THE COUNTY OF CHITTENDEN THE SUM THEREIN MENTIONED

NOVEMBER 2ND, 1799

It is hereby Enacted by the General Assembly of the State of Vermont, That the treasurer of this State be, and he is hereby directed to credit the town of Burlington the sum of twenty dollars on the state tax granted by the Legislature in October, A.D. 1798.

Passed November 2, 1799.

A true record,

Attest, Ros. Hopkins, Sec'y.

AN ACT INCORPORATING CERTAIN PERSONS THEREIN NAMED BY THE NAME OF THE GREEN MOUNTAIN TURNPIKE COMPANY

NOVEMBER 2ND, 1799

Whereas, the public road leading from the east line of Clarendon, in the county of Rutland, to Bellows Falls in Rockingham is circuitous, rocky and mountainous, and the expense of shortening, making, and repairing a road over said ground would be much greater than ought to be bourne by the towns through which the same may pass, Therefore,

Sec. 1. *It is hereby Enacted* by the General Assembly of the State of Vermont, That Salmon Dutton, Calvin Robinson, Lyman Clark, Jeffery A. Barney, Peter Reed, Jesse Gilbert, Ichabod Robinson, Royal Crafts, John Willoughby, John Atkinson, William Page, Daniel Farrand, Salmon Dutton, Junr., Asa Wheeler, Martin Cavenaugh, Stephen Clark, and such persons as shall be associated with them and their successors, shall be a body corporate and hereby are incorporated by the name of the Green Mountain Turnpike Company; and by that name may sue and be sued; may purchase and hold property; may have a common seal; and shall have and enjoy all the privileges which by law are incident to corporation[s]. And the said corporation shall have power to cause to be laid out in the manner herein after directed a road from the east line of Clarendon, to the post road on Connecticut River in Rockingham; and when laid out to open, make, and keep the same in good repair.

Sec. 2. *And it is hereby further Enacted,* that the mode of laying out said road shall be as follows, to wit, the judges of the supreme court are hereby empowered, on application of said corporation to appoint a committee to consist of three judicious disinterested persons, who shall, at the expense of said corporation, view the said ground, and shall lay out the said road, as will in their judgment best accommodate the public and promote the general object and design of the corporation; which road shall be laid our four rods wide, and the path for travelling be made at least eighteen feet wide. And the said corporation may purchase and hold the lands for said road, of the owners, and if they cannot agree on the price of the same, the said committee shall appraise the damage which may be done to any person or persons by having said road laid on his or their lands, which sum being paid by the said corporation, on demand, to the person owning or being in possession of said lands shall forever discharge them from any action on account of said road being laid as aforesaid. *Provided,* That no allowance shall be made to the owners of land taken up by said road, if the same are not improved, but in a wild state, nor in cases where the said road shall be laid, on any other already laid out.

Sec. 3. *And it is hereby further Enacted,* That when said road shall be completed and appraised by the judges of the supreme court, or a majority of them, who may examine the same by themselves, or by a committee of three judicious men by them appointed for that purpose, it shall be lawful for the corporation to erect four turnpike gates; one at or near the east end of said road in Rockingham; one in Cavendish, south of the road leading to Weathersfield; one in Ludlow in the most convenient place, and one in Shrewsbury, southwardly of Captain Finney's now dwelling house; and shall be entitled to received from each passanger, at each of said gates, the following rates of toll, to wit, for each coach, phaeton, chariot, or other four wheeled pleasure carriage drawn by two horses, fifty six cents, and if drawn by more than two horses for each additional horse ten cents; for every chaise, chair, sulkey [sulky] or other two wheel pleasure carriage drawn by one horse, thirty cents, and for each additional horse, nine cents; for every cart or waggon drawn by two oxen or horses, twenty five cents, and if drawn by more then two oxen or horses, for every additional ox or horse, four cents; for every sled or sleigh drawn by two oxen or horses, twelve and half cents, and for each additional ox or horse, three cents, and if drawn by one horse, eight cents; for every man and horse, six cents; for all horses led or driven, exclusive of those in teams or carriages, two and an half cents, if under ten, if over ten, one cent each; for all neat cattle in droves of the number of ten or under, the sum of two cents each, if over ten, one cent for each additional creature; and for all sheep or swine to the number of twelve, half a cent each, if over twelve, at the rate of three cents per dozen. *Provided always,* that no person shall be obliged to pay any toll at either of said gates, who shall be going to or from public worship or to or from any grist mill or saw mill or on militia duty or on the ordinary domestic business of family concerns.

Sec. 4. *Provided also,* and it is hereby further Enacted, That when the said corporation shall have completed one fourth part of the said road, and such fourth part as the committee of the supreme court aforesaid shall determine, they shall have right to erect one gate thereon and receive toll as prescribed in this act, and so on in like manner for the remaining three fourths of said road.

Sec. 5. *And it is hereby further Enacted,* That the said corporation at any legal meeting, shall have power to divide the said grant into as many shares as they shall agree. And each town through which the said turnpike road shall pass shall be allowed the privilege of taking as many shares as they shall chuse [choose]. *Provided,* That no town shall be at liberty to take more than one sixth part of the whole number of said shares; nor have liberty to take any share in the road, unless application be made to the corporation at their first meeting. And said corporation shall have power to agree upon the mode of transferring such shares. And when any person shall purchase any share or shares, he shall be a proprietor according to the number of shares which he shall hold. And the said corporation shall at such meeting have power to make bye-laws not inconsistent with the constitution and laws of this State for the due regulation of the common interests and concerns. And shall have power to raise taxes, or by vote to impower their director or agent to raise and assess the same for the purpose of making and repairing such roads or gates, and for any other purpose which they may deem necessary; which tax or taxes shall be assessed equally on the several shares, and to appoint such number of directors or agents to manage the affairs of said corporation as they may deem necessary, a treasurer and collector and such other officers as they shall judge expedient.

Sec. 6. *And it is hereby further Enacted,* That when any tax shall be assessed on the shares by direction of the proprietors, and the owner of any share or shares shall neglect or refuse to pay the said assessment, it shall be lawful for the proprietors, in pursuance of their bye laws, to sell such share or shares, and the person purchasing such share or shares shall be a proprietor in the said corporation, and shall stand fully in the place of the first proprietor.

Sec. 7. *And it is hereby further Enacted,* That if the said corporation, their toll gatherers or any person in their employment shall unreasonably delay or hinder any traveller or passenger at said gate or gates, or shall demand and receive more toll than is by this act allowed, the said corporation shall forfeit and pay to the person so injured a sum not exceeding ten dollars, nor less than one dollar, to be recovered before any court having competent jurisdiction. And the said corporation shall be liable to pay to any person from whom toll is demandable, all such damage as shall happen to him in travelling said road, for any defect or want of repairs in the same. And shall also be liable to presentment by the grand jury for not keeping said road and bridges thereon in repair.

Sec. 8. *And it is hereby further Enacted,* That if any person shall cut, break down, or destroy any of said turnpike gates, or dig up or carry away any earth from said road, or in any manner wantonly and maliciously damage the same, or shall attempt forcibly to pass any gate on said road without having paid the legal toll at said gate, such person shall forfeit and pay a sum not exceeding fifty dollars, nor less than one dollar, together with double damages and costs, to be recovered by the treasurer of said corporation, to and for the use thereof, in an action of the case before any court having competent jurisdiction. And if any person or persons with his or their carriage, team or cattle shall turn out of said road to pass the gate or gates, with intent to avoid the toll due by virtue of this act, such person shall forfeit and pay treble toll to be recovered by the treasurer of said corporation to the use thereof, in an action of the case, to be by him brought for that purpose.

Sec. 9. *And it is hereby further Enacted,* That the shares in said turnpike road shall be taken and deemed to be personal estate; and the mode of attaching the same shall be by leaving a true and attested copy of the attachment with the officer's return, with the clerk of said corporation. And a copy of an execution, with the officer's return thereon, that he has sold any share, lodged with the said clerk for record, within fourteen days after such sale, shall be good to pass the same to the purchaser.

Sec. 10. *And it is hereby further Enacted,* That the first meeting of said corporation shall be holden at the house of Salmon Dutton, Esqr., in Cavendish on the first Monday of January next, for the purpose of choosing such officers as may be necessary, and for transacting any other business which the said corporation, by this act, are empowered to transact for regulating the concerns thereof. And said corporation may then and there agree on the mode of calling any future meetings of said corporation, and the same mode from time to time alter, as the said corporation may judge expedient.

Sec. 11. *And it is hereby further Enacted,* That it shall be the duty of said corporation, within one year after the completion of said road to deliver to the secretary of this state an account of the expenses of making the same.

Sec. 12. *And it is hereby further Enacted,* That at the expiration of the term of fifteen years from and after the completion of said road, and thereafter at each successive period of fifteen years as the case shall require, it shall be the duty of said corporation to lay all their accounts before the judges of the supreme court, for the time being, who shall have power to examine the accounts and books of said corporation, and if they shall find that the toll received shall have paid all the expenditures of making, repairing, and taking care of said road, together with an annual interest on the same at the rate of twelve per cent per annum, then and in that case the said supreme court may dissolve said corporation. And thereupon the property of said road shall vest in this State, and be at the disposal of the Legislature.

Sec. 13. *And it is hereby further Enacted,* That at the several gates where toll shall be taken, there shall be erected and kept exposed to view a sign or board with the rates of toll with all the tollable articles fairly written thereon in large letters.

Sec. 14. *And it is hereby further Enacted,* That if the said corporation shall neglect to complete the said road for the space of five years from and after the passing of this act, then this act shall become null and void.

Sec. 15. *Provided nevertheless,* and it is hereby further Enacted, that if the said corporation shall not enter into bonds, with sufficient sureties, in the penal sum of one thousand dollars, to the treasurer of this State, to the acceptance of the judges of the supreme court, on or before the first day of October next, conditioned that the said corporation shall complete said turnpike road, agreeable to the true intent and meaning of this act, this grant shall be, and hereby is declared to be forfeited, from and after the said first day of October next.

Passed November 2, 1799.

    A true record,

        Attest, Ros. Hopkins, Sec'y.

AN ACT EMPOWERING RUTH STEARNES, ADMINISTRATRIX OF THE ESTATE OF REUBEN STEARNES, LATE OF SHREWSBURY, IN THE COUNTY OF RUTLAND, DECEASED, TO DEED A CERTAIN LOT OF LAND

NOVEMBER 2ND, 1799

It is hereby Enacted by the General Assembly of the State of Vermont, that Ruth Stearnes of Wallingford, in the county of Rutland, sole administratrix on the estate of Reuben Stearnes, late of Shrewsbury in said county, deceased, be, and she is hereby empowered, under the direction and with the approbation of the judge of probate for the probate district of Rutland, to sell, and by deed convey the real estate of the said deceased, situate in Shewsbury aforesaid, to wit, one lot of land containing one hundred acres, lying west of and adjoining James Parker's farm, and easterly of the beaver meadow lot, so called. And the avails of such sale, excepting such part as shall, by the judge of probate aforesaid, be assigned to the widow of the deceased, in lieu of her dower, shall be for the sole use and benefit of Lucy Stearnes, a minor and sole heiress of said estate. And the deed of land so given by said administratrix under the direction and with the approbation of said judges as aforesaid, shall be good and valid in law, to all intents and purposes, as if the same had been given by the said deceased in his life time.

Sec. 2. *Provided nevertheless,* and it is hereby further Enacted, That a mortgage deed shall be executed by the purchaser, at the time of his receiving such deed, as aforesaid, to the said heiress, by name, reconveying to her the said lands for the security of the payment of the purchase money (except such part as shall be assigned to said widow as aforesaid), on her arriving at lawful age, and conditioned that upon such payment the said mortgage deed shall be null and void.[1]

Passed November 2d, 1799.

A true record,

Attest, Ros. Hopkins, Sec'y.

AN ACT IN ADDITION TO AN ACT ENTITLED "AN ACT TO ENABLE THE PROPRIETORS AND LANDOWNERS OF THE TOWN OF JERICHO TO DIVIDE THEIR LANDS INTO SEVERALTY" PASSED NOVEMBER 7, 1798

NOVEMBER 2ND, 1799

It is hereby Enacted by the General Assembly of the State of Vermont, That if the former clerk or clerks of the town of Jericho, their successor or successors in said office, or any other person or persons whatsoever, that may have in their possession, the records, files or papers appertaining or belonging to the said proprietors' office, or who shall have in his or their possession any bill of survey that may have been made of lands in said town, do refuse or neglect to deliver over the records, files and papers as aforesaid, to the town clerk of the town of Jericho, for the time being, on or before the day of a proprietor's meeting, warned and held agreeable to the act passed November, 1798, as aforesaid, shall forever thereafter be debarred from producing them as evidence of any division or allotment of said proprietors whatever.

Sec. 2. *And it is hereby further Enacted,* That if the records, files, or papers of the former proprietors' clerk, or any part of them, should be delivered over agreeably to the directions of this act upon

---

1. State Papers of Vermont, Vol. XI, *General Petitions,* 1797-1799, "For Authority to a Widow to Sell Real Estate," 402.

notice as aforesaid, and should be found to be incomplete, the proprietors and landowners of the said town of Jericho are hereby empowered to complete and establish the same according to the true
intent and meaning of this act.

AN ACT FOR ASSESSING A LAND TAX IN BRIDG[E]WATER IN THE COUNTY OF WINDSOR

NOVEMBER 2ND, 1799

It is hereby Enacted by the General Assembly of the State of Vermont, That a tax of one cent on the acre on all the lands in said Bridgewater, except public rights, is hereby assessed for the purpose of making
and repairing road through said Bridgewater leading from Woodstock
to Rutland, and for building and repairing bridges thereon, all of which
tax is to be appropriated on the river road, so called, between the
bridge known by the name of the North Branch bridge and west line
of said Bridgewater, to be expended under the direction of John
Hawkins and Nathan Avery, both of the same Bridgewater, and
Phinehas Williams, of Woodstock, in said Windsor county, who are
hereby appointed a committee to superintend the expenditure of said
tax. And any justice of the peace within the said county of Windsor
is hereby empowered to issue his warrant to Joseph Hawkins of said
Bridgewater, who is hereby appointed a collector to collect said tax.
And said committee and collector are hereby directed in the collection,
expenditure, and accounting for the monies raised by said tax, to
govern themselves in all things by the directions of the statute of this
State in that case made and provided. And,

It is hereby further Enacted, That the act passed at the session of
the Legislature in October, 1798, assessing a road tax on the lands in
said Bridgewater be, and the same is hereby repealed.

AN ACT ASSESSING A TAX OF ONE CENT PER ACRE ON THE TOWN OF MANSFIELD

NOVEMBER 2ND, 1799

It is hereby Enacted by the General Assembly of the State of Vermont, That there be, and hereby is assessed a tax of one cent per acre
on all lands in the town of Mansfield, in the county of Chittenden,

public rights excepted, for the purpose of making and repairing roads and building bridges in said town, to be expended under the direction of Ebenezer Wakefield & David Moody, both of Stowe, and Isaac Chamberlain of Richmond, who are hereby appointed a committee to superintend the expenditure of said tax. And any justice of the peace within the county of Chittenden is hereby empowered to issue his warrant to Joshua Chamberlain of Richmond, who is hereby appointed a collector to collect said tax; and said committee and collector are hereby directed in the collecting, expending, and accounting for the monies raised by said tax, to conform themselves in all things to the directions of the statute of this State, in that case made and provided.[1]

AN ACT DIRECTING THE TREASURER OF THIS STATE TO CREDIT THE TOWN OF BETHEL THE SUM THEREIN MENTIONED

NOVEMBER 4TH, 1799

It is hereby Enacted by the General Assembly of the State of Vermont, That the treasurer of this State be, and he is hereby directed to credit the town of Bethel, the sum of ten dollars on the tax of 1798.

Passed November 4, 1799.

A true record,

Attest, Ros. Hopkins, Sec'y.

AN ACT TO EMPOWER THE PROPRIETORS OF THE TOWNSHIP OF LUTTERLOCK[LUTTERLOH][2] IN THE COUNTY OF ORANGE, TO ESTABLISH THE SURVEY OF SAID TOWN TO PROCEED TO A DIVISION OF SAID TOWN INTO SEVERALTY AGREEABLY TO ANY EXISTING WRITTEN AGREEMENT BETWEEN THE PROPRIETORS

NOVEMBER 4TH, 1799

Whereas, a survey of said town into lots has already been effected without any proprietors' meeting being previously had as the law

---

1. State Papers of Vermont, Vol. XI, *General Petitions,* 1797-1799, "For a Tax on Land to Build Roads and Bridges," 408.

2. Ibid., Vol. 1, *Index to the Papers of the Surveyors General:* Lutterloh, Vermont Grant to Col. Antipas Gilman and associates, June 26, 1782; name changed to Albany, 1815.

directs. And whereas there are certain written agreements between the proprietors of said town of Lutterloh, relative to a division of said town, different from the mode pointed out in the act regulating proprietors' meetings and the proceedings therein. Therefore,

It is hereby Enacted by the General Assembly of the State of Vermont, That the proprietors of the said town of Lutterloh, at a meeting legally to be warned and holden, may proceed to ratify the survey of said town, so far as they shall be satisfied therewith, and may further proceed to a division of said town into severalty, agreeably to any existing written agreements by and between them entered into, any law, usage, or custom to the contrary notwithstanding.

Passed November 4, 1799.

A true record,

Attest, Ros. Hopkins, Sec'y.

AN ACT ASSESSING A TAX OF THREE CENTS ON EACH ACRE OF LAND IN THAT PART OF THE TOWN OF GOSHEN WHICH LIES IN THE COUNTY OF ADDISON

NOVEMBER 4TH, 1799

It is hereby Enacted by the General Assembly of the State of Vermont, That there be, and hereby is assessed a tax of three cents on each acre of land in that part of the town of Goshen which lies in the county of Addison, public lands excepted, for the purpose of making and repairing roads and building bridges in that part of the town of Goshen aforesaid, to be expended under the direction of Joshua Hyde, Jabez Rogers, Junr., and Joel Boardman, all of Middlebury, in said county of Addison, who are hereby appointed a committee for that purpose. And any justice of the peace within the county of Addison is hereby empowered to issue his warrant to Samuel Miller of Middlebury in said county of Addison, to collect said tax, who is hereby appointed a collector for that purpose. And the said committee and collector are hereby directed to govern themselves in all things in the collecting, expending, and accounting for the monies raised by said tax conformably to the directions of the statute of this State, in that case made and provided.[1]

---

1. State Papers of Vermont, Vol. XI, *General Petitions,* 1797-1799, "For Revival of an Act granting a Land Tax," 312.

AN ACT GRANTING THE EXCLUSIVE RIGHT OF A FERRY TO JOHN S.
LARRABE FOR THE TERM OF TEN YEARS

NOVEMBER 4TH, 1799

It is hereby Enacted by the General Assembly of the State of Vermont, That there be, and hereby is granted to John S. Larrabe of
Shoreham, in the county of Addison, in this State, the exclusive right
and privilege of keeping a ferry for the term of ten years, from Rowley's
Point in this State, to a place in the State of New York, commonly
known by the name of the Sandy Battery; said privilege to be considered to extend, to the distance of one mile each way up and down
the lake. *Provided,* That the said John shall furnish himself with a
good scow fit to carry a loaded waggon with four oxen, and one good
and convenient new boat, and keep the same in good repair; and within
one year from the passing hereof shall build a wharf sufficient to guard
against the winds and swell so that passengers can land with ease and
safety.

Sec. 2.   *And it is hereby further Enacted,* That the selectmen
of the town of Shoreham, be, and they are hereby authorised to examine the said wharf and boats, and if they shall judge them to be
sufficient, and agreeably to the intent of this act, and that said wharf
shall be compleated within the year as aforesaid, to give their approbation of them, and certify the same under their hands. And the rates of
ferriage to be received by the said John shall be affixed and determined
by the said selectmen, subject however, so far as respects the rates of
ferriage, to the future alteration and controul of the Legislature of
this State.[1]

Passed November 4, 1799.

A true record,

Attest, Ros. Hopkins, Sec'y.

AN ACT ASSESSING A LAND TAX IN THE TOWNSHIP OF WINHALL IN THE
COUNTY OF BENNINGTON

NOVEMBER 4TH, 1799

It is hereby Enacted by the General Assembly of the State of Ver-

---

1. State Papers of Vermont, Vol. XI, *General Petitions,* 1797-1799, "For the Right
to Operate a Ferry, 430.

mont, That there be, and hereby is assessed a tax of two cents on each acre of land in the township of Winhall, in the county of Bennington (public rights excepted), for the purpose of repairing roads and making bridges in said town, to be expended by the order and under the direction of Jonathan Sprague, Joseph Rose, and Asa Beebe, Junr., of Winhall, who are hereby appointed a committee to superintend the expenditure of said tax. And any justice of the peace of the county of Bennington, is hereby empowered to issue his warrant to Isaac Sprague to collect said tax; and the said collector is hereby made accountable to said committee for the amount of said tax. And said collector and committee are hereby directed to govern themselves in the collecting, disposing, and accounting for the monies raised by said tax, agreeably to the directions of the statute of this State, in that case made and provided.

AN ACT EMPOWERING THE COMMITTEE APPOINTED ON A LAND TAX IN THE TOWN OF STOWE TO PUBLISH NEW ADVERTISEMENTS

NOVEMBER 4TH, 1799

Whereas, the advertisement to proprietors to pay their tax by labour published by the committee appointed to superintend the expenditure of a tax of one cent per acre on the town of Stowe for making and repairing roads &c., assessed by the Legislature at their last session at Vergennes, by an accident of the press or otherwise, proved not to be, in respect to a limitation of time, as the law directs. Therefore,

It is hereby Enacted by the General Assembly of the State of Vermont, That the said committee are hereby authorised and empowered to make a new publication of the said advertisement in the same manner as though the said act assessing the said tax had been passed at the present session of the Legislature. *Provided,* nevertheless, that such proprietors as have worked out their tax, in whole or in part, in pursuance of such first advertisement, shall not have right to demand the privilege of doing additional labour in pursuance of such second advertisement, otherwise, or more than for the simple payment of their said tax.

AN ACT TO REVIVE AN ACT ENTITLED "AN ACT ASSESSING A TAX OF TWO
CENTS PER ACRE ON THE TOWN OF PLAINFIELD, LATE ST. ANDREWS
GORE, FOR THE PURPOSE THEREIN MENTIONED"

NOVEMBER 4TH, 1799

Whereas, the statutes of this State make it necessary that advertisements from committees on land taxes, giving an opportunity for proprietors to pay their taxes in labour shall be published previous to a certain time; and whereas a failure happened to that effect in the case above alluded to. Therefore,

It is hereby Enacted by the General Assembly of the State of Vermont, That the act entitled, "An act assessing a tax of two cents per acre on the town of Plainfield (late St. Andrews Gore) for the purpose therein mentioned," passed at the last session of the Legislature, be, and the same is hereby revived, and shall have the same force and effect as though it had been passed at the present session of the Legislature.

AN ACT EMPOWERING ZEBULON SPAULDING & MARTHA DAVIS
ADMINISTRATORS TO THE ESTATE OF DAVID DAVIS, LATE OF
HUBBARDTON, DECEASED, TO CONVEY CERTAIN LANDS
THEREIN MENTIONED

NOVEMBER 4TH, 1799

Whereas, it appears to this Assembly that David Davis, late of Hubbardton, deceased, did in his life time make out, well execute and deliver to Israel Dewey, late of Hubbardton, his deed of conveyance for seven acres of land in said Hubbardton, bounded and described as follows, to wit, beginning at a stake and stones in the north east corner of Bigelow Lawrence's lot, thence south 80 d. East 20 rods, to the north west corner of Jonas Selick's lot, thence south 10 d. west 50 rods on the west line of said Jonas's lot, to the south west corner thereof, thence north 80 d. west 20 rods, to a stake and stones, thence north 10 d. east 50 rods, to the first mentioned bound, containing seven acres. Since which transaction the said David and the said Israel have both died, and the deed so made and delivered by the said David, to the said Israel, hath since been lost and cannot be found. Therefore,

It is hereby Enacted by the General Assembly of the State of Vermont, That Zebulon Spaulding, administrator, and Martha Davis, administratrix, upon the estate of the aforesaid David Davis, be, and they are hereby authorised and empowered, with the approbation and under the direction of the judge of probate for the district of Fairhaven, to make and deliver a well executed deed of conveyance of the above described lands to Peter Dewey, administrator of the estate of the aforesaid Israel Dewey; which deed, so made and delivered, shall be good and valid in law, to all intents and purposes as though the same had been made and delivered by the said David Davis in his life time.[1]

Passed November 4, 1799.

A true record,

Attest, Ros. Hopkins, Sec'y.

AN ACT EMPOWERING JOSIAH HUBBARD TO SELL THE REAL ESTATE OF JUDAH SWIFT, LATE OF THETFORD, COUNTY OF ORANGE & STATE OF VERMONT, DECEASED

NOVEMBER 4TH, 1799

Whereas, it appears that the real estate of the said Judah Swift, deceased, being small, and the widow's third being set off, and the same being divided to and among the heirs of the said deceased, who are four small children, it will become unprofitable, both for the widow and heirs, and that the said real estate being sold for the value thereof, together and the widow receiving such share of the interest as shall be adjudged equitable by the judge of probate for the district of Bradford. And the residue thereof, laid out to purchase new lands, or put to use as the said judges shall order, will be more beneficial to the said heirs than to rent the same as it now is. Therefore,

It is hereby Enacted by the General Assembly of the State of Vermont, That Josiah Hubbard of Thetford, aforesaid, administrator on the estate of the said deceased be, and he is hereby empowered to sell and convey all the real estate of which the legal heirs of the said Judah, deceased, are seized, situate in Thetford aforesaid, and to make and execute good and valid deed or deeds of the same, conveying, and securing to the purchaser or purchasers the fee of the premises and privileges thereof in his capacity as fully as the deceased in the time of his life could have done. *Provided nevertheless,* That the said Josiah Hubbard shall, within one month after the sale of the real estate of

---

1. State Papers of Vermont, Vol. XI, *General Petitions,* 1797-1799, "For Authority to an Administrator to give a Deed of Real Estate," 427.

the said Judah, deceased, or any part thereof, make out a true and correct return of his proceedings, subscribed with his name to the judge of probate for the district of Bradford.

Sec. 2. And it is hereby further Enacted, That the said judge of probate be, and he is hereby directed and empowered to enter the return so made and subscribed by the said Josiah on the files and records of his office; and proceed forthwith to make such order or orders as he shall adjudge to be just and equitable in the premises for the benefit of the heirs aforesaid. *Provided nevertheless,* That the said Josiah Hubbard, before any sale by him made shall be valid in law, shall enter into bonds with sufficient surety in such sum as the said judge shall order, which shall be at least double the value of the interest to be by him so sold, which bond shall be lodged in said probate office.[1]

Passed November 4, 1799.

A true record,

Attest, Ros. Hopkins, Sec'y.

AN ACT ASSESSING A TAX OF ONE CENT ON EACH ACRE OF LAND IN THE TOWNSHIP OF MEDWAY[2] IN THE COUNTY OF RUTLAND

NOVEMBER 4TH, 1799

It is hereby Enacted by the General Assembly of the State of Vermont, That there be, and hereby is assessed a tax of one cent on each acre of land on the township of Medway, in the county of Rutland (public rights excepted), for the purpose of making and repairing roads and building bridges in said town, to be expended under the direction of William Tripp of Killington, Jonathan Wells and Matthew Fenton of Rutland, who are hereby appointed a committee for that purpose, and any justice of the peace within the county of Rutland is hereby empowered to issue his warrant to Jonathan Parker, Junr., of Clarendon, who is hereby appointed and empowered to collect said tax. And the said committee and collector are hereby directed to

---

1. State Papers of Vermont, Vol. XI, *General Petitions,* 1797-1799, "For Authority to Administrators to Sell Real Estate," 401.

2. Ibid., Vol. I, *Index to Papers of the Surveyors-General of Vermont:* Medway, Vermont Grant to Joseph Bouker and Associates, 1781; Parker's Gore annexed, and name changed to Parkerstown, Nov. 7, 1804; name changed to Mendon, 1827.

govern themselves in all things, in the collecting, expending, and accounting for the monies raised by said tax, agreeably to the directions of the statute law of this State, in that case made and provided.

And it is hereby further Enacted, That an act passed at the session of the Legislature in October, 1797, assessing a road tax on the township of Medway aforesaid, be, and the same is hereby repealed.

AN ACT ASSESSING A TAX OF ONE CENT PER ACRE ON THE TOWN OF MIDDLESEX IN THE COUNTY OF CHITTENDEN

NOVEMBER 4TH, 1799

It is hereby Enacted by the General Assembly of the State of Vermont, That there be, and hereby is assessed a tax of one cent on each acre of land in said town of Middlesex, (public rights excepted), for the purpose of making and repairing roads and building bridges in said town, and that Charles Bulkey of Montpelier, Henry Perkins and Joseph Stoughton of said Middlesex, be a committee to superintend the expenditure of said tax for the purposes aforesaid. And that said committee, or either two of them be, and are hereby empowered to appoint a collector to collect said tax. And that said committee shall stand accountable for the faithful discharge of the duties of such collector. And any justice of the peace for said county is hereby authorised to issue his warrant to such collector, when appointed as aforesaid to collect said tax. And said committee and collector are hereby directed in the expenditure, collection and accounting for the monies raised by said tax, to govern themselves in all things agreeable to the act entitled, "An act regulating the disposition of monies raised by tax on lands in the several towns for the purpose of making and repairing roads and building bridges."

AN ACT AUTHORISING FRANCIS DAVIS, ADMINISTRATOR TO THE ESTATE OF ROGER KINSLEY, TO SELL CERTAIN LANDS THEREIN MENTIONED

NOVEMBER 4TH, 1799

Whereas, Roger Kinsley, late of Fairfax, deceased, was at the time of his decease, seized of thirty nine acres of land, being so much of the south east part of the governor's right of land in Fairfax, for the estate of the deceased stands indebted, in the sum of 372 dollars (which is the whole of the purchase money for said premises), to be paid with interest on the tenth day of October, 1805; which sum when it shall become due will amount to more than the personal estate of the said deceased, by means of which the administrator of said estate cannot make a division of the personal property of the deceased. Therefore,

It is hereby Enacted by the General Assembly of the State of Vermont, That Francis Davis, administrator of the estate aforesaid, be, and he is hereby fully authorised and empowered, under the direction of the judge of probate for the district of Georgia, to sell the aforesaid premises to any person or persons who shall appear to purchase the same, and will pay up and cancel the aforesaid obligation. And said deed, so executed by the said Francis Davis, shall be good and valid in law to pass to the purchaser in fee, to all intents and purposes whatever.

Passed November 4, 1799.

A true record,

Attest, Ros. Hopkins, Sec'y.

AN ACT TO ENABLE ALLEN HAYES AND ABNER FORBES TO SELL AND CONVEY ALL THE REAL ESTATE OF LEWIS R. MORRIS WEST, A MINOR

NOVEMBER 4TH, 1799

Whereas, it appears that Lewis R. Morris West, a minor, is seized of certain real estate in the town of Windsor, county of Windsor, and other parts of the State of Vermont, as one of the legatees to the estate of his late father, Elijah West, late of said Windsor, deceased, and as grantee from his late mother, Hannah West, which, if the same be sold and the monies arising therefrom be put out to use, would much benefit the said minor in his subsistance and education. Therefore,

It is hereby Enacted by the General Assembly of the State of Vermont, That Allen Hayes and Abner Forbes, administrators on the estate of the said Elijah West, with the will annexed, be, and they are hereby empowered to sell and convey all the real estate of which the said minor is seized as aforesaid, within the town of Windsor and State of Vermont, and to make and execute and acknowledge good and sufficient deed or deeds, convey the said real estate, together or in parcel, in fee, to any person or persons who may appear to contract and purchase the same. *Provided nevertheless,* That within one month after such sale and conveyance of the whole, or any part of such real estate, the said Allen Hayes and Abner Forbes shall make due and correct returns of their doings in the premises by them subscribed, to the judge of probate for the district of Windsor.

Sec. 2. *And it is hereby further Enacted,* That the said judge of probate be empowered, and he is hereby directed and empowered to enter said return by said Hayes and Forbes, to be made upon the files and records of his office. And to proceed forthwith to make such [order] or orders for the disposition of monies arising from such sale or sales, as if the same were personal estate of the property of the said minor.

Provided nevertheless, That the said Allen Hayes and Abner Forbes, before any sale by them made shall be valid in law, shall enter into bonds with sufficient surety, in the sum of three thousand dollars, to the acceptance of the judge of probate for the district of Windsor.[1]

Passed November 4, 1799.

A true record,

Attest, Ros. Hopkins, Sec'y.

AN ACT EMPOWERING THE INHABITANTS OF HUBBARDTON AND SUDBURY
IN THE COUNTY OF RUTLAND, TO DRAW THE WATERS OF CERTAIN
MILL PONDS RAISED IN HUBBARDTON AND SUDBURY TO
THEIR ANCIENT AND NATURAL LEVEL AT CERTAIN
SEASONS OF THE YEAR

NOVEMBER 4TH, 1799

Whereas, it appears to this Assembly, That the rising of the waters in the ponds commonly called Greggory's [Gregory's] Pond, partly situate in Hubbardton and partly in Sudbury, at the outlet of which stands the mill now occupied by Dyer Waterous [Waters]; and the pond principally situate in Hubbardton, flowed as a reserve of water for the use of the mills now occupied by Nathan Rumsey, and the

---

1. State Papers of Vermont, Vol. XI, *General Petitions,* 1797-1799, "For Authority to Administrators to Sell Real Estate," 425.

pond called Burr's Pond, situate in Sudbury at the outlet of which stands the saw mill occupied by Roger Burr.

It is hereby Enacted by the General Assembly of the State of Vermont, That the inhabitants of the towns of Hubbardton and Sudbury, in the county of Ruland, shall yearly and every year hereafter, as long as said dams shall continue, have full power and lawful authority to draw the gates of said dams, and also at their own cost and expense, to erect such flooms [flumes] and sluice ways in said dams as may be necessary and convenient to draw the waters of said several ponds to their ancient and natural level; and to open and keep open the gates and flooms [flumes] of said dams from the first day of May annually hereafter, until the first day of September, unless the owners thereof shall, on the said first day of May annually as aforesaid, draw the aforesaid gates, and continue the same drawn for the purposes aforesaid, until the first day of September annually.[1]

Passed November 4, 1799.

A true record,

Attest, Ros. Hopkins, Sec'y.

AN ACT TO ENABLE THE PROPRIETORS OF THE TOWN OF PAWLET TO COMPLETE THEIR SIXTH DIVISION OF LANDS BY PITCHING

NOVEMBER 4TH, 1799

Whereas, it is found inconvenient, and almost impracticable, for the proprietors of Pawlet to complete their last division of lands in said town, in the present legal mode of allotting & drawing. Therefore,

It is hereby Enacted by the General Assembly of the State of Vermont, That the proprietors of the town of Pawlet be empowered, and they are hereby authorised and empowered to complete their sixth division of lands in said town, which was voted by the proprietors at a meeting of the said proprietors on the fourth of September, A.D. 1795. And when any proprietor or owner of any undivided share in said town, shall have surveyed his lot aggreeable to the vote of said proprietors, and recorded his survey in the proprietors' clerk's office,

---

1. State Papers of Vermont, Vol. XI, *General Petitions,* 1797-1799, "For Seasonal Lowering of the Water Level in Mill Ponds," 386.

the same shall be considered as a legal division of said lot or pitch, any law to to the contrary notwithstanding.[1]

Passed November 4, 1799.

A true record,

Attest, Ros. Hopkins, Sec'y.

AN ACT AUTHORISING THE PROPRIETORS AND LANDOWNERS OF WILLISTON TO CONFIRM AND COMPLETE THE DIVISION OR PITCHES OF THEIR LAND

NOVEMBER 4TH, 1799

Whereas, the proprietors of Williston, in the county of Chittenden, formerly attempted to make a division of the lands in said town by the mode of pitching, in consequence of which many of said proprietors made pitches and surveys of lots in said town, and many settlements and large improvements have been made thereon. And it appears that said divisions, so attempted to be made, were not made conformably to any existing law of this State. And whereas through the loss of papers, and the inaccurate manner in which the proceedings of the proprietors have been recorded, disputes may hereafter arise respecting the several divisions of the lands pitched and laid out in said town, which evil to prevent,

Sec. 1. *It is hereby Enacted* by the General Assembly of the State of Vermont, That the proprietors and landowners of said town of Williston be, and they are hereby authorised and empowered at any legal meeting by them already warned, or to be warned hereafter for the purpose, to confirm any prior or former division or divisions, or any pitch or pitches of the lands in said Williston, among the said proprietors, and to pass any vote for completing any division or divisions, or any pitch or pitches of said lands already begun, any law, usage, or custom to the contrary notwithstanding.

Sec. 2. *And whereas,* the land which remains common and undivided in said Williston cannot conveniently be divided in the mode prescribed by the existing laws of this State. Therefore,

It is hereby further Enacted, That the said proprietors and land-

---

1. State Papers of Vermont, Vol. XI, *General Petitions,* 1797-1799, "For Confirmation of Proprietors' Proceedings, 429.

owners of said Williston be, and they are hereby fully authorised and empowered, at any legal meeting already warned or to be warned, and holden for the purpose, to complete the division of such common and undivided lands by pitching the same. *Provided nevertheless,* That there be accounted and recorded but one vote, to any one original proprietor's right; and where there shall be a number of persons claiming under the same original right, such persons shall be allowed their vote according to the interest they so claim. And a majority of interest so claimed shall determine the vote for said right under which said several persons shall so claim.[1]

Passed November 4, 1799.

A true record,

Attest, Ros. Hopkins, Sec'y.

AN ACT DECLARING THE WIDOWS OF TESTATORS ENTITLED TO DOWER

NOVEMBER 4TH, 1799

It is hereby Enacted by the General Assembly of the State of Vermont, That the widow of any testator may, within sixty days after the will of her deceased husband shall be approved by the judge of probate, before such judge, wave any provision made for her in such will and have her dower assigned her, in the same manner as though her husband had died intestate; in which case she shall have no benefit from such provision unless it shall appear to have been the testators intention that such provision should be in addition to her dower.

Passed November 4th, 1799.

A true record,

Attest, Ros. Hopkins, Sec'y.

AN ACT FOR THE PURPOSE OF ESTABLISHING A COUNTY GRAMMAR SCHOOL AT ST. ALBANS IN THE COUNTY OF FRANKLIN

NOVEMBER 4TH, 1799

Sec. 1. *It is hereby Enacted* by the General Assembly of the

---

1. State Papers of Vermont, Vol. XI, *General Petitions,* 1797-1799, "For Confirmation of Proprietors' Proceedings," 440.

State of Vermont, That there be, and hereby is instituted and established a grammar school at such place at St. Albans, in the county of
Franklin, as the corporation hereinafter named shall think most convenient for that purpose, to be known and designated by the name of
Franklin county Grammar School.

Sec. 2. *And it is hereby further Enacted,* That Silas Hathaway,
Levi House, Joseph Jones, Nathan Green, Seth Pomeroy, Jonathan
Hoyt, Elisha Sheldon, Joseph Robinson and such others as shall be
appointed in manner, and to the number herein after directed, shall
at all times hereafter form and constitute the board of trustees for
the said institution, and to be known by the name and stile [style] of
the corporation of Franklin County Grammar School. And the said
corporation and their successors in office are hereby declared, constituted, ordained and appointed a body corporate and politic to all
intents and purposes, in name and in fact. They shall have full power
to take by gift, grant, purchase or devise any estate either real or
personal for the use of said grammar school, and also to receive and
appropriate all such donations as have been or hereafter shall be made
for the use of said institution; and by themselves or their attornies,
to institute, maintain, and defend any suit or suits which may or
shall be sued, prosecuted, or impleaded either in law or equity
for the recovery or defense of any of the rights of property of the
said institution as they shall find necessary. And also to appoint, elect,
support, and remove from time to time, all such instructors as they
shall find necessary.

Sec. 3. *And it is hereby further Enacted,* That when and so
often as they find it necessary for the interest of said institution that
addition should be made to the number of trustees, or supply any
vacancy occasioned by death or otherwise of any of the members of
said corporation, it shall and may be lawful for the said corporation
at any stated regular meeting, or when specially notified to attend for
that purpose, to elect by ballot such and so many as they shall judge
proper, so as that the whole number appointed shall not exceed twelve,
and a majority of the trustees shall be a quorum to act in all cases.

Provided always, that the inhabitants of St. Albans aforesaid, and
such others as may voluntarily subscribe therefore, shall build and
furnish a good sufficient house for said grammar school, of the value

of 800 dollars, within two years from the passing of this act, and shall forever after keep the same in good repair.

Passed November 4, 1799.

A true record,

Attest, Ros. Hopkins, Sec'y.

AN ACT TO ESTABLISH FOR THE TIME BEING THE JURISDICTIONAL
LINES OF THE TOWNS THEREIN MENTIONED

NOVEMBER 4TH, 1799

Whereas, disputes exist relating to the lines of property and jurisdiction of the towns of Newbury, Topsham, Orange, Barre, Corinth, Washington, and Williamstown, in the county of Orange, whereby the inhabitants of said towns are greatly discommoded. Therefore,

Sec. 1. *It is hereby Enacted* by the General Assembly of the State of Vermont, That until further order of this Legislature, the said towns of Newbury, Topsham, Orange, Barre, Corinth, Washington, and Williamstown shall severally have, hold and exclusively exercise jurisdiction as town corporations agreeably to the lines and bounds made for the said towns in the year 1784, beginning at a birch tree, the former reputed southwest corner of Newbury, by James Whitelaw, then deputy to the surveyor general of this State.

Sec. 2. *Provided nevertheless, and it is hereby further Enacted,* That the following shall be the lines between Orange and Barre; beginning one hundred rods east of the south west old corner of Orange, thence northerly parallel with the town line, 315 rods; thence easterly on the line of lots as surveyed by Orange, 120 rods; thence northerly 120 rods; thence westerly 220 to the old town line; thence northerly on said town line, 470 rods; thence easterly turning on right angles, 160 rods; thence northerly on the line of lots as surveyed by Orange to the north line of No. 14 in the first range; thence westerly to the town line; thence northerly on said town line to Plainfield.

Sec. 3. *Provided also, and it is hereby further Enacted,* That nothing in this act contained shall be construed in any wise to affect the right of property, in any of the lands between the proprietors of said town or individuals.

Passed November 4, 1799.

A true record,

Attest, Ros. Hopkins, Sec'y.

AN ACT ASSESSING A TAX OF ONE CENT PER ACRE ON THE TOWN OF DUNCANSBOROUGH

NOVEMBER 4TH, 1799

It is hereby Enacted by the General Assembly of the State of Vermont, That there be, and hereby is assessed a tax of one cent per acre on all the lands in the town of Duncansboro', in the county of Orleans, public rights excepted, for the purpose of making and repairing roads and building bridges in said town, to be expended under the direction of Calender Adams of Duncansboro' and Nath¹. P. Sawyer of Hyde Park, who are hereby appointed a committee to superintend the expenditure of said tax. And any justice of the peace within the county of Caledonia, is hereby authorised to issue his warrant to John Bean of Wheelock, who is hereby appointed a collector to collect said tax. And said committee and collector are hereby directed to conform themselves in the collecting, expending, and accounting for the monies raised by said tax, in all things, to the directions of the statute of this State in that case made and provided.[1]

AN ACT RELATING TO THE STAGE ROAD AS LAID OUT BY THE COMMITTEE FOR THAT PURPOSE THROUGH THE TOWN OF HARTLAND

NOVEMBER 5TH, 1799

It is hereby Enacted by the General Assembly of the State of Vermont, That the town of Hartland in the county of Windsor, shall not incurr any penalty under the second section of the act entitled "An act in addition to and alteration of an act, entitled 'An act empowering and directing certain persons therein named to lay out and survey a post road from the Massachusetts line to the north line of the town

---

1. State Papers of Vermont, Vol. XI, *General Petitions,* 1797-1799, "For a Tax on Land to Build Roads," 317.

of Newbury, in the county of Orange'," passed on the 10th day of March 1797, until the first day of October, 1801.

Sec. 2. *Provided nevertheless, and it is hereby further Enacted,* That the town of Hartland, shall not take any benefit from this act, unless they make and repair all the remaining part of the road laid out by the committee appointed in and by said act, to lay out and survey a post road as aforesaid, which lies north of the dwelling house where Isaac Stevens formerly lived, to the north line of said town of Hartland, to the acceptance of the committee appointed to lay and survey said road, on or before the first day of November, 1800.

Passed November 5, 1799.

A true record,

Attest, Ros. Hopkins, Sec'y.

AN ACT TO REPEAL AN ACT PASSED IN OCTOBER 1794 DIRECTING THE USES OF THE RIGHTS OF LAND IN THIS STATE HERETOFORE GRANTED BY THE BRITISH GOVERNMENT AS GLEBES FOR THE BENEFIT OF THE CHURCH OF ENGLAND AS BY THEIR LAW ESTABLISHED

NOVEMBER 5TH, 1799

It is hereby Enacted by the General Assembly of the State of Vermont, That an act directing the uses of the rights of land in this State, heretofore granted by the British government as glebes for the benefit of the church of England, as by their law established, be, and hereby is repealed. *Provided nevertheless,* and it is hereby expressly declared, that the repealing clause aforesaid, shall not be construed to extend to, or in any way affect any person or persons who are in possession of any lot belonging to any such glebe right, by virtue of a lease from the selectmen, as directed by law, of any town where any such lands lie; and it is hereby declared, that the selectmen where any such lands lie, are prohibited from leasing any such lands in future.

Pased November 5, 1799.

A true record,

Attest, Ros. Hopkins, Sec'y.

AN ACT IN ADDITION TO AN ACT ENTITLED "AN ACT DIRECTING THE
PUBLICATION OF ADVERTISEMENTS IN THE NEWSPAPERS
THEREIN MENTIONED"

NOVEMBER 5TH, 1799

It is hereby Enacted by the General Assembly of the State of Vermont, That in addition to the mode of printing advertisments pointed out in said act, that all lands so to be advertised, being in the county of Bennington, be advertised in the "Vermont Gazette," printed at Bennington; and if such land be in the county of Windham, they shall be advertised in the "Federal Galaxy" printed in Brattleborough; and if such lands shall be in either of the counties of Caledonia, Orleans, or Essex, they shall in like manner be advertised in the "Green Mountain Patriot" printed at Peacham; and if such lands be in either of the counties of Addison, Chittenden, and Franklin, the same shall, in like manner, be advertised in the "Vergennes Gazette" printed at Vergennes.

Provided nevertheless, That this act shall not be in force until the first day of February next.

Passed November 5, 1799.

A true record,

Attest, Ros. Hopkins, Sec'y.

AN ACT REVIVING AN ACT ASSESSING A TAX OF TWO CENTS PER ACRE ON
THE TOWN OF BRAINTREE

NOVEMBER 5TH, 1799

Whereas, an act was passed at the last session of this Legislature assessing a tax of two cents per acre on the town of Braintree, for making and repairing roads and building bridges, and the committee appointed therein neglected to advertise the same according to law. Therefore,

It is hereby Enacted by the General Assembly of the State of Vermont, That the act passed at the last session of this Legislature assessing a tax of two cents per acre on the town of Braintree for the purpose aforesaid, be, and the same is hereby revived and declared to be in full force and effect as though the same had passed at the present session of the Legislature.

AN ACT DIRECTING THE TREASURER OF THIS STATE TO PAY TO THE
PROPRIETORS OF SALEM THE SUM THEREIN MENTIONED

NOVEMBER 5TH, 1799

Whereas, the proprietors of Salem, in that part of the county
of Orleans annexed for the time being to the county of Caledonia,
in this State, paid into the treasury of the State, as granting fees for
said township, the sum of $536.66 cents, more than of right and justice
they ought. Therefore,

It is hereby Enacted by the General Assembly of the State of Vermont, That the treasurer of this State be, and he is hereby directed to
repay to James Whitelaw, Esqr., agent of the proprietors of said
Salem, the said sum of $536.66, with interest on the same, from the
28th day of September A.D. 1781, being $579.60 cents, amounting in
the whole to the sum of $1116.26 cents, to be equally divided among
the orginal proprietors of said Salem, in proportion to their property
therein, which sum the treasurer is hereby directed to pay on the first
day of August next with interest.

Sec. 2. *And it is hereby further Enacted,* That the said Agent
on receiving the said money from the said treasurer, shall make and
execute a bond to the said treasurer in the penal sum of $2232 dollars,
conditioned that if the said bounden agent shall, when thereunto demanded by the said treasurer, at any time after four years from and
after the passing of this act, produce to the said treasurer the receipt
of the original proprietors of said Salem, or their lawful agent or
representatives; which receipt shall, in every instance, include a discharge to the state of all demands of such proprietor or proprietors (in
consequence of the interference of Derby upon Salem); and in default
of such receipts, shall refund the monies to the said treasurer, to the
amount of the said sum of $1116.26 cents; then the said obligation to
be null and void, otherwise to remain in full force and virtue.

Passed November 5, 1799.

A true record,

Attest, Ros. Hopkins, Sec'y.

AN ACT TO PAY HIS EXCELLENCY THE GOVERNOR OF THIS STATE
THE SUM THEREIN MENTIONED

NOVEMBER 5TH, 1799

Whereas, his Excellency the Governor has been at unusual expense in postage and in making two journeys to the northern part of this State, relative to the accommodation of the difficulties with the government of Canada, respecting the death of John Griggs; and enquiring into the claims of the Indians, &c. [Therefore,]

It is hereby Enacted by the General Assembly of the State of Vermont, That the treasurer of this State be, and he is hereby directed to pay his Excellency, Isaac Tichenor, Esquire, the sum of $200., for his expense and trouble in the aforesaid business.

Passed November 5, 1799.

A true record,

Attest, Ros. Hopkins, Sec'y.

AN ACT FOR THE RELIEF OF ZADOCK HARD AND OTHERS

NOVEMBER 5TH, 1799

Whereas, the aforesaid Zadock Hard, Abel Aylesworth, Levi Hill, Ozi Baker, Ephraim Knapp, and Benjamin Boardman, did in the year 1788 become bail for Israel Burrett, and in consequence of the said Burrett having broken his bond, became indebted to this State in a certain sum which amounted in the month of August, 1794, by a judgment rendered against them in the supreme court of this State, to the sum of 390 pounds, 8 shillings, 7 pence. And whereas it appears that the said court in rendering their judgment as aforesaid, had not deducted any part of 100 pounds from which the said Hard & those others as before mentioned, had been relieved by an act of the Legislature of this State, previous to the rendition of said judgment. And whereas, it appears that part of the debt justly due by the said Zadock Hard and others as aforesaid, has been paid to the treasurer of this State.

It is hereby Enacted by the General Assembly of the State of Vermont, That the said Zadock Hard, and those others who became bound with him as aforesaid, shall be liberated and totally exonerated from all and every demand of this State on the treasury thereof, against any or all of them on account of their having become bail as aforesaid, on their paying into the treasury of this State the sum of $658.17 cents, and freeing and exonerating this State from all and every expense which has accrued to this state in the prosecution of him, the said Zadock and others, since the month of August, in the year 1794, as aforesaid.

Provided also, and it is hereby further Enacted, That if the aforesaid Abel Aylesworth and Zadock Hard shall give a bond to the treasurer of this State for the aforesaid sum of $658.17 cents, together with the costs accruing on said demand since the year 1794, conditioned for the payment of one half the said sum, on or before the first day of October, 1800, and the other half on or before the first day of October, 1801, with interest; which bond the treasurer is hereby directed to take; that then the said Abel Aylsworth, Zadock Hard and others mentioned in the preamble to this act, shall be discharged from any further demand in favor of this State on account of the aforementioned demand.

Passed November 5, 1799.

A true record,

Attest, Ros. Hopkins, Sec'y.

AN ACT MAKING APPROPRIATIONS FOR THE SUPPORT OF GOVERNMENT
FOR THE PRESENT SESSION AND FROM THENCE TO THE SESSION
OF THE GENERAL ASSEMBLY IN OCTOBER 1800 AND FOR
OTHER PURPOSES

NOVEMBER 5TH, 1799

It is hereby Enacted by the General Assembly of the State of Vermont, That there be paid out of the treasury of this State for the salary of the Governor, $500; for the salary of the treasurer, $400; also for the debenture of the Lieutentant Governor, Council and General Assembly and the necessary officers attending the same, including the auditor of accounts against the state, $9,105.98 cents; and to Robert Grandy $5.50 for his room, candles, and firewood; and to Stephen Conant $5. for ringing the bell; and also to Samuel Patrick $10. for his room, firewood, and candles; also the debenture of the Lieut. Govr. and Council for their special session at Rutland in March last, the sum of $110.88 cents.

Sec. 2. *And it is hereby further Enacted,* That there be appropriated a sum not exceeding three thousand dollars for the purpose of paying the demands of this State, which may be allowed by the auditor of accounts against the State, and the orders drawn by and under the direction of the supreme court, which several sums of money shall be paid by the treasurer. And if there shall not be sufficient monies in the treasury, the treasurer shall issue hard money orders for the residue of such appropriations.

Passed November 5, 1799.

A true record,

Attest, Ros. Hopkins, Sec'y.

AN ACT DIRECTING COLLECTORS OF LAND TAXES IN THEIR OFFICE AND DUTY

NOVEMBER 5TH, 1799

It is hereby Enacted by the General Assembly of the State of Vermont, That every collector of land taxes shall, within thirty days after compleating the sale of any township, cause his proceedings to be recorded in the proper office for the recording of deeds, and within thirty days, after the expiration of the time allowed by law for the redemption of land so sold, shall cause a list of all lands not redeemed, to be recorded in the same office.

Sec. 2. *It is hereby further Enacted,* That within one year after the time appointed by the collector for the sale of lands he shall present at the office, where the proceedings of his sale are recorded, all the newspapers containing advertisements respecting the land so sold, whether concerning the labor to be performed or the sales of said lands, and the clerk shall record the advertisements at length, and the title, the volume, the number, and the date of the papers wherein they were inserted. And a copy of this record, certified by the clerk, shall be full evidence of such advertisement in any court in this State.

Sec. 3. *It is hereby further Enacted,* That for making the above records each collector shall be allowed five dollars together with his travel, in going and returning twice from the place of sale to the place where the record is made, which sum shall be equally charged on the delinquents.

Passed November 5, 1799.

A true record,

Attest, Ros. Hopkins, Sec'y.

AN ACT SUSPENDING CIVIL PROCESS AGAINST ELI COGGSWELL

NOVEMBER 5TH, 1799

Whereas, it appears to this Assembly That Eli Coggswell of Castleton, in the county of Rutland, by misfortune and the unexpected failure of divers persons for whom he became bound as surety, and by the violation of faith reposed in, and bankruptcy of others, is now embarrassed with numerous demands and law suits by reason whereof he is liable to large and numerous bills of cost; and is now imprisoned in Rutland county gaol on an execution for a large amount; and said Eli is unable to pay or satify the demands against him, or to free himself from said imprisonment. Therefore,

It is hereby Enacted by the General Assembly of the State of Vermont, That from and after the passing of this act, the body of the said Eli Coggswell shall not be liable to be attached, arrested or imprisoned, by any civil process in law or equity, whether mesne or final, for and during the term of three years from the first day of December next ensuing, on any judgment, debt, obligation, contract, or demand whatever, which has accrued, been entered into, or arisen before the passing of this act, but that he shall be exempted therefrom, for and during the term aforesaid. And if any person or persons whatever, shall, during or within the time aforesaid, arrest, attach, or imprison the body of said Eli by virtue of any civil process or execution whatever, such arrest shall be void and of no effect. And the said Eli shall be discharged and liberated therefrom.

Sce. 2.. *And it is hereby further Enacted,* That the property of said Eli, whether real or personal, shall be exempted from and not liable to any attachment, levy, extent or civil process whatever, within and during the term of three years as aforesaid, upon his the said Eli's procuring and giving to the sheriff of Rutland county, his successors in said office, or assigns, good and sufficient security in the sum of ten thousand dollars; conditioned that the said Eli shall not waste, embezzle, or secrete any of his property during the time aforesaid, which bonds shall be taken for the benefit of said Eli's creditors, and be assignable to them or either of them, and action or actions thereon maintained, in case of forfeiture, as in the case of jail bonds for the liberty of the prison yard. *Provided always,* That in all cases where any creditor heretofore has legally attached or levied upon any property, by any process in law, and the action is sustainable, the property so attached or levied upon, shall remain in the possession and improvement of the said Eli during the term aforesaid, for the use and benefit of the creditor or creditors having so attached or levied upon the same, and be disposed of in the same way and manner as if this act had not passed.[1]

Passed November 5, 1799.

A true record,

Attest, Ros. Hopkins, Sec'y.

AN ACT GRANTING TO EZRA BUTLER, JABEZ JONES, GEORGE KENNAN, AND THEIR ASSOCIATES THE EXCLUSIVE PRIVILEGE OF BUILDING A TOLL BRIDGE OVER ONION RIVER, AGAINST WATERBURY

NOVEMBER 5TH, 1799

It is hereby Enacted by the General Assembly of the State of Vermont, That Ezra Butler, Jabez Jones, and George Kennan, and their associates be, and they are hereby formed into, constituted and made a body politic and corporate by the name of the Onion River Bridge company. And that they and their successors, and such other persons as shall be admitted members of said company shall be, and continue a body politic and corporate by the same name for the term of one hundred years from the first day of January next. And that the same company have the exclusive privilege of erecting and continuing a bridge over Onion River, within three miles each way of the said Ezra Butler's now dwelling house in said Waterbury.

Sec. 2. *And it is hereby further Enacted,* That it shall and may be lawful for the said company to demand and receive toll at the following rates, for crossing said bridge, to wit: for each foot passenger,

---

1. State Papers of Vermont, Vol. XI, *General Petitions,* 1797-1799, "For a Temporary Suspension of Civil Suits," 411.

two cents; for each man and horse, five cents; for each horse or colt, or cow or other horned creature, excepting sucking colts and calves, not exceeding ten in number, two cents; for each additional horse or colt, or cow or other horned creature, one cent; for each chair, chaise, or sulkey [sulky] drawn by one horse, twenty cents; for each cart or waggon drawn by two horses or oxen, twelve cents; for each additional horse or ox, three cents; for each coach or chariot or other four wheeled pleasure carriage drawn by two horses, fifty cents, for each additional horse, five cents; for each cart or sleigh drawn by one horse, six cents; for each sheep or swine, if under twenty, half cent; for each additional sheep or swine at the rate of three cents per dozen; for each jack or mule, three cents; for each sled or sleigh drawn by two horses or oxen, ten cents; for each additional horse or ox, two cents.

Sec. 3. *It is hereby further Enacted,* That at the expiration of twenty years from the first day of January which will be in the year of our Lord, one thousand eight hundred and one, it shall be the duty of the judges of the supreme court to examine into the accounts of the said company for and on account of the said bridge, and the proceeds thence arising, for which purpose the said judges are hereby empowered to appoint one person wholly disinterested, who shall be sworn to the faithful discharge of his trust, as commissioner to examine into the state of the accounts of the said company. And the said commissioner, for the purpose aforesaid, shall have free access to all the books and accounts of the said company, and is hereby empowered to call before him and examine under oath such person as he may think fit, and make out a fair statement of the cost of erecting, maintaining and attending the said bridge, and of the proceeds thence arising to the said company from the same, by the rates of toll aforesaid, during the said term, and make report thereon to the said judges at the stated session of the supreme court in the county of Chittenden, next after his appointment. And the said commissioner shall receive from the said company such compensation for his services as shall be allowed by the judges of the said court. And if it shall appear to the said judges by the report of the commissioner made as aforesaid, that the neat proceeds during the term of twenty years as aforesaid shall average at a larger sum than twelve per centum per annum, on all actual expenditures, it shall be the duty of said judges to lessen the toll to such sum as to them shall appear reasonable, provided it shall not be in the power of said judges to reduce the toll to such sum as shall prevent the proprietors from receiving twelve per centum per annum for all actual expenditures.

Sec. 4. *And it is hereby further Enacted,* That said company are hereby made capable of suing and being sued, of prosecuting and defending suits in their corporate capacity; may have a common seal; and make bye laws for their company concerns. And at any meeting warned for that purpose may choose a president and two directors who shall continue in office two years from the time of their election, and until others shall be chosen in their place; a majority of whom, including the president, shall be a quorum to transact business. That at any election of officers in said company, every owner shall be entitled to as many votes as he shall own shares in said bridge. That a secretary shall be appointed by said company whose duty it shall be to make and keep necessary records and make regular entries of the transfers of all shares. And no person shall be allowed to vote at any meeting upon any share unless it shall appear by the books and entries of the secretary, that he has owned said share at least twenty days previous to said meeting. That the first meeting shall be warned by the said Ezra Butler, within one year from the passing of this act, in such manner as he may judge expedient; and that all future meetings shall be warned by the president unless there shall be a vacancy, in which case it may be warned by the secretary.

Sec. 5. *And it is hereby further Enacted,* That the said company shall keep the bridge to be by them erected, and continued in manner aforesaid, in good repair during the term of this grant, and in case of neglect shall be liable to the same penalties to which towns by law are subjected for not keeping roads and bridges in repair, and shall be liable to a presentment by a grand juror for the same. And in case they shall neglect for the space of six months after complaint be made, they shall forfeit all the rights and privileges granted by this act, unless it shall appear that said bridge was destroyed by accident, in which case they shall have eighteen months for rebuilding the same.

Provided nevertheless, That if the said company shall not, within three years after such time as the selectmen of Duxbury or Moretown, under the direction of the president and directors of the said company, lay out and survey a road across said river (within the bounds heretofore described in this act), build said bridge and render the same passable, they shall receive no benefit by this act.

Passed November 5, 1799.

A true record,

Attest, Ros. Hopkins, Sec'y.

AN ACT ESTABLISHING A CORPORATION BY THE NAME OF WINDSOR AND WOODSTOCK TURNPIKE COMPANY

NOVEMBER 5TH, 1799

Sec. 1. *It is hereby Enacted* by the General Assembly of the State of Vermont, That Stephen Jacob, Jesse Williams, William Leveret, Charles March, Perez Jones, Benjamin Swan, Amasa Paine, Jonathan H. Hubbard, Allen Hayes, William Rice, and Abner Forbes, and their associates, and their heirs and assigns, be, and they are hereby constituted a corporation by the name of Windsor and Woodstock turnpike company; and shall by that name sue and be sued, and shall have a common seal, and shall enjoy all the privileges and powers, that are by law incident to corporations for the purpose of laying out and making a turnpike road from the east parish in Windsor, in the county of Windsor, to or near to Woodstock court house in said county, in such place or places as the said corporation shall choose. *Provided,* That said corporation shall not erect any toll gate on the present post road leading from said East-parish in Windsor to said Woodstock court house.

Sec. 2. *And it is hereby further Enacted,* That so soon as said turnpike road shall be sufficiently made, and shall be allowed and approved by the judges of the supreme court or a committee by them appointed, said corporation shall be at liberty to erect two gates on the same, and they be, and are hereby entitled to receive from each traveller or passenger the following rates of toll, at each of said gates, to wit, for every four wheeled pleasure carriage, drawn by one beast, thirty one cents, and for each additional beast, three cents; for every two wheeled pleasure carriage drawn by one beast, seventeen cents, and for each additional beast, three cents; for each waggon or cart drawn by two beasts, fifteen cents; for each additional beast, three cents; for each waggon or cart drawn by one beast, ten cents; for each sled or sleigh drawn by two beasts, twelve cents and one half, for each additional beast two cents; for each sled or sleigh drawn by one beast, ten cents; for each man and horse, six cents and one quarter; for all horses, mules or neat cattle led or driven, besides those in teams or carriages, one cent each; for all sheep and swine, three cents per dozen. *Provided,* That the said corporation may, if they see fit, commute the rate of toll with any person or persons by taking of him or them a certain sum monthly or annually to be mutually agreed upon in lieu of the toll aforesaid.

Sec. 3. *And it is hereby further Enacted,* That the said corporation be, and they hereby are empowered to erect any additional gate or gates on said road, and to average the toll by this act allowed to the respective gates but shall receive no additional toll.

Sec. 4. *And it is hereby further Enacted,* That the said corporation, or a committee by them appointed, be, and they are hereby authorised to lay out, make, & alter said road through any lands where it shall be necessary or convenient, under the same regulations and restrictions which the selectmen in the several towns are under, in laying out and altering highways, which road shall be laid out four rods in width. *Provided,* That no pay shall be allowed to any land owner for laying out or altering said road through his lands where the same shall not be improved at the time of such laying out or altering, or for extending said road to the width of four rods in any place where the highway is now laid; and the path to be travelled in shall not be less than eighteen feet in width.

Sec. 5. *And it is hereby further Enacted,* That if said corporation, or their toll gatherer, or any other person in their employment, shall unreasonably delay or hinder any traveller or passenger, at either of said gates, or shall demand and receive more toll than is by this act established, the corporation shall forfeit and pay a sum not exceeding ten dollars nor less than one dollar to be recovered before any court proper to try the same. And the said corporation shall be liable to pay all damages which may happen to any person from whom the toll is demandable for any damages which shall arise from neglect of any bridge or want of repairs in said road, and shall be liable to presentment by grand jury for not keeping the same in good repair.

Sec. 6. *And it is hereby further Enacted,* That if any persons shall cut, break down, or otherwise destroy any of said turnpike gates, or shall dig up or carry away earth from said road to the damage of the same, or shall forcibly pass, or attempt to pass by force, the gate, or any of them without first having paid the legal toll at such gate, such person shall pay all damage which said corporation shall thereby sustain, and shall forfeit and pay a fine not exceeding fifty dollars, nor less than one dollar, to be recovered by the treasurer of said corporation, to their use in an action of trespass on the case. And if any person with his carriage, cattle or horse shall turn out of said road to pass any of the turnpike gates, and again enter the said road, with intent to evade the toll due by virtue of said act, such person shall forfeit and pay three times so much as the legal toll would have been, to be recovered in manner aforesaid, to the use of said corporation. *Provided,* That nothing in this act shall extend to entitle the said corporation to demand and receive toll of any person who shall be passing with his horse or carriage to and from public worship, or on militia duty, or with his horse, team, or cattle to or from his common labour on his farm, or to or from any grist mill or other ordinary business of family concerns.

Sec. 7. *And it is hereby further Enacted,* That the shares in said turnpike road shall be taken, deemed and considered personal estate to all intents and purposes, and shall and may be transferable in such manner as the corporation may, by their bye laws, establish. And when any share shall be attached on mesne process, an attested copy of such process shall be, at the time of the attachment, left with the clerk of the corporation, otherwise the attachment shall be void. And such shares may be sold on execution in the same manner as is, or may be by law provided, for making sale of personal property on execution, the creditor leaving a copy of the execution, and the officer's return thereon, with the clerk of said corporation, within fourteen days after such sale, and paying for recording the same. And such share or shares so sold as aforesaid, shall to all intents and purposes vest in the purchaser.

Sec. 8. *And it is hereby further Enacted,* That there shall be a meeting of said corporation, held at the house of Samuel Patrick in Windsor on the first Monday of December next, at ten oclock in the forenoon, for the purpose of choosing a clerk and such other officers as may be considered necessary by the said corporation, and the said corporation may establish such rules and regulations as the said corporation may judge necessary for regulating the concerns thereof. *Provided,* the same shall not be repugnant to the laws of this state, and the said corporation may from time to time establish such method of calling meetings as they shall judge proper.

Sec. 9. *And it is hereby further Enacted,* That when any proprietor shall neglect or refuse to pay any tax duly assessed, by said corporation to their treasurer, within twenty days after the time appointed for the payment thereof, the treasurer is hereby authorised to sell at public vendue, the share or shares of such delinquent proprietor, under such regulations as the said corporation may by their bye laws direct; and such purchaser on producing a certificate of such sale from the treasurer to the clerk of said corporation, in the name of such purchaser, with the number of shares so sold, shall be by the clerk entered in the books of said corporation; and such purchaser shall thereupon be considered to all intents and purposes the proprietor thereof. And the overplus, if any there shall be, shall be paid on demand, by the treasurer to the person whose share or shares shall have been sold as aforesaid.

Sec. 10. *And it is hereby further Enacted,* That the said corporation shall, at all places where the said toll shall be collected, erect and keep constantly exposed to view a sign or board, with the rates of toll fairly and legibly written in large or capital letters.

Sec. 11. *And it is hereby further Enacted,* That after the expiration of twenty years from the completion of said road it shall be the duty of the judges of the supreme court, for the time being, to examine the books, and accounts of said corporation, and if they shall find that the toll received shall have reimbursed to said corporation all expenditures for making and keeping said road in repair, and all expenses incident thereto, with an interest at the rate of twelve per centum upon said expenditure, it shall be the duty of said judges to dissolve said corporation, and thereupon the property of said turnpike shall vest in this State. And if the said judges shall find on such examination that the toll so received as aforesaid, shall not have reimbursed said expenditures and have given an interest upon said expenditures at the rate of twelve per cent per annum, then it shall become the duty of the judges of the said supreme court, thereafter, once in five years, to make examination as provided above. And when upon such examination, said expenditures shall be reimbursed, and said interest paid as aforesaid, said judges shall dissolve said corporation as aforesaid, and said turnpike shall vest in this state as above provided. And the said corporation shall within one year after said road is completed, make out a correct statement of all the expenditures thereof, and present the same to the judges of Windsor county court, to be by them approved, after which the same shall be immediately lodged in the office of the secretary of state.

Sec. 12. *And it is hereby further Enacted,* That if the said corporation shall not complete said turnpike road, to the acceptance of the said judges of said Windsor county court, within the term of three years from and after the passing of this act, the same shall be null and void. *Provided,* however, that when said corporation shall at any time within three years have completed not less then one half of said road, to the acceptance of the judges aforesaid, said corporation may erect one toll gate as is heretofore comtemplated by this act, and may receive at such gate the same toll as is heretofore provided by this act.[1]

Passed November 5, 1799.

A true record,

Attest, Ros. Hopkins, Sec'y.

AN ACT TO PREVENT THE HAWKING AND VENDING OF FEATHERS EXCEPT
IN THE MANNER THEREIN DIRECTED

NOVEMBER 5TH, 1799

Whereas, there is great reason to believe that sundry evil minded persons import into this State, quantities of feathers on which persons who were afflicted with the putrid or yellow fever, in the cities of New York, Philadelphia, and other places have actually died, by which the infection may be brought into this State.

Sec. 1. *It is hereby Enacted* by the General Assembly of the State of Vermont, That every hawker and pedlar, or every other person who shall, from and after the first day of January next, be found going from town to town on foot, with an horse or horses or any carriage whatever, exposing to sale any feathers, not produced in this State, or which he shall not be able to prove were imported through the province of Canada, immediately into this State, shall forfeit a sum not exceeding seven dollars, nor less than three dollars, also the whole of such feathers, so exposed to sale, or so conveyed or transported as aforesaid, to be destroyed by the magistrate before whom a conviction shall be

---

1. State Papers of Vermont, Vol. XI, *General Petitions,* 1797-1799, "For Authority to Build a Turnpike Road," 441.

had by information or complaint to any justice of the peace within the county in which such feathers shall have been first detected. And all tavern keepers or any other person who shall knowingly entertain any person hawking feathers as aforesaid, for the space of four hours together, shall forfeit and pay a sum not more than seven dollars, nor less then one, to him or them who will prosecute and sue therefore by action of debt, unless the departure of such person from such tavern keepers or other person's house shall be prevented by sickness or some other unavoidable necessity.

Sec. 2. *And it is hereby further Enacted,* That the secretary of the state be, and he is hereby directed to publish this act in all the newspapers printed in this State immediately after the rising of this assembly.

Passed November 5, 1799.

A true record,

Attest, Ros. Hopkins, Sec'y.

AN ACT IN ADDITION TO AN ACT ENTITLED, "AN ACT FOR THE DISTRIBUTION OF LAWS, JOURNALS, AND OTHER PUBLIC PAPERS"

NOVEMBER 5TH, 1799

Whereas, the law directing the printing and distribution of the laws, journals, and other public papers appears to be insufficent to answer that desirable end, and by reason whereof, the laws and journals have been heretofore very unequally distributed, which evil to prevent.

Sec. 1. *It is hereby Enacted* by the General Assembly of the State of Vermont, That from and after the rising of this assembly, it shall be the duty of the printer, after having received from the Secretary of State and Clerk of the General Assembly attested copies of the laws and journals of the Legislature, to print and deliver the same to the sheriffs of the several counties in this State within three months after receiving such copies from said Secretary and clerk respectively, on penalty of forfeiting and paying into the treasury of this State, the sum of fifty dollars, and the sum of twenty dollars for every month of delinquency afterwards, to be recovered by an action on the case to be brought on this statute and prosecuted by the state's attorney for Addison county, in the name of the Treasurer of this State, before any court in this State proper to try the same.

Sec. 2. *And it is hereby further Enacted,* That it shall be the duty of the Secretary of State, to furnish the state printer with a copy of the laws within one month; and the clerk of the House the journals within two months after the rising of each session of Legislature, under the same penalties, and to be recovered in the same manner, as is provided in the preceding section of this act.

Passed November 5, 1799.

A true record,

Attest, Ros. Hopkins, Sec'y.

AN ACT FOR THE RELIEF OF THE TOWN OF SPRINGFIELD AS THEREIN MENTIONED

NOVEMBER 5TH, 1799

It is hereby Enacted by the General Assembly of the State of Vermont, That the town of Springfield, in the county of Windsor, shall not incur any penalty under the second section of the act entitled, "An act in addition to and alteration of an act empowering and directing certain persons therein named, to lay out and survey a post road from the Massachusetts line, to the north line of the town of Newbury, in the county of Orange," passed on the tenth day of March A.D. 1797, until after the first day of October, 1801. *Provided,* said town shall complete one half of said road previous to the first day of October next, any thing in the above recited act to the contrary notwithstanding.[1]

Passed November 5, 1799.

A true record,

Attest, Ros. Hopkins, Sec'y.

---

1. State Papers of Vermont, Vol. XI, *General Petitions,* 1797-1799, "For Appointment of a Committee to Make Alterations in a Post Road," 424.

AN ACT DIRECTING THE TREASURER OF THIS STATE TO PAY WILLIAM
RICE $8.25

NOVEMBER 5TH, 1799

It is hereby Enacted by the General Assembly of the State of Vermont, That the treasurer of this State be, and hereby is directed to pay to William Rice the sum of $8.25 cents; it being for doctoring and nursing one John Morehouse, a state prisoner.[1]

Passed November 5, 1799.

A true record,

Attest, Ros. Hopkins, Sec'y.

AN ACT DIRECTING THE TREASURER OF THIS STATE TO PAY THE SUM OF
MONEY HEREINAFTER MENTIONED

NOVEMBER 5TH, 1799

It is hereby Enacted by the General Assembly of the State of Vermont, That the treasurer of this State be, and he hereby is directed to pay Daniel Heald, Junr., sheriff's deputy for the county of Windsor, the sum of $8.25 cents for his extra services in taking and securing for trial John Morehouse, a state prisoner.[2]

Passed November 5, 1799.

A true record,

Attest, Ros. Hopkins, Sec'y.

AN ACT IN ADDITION TO AN ACT ENTITLED, "AN ACT DIVIDING THE STATE
INTO DISTRICTS FOR ELECTING REPRESENTATIVES TO THE
CONGRESS OF THE UNITED STATES, AND DIRECTING
THE MODE OF THEIR ELECTION"

NOVEMBER 5TH, 1799

It is hereby Enacted by the General Assembly of the State of Vermont, That the district or territory now constituting the county of

---

1. State Papers of Vermont, Vol. XI, *General Petitions,* 1797-1799, "For Compensation to a Deputy Sheriff for Keeping a Prisoner," 439.
2. Ibid., "For Compensation to a Sheriff for caring for a Sick Prisoner," 447.

Orleans be, and the same hereby is annexed to the first or western district for the purpose of electing a Representative to Congress, any law, usage, or cutom to the contrary notwithstanding.

Passed November 5th, 1799.

A true record,

Attest, Ros. Hopkins, Sec'y.

AN ACT IN ADDITION TO "AN ACT RELATING TO GAOLS AND GAOLERS AND FOR THE RELIEF OF PERSONS IMPRISONED THEREIN"

NOVEMBER 5TH, 1799

It is hereby Enacted by the General Assembly of the State of Vermont, That the common gaol in Burlington in the county of Chittenden, and also the common gaol in Danville in the county of Caledonia, in addition to the purposes for which they are now used, shall be gaols for receiving and safekeeping such prisoners as shall be committed under the authority of the United States, until they shall be discharged by due course of law.

Passed November 5, 1799.

A true record,

Attest, Ros. Hopkins, Sec'y.

END OF ACTS PASSED AT WINDSOR
1799

INDEX OF LAWS

INDEX

LAWS OF VERMONT

1796 - 1799

— A —

— D —

— G —

— L —

— M —

— N —

— P —

— R —

— S —

— V —

— W —